Education, Information, and Transformation

Essays on Learning and Thinking

JEFFREY KANE
Long Island University

MERRILL,
an imprint of Prentice Hall

Upper Saddle River, New Jersey *Columbus, Ohio*

Library of Congress Cataloging-in-Publication Data

Education, information, and transformation : essays on learning and thinking/ [edited by] Jeffrey Kane.

p. cm.

Includes bibliographical references.

ISBN 0-13-520594-8

1. Thought and thinking. 2. Knowledge, Theory of. 3. Learning, Psychology of. I. Kane, Jeffrey

BF441.E25 1999

153—dc21 97-45706

CIP

Cover art: © Diana Ong/Superstock
Editor: Debra A. Stollenwerk
Production Editor: Mary M. Irvin
Design Coordinator: Karrie M. Converse
Text Designer: Mia Saunders
Cover Designer: Linda Fares
Production Manager: Pamela D. Bennett
Electronic Text Management: Marilyn Wilson Phelps, Karen L. Bretz, Tracey B. Ward
Director of Marketing: Kevin Flanagan
Advertising/Marketing Coordinator: Krista Groshong
Marketing Manager: Suzanne Stanton

This book was set in Garamond by Prentice-Hall, Inc., and was printed and bound by R. R. Donnelley & Sons Company. The cover was printed by Phoenix Color Corp.

Printed in the United States of America

10 9 8 7 6 5 4 3 2 1

ISBN: 0-13-520594-8

Prentice-Hall International (UK) Limited, *London*
Prentice-Hall of Australia Pty. Limited, *Sydney*
Prentice-Hall of Canada, Inc., *Toronto*
Prentice-Hall Hispanoamericana, S. A., *Mexico*
Prentice-Hall of India Private Limited, *New Delhi*
Prentice-Hall of Japan, Inc., *Tokyo*
Simon & Schuster Asia Pte. Ltd., *Singapore*
Editora Prentice-Hall do Brasil, Ltda., *Rio de Janeiro*

PREFACE

We have come to accept that the acquisition of knowledge is quite distinct from the accumulation of facts or information. The concepts of learning and of knowing now imply that one has integrated information in some cohesive fashion into an interpretive framework that an individual will use in understanding her- or himself and the world. Correspondingly, in education, the focus on fixed information has been balanced with the recognition of the importance of cognitive skills. The question arises, however, what these cognitive skills might be.

At the same time, information processing technologies have been advancing substantially on a day-to-day basis. These information processing technologies provide a coherent and cohesive framework for the storage, management, analysis, and application of information. In this regard, they seem to embody cognitive attributes we would hope to find in human thinkers. This view is further extended by advances in cognitive psychology and neuropsychology that use computer models to interpret human thinking.

Under the circumstances, popular culture and education alike have adopted what might be called a "computational paradigm," the use of computer metaphors, to understand how human beings cognize themselves and the world. The model of thinking that empowers information processing technology may also limit it, however, and those limitations may, when applied educationally, significantly limit the way students learn to think. This book asks the critical questions Is there more to thinking than information processing? What more is there? and What difference does it make to educators?

This book contains chapters by authors from widely disparate orientations and disciplines who explore "the more." They also explicate the human cognitive capacities that transcend computation, as well as substantially affect our judgment and action, individually and collectively. In so doing, they address numerous crucial issues from educational standards to the environmental/social and moral dimensions, to the role of the senses in human development. Indeed, our thinking about thinking governs much of educational theory and practice. We are deeply influenced by tacit, deeply held assumptions . . . assumptions that may turn out to be severely limited and limiting. What are these assumptions, and what do they mean for us as educators?

The goal of this volume is less to provide specific information than it is to present readers with images and ideas. These images and ideas are intended to provide broad perspectives, to offer alternative contexts for viewing the world and the way we think about it. These perspectives will challenge readers to examine deeply held beliefs and assumptions about what the world is, who we are, and how both may be known. Each chapter is designed to engage the reader in the exploration of ideas, and this very activity of thinking itself forms an experiential base for examining the thinking processes. Thus, the activity that the reader brings to the text is as significant as the explicit text itself.

Each chapter is contextualized with a brief introduction written by the editor. These introductions provide an overview of the central issues in each chapter and serve to maintain continuity throughout the book.

In Chapter 1, Jeffrey Kane introduces one central theme of the book: that our thinking is often based on deeply held but unexamined cultural assumptions. He explains that these assumptions, rather than the explicit content of thought, often determine the conclusions we reach and the judgments we make. One of the most basic and pervasive root metaphors in contemporary education is that thinking can be reduced to the formal processing of symbols, as in information processing. Kane describes the limitations of this perspective and traces them back philosophically to what he perceives as an error in Descartes's *cogito*.

Chet Bowers, in Chapter 2, further clarifies the computational metaphor and demonstrates its power in shaping contemporary notions of human nature and the potential of technology. Bowers critically analyzes the related notions of individuality and intelligence relative to the computational framework. His analysis reveals a direct relationship between the mechanistic assumptions in our thinking and the educational, social, and ecological crises of our time.

Dale Snauwaert, in Chapter 3, offers a historical overview of the evolution of Western thought as it relates to the detachment of the person from the world or the knower from the known. He introduces an alternative concept of thinking and an alternative concept of education based on Martin Buber's concept of the I-You relation as a way of overcoming the narrowness and detachment of much of contemporary thought.

David Purpel, in Chapter 4, provides a specific, immediate account of the moral and social failure of abstract and detached thinking. He contends that one cannot process discrete bits of information to recognize the moral and social responsibilities of human beings. Rather, he emphasizes the need in education for affirmation, for a personal rootedness in traditions that recognize meaning, purpose, and identity, beyond what may be calculated. Purpel describes some of the wisdom he has found in the mystical traditions of his own Jewish heritage. This emphasis on affirmation of cultural heritage is mirrored by Gregory Cajete (chap. 9) describing his educational experiences as an American Indian.

In Chapter 5, Diana Muxworthy Feige addresses the concept of detached intellectual thinking in the domain of the physical sciences. Following Gregory Bateson, she explores the notion that patterns and relationships run through nature, giving it its particular order and form. She explains that these underlying patterns of nature are aesthetic and may be revealed only through an act of creative imagination. In this context, the educational task is to spur and nourish the creative imagination, not as an act of fantasy but as a foundation for scientific insight.

Howard Gardner, in Chapter 6, both demonstrates how new intelligences may be identified and examines two candidates: naturalist and spiritual intelligence. In his analysis of naturalist intelligence, Gardner reflects many issues addressed by Muxworthy Feige (chap. 5), specifically with reference to the recognition of patterns in nature. Gardner concludes that an eighth distinctive intelligence does indeed exist. The question of spiritual intelligence proves more complex because it includes questions of metaphysics and strains the limits of knowledge. In this respect, he revisits, within the context of his inquiry, fundamental issues raised by Purpel (chap. 4) and Snauwaert (chap 3).

In Chapter 7, Mary Catherine Bateson explores the virtues of ambiguity. Although contemporary thought values clarity, Bateson contends that the vagaries that allow for the play of the imagination in recognizing the patterns and relationships give things their meaning and form. The generation of meaning requires a high degree of personal engagement, and the patterns of meaning that emerge bear an individual's interpretive stamp. Consequently, ambiguity allows for communication, continuity, and change within a community.

Following a similar theme, Madhu Suri Prakash, in Chapter 8, challenges the value of abstract academic study. Focusing on doctoral-level inquiry, she explains that students are initiated into a culture where local, specific, and multidimensional problems have no place. Rather, students are required to work in the context of theoretical generalizations and abstractions removed from messy local reality. Prakash explains that such study, removed from specific places and persons, does not generate sound social or ecological insight or action.

In Chapter 9, Gregory Cajete, speaking from American Indian tradition, echoes many concerns raised by Prakash (chap. 8), Bowers (chap. 2), Purpel (chap. 4), and others, particularly with respect to moral and ecological thinking. He offers a model of thinking radically different from the root metaphor described by Kane (chap 1). Cajete's model emphasizes local, natural, and cultural continuity as a foundation for understanding what the world is, who we are, and our responsibilities as human beings. He describes the importance of community, art, music, story, and the study of nature in developing whole human beings.

Robert Samples places the growth of the individual mind within the context of biological and cultural evolution. In Chapter 10, he suggests that all learning is a form of adaptation, a transformation of mind, to cope with new and varied circumstances. This process of adaptation is part of a larger evolutionary process of one's culture, our species, and the ecosystems of nature. Given this perspective, Samples identifies the factors conducive to evolving ecosystems and applies them to the creation of environmental opportunities for the growth of the mind to participate in this continuous cycle of creation.

In Chapter 11, John Miller, building on American transcendentalism and, most notably, the work of Ralph Waldo Emerson, emphasizes a spiritual unity that unites each and all of us with one another and the world. Miller explains that, beyond all the computational skills one may acquire to work in the information age is a personal, social, and moral necessity to perceive what unifies us, rather than what separates us. This unfolding of the soul is best achieved through an education devoted to the growth of the imagination, the centrality of the arts, and the study of nature. These, Miller contends, are the foundations on which to develop a capacity for wisdom, rather than mere practical skill.

Chapter 12, by Robert Sardello and Cheryl Sanders, presents a unique picture of the unity of mind and body. They respond to the problem of the separation of the knower from the known, not by describing a physiology of mind as is common, but through the spiritualizing of the body. They contend that 12 senses, rather than 5, serve as bridges, not only of information but also of form and substance between the physical body, soul, and spirit. They present a vivid and detailed account of how education can provide for a unity of thinking and being.

The perspective offered by Sardello and Sanders has been integrated into a pedagogical perspective known worldwide as *Waldorf education.* In Chapter 13, Joan Almon introduces Waldorf education, with particular emphasis on the early childhood years. The picture of education that emerges is based on children engaged in creative encounters (as described by Snauwaert, chap. 3), whether through art, music, story, or nature study—the very emphases identified by Gregory Cajete (chap. 9) and John Miller (chap. 11). Through such encounters, Almon explains, the child is educated or drawn forth as a person, rather than merely informed as a processor of information.

These same concerns are addressed by David Sobel in Chapter 14, where he presents a curricular model incorporating Piagetian developmental stages; some common, almost universal interests in childhood; and the circumstances of particular places and particular times—serendipity. Sobel suggests that curricula must be

responsive to the integration of these factors if they are to provide a vital place for children to learn and sustain their interest in continuing their explorations of the world and of themselves.

Continuing the developmental emphasis of previous chapters, Kieran Egan, in Chapter 15, presents a developmental view of consciousness that integrates sociocultural influences. He explains that various modes of understanding unfold within cultures and individuals relative to the introduction of various forms of literacy. Each new form of literacy introduces new cognitive skills and frameworks for both the exercise and the intellect of the imagination. Egan describes the development of what he calls a romantic mode of understanding that develops with the introduction of written literacy. In this context, human understanding develops, not with reference to the processing of information alone, but relative to the form of consciousness created by the given constellations of literacy.

Chapter 16, by Nel Noddings, also focuses on literacy—specifically, the simple but vital art of conversation. Noddings suggests that conversation, which may include various levels of formality, can serve as a foundation for engaged academic studies and for the development of community within a school. In a manner reminiscent of Mary Catherine Bateson's discussion (chap. 7) of the virtues of ambiguity, she adds that conversation allows for the creation of meaning, identity, and morally conscious school communities.

* * *

This book is a result of the efforts of many individuals working together. First and foremost, I gratefully acknowledge the contributing authors, who not only created this text but also endured my editing. I also acknowledge all those who helped me organize this text and write my own chapter: Dale Snauwaert, David Purpel, Howard Gardner, Madhu Prakash, and Huston Smith.

I also acknowledge the contributions of Assistant Dean Joanne Blas for her critical and careful analysis of the book as a whole and the introductory texts in particular. My graduate assistant, James Perez, was tremendously helpful in working through the various details of the publication process. A special thanks is owed to my secretary, Joan McCarthy, who endured endless hours of close work with me while I continuously changed my mind. Last, this book would not have been possible if not for the patience, strength, and guidance I received from my wife, Janet.

Thanks also to the reviewers of the manuscript for their insights and comments: Timothy J. Bergen, University of South Carolina; George Bernstein, Montclair State University; Marylou Brotherson, Nova Southeastern University; John Dahlberg, Western Oregon State College; Vicky L. Gilliland, Southwestern Oklahoma State University; Patricia A. Gross, Ursinus College; W. Thomas Jamison, Appalachian State University; John E. Merryman, Indiana University of Pennsylvania; and Ann H. Stoddard, University of North Florida.

Contents

5 THE LEGACY OF GREGORY BATESON: ENVISIONING AESTHETIC EPISTEMOLOGIES AND PRAXIS 77

6 ARE THERE ADDITIONAL INTELLIGENCES? THE CASE FOR NATURALIST, SPIRITUAL, AND EXISTENTIAL INTELLIGENCES 111

7 In Praise of Ambiguity 133

8 Understanding Ourselves: Beyond Information Explosion, Hypertext, or Mechanical Memory 147

9 The Making of an Indigenous Teacher: Insights Into the Ecology of Teaching 161

10 LEARNING AS TRANSFORMATION 185

11 EDUCATION AND THE SOUL 207

12 CARE OF THE SENSES: A NEGLECTED DIMENSION OF EDUCATION 223

INTRODUCTION

This book asks the question: If there is more to human thinking than information processing, what more is there? The question has become increasingly important as computers have become more integral in daily life and the economy. In the workplace, home, and school, we have become accustomed to working with computers of one sort or another, and the computers themselves have become so sophisticated that it seems as though they perform the same cognitive functions as we. They are much faster and much more precise and do not suffer from the all-too-human capacity to err.

Some applications of computers leave us only to marvel at their power. They can perform complex operations that we struggle to imagine. Consider, for example, the sophistication required to generate three-dimensional pictures of our bodies as in magnetic resonance imaging. Given such circumstances, it is easy to conclude that computers possess the highest qualities of human thinking.

In this context, it is critically important to understand that computers operate exclusively in accord with formal rules. They can store and manipulate vast amounts of information, but the information itself is irrelevant. Depending on the program used, all data are assigned codes for storage and use. A word processing program, for example, will treat the story of a massacre according to the very same rules as one about a celebrity's wardrobe. The words have no more meaning to a computer than they would to a book. For all the practical utility of the computer, it has no facility to see meaning or purpose in a word, idea, person, action, or event.

The argument has been advanced in a variety of quarters (see chaps. 1 and 2, this volume) that human beings think according to the same kinds of formal rules. The meaning that we assign to things is said to be a function of the programs in our brains, with neurons serving as silicon chips. The "wetware," the brain, is assumed to process information in the same fashion as programmed hardware in computers. The implication here is that every thought we have ever had, every idea about the relative or absolute value of things, every word we have ever spoken in joy or in anger, is considered nothing more than biologically produced output. By extension, we can conclude that if we could replicate the complexity of neural activity and enough information, a computer could write *Hamlet.*

The implications of this perspective penetrate to the fundamental questions of what the world is, how it can be known, and who we are as conscious inhabitants. Are we chemical machines and nothing more? Is our thinking simply the firing of neurons as can be studied in a laboratory (rather than as experienced in thinking)? Can we know the world only as we reduce it to describe bits that we then put together in accordance with the explicit operational rules of "cultural software"? Do foundations for human thinking exist that, in the final analysis, transcend the notions of information and processing as they are defined in computers? Do principles operate in our attempts to understand the world, ourselves, and one another that cannot be reduced to the manipulation of data?

We can clarify the issues by considering the difference between the universe as understood by Isaac Newton and by Albert Einstein. Newton assumed that the world was composed of fixed bits of matter and that the task of science was to create precise mathematical descriptions accounting for their interaction. He further assumed that these bits of matter existed within a fixed framework of time and space. In this model of the universe, energy and matter were separate and distinct; there was no such thing as absolute terminal velocity.

Much of Newton's model of the universe is pretty useful. It provides the foundation for the scientific understanding of the gravitational forces governing everything from the movement of the planets to the flight of a baseball. It has been said that Newton's model of universal mechanics was sufficient to get us to the moon. For all practical intents and purposes, with the exception of the generation of nuclear power, Newton's theoretical framework is effective in describing the world as we know it in daily life.

By contrast, Einstein assumed that matter and energy were interchangeable and that time and space existed in a seamless continuum. Space curves with gravitational

force, and time moves at varied rates, depending on the speed at which an object is traveling. In his model of the universe, the only absolute is the speed of light. Einstein imagined that the physical characteristics of the world that he observed were not fixed, but relative to the speed at which he was traveling. At speeds beyond those we can attain, time slows and space expands sufficiently to change everything we see. Einstein may not have been necessary to get us practically to the moon, but Newton would not have been able to explain the power of the atom or the mysteries of the expanding universe.

Newton's theoretical framework was powerful, but Einstein revealed that it was wrong. For all its ability to describe physical phenomena, it was based on reasonable, sensible assumptions that were fundamentally false. Einstein sought to understand the properties of matter, energy, time, and space in conditions beyond what could be observed and available only to his imagination. Philosopher Karl Popper (1965) explains that Einstein's formulations assumed elements that were "highly speculative and abstract, and very far removed from what might be called their 'observational basis.' All attempts to show that they were more or less directly based on observations were unconvincing" (p. 255).

The point of this discussion is to illustrate that a theoretical framework may indeed be reasonable and useful but inadequate. Where basic assumptions are faulty, the framework may not be able to penetrate into phenomena to see what principles are operating beyond what we can perceive. Furthermore, it is intended to illustrate that fluid, imaginative thinking may be necessary to see the principles at work in phenomena beyond what is immediately empirically available. This imaginative element in our thinking is necessary to grasp the phenomena, not as fixed and separate entities, but as dynamic systems only partially revealing themselves to us in our limited observational perspective.

Physicist David Bohm (1980) reaches much the same conclusion in his work on particle research:

> [T]he idea of a separately and independently existent particle is seen to be, at best, an abstraction furnishing a valid approximation only in a certain limited domain. Ultimately, the entire universe (with all its "particles," including those constituting human beings, their laboratories, observing instruments, etc.) has to be understood as a single undivided whole, in which analysis into separately and independently existent parts has no fundamental status. (p. 174)

Undoubtedly, much of what we do and can do on a practical level is a consequence of our ability to break things down into manageable parts and rearrange them to solve a particular problem. There is a vast difference, however, between breaking these down into fragments and assuming that the field we are studying is composed of these separate entities. If our aim is to understand, rather than to achieve ways to do something, then reductive thinking may be inadequate, especially when our subject is human beings. Rather, it is essential to "dwell" in phenomena (as philosopher/scientist Michael Polanyi would say), to let our imaginations roam into phenomena, to create an intuitive context for recognizing the patterns and relationships governing our subject beyond the confines of what we perceive immediately.

The central thesis of this book is that fragmentary models of knowledge and thinking are widely assumed in studying human thinking and in teaching children how to think. In years past, much of educational practice and theory was guided by a reductivist conception of knowledge. Knowledge was thought to consist of discrete bits of information, data that, as public property, were stored in books, machines, and human minds. Learning, behaviorist B. F. Skinner explained, was the process by which an individual acquired the capacity to exhibit such data, given appropriate stimuli. Thus, the key to education was to develop mechanisms that could effectively transmit specific items of data as efficiently as possible. The learner, despite having individual learning characteristics, did not create or reconstitute information. Knowledge was ready-made, final, complete, and unique unto itself; there was no room for the knower in the known.

More recently, the underlying conception of knowledge applied in educational practice and theory has undergone a revolution. As information processing technologies have advanced, the metaphors for knowledge have been shaped by the language systems theory. In this context, knowledge remains discrete information but is embedded in an information system. System theory allows for the development of a cognitive map so that information is not merely stored but located; that is, each bit of information exists in relation to other bits of information. Thus, a knower may systematically integrate bits of information to create new knowledge structures. In this broad context, learning is viewed in terms of growth of an individual's capacity to animate systems of information. To know is to be an active information processor.

This theoretical perspective has led to development of a variety of new educational priorities. Curricula now abound with references to "problem-solving skills" or "critical thinking." The evaluation of students now employs more "authentic assessment" practices that measure learning through reference to an individual's capacity to apply, rather than merely to exhibit, information. Students are now challenged to be "active learners"—to adapt acquired information to new and varied circumstances.

As refreshing and important as these educational innovations have been, the underlying model of knowledge has defined the knower as an information processor. The question persists: What differences exist between mechanical and human information processors? Are human beings "personnel subsystems" in a technological infrastructure (Noble, 1993, p. 6)?

Such questions require that we consider the nature of the intelligence that permits us to acquire, retain, and adapt knowledge. In this regard, Robert Sternberg's (1985) "triarchic theory" of human intelligence and Howard Gardner's seminal work on multiple intelligences (1983) are particularly edifying. In particular, Gardner begins with an extraordinarily penetrating and simple definition of intelligence, one that is particularly pertinent to the questions above. He defines an **intelligence** as "the ability to solve problems, or to create products, that are valued within one or more cultural setting" (p. x).

This definition is critical because it allows for intelligence to operate in nonlinguistic modes. It permits us to address problems in music, art, intrapersonal relationships, and the like without confining us to the use of linguistic symbols and processes. No longer is knowing confined to the symbol of the word; no longer is knowing confined by the processes of ratiocination. Thus, multiple modes of knowledge are possible in multiple domains. As we move away from the manipulation of linguistic and mathematical symbols, the knower increasingly becomes one of the defining characteristics of knowledge. Knowledge, as such, cannot be found in words, books, or computers, but only as it is animated by intelligence.

Yet, despite Gardner's remarkable accomplishments in describing and expanding our conceptions of intelligence and knowledge, he nonetheless leaves us with our original question: Are we, as knowers, mere information processors? Is it possible that the modes of knowing that may be associated with each of the intelligences amount to "computational mechanisms"—varied means in varied contexts for problem solving and problem solving only (Gardner, 1983, pp. 64–65, 243)?

Let us keep in mind the various kinds of machines that are designed to solve diverse problems. From the steam engine, to Turing machines, to word processors, to self-correcting industrial robotic devices—machines solve problems—some physical, some computational, some linguistic, and some working in many contexts all at once. What makes the human capacity to solve problems different from all the others—not only in terms of degree but also in kind?

The most obvious response to the question is, of course, that machines respond to problems by design, whereas human beings may select problems and create new solutions. Of course, the selection of problems requires that we have the capacity to identify something as problematic and something as more problematic than something else. In other words, intelligence must be *more* than the capacity to solve problems; our definition must include the capacity to recognize that problems exist.

To recognize that a problem exists, it is necessary to recognize that something is in a state of disequilibrium, that something requires our attention, that something should be different from what it now is. Problems do not exist in a vacuum; they're defined in terms of objectives, intentions, and purposes beyond themselves. Problems arise when we seek physical basics, coherence, or social power, to name but a few contexts. Whether we seek to understand the physical laws governing energy and matter or to refine the kinesthetic motion of our own bodies to snap a sharp-breaking curve ball or to express in color and form the aesthetic dimensions of a sunset, we perceive problems as problems relative to some sense that thought or action is required. Such drive may come from such diverse sources as instinctive impulse, aesthetic sensibility, existential recognition, or spiritual realization. Our capacity for tacit experience defines what we see as a problem and what possibilities we will entertain regarding possible solutions.

As we attend to problems, alternation of emphasis is constant, a continuous interplay of information processing strategies and underlying experience. As information processing computes possibilities, we experience an increase of relative degrees of satisfaction or dissatisfaction with the possibilities that unfold.

Throughout, we are guided by our capacity for experience, the nature and extent of both problems and solutions. If our capacity for experience is shallow, so shall be our problems and solutions. If we learn to experience with depth, so all else shall follow.

Information is processed in a context that transcends the information itself—whether the context be profound or profane, existential or pragmatic. This context is equivalent in human thinking to relativity in the physical universe. It is essential in understanding not only the world but also ourselves. As we lose sight of it, we diminish the world and reduce ourselves.

Computer paradigms for researching human cognition, as stated earlier, base their simulations of thinking on discrete bits of data. The use of such approaches to understanding human thinking has extraordinary value, but they, when we lack more global vision, fragment our conceptions of who we are, as well as our relations with others and the environment. In this case, Bohm (1980) explains:

> [W]hen this mode of thought is applied more broadly to man's notion of himself and the world in which he lives . . . then man ceases to regard the resulting divisions as merely useful or convenient and begins to see and experience himself and his world as actually constituted of separately existent fragments. (p. 2)

In this context, our concern in this volume is not about computers or, more narrowly, computers in education. Rather, it is about how we think about our thinking and ultimately ourselves as human beings.

The perspective that human thinking can be reduced to the electrochemistry of the brain or absolutely explicit propositions without ambiguity has profound consequences relative to the way we define our humanity, as well as our social, moral, and ecological responsibilities. It has profound implications on the way we approach education—the kinds of experiences we would create for students, the kinds of cognitive capacities we would have them develop, the kinds of relationships with others, and the environment we would foster.

The purpose of this book is to explore the limitations of models of thinking reducible to the processing of separate and distinct bits of information according to prescribed rules, to suggest other possible perspectives for understanding who we are and how we think, and to consider some implication of these considerations for education. The contributors to the volume offer a wide, and by no means cohesive, variety of perspectives. Together, the chapters introduce a host of questions that require much further critical review and imaginative insight.

The reader will find themes that ebb and flow through the chapters. These themes provide the contexts for exploring key educational issues. The authors, in various contexts, address the role of community in constructing knowledge, the ecological dimensions of modes of thinking, the spiritual aspects (variously defined) of the world and ourselves, and the moral implications of the assumptions embedded in our thinking. These themes, each in their own way, arise from the effort to transcend the limitations of an information processing paradigm.

References

Bohm, D. (1980). *Wholeness and the implicate order.* London: Kegan Paul.

Gardner, H. (1983). *Frames of mind: The theory of multiple intelligences.* New York: Basic Books.

Noble, D. (1993, Summer). The regime of technology in education. *Holistic Education Review.*

Popper, K. (1965). *Conjectures and refutations: The growth of scientific knowledge.* New York: Basic Books.

Sternberg, R. (1985). *Beyond IQ: A triarchic theory of human intelligence.* Cambridge UK: Cambridge University Press.

1 On Education With Meaning

Jeffrey Kane

INTRODUCTION

Information technologies not only provide enormous capacities in storing, managing, and accessing data but also have become models for studying and understanding human thinking. They process information with such speed and precision that they seem to exhibit the highest standards of thinking without the vagaries and errors that abound as humans assume the task. Furthermore, these technologies have taken a central place in the world economy, performing operations once reserved for human beings and opening previously unimaginable possibilities. By contrast, human thinking seems more anemic than vital, more the flawed copy than the unmatched original.

These images of the virtues of information technologies and the frailties of human thinking are a consequence of an overstatement of the possibilities of the systems governing the operations of the former and an understatement of the subtle but profound qualities of the latter. The overestimation results, in part, from the brute fact that the machines can do amazing things. A second factor is that these technologies drive the economy and have redefined national educational policy. The underestimation is a consequence of the continued evolution of some deeply held cultural assumptions beginning, most notably, with the writings of René Descartes in the 17th century.

In this chapter, educational philosopher Jeffrey Kane examines the operational principles underlying information processing technologies and some of the cultural assumptions we carry as Descartes's intellectual heirs. In more specific terms, Kane explains that information processing is based on the use of prescribed operational procedures irrespective of the content of the data being considered. The data have no meaning other than to open or close microcircuits embedded in silicon. These machines derive their power from this unambiguous and precise routing of information, but they do so by eliminating the possibility that the meaning of a fact or figure could actually affect the course of the process. This limitation becomes important when applied to the study of human thinking where the meaning of ideas would seem to play a role in determining the judgments we make. The problem here, Kane suggests, is in understanding the nature of "meaning." Cognitive neuropsychologists claim that meaning is a matter of the activation levels and the particular neural pathways of the brain. In other words, the content of the idea has nothing to do with the idea itself any more than data could have intrinsic meaning for a computer. In this context, human beings amount to no more than biological computers.

Kane's thesis is that this model of human thinking begins with the thinker as an object, rather than as a thinking subject. The perspective precludes the possibility that directly experiencing an idea (say, the eventuality of death) might actually have intrinsic meaning and exert a powerful influence on the course of determining what we believe, decide, and act on. Kane traces this view of the human being as a "thinking thing" back to Descartes's *cogito:* "I think, therefore I am." With this sentence, Descartes defined the human being as an abstraction, as a conclusion rather than a person of flesh and blood experiencing and trying to make sense out of life.

Kane maintains that this view of human thinking and human being, however vague and inexplicit in the minds of most educators, is becoming increasingly prevalent in educational theory and practice. Kane provides a variety of examples of how our educational focus has narrowed and how we may lead children to acquire information without giving them the experiences and skills to create or discover meaning in the world, in others, and in their own lives.

—*Jeffrey Kane*

Imagine there is a planet where the inhabitants have very refined skills equivalent to those we normally associate with inquiry in the physical sciences. They have the ability to observe with precision, identify discrete variables, and apply a calculus to describe the interactions of things they observe. The inhabitants have honed these skills but no other cognitive or expressive capacities. On their planet, the arts do not exist. There is no music.

Now imagine that one of these extraterrestrials visits our planet and finds himself or herself outside a building listening to someone inside playing a violin. Using his or her skills, the visitor begins a study by listening carefully to each of the notes, identifying each of their characteristics and attempting to find explicit patterns in their relationships. Our visitor takes each note and defines it in terms of its duration, amplitude, and frequency. With this information, the visitor constructs a mathematical model to describe to colleagues "back home" exactly what was discovered.

However, this visitor would not be able to describe anything more than sound or vibrations in the air. He or she would not be able to observe or understand that each of the notes heard carried meaning. This exacting scientist would not be able to discern that each of the notes, each characteristic of each of the notes, and the configuration of all the notes together, including the intervals of silence between them, were governed by a meaning transcending physical characteristics.

Leaving our planet, this observant alien would not have a clue that there is music on our planet or that what he or she heard ultimately was more a creation of a musician's vision than simply the vibration of air.

Neil Scott, a senior researcher at Stanford University's Center for the Study of Language and Information, is working on a new technology that will allow individuals to interact with computers through electrical activity in the brain (Madison, 1995). The evolving system, sensing primarily brain wave patterns, allows a person to move a cursor on a monitor simply by thinking "right" or "left." No physical action is required—not so much as a movement of an eye. Scott explains that the system reads brain wave patterns, electrical activity on the forehead, and electrical charges on the surface of the eye. Given the data, the intent is to identify the unique configurations for the thoughts "right" and "left."

This technology puts a fine edge on the question of the relationship between human thinking and information processing in computers. It establishes a completely electronic linkage between neural activity in the brain and the racing of electrical impulses through silicon chips. The connection is seamless. In this context, we may ask what differences might there be (aside from issues of voltage and the like) between an electrical stream as it moves "within the skin" and the technology without?

The question is crucial for educators in that it requires us to explore some of our basic assumptions not only about human thinking but about human being as well.

What are we to teach, to whom, and toward what end? We can address these issues directly by exploring some effects of the growth of information technologies in our understanding of human thinking and some fundamental assumptions about human thinking deeply embedded in Western culture since the days of René Descartes.

THE SHIFT FROM MEANING

The last half century has witnessed a revolution in the nature of machines. Where once machines were designed to perform specific mechanical functions, they now often have the flexibility to respond to contingencies. Philosopher William Lycan (1995) explains that such flexibility is a function of a sensitivity to information—an ability not only to register information through receptors but also to store, manage, and finally use that information (p. 123). As machines have become more subtle, complex, and rapid in their processing of information, cognitive science has emerged to adopt their functional operation as the framework for understanding the processes used in human thinking. The machines' mimicking of some human cognitive processes and functions has become the prototype for understanding all human thinking.

The eminent psychologist Jerome Bruner (1990) recalls the origins of the cognitive revolution as an attempt

> to discover and to describe formally the meanings that human beings created out of their encounters with the world. It focused upon the symbolic activities that human beings employed in constructing and in making sense not only of the world, but of themselves. . . . Very early on . . . emphasis began shifting from "meaning" to "information," from the *construction* of meaning to the *processing* of information. . . . The key factor in the shift was the introduction of computation as the ruling metaphor and of computability as a necessary criterion of a good theoretical model. (p. 2)

To assess the importance of this shift in perspective, we need to define the terms *information* and *processing* in contrast to the notions of "meaning" and the "construction of meaning." In a computational context, **information** is a message consisting of a code that serves to store it at a specific location and to manage its functional relationships within a system of formal syntax. **Processing** consists of formal rules that manage information. A bit of information entered into a system is assigned codes about its location, rules of access, and use relative to a given processing program. "The system that does all of these things is blind with respect to whether what is stored is words from Shakespeare's sonnets or numbers from a random number table" (Bruner, 1990, p. 4). Information is an empty symbol; it has no content, it has no semantic meaning. A bit of information is a sign directing continued processing to one alternative or another within the governing syntactic rules of a particular program. A bit of information is as unambiguous as a flick of a light

switch. It determines whether an electrical impulse traveling through a computer opens or closes a circuit. All information amounts to zeros and ones, which philosopher John Searle (1984) explains, "are just numerals; they don't even stand for numbers. Indeed, it is this feature of digital computers that makes them so powerful" (p. 31).

The processing—the manipulation of information to achieve some end—does not depend in any way on significance, beauty, or capacity to illuminate something that might be called substance of an idea. The processing of ideas relative to syntax is clearly illustrated in a sample of "computer poetry" cited as exemplary by computer scientist and educator Seymour Papert. His book *Mindstorms: Children, Computers, and Powerful Ideas* includes a "poem" generated by a 13-year-old girl programming a computer to place random nouns, verbs, and so forth in a syntactically prescribed framework. The poem:

INSANE RETARD MAKES BECAUSE SWEET SNOOPY SCREAMS
SEXY WOLF LOVES THAT WHY SEXY LADY HATES
UGLY MAN LOVES BECAUSE UGLY DOG HATES
MAD WOLF HATES BECAUSE INSANE WOLF SKIPS
SEXY RETARD SCREAMS THAT WHY SEXY RETARD HATES
THIN SNOOPY RUNS BECAUSE FAT LADY HOPS
SWEET FOGINY SKIPS A FAT LADY RUNS[1]

The poem is a syntactic exercise that, in effect, expresses nothing because there is literally nothing to express. Words are coded signals and have no meaning other than their function in the logic of the syntax. The fact that computer poetry is pedagogical history is of no account here. The poem illustrates the way computers process information. The meaning of the words *love* and *hate* are interchangeable, irrelevant; they have no relevance to the way the poem evolves or anything else (Kane, 1984; Roszak, 1994).

A more subtle but profoundly problematic example of information processing, as opposed to the construction of meaning, is provided by computer scientist Joseph Weizenbaum. In the early 1970s, Weizenbaum developed a program with which an individual could interact with a computer using English. To demonstrate its ease, he designed a Rogerian psychotherapist (Doctor) script to mimic some basic therapeutic techniques. When a person typing at the keyboard entered a message that he or she was upset about, let us say an argument with a spouse, Doctor might have responded by noting that the typist was upset about an argument and asking why. Weizenbaum was astounded that several practicing psychiatrists, thinking of therapists as information processors, suggested that Doctor could be used therapeutically.

---

1. Excerpt as submitted from *Mindstorms: Children, Computers and Powerful Ideas* by Seymour Papert. Copyright © 1980 by Basic Books, Inc. Reprinted by permission of BasicBooks, a division of HarperCollins Publishers, Inc.

The fact was that Doctor was operating in a syntactic fashion, according to formal rules, and could not interpret the importance of the message in terms of the personal meanings driving the person's expression. The program would respond in virtually the same way to a "story" of nonsense syllables. If someone entered, "I feel xprqmz!" Doctor could likely have responded, "Why do you feel xprqmz?" For the person, the discourse was a method of conveying meaning with words as symbols; for Doctor, the interaction was a string of signs directing electrical impulses through circuitry. Weizenbaum (1976) wonders,

> What must a psychiatrist who makes such a suggestion think he is doing while treating a patient that he can view the simplest mechanical parody of a single interviewing technique as having captured anything of the essence of a human encounter? (p. 6)

It seems that the shift from constructing meaning to processing information had, by that time, taken hold. An information processing paradigm had established itself as *the* interpretative framework for understanding human thinking. The difference between "meaning" and "information," between semantic and syntactic systems, seemed increasingly irrelevant as technology advanced and cognitive psychology opened new domains of competence and of inquiry.

Today, the capacity of machines to process information has become so sophisticated, so flexible, that their syntactic mode of processing is virtually transparent. Where once technology presented a crude illusion of human thinking, current technology provides what in many quarters is seen as the actual foundation for cognition. The response to Weizenbaum's question might now come in the form of a new question. What makes us think that something regarded as human encounter is in any way different from the processing operations performed by computers?

The Chinese Room

Nowhere is this question more pressing than in the emerging field of cognitive neuroscience. This field of inquiry begins with the principles that neurons are essentially electrical devices, and that the characteristics of systems of neurons depend on individual cells. It employs computer models and information processing frameworks as the theoretical basis for research. The computational paradigm extends beyond an approach to research to a fundamental belief that the brain is a biological computer. Patricia Churchland and Terrence Sejnowski (1992), two researchers in the field, speak of a

> deep-seated conviction that what is being modeled by a computer is itself a kind of computer, albeit one quite unlike the serial, digital machines on which computer science cut its teeth. That is, the nervous systems and parts of nervous systems are themselves naturally evolved computers—organically constituted, analogue in representation, and parallel in their processing architecture. (p. 7)

Again, it is essential to note here the transition in the notion of meaning. Cognitive scientists, in applying computer-based models, opened the definition from a fixed, universal unit of communication to anything that may be said to be a message. Theodore Roszak (1994) observes,

> Following the lead of information theorists, scientists and technicians felt licensed to make even broader and looser use of the word. It could soon be applied to any transmitted signal that could be metaphorically construed as a "message"—for example, the firing of a nerve impulse. To use the term so liberally is to lay aside all concern for the quality or character of what is being communicated. The result has been a progressive blurring of intellectual distinctness. (p. 14)

The cognitive neuropsychologist's model for research precludes the possibility that a message being communicated has a meaning that, itself, has significance and that can determine the course of thinking. The change in definition of information from codes governing the movement of electrical impulses through the circuitry of a machine and the electrochemical activity within and between neurons in the brain does not account for our ability to grapple with semantic meaning. Philosopher John Searle (1984) writes, "If my thoughts are to be *about* anything, then the strings [of symbols] must have *meaning* which makes the thoughts about those things. In a word, the mind has more than a syntax, it has a semantics" (p. 31).

Searle illustrates this point with a "thought experiment" in which he asks us to imagine that a computer has been programmed to simulate an understanding of Chinese. The computer might be able to process syntactically questions written in Chinese and, with a large enough database, conceivably generate responses as good as those of a native Chinese speaker. Searle asks whether we would then say that the computer understands Chinese as do native speakers.

To address this question, Searle asks us to imagine that we are locked in a room with basketfuls of Chinese symbols and that we do not understand a word of Chinese. In this room, we find a rule book, written in English, explaining how to manipulate Chinese symbols. A rule might say "Take a squiggle-squiggle sign out of basket number 1 and put it next to a squoggle-squoggle sign from basket number 2." Searle asks us to suppose further that some Chinese symbols are passed into the room and that we manipulate them according to the rules we have learned. Unbeknownst to us, those coming in would be called "questions," and those we send out, "answers."

Searle concludes that even if our answers cannot be distinguished from those of a native Chinese speaker, we would not have learned to speak a word of Chinese. Nor, obviously, would we have any understanding of the meaning of the Chinese symbols we manipulated other than relative to the procedures and processes we followed. The Chinese room illustrates that "understanding a language, or indeed, having mental states at all, involves more than just having a bunch of formal symbols. It involves having an interpretation or a meaning attached to those symbols" (Searle, 1984, p. 33).

Herein lies our first response to the question occasioned by Neil Scott's research. For a person thinking, there are semantic meanings, whereas only syntactic rules once the information technology receives the signal. There is more to the story, however. As cognitive neuroscience has progressed, it has developed a highly sophisticated and refined computational theoretical framework for understanding the brain to the point where it includes assertions about the very nature of human being.

TELEVISION WITHOUT SOUL

Paul Churchland, also a cognitive neuroscientist, elaborates a computational paradigm in his book *The Engine of Reason, the Seat of the Soul* (1995). He likens neurons in the brain to pixels on a television screen. The neurons, like pixels, represent the "general and lasting features of the external world." Churchland describes the capacity of the neurons relative to a television screen. "Counting each neuron as a pixel then, and dividing the TV screen's capacity (200,000) into the brain's capacity (100 billion), we must reckon that the brain's representational capacity is about 500,000 times greater than a TV screen's" (p. 7). When discussing who may be watching the pixilated show, Churchland concludes, "no one." "There is no distinct 'self' in there, beyond the brain as a whole" (p. 8). Various parts of the brain monitor each other at all times, but no "person," as such, is involved except as he or she may be defined as an organic computer with a unique pattern of neural pathways governing the activation levels of individual and nets of neurons.

Given this perspective, Churchland (1995) argues that the widely held notion of a mind or soul beyond the "picture" of the human being stated above is all but proven false. "The doctrine of an immaterial soul looks, to put it frankly, like just another myth, false not just at the edges, but to the core" (p. 17).

In a different context, but using a binary information processing or computational perspective, Bill Gates is quoted in *Time* as stating,

> All the neurons in the brain that make up perceptions and emotions operate in a binary fashion. . . . We can someday replicate that on a machine. . . . Eventually, we'll be able to sequence the human genome and replicate how nature did intelligence in a carbon-based system. (Isaacson, 1997, p. 47)

The computational human being image is clearly reflected in Gates's (1997) coworkers' description of his thinking with observations about his "incredible processing power and 'unlimited bandwidth,' as well as an agility at 'parallel processing' and 'multitasking'" (Isaacson, 1997, p. 46). The metaphors carry over into the way the reporter begins to describe Gates's capacity to think—that is, his received ability to process information. "He can be so rigorous as he processes data that one can imagine his mind indeed be digital: no sloppy emotions or analog fuzziness, just trillions of binary impulses coolly converting input into correct answers" (p. 46).

The speed, sophistication, and capacity of new technologies raise questions about human thinking and human beings not only for researchers and experts but also for the general population. For example, commenting on a chess match between grand master Gary Kasparov and IBM's Big Blue, a *Time* reporter concludes, "The better these seemingly soulless machines get at doing things people do, the more plausible it seems that we could be soulless machines too" (Wright, 1996, p. 50).

The point here is not to engage in a debate about the existence or nonexistence of the soul. It is not to suggest that those who use computers must agree that we are nothing but biological computational machines. Rather, the foregoing discussion illustrates how the shift Bruner noted from constructing meaning to information processing shapes not only the way we think about thinking but also the way we understand the world and define ourselves. Our assumptions about the nature of human thinking do not necessarily end in explicit conclusions regarding human nature. Some individuals may study computers, computational systems design, and the logic of syntactically based information processing programs without a twinge of doubt about the soul, God, or moral truth. Yet, even if unrecognized, the issue raised by the *Time* reporter illustrates how our collective cultural assumptions are changing. The shift to an information processing concept of human thinking was an outgrowth of long-evolving cultural assumptions that first took root during the Age of Enlightenment. The recent growth in technology and the effect of technology on the economy as the century draws to a close has refined and reinforced fundamental cultural assumptions about the nature of thinking.

In the 1970s, Weizenbaum could wonder what had gone wrong without thinking that we could confuse artificial intelligence with the real thing. He assumed, as did many of his readers, that something was amiss in our understanding of the nature of human thinking. Today, the assumption is increasingly widespread that we do indeed process information and, by extension, that we are information processors. Today's machines fit so seamlessly with the intentions of the people working with them, they are so "user friendly," that they seem to operate using the same essential systems we do. Conversely, we assume that they use the same systems as we.

Most of us do not see information in the stark zeros and ones (or analogical equivalents) even if it would seem to make sense that everything we think comes down to the firing of neurons or groups of neurons in the brain. The actual operations of the brain are extraordinarily complex, and the theory holds that what we experience as thinking is simply the cumulative effect of the firing of enormous numbers of neurons. We do not experience the zeros and ones (or threshold limits in analogical models) any more than we experience the digitalization of a voice carried over a telephone line. We might find ourselves wondering, however, how any analysis of the digital operations in a telephone system could ever reveal what it is we are talking about or what we are saying means to us.

The general notion of our being information processors is implicit and far more ambiguous than that of cognitive neuropsychologists. It exists in the form of tacit assumptions—a framework for thinking, rather than a conclusion reached after reflection. Where Weizenbaum (1976) wondered in amazement, we might read the

Time stories that suggest the only difference between our thinking and computers' processing is that they are more precise and much faster. Our emerging framework is still ambiguous enough, and we still hold a sufficient number of other cultural assumptions to obscure the contradiction of our being "soulful machines." In other words, we can hold contradictory assumptions because they are vague and enmeshed in the complex of deeply held assumptions that constitute our cultural worldview. Deeply held cultural assumptions do not shift overnight; they evolve over time. Over time, we develop new tacit perspectives that guide our thinking; we do not reach new conclusions simply by reason alone. We persue this in our later discussion of René Descartes, but the point for now is that the notion of human thinking as information processing has a profound impact on how we view ourselves and the world even if we may not now agree with the explicit conclusions of those on the leading edge.

ECONOMIC AND EDUCATIONAL IMPLICATIONS

Not only are the advances of technology and the information processing metaphor shaping the way we see the world, but they also are changing the world we see. Everything from the way we spend leisure time to the nature of our social interactions to the tasks we assume in the workplace are changing with the advancing of "everyday" technology. In this context, educational policy in the United States in the early 1980s began to focus on the need to provide the intellectual skills necessary to serve an information-based economy. In 1983, the National Commission on Excellence in Education issued its report, *A Nation at Risk*, stating,

> Knowledge, learning, information and skilled intelligence are the new raw materials of international commerce and are today spreading throughout the world as vigorously as miracle drugs, synthetic fibers, and blue jeans did earlier. If only to keep and improve on the slim competitive edge we still retain in world markets, we must dedicate ourselves to the reform of our educational system. . . . Learning is the indispensable investment required for success in the "information age" we are entering. (p. 7)

The report concluded that it is "essential . . . for government at all levels to affirm its responsibility for nurturing the *Nation's intellectual capital* [italics added]" (p. 17).

This intellectual capital is nothing less than the minds of children. In an industrial economy, the raw materials were coal, iron and other minerals, lumber, and of course, an adult population to provide physical labor. In the information economy, the primary resource is a population capable of collecting, sorting, storing, analyzing, and applying data in an efficient and systematic fashion. In the late 1980s, noting the relative failure of educational reform in the 1950s, President Bush called an "education summit" with the nation's governors to map a more effective strategy to achieve "the maximum return possible from our investment in the nation's educational system" (U.S. Department of Education, 1989, p. 3). The goal was to find how to reform the American education system to produce adult minds capable of meeting the information processing needs of the economy; the focus of policy was not the needs of children seeking to understand the world, to discover meaning, to develop a sense of connection or place, or simply to guide children in their growth as human beings. President Bush's strategy for national education reform in 1991, "America 2000," cites the need to rectify "America's skills and knowledge gap" (U.S. Department of Education, 1991, p. 5). It explains that "in the eight years since *A Nation at Risk,* we haven't turned things around in education. Almost all of our education trend lines are flat. Our country is idling its engines" (p. 5). The Clinton administration continued the initiative with the passage of "Goals 2000: Educate America Act," which is intended to assist "in the development and certification of high-quality assessment measures that reflect the internationally competitive content of student performance standards" and to provide the education necessary *"to meet high academic and occupational skill standards and to succeed in the world of employment and civic participation* [italics added]" (U.S. Department of Education, 1994, p. 5). The president's more recent call for a computer in every classroom (Isaacson, 1997) demonstrates the belief that computers are effective educational tools (or that their sale is good for the economy) and that there is a perceived need to educate children to fill the cognitive bill for an information economy.

Although much can be said for preparing children to participate in the economy, there is more to education than training intelligence for the job market or the maintenance of corporate profits. What is lost in all this is that children are human beings whose minds are not a *public* or *corporate* resource. The source of the error is in assuming that children *have* intelligence, rather than that they *are* the embodiment of intelligence. Children not only process information but also exist as self-conscious human beings who construct meaning in their thinking. In a very immediate sense, their thinking is part of who they are. As children learn to think, they acquire not only facts and skills but also assumptions about what the world is, who we are, how things are to be known, and what we need do. These lessons are not explicit, but implicit; they are not reasoned conclusions, but root metaphors, fundamental frameworks for thinking. Through education, we exert profound influence on the kinds of cognitive skills children develop and the kinds of things they think about. We thus shape much of their experience and the articulate contexts to construct meaning. Every fact imparted, every thinking skill emphasized, however subtle, opens some possibilities for meaning and may close others. The effects of education on children are cumulative and cannot be represented or understood in unambiguous, clear, and specific terms.

We may think we simply teach the facts and processes, but we speak to the very being of the child as he or she attempts to discover or create meaning. The models that cognitive scientists use have no place for being or for its role in shaping the meaning an individual may experience in or through an idea. In adopting their framework, we would have as much hope in understanding the meaning of education as the extraterrestrial at the beginning of this chapter would have in understanding the power, beauty, or sadness conveyed in a piece of music by analyzing the wavelength and amplitude of the sound waves emitted by the vibrations of a violin.

A specific educational trend stemming from the computation paradigm is in teaching children to think in specific terms within systems with formal rules. Perhaps the clearest example is found in Papert's work with LOGO in the early 1980s. The language of LOGO was designed to enable children to program a computer to create, among other things, geometric figures on a monitor. The creation of a figure required children to break the task into discrete steps. The calculations made by children immediately affected the movement and direction of the cursor. The action of the cursor gave children specific feedback to their decisions. Papert (1980) explains that his intent in creating LOGO was to "invent ways to take educational advantage of the opportunities to master the art of *deliberately* thinking like a computer, according, for example, to the stereotype of a computer program in step-by-step, literal, mechanical fashion" (p. 27). Papert explains, "they program the computer to make more complex decisions and find themselves engaged in reflecting on more complex aspects of their own thinking" (p. 28).

Although children may be said to master "the art" of thinking like a computer and to achieve increasingly sophisticated insights into their own thinking in this fashion, Theodore Roszak (1994) reminds us that "the mastery comes through adapting to the machine's way of doing things" (p. 76). What may appear as power over the computer is a function of conforming to its framework for processing.

Today, LOGO is more an educational artifact than anything else, rather like the original Pong games in contrast to the 64-bit technology. Today, variables have become more complex, flexible, and contextual, but the "power" provided by computers still requires that we learn to conform the way we think to the design of the technology itself. The operational architecture requires one to learn how various operating systems, drives, programs, functions, and so forth integrate. One has to develop a functional understanding of how programs work, how data are stored, how they may be accessed, and the like.

Recently, I visited a sixth-grade classroom where children were studying the Renaissance. They used the Internet to find information about the period. They prepared their reports by using word processing and graphic programs, including video and audio components. The children proudly demonstrated their reports, and the teacher complimented their work by telling me that they knew more about the software used than did she. The reports contained a reasonable amount of information, the kind that would be available in any text, and they showed a great deal of effort in combining the various media. However, I did not get the sense in talking with them that they internalized much of the drama and cultural richness of the Renaissance. They did not get a vivid picture of the lives of the painters, their motivations, pains, and imaginations. They did not acquire the compelling insights that would come from reading a book such as Giorgio Vasari's *Lives of the Most Eminent Italian Painters, Sculptors, and Architects,* a collection of firsthand biographical sketches written during the Renaissance. The Internet and databases the children used were not conducive to reading such a book. From what I've seen in classrooms, the technologies used have almost no place for books at all. In this case, the children looked for information, got it, and moved on to the presentation. The teacher did not guide them further to experience some of the inner meaning of the period, of the unfolding of new aesthetic and intellectual capacities played out on the scale of individual lives. Rather than pursue the richness of the Renaissance as a foundation for new visions and insights within themselves and in the world, the children learned to use the software programs available. They learned more about how to think like computers than like the people of the Renaissance. Although one may argue that the Internet and computer searches of various sorts could produce the information I describe, the fact remains that neither the teacher nor the students had any sense that something was missing. The "lessons" reflected a fascination with technology, rather than with the capacities for human experience and vision identifying the Renaissance.

The problem here is not computers themselves or a lack of training or commitment on the part of the teacher. The children were far more enthusiastic about learning than if they had read a text or an encyclopedia. The deeper issue is the concept of thinking underlying study in this and most other classrooms. The emphasis was on the acquisition of computer skills, the facts, and an analysis of the facts, rather than on history as a source of experience or reflection upon experience on seeing art, science, life, and self in new ways. The underlying concept behind the assignment was to learn about the Renaissance as a detached set of facts, rather than as a foundation for the growth of a new form of consciousness in children. Certainly, the children could have read Vasari in addition to their Internet sites, but what was the educational intent in studying the Renaissance to begin with? The object, like much of the thinking underlying that embodied in computers, was not a search for meaning, but rather information and skill in processing information.

Those familiar with classroom life recognize that teachers, schools, and communities do not claim to be interested exclusively in teaching children information and information processing skills. Other factors are involved as well. If we do not explore these issues in clear relief, however, we likely will not see them at all. The paradigm is so deeply ingrained and so pervasive that it cannot be separated out as we might look at a model of curriculum. We need to be very clear about what we're looking for to see the patterns these assumptions weave through educational policy and practice.

The computational paradigm has a great deal to commend itself so that its limitations can be obscured. Aside from the effective marketing of information techniques for educational purposes, their capacities are beguiling. Some newer technologies seem almost magical, wowing teachers and parents alike with endless possibilities. Children show a fascination with the stuff and a remarkable ability to pick up the functions with ease. All this can make for an active classroom. Under the circumstances, it is difficult to see the limitations as explored in the previous discussion of the teaching of the Renaissance. It is difficult to imagine what is meant by "meaning" as a form of inner awakening in response to an encounter.

Furthermore, other deeply held cultural assumptions in daily life soften the edge of the paradigm. For example, many educators hold to the belief that music and art ought to be essential components of a child's education. Not many are clear about why, however. There seems to be a vague sense that the arts are important expressive modes, but they are still relegated to the "affective sphere" despite Howard Gardner's (1991) insights into the variety of human intelligences. (Elliott Eisner, in his work on the arts and human cognition, offers an articulate and compelling model of cognition based in "meaning" in contrast to the information processing paradigm.)

Last, let us not forget the teacher as a person. Many teachers care deeply about their students as growing human beings. One had only to glance at the sixth-grade teacher of the Renaissance to know the depth of her devotion to her students and the guidance they find in her. The unspoken aspects of the relationship between the teacher and the students itself carries meanings that can transcend the subject matter covered by the curriculum. However, the curriculum can provide for encounters with the world, others, and oneself. In this context, the subject matter itself can be a source of inner experience and meaning. The task of educatioin in which the balanced growth of children is central might well be to help children unfold the possibilities of meaning they might find through encounters with the world otherwise known as the curriculum.

The intellectual capital conception of education is particularly problematic because it, by definition, is not concerned with the education relative to the growth and development of students as persons, but as resources in an information-based economy. It doesn't frame policy or practices focused on students' experiences as a foundation for discovering or creating lives of meaning.

A Wink and a Blink

In daily life, a sufficient number of variables soften the hard edge of the computational paradigm. It may seem to be far removed from what we experience, think, and do. Yet, we are hard-pressed when we are confronted with Churchland's picture of who we are and how we think. We previously noted the gulf between syntax and semantics but need now to explore how we can know semantic meanings whereas machines may not. If the brain is simply a biological computer, what characteristics does it have that we cannot replicate mechanically? In Churchland's (1995) terms, "If high-dimensional activation vectors can have intrinsic meaning within the human neural architecture, then why can't their vector analogs have intrinsic meaning in a silicon recapitulation of that architecture?" (p. 244). The question has been the subject of much academic debate, but we may find some help if we focus on something as simple as the difference between a wink and a blink. In many respects, they seem the same, but the whole course of human evolution stretches between the two.

Noted philosopher Gilbert Ryle (1971) explains that blinking is an involuntary movement of the eyelid, which, from a phenomenalistic perspective, cannot be distinguished from a wink, a signal to someone else. The wink is intended as a form of communication that is richly contextualized. Ryle offers scenarios in which winks were used to acknowledge, mislead, mimic, or satirize, depending on a complex set of conditions and cultural norms. In all cases, he notes, "[T]he 'signaler' (1) had deliberately winked, (2) to someone in particular, (3) in order to impart a particular message, [and] (4) according to an understood code" (p. 481). A complex set of factors allow winks to carry meaning that could not be recognized or understood simply by observing the closing of someone's eyelids.

A wink does constitute a transmission of information, but what is more—something Ryle does not address—is the fact that *someone* is indeed attempting to communicate with someone else. A wink is a personal interaction, an effort by *someone* to share in *someone* else. There is a personal dimension beyond the transference of information. The wink is, at a very subtle level, given meaning by the fact that the message is a sharing of experience, a communion in what is communicated.

This personal element, this element of being, is a source of meaning for which information processors, no matter how sophisticated, cannot account. No computational analysis will reveal meaning as an experience of being, nor can it begin to comprehend such experience as it plays out in the way we perceive ourselves and the world. What is true for the wink is infinitely richer and more substantive for much of human cognitive activity.

We cannot escape the fact that we exist; ask Descartes! The fact that we exist and that we are conscious of our own existence sets the context, the foundation, for all thinking. Although one may spend the course of a lifetime without a moment of reflection on these matters, the experience of being is at the root of one's thinking and judgment. This experience varies from person to person and culture to culture. It is the source of everything from the desire for food to the desire for communion, from the search for truth to the search for advantage, from the pain at the suffering, to the desire to inflict it, from the sense of the mystery and wonder of existence to the sense that "all is machine," from a commitment to moral agency to indifference to others. The fact that we *are,* that we experience being, is not reducible to a bit of information. It is infused within all that we know and do. We cannot deny being without denying ourselves. We cannot know meaning without it.

This existential foundation does not depend on an individual identifying him- or herself as an autonomous person. The frame of existential reference need not be based on a recognition of separateness. Notions of self or soul may evolve from it as an individual interacts with environment and culture. As noted earlier, we, as we are educated, do not simply receive information or acquire skills in accessing it. With each lesson, formal and informal, our existential frame of reference takes form. As we learn, we do not simply place ideas in storage and call them forth when we wish to use them—no matter how dry and abstract the context. We always, to lesser or greater extents, learn implicitly how to orient ourselves physically, socially, and intellectually. The ways we learn to experience give us cognitive modalities—ways to discover, create, and understand, in however vague a fashion, who we are and what the world is. We acquire dispositions—"ways of relation" as Martin Buber would say. We learn to objectify the world or dwell within it, to see things through detached analysis or imagination, to seek the exercise of control or open encounter. Education in this context is the process of gradually unfolding and giving form to the student; it is a process of transformation.

If education primarily and prematurely focuses on the acquisition of information and the skills to manipulate it in one way or another—that is, if education is an abstract exercise—students will not likely develop the capacity to explore, articulate, or create meaning. The extrinsic rewards that students may receive in the form of grades or personal recognition will not substitute for the lack of meaning that they experience in their studies. Eventually, the sterility of study in terms of being will take its toll in cynicism, a sense that nothing has any meaning, or in a search for meaning in extrinsic rewards for themselves (status, grades, money). The cognitive modalities that students learn are limited in their capacity to know themselves, and the world in varied contexts suffers. Art, music, story, imaginative play, physical movement, and other contexts for growth and transformation get short shrift. Students learning in limited environments relative to the exploration and unfolding of being may find school both very informative and meaningless.

IT ALL STARTED WITH A DREAM

The dissociation of being and thinking is not, once again, a recent historical event. It has its origins most clearly in René Descartes (1596–1650). Searle (1990) comments:

> Few people in cognitive science think that the study of the mind is essentially or in large part, a matter of studying something that is conscious; consciousness is rather a "problem," a difficulty that functionalist or computational theories must somehow deal with. Now, how did we get into this mess? There are complicated historical reasons, but one primary factor is that since Descartes, we have, for the most part, thought that consciousness was not an appropriate subject for a serious science or scientific philosophy of mind. (p. 585)

Ironically, Descartes's effort to establish a methodological foundation for scientific understanding began with dreams. Roszak (1994) details:

> On the night of November 10, 1619, René Descartes, then an aspiring philosopher still in his early twenties, had a series of three dreams which changed the course of his life and of modern thought. He reports that in his sleep, the Angel of Truth appeared to him and, in a blinding revelation like a flash of lightning, revealed a secret which would lay the foundation of a new method of understanding and a new and marvelous science. (p. 234)

Years later, Descartes completed his philosophical effort to create a clear methodological approach to inquiry in his *Discourse on Method* (1637) and *The Meditations* (1644). These works are widely recognized as the foundation of modern philosophy. The essence of his method was to lay bare the foundations of thought of anything that could in any way be doubted and to build upon those things beyond doubt with precise mathematical reasoning. His aim was to ensure that any statement generated would be absolutely true. Using precise reasoning, he demonstrated how all natural things could be doubted and even how mathematics could fail the test. (He explains that God could, for example, cause us to make a mistake in calculating the sides of a square.) Of particular note, he applies his skepticism to his own existence. Descartes reasons that he may think he is in his room before a fire, while he indeed may be dreaming asleep in his bed. It also is possible that he, like one who is mad, may be subject to illusion.

In this context, there is but one certainty Descartes can find. Even if his thoughts may be misguided, even if he is lost in a dream, he undoubtedly thinks. He concludes, "I think, therefore I am" (*cogito ergo sum*). With these words, Descartes ushered in the modern era. With this seemingly unshakable foundation, he began to rebuild the edifice of knowledge and to set the context for the subsequent development of Western thought and science.

The literature on Descartes has focused on the dualism created between the mind and the body. The "I am" to which Descartes refers is not in the body but in the mind. When he inquires as to the nature of the self he has discovered, he concludes that it is a "thinking thing," a thing that thinks. However, he did not recognize, nor have the vast majority of scholars who have studied his work, that the mind, "the thinking thing" was not the "I," the thinking subject, but the "I" as an object of thought. Varela, Thompson, and Rosch (1993) conclude, "Descartes did infer that the 'I' is fundamentally a thinking thing, but here he went too far: the only certainty that 'I am' carries is that of being a thought" (p. 2).

The problem lies in the fact that the "I" at the beginning of the sentence is entirely different from the "I" in the closing phrase. The first is the one using the method; the second is a result of its use. The first experiences thinking as a process, the second is an object that had to be *explicitly* defined; the first is the thinker, and the second a thought. The "I am" in Descartes's system is a logical necessity, given his method. It is a logical category, rather than an affirmation of the experience of being. Descartes refers to the self as a thinking thing but does not address why a thinking thing would seek truth even though he saw the pursuit of truth as his most essential task. The "I am" at the end of the sentence is not the "I" motivated to use the method in the service of truth. Certainly, it is not the one stirred by the Angel of Truth.

Philosopher William Barrett, in his pointedly titled book *Death of the Soul: From Descartes to the Computer* (1986), writes that Descartes did not bring the "I" that cogitates into philosophy. He observes that Descartes, in his search for certainty, arrived at "the poor ego" as "only a thematic instrument, though an indispensable one in the search" (p. 17). Descartes's "I am" is an abstraction and not the "I that lives and breathes in intimacy with its body enmeshed in memories, anxious about death, and possibly hoping, if it dare, for some kind of salvation" (p. 17).

Barrett (1986) continues, "But having thus abstracted the mind from its world, Descartes is hard put to get it back into the world. For that purpose, he must have invoked the help of God" (p. 17). Descartes reasoned that because he had the idea of a perfect being and because he himself was imperfect, the idea could not have come from him. Therefore, God must exist. Descartes's notion of God enabled him to place the "I" in an all-embracing reality, a context that gives it some place, some point of reference, rather than to leave it adrift in a void. Barrett concludes, however, that Descartes's argument for the existence of God is not an argument at all, but rather an intuition "valid and compelling for some minds as soon as they begin to reflect upon the mystery of existence." He continues, "This is the intuition that finite existence cannot just float but must be grounded in some all-encompassing and self-grounded Being" (p. 18). (The term *Being* for our present purposes need not be theistic or related to religious belief. For purposes of this chapter, *being,* in the lowercase, refers to that which animates each of us individually; in the uppercase, *Being* refers to the whole of existence in which we dwell.)

The notion of being, without participating in Being, without some place or purpose in existence, is empty, without meaning. Only through participation in Being can an individual being begin to imagine or intuit some purpose in existence. Descartes's "I" and "God" were abstractions, however. They were not animate as was the "I" of Descartes himself as he pursued truth. Meaning for the living, breathing "I" does not come through abstraction any more than music can be revealed through the analysis of sound in our opening story. The context he created for thinking had no place for the vital, inquiring Descartes as a being. In this context, Descartes cut himself off from sources of insight into the question of purpose, identity, and meaning as a human being.

This is the central dilemma of modern Western thought: For all the abstract information we can generate and apply, we employ systems of thought that have no place for us—no place for us to relate our experience of existence or our experience of being. This is true not only in a personal sense but socially as well. Others are abstractions in our thinking. We ascribe everything else to a separate "affective sphere"—an aspect of our experience of low regard when it comes to thinking. More often, we see ourselves as separate as the facts we employ and are lost when we are called on to explain our social and moral connections to others. As we are isolated, adrift in Being, so are they. This estrangement of thinking and being reduces questions of value to word games. No fact or set of facts, no system of logic or call to reason, can ever convey the value of a single human being. There is no being embedded in our abstract system of thought. Human beings have the same epistemological status as any other object. The idea of moral responsibility or agency seems like a matter of personal taste; there is no common ground, only separate choice. We, as Descartes's heirs, in subscribing to his system of doubt and the construction of ideas from atomized premises woven together with strings of mathematical reasoning, are often cut off from these deeper streams of understanding.

The computational paradigm of today is constructed on a system of information processing that can be modeled by computers. It has no place for the experience of being, of participating in Being. This experience is difficult to grasp because it is at the root of our thinking, rather than explicitly in the ideas we create. It is generative—giving substance and direction in our thinking and judgment. The computational paradigm cannot recognize the experience of being as it affects what we think about, how we think, or the significance that ideas hold for us.

Certainly, computation plays a great role in helping us sort and analyze ideas, but it does not serve as the foundation for judgment except as we intuitively allow it to. Philosopher scientist Michael Polanyi (1969) explains that, even in the most sophisticated scientific research, there is an informal or personal foundation for judgment that cannot be expressed in words. This "tacit dimension" of thinking, as he calls it, is greatly affected by experience and culture generally but is bound up in our very sense of ourselves and the world as a whole. Polanyi writes,

> [W]e can use our formulas only after we have made sense of the world to the point of asking questions about it and have established the bearing of the formulas on the experience that they are to explain. Mathematical reasoning about experience must include, besides the antecedent non-mathematical finding and shaping of experience, the equally non-mathematical relating of mathematics to such experience, and the eventual, also non-mathematical, understanding of experience elucidated by the theory. It must also include ourselves, carrying out and committing ourselves, to these non-mathematical ways of knowing. (p. 179)

In this generative, fluid, personal sense of being, all things we think have their place and take their meaning.

This is not to say that information processing or computational thinking is of little value. One has only to observe the technological advances in the last century to appreciate its power. Conversely, one has only to look at the social, environmental, and cultural problems that have arisen to see that it is, in equal or superior measure, dangerous and inadequate. Just as it enables us to focus on discrete problems, it obscures the larger questions of meaning and purpose in our choices, as well as in the whole of existence. For all the capacity it provides for us to effect control, it masks the questions of what is truly worth doing and why.

Thinking grounded in a rich, substantive exploration of both Being and being through multiple modalities reveals an expansive picture of education and a dynamic insight into children as growing human beings. The educational imperative of our day is not to cultivate intellectual capital for the economy; it is not to teach children to process bits of information in formal ways to solve problems; and it is not to get them to store as much discrete information where "more" and "earlier" are the rule. It is to guide children in their development as whole persons; it is to help them learn through direct and varied forms of encounter with the world as a foundation for clear, rigorous thinking; it is to bring all the resources of the culture to help them experience meaning, identity, purpose, and responsibility in the whole of life; and it is to address the "I am" as being, rather than as abstraction or capital.

REFERENCES

Barrett, W. (1986). *Death of the soul: From Descartes to the computer*. Garden City, NY: Doubleday.

Bruner, J. (1990). *Acts of meaning*. Cambridge, MA: Harvard University Press.

Churchland, P. M. (1995). *The engine of reason, the seat of the soul: A philosophical journey into the brain*. Cambridge: MIT Press.

Churchland, P. S., & Sejnowski, T. J. (1992). *The computational brain*. Cambridge: MIT Press.

Descartes, R. (1989). *Discourse on method (1637) and the meditations (1644)* (John Veitch, Trans.) Buffalo, NY: Prometheus Books.

Gardner, H. (1991). *The unschooled mind: How children think and how schools should teach*. New York: Basic Books.

Isaacson, W. (1997, January 13). In search of the real Bill Gates. *Time, 149*(2), 44–57.

Kane, J. (1985). Of emerging minds in microworlds. In *Philosophy of education 1985*. Proceedings of the Forty-First Annual Meeting of the Philosophy of Education Society. Normal, IL: Philosophy of Education Society.

Madison, M. (1995, December 2). Mind control for computers. *San Francisco Chronicle*, final edition, p. A1.

National Commission on Excellence in Education. (1983). *A nation at risk: The imperative for educational reform*. Washington, DC: Government Printing Office.

Papert, S. (1980). *Mindstorms: Children, computers, and powerful ideas*. New York: Basic Books.

Polanyi, M. (1969). *Knowing and being* (Marjorie Grene, Ed.). Chicago: University of Chicago Press.

Roszak, T. (1994). *The cult of information: A neo-Luddite treatise on high tech, artificial intelligence, and the true art of thinking*. Berkeley: University of California Press.

Ryle, G. (1971). *Collected papers: Volume II. Collected essays 1929–1968*. New York: Barnes & Noble.

Searle, J. (1984). *Minds, brains, and science*. Cambridge, MA: Harvard University Press.

Searle, J. R. (1990). Consciousness, explanatory inversion, and cognitive science. *Behavioral and Brain Sciences, 13,* 585–642.

U.S. Department of Education. (1989, September 27–28). *The president's education summit with governors*. A joint statement issued by the Education Summit.

U.S. Department of Education. (1991). *America 2000: An educational strategy*. Washington, DC: Government Printing Office.

U.S. Department of Education. (1994). *Goals 2000: Educate America act*. Washington, DC: Government Printing Office.

Varela, F. J., Thompson, E., & Rosch, E. (1993). *The embodied mind*. Cambridge: MIT Press.

Weizenbaum, J. (1976). *Computer power and human reason: From judgment to calculation*. San Francisco: W. H. Freeman.

Wright, R. (1996, March 25). Can machines think? *Time, 147*(13), 50–56.

Biography

Jeffrey Kane received his doctorate in philosophy of education at New York University. He currently serves as Dean of the School of Education at the C. W. Post Campus of Long Island University. Dr. Kane has written numerous articles on knowledge theory and the interaction of human and artificial intelligences. His book, *Beyond Empiricism: Michael Polyani Reconsidered,* provides a foundation for much of his work on the tacit foundations of human knowledge. He has made presentations nationally and internationally and has served for 6 years as editor of *Holistic Education Review,* now known as *Encounter: Education for Meaning and Social Justice.*

2 Why Culture Rather Than Data Should Be Understood as the Basis of Intelligence

C. A. Bowers

Introduction

Information processing technologies have been developing so rapidly that it is increasingly difficult to understand the distinction between artificial intelligence and "the real thing." As Chet Bowers explains in this chapter, leading cognitive theorists, artificial intelligence experts, and even anthropologists are beginning to see modern machines as "silicon brains" that, with soon-to-be-realized capacities for self-refinement, may usher in a new age of "postbiological evolution."

Although such images evoke amazement and perhaps some fear, Bowers is less concerned with technology per se than with the dangerously limited understanding of human intelligence. Limitations of the prevailing views of intelligence are found in the root metaphors of Western culture that at once define intelligence in terms of an individual's power to store, evaluate and generate information, and effectively obscure the fact that such a definition is an expression of cultural bias. The bias is so ingrained in our thinking that we cannot imagine other reasonable possibilities. What else could intelligence be than a measure of individual cognitive capacity?

Bowers's answer is that intelligence is a cultural phenomenon. The particular constellations of cognitive capacities that one develops and the schemata that shape our cognitive efforts are products of deep cultural metaphors embodied in everything from language to architecture. The beliefs we hold, the values we cherish, and the understandings we develop are not simply choices we have made as autonomous human beings, but rather are most fundamentally variations on cultural themes. The notion of the human being as a free agent, as a self-directed individual, is itself one of our key cultural assumptions.

Although many educators see new information and communication technologies as freeing students to pursue their own interests and to construct their own unique insights, Bowers argues that educators are merely perpetuating a deep cultural myth of individualistic intelligence that does not account for the ecological and social dimensions of human experience. He maintains that the notion of the self-directed individual is, in part, responsible for an excessive competition and consumption of resources. Computer technology, with its capacity to "free" individuals to direct their studies and interests, serves to perpetuate and extend the metaphor.

In this chapter, Bowers calls us to reflect on the root cultural metaphors in technology and to see their implications for the social and ecological crises of our time.

—*Jeffrey Kane*

Information Processing: Human and Artificial

During a recent flight to Washington, DC, I read a magazine article about a new "wonder chip" being developed by an industry that is having a far more profound influence on how the public and, increasingly, teachers understand the nature of intelligence than any book written by educational psychologists. According to Hugo de Garis (1994), a researcher at the Human Information Processing Research Laboratory in Kyoto, Japan, the new gigabit technology will lead to the development of "silicon brains" that are as intelligent as humans. Whereas the human brain has about 10 quadrillion *synapses,* or connections between neurons, gigabit technology would have billions of times more synapses, each faster than the brain's (p. 88). De Garis's prediction of machine intelligence surpassing that of humans is being increasingly echoed by reputable scientists working in the converging fields of brain research and artificial intelligence. For example, Hans Moravec (1988), a professor at Carnegie Mellon University, argues that the "postbiological world dominated by self-improving, thinking machines" is part of the evolutionary process. As he put it,

> [O]ur culture still depends utterly on biological human beings, but with each passing year our machines, a major product of the culture, assume a greater role in its maintenance and continued growth. Sooner or later our machines will become knowledgeable enough to handle their own maintenance, reproduction, and self-improvement without help. When this happens, the new genetic takeover will be complete. Our culture will then be able to evolve independently of human biology and its limitations, passing instead directly from generation to generation of ever more capable intelligent machinery. (p. 4)

Gregory Stock's book *Metaman: The Merging of Humans and Machines Into a Global Superorganism* (1993) makes essentially the same argument. The following promotional statements appeared on the back cover of his evolutionary and technologically deterministic book: Steven M. Stanley, professor of paleobiology at Johns Hopkins University, wrote that "Stock reformulates the human enterprise in a way that may well cause us to rethink the future or our species." In addition to equally supportive statements by scientists from Princeton University and the University of Chicago, Susan Bryant, professor of developmental biology at the University of California at Irvine, wrote that "this book is a marvelous antidote to the gloom and doom predictions of most futurists. Stock's vision of the future is optimistic and appealing and at the same time it resonates with truth and intelligence."

Spokespersons for the computer industry do not frame the significance of computer-mediated thinking and communication in terms of entering the "postbiological stage" in the evolutionary process. Nor do they use Donna Haraway's metaphor of "cyborg" to represent the merging of machine and human intelligence. To avoid alarming religious fundamentalists, Third World thinkers concerned with the spread of a new technological form of colonialism (Sachs, 1992), and Western intellectuals who would object on different grounds, they use the more general and taken-for-granted language of progress to give legitimacy to expanding the use of computers into all areas of cultural life—including all ages and phases of formal education. The equating of computer-mediated thinking and communication with progress can be seen in Larry Ellison's (president and CEO of Oracle; 1994) claim that "the information highway promises to democratize information and profoundly affect the way we educate our children . . . [to provide] vast stores of information . . . [and to connect] schools across the country and around the world" (p. 18). Teacher mailboxes are now being flooded with promotional literature for the latest educational software that promises some new form of "mind power breakthrough" for preparing students for the emerging information age. And articles appear with increasing frequency in national and local newspapers, praising the latest development in getting classrooms wired to the Internet and putting "whole giant libraries of information at the fingertips of students"—to quote from a memorandum circulated by a local school district in Oregon.

An article titled "Rethinking the Curriculum for the Digital Age" reflects the increasing tendency within universities to represent information as the basis of human intelligence. In discussing how computers will transform Washington State University into a "virtual paperless and buildingless" educational experience, Tom George (1995) holds out the promise that "information access through state-of-the-art technology will permit greater focus on the learner's inquiry process and will facilitate learning by matching the delivery [of information] to the students' multiple cognitive skills and styles" (p. 16). The "Information Technology" section in *Chronicle of Higher Education*, which appears weekly with articles such as "Classes on the Web" and "Campuses in Cyberspace: Western Governors Will Explore the Establishment of 'Virtual Universities,'" is a sign of the educational significance being afforded computers. Indeed, anyone who claims that the public, including classroom teachers and teacher educators, is not being indoctrinated with a new orthodoxy that is both "scientifically" based and heavily promoted by the computer industry is in a state of deep denial about the scale and significance of the cultural change now being legitimated in the name of progress. Whereas educational psychology textbooks continue to present different theories of intelligence and educational psychologists continue to teach and write about the view of intelligence that has been the basis of their careers, the popular media and the sciences that range from sociobiology to cognitive neuroscience are increasingly associating intelligence with information processing. How this view of intelligence is being promoted at the level of popular culture can be seen in the *Time* magazine article (Lemonick, 1995) that summarized the current scientific research into what they considered the human brain's "best kept secrets," announcing in bold red typeface that "the brain craves information" (pp. 48–49).

Books by scientists also represent thinking as based on information. For example, Steven Pinker, director of the Center for Cognitive Neuroscience at the Massachusetts Institute of Technology, writes in *The Language Instinct* (1994) that "once you begin to look at language not as the ineffable essence of human uniqueness but as a *biological adaptation to communicate information* [italics added], it is no longer tempting to see language as an insidious shaper of thought, and, we shall see, it is not" (p. 19). Later in the book, he explains that thinking depends on a network of neurons firing in different patterns, with the patterns serving as a "processor" that organizes representations (information) from the senses into ideas and ways of understanding relationships. This "computational" or "representational" theory of mind, he writes, "is as fundamental to cognitive science as the cell doctrine is to biology and plate tectonics is to geology" (pp. 77–78). Antonio R. Damasio gives a similar explanation of how stimuli (information or, in Bateson's language, "a difference which makes a difference") is processed by the brain. As Damasio (1994) put it,

> [T]he mind arises from activity of neural circuits, but many of those circuits were shaped in evolution by functional requisites of the organism. . . . In brief, neural circuits represent the organism continuously, as it is perturbed by stimuli from the physical and sociocultural environment, and as it acts on these environments. (p. 226)

And Francis Crick (1994), the co-winner of the Nobel Prize for the discovery of the molecular structure of DNA, concludes a long explanation of how mental processes involve vast numbers of neurons acting together in parallel with the following statement: "I have described the general workings of an intricate machine—the brain—that handles an immense amount of *information* [italics added] all at once, in a perceptual moment" (p. 256).

Harvard University's E. O. Wilson provides a more inclusive and, I think, more dangerous way of understanding the nature of intelligence. His explanation of the genetic evolution of language and intelligence also purports to explain how all aspects of cultural development are determined by the "epigenetic rules" that govern which genes will survive and which lack the capacity to adapt to changes occurring in the environment. As all the explanations of intelligence and the functions of the brain just cited are based on the evolutionary model now dominant within the sciences and are consistent with Wilson's more expanded theory of sociobiology (which can also be called neo-Social Darwinism), I want to conclude this overview of how scientists represent the mind with a quotation from Wilson. In *On Human Nature* (1978), Wilson observes that "the mind might well receive all of its *information* [italics added], originating from both outside and inside the body, through such [information] coding and abstraction processes" (p. 74). He further suggests that we should understand that "consciousness consists of immense numbers of simultaneous and coordinated, symbolic representations by the participating neurons of the brain's neocortex" (p. 74). Although his way of explaining the neurological and genetic basis of thought, which he wrote more than 20 years ago, represents a reductionist tradition of thinking within the scientific community that has been further refined rather than questioned in any fundamental way, what I find even more important is that he was able to enfold the theory that equates neural networks with information processing (thinking) within an evolutionary framework that equates survival with genetic fitness and the "selfish gene." The acceptance of this evolutionary framework enables both Moravec (1988) and Stock (1993) to predict that cultures that do not evolve in a way that leads to a computer-based form of intelligence will disappear as a natural and thus inevitable consequence of the process of evolution. Before turning to the educational issues surrounding how the educational computing industry is able to capitalize on the scientific paradigm that represents the connections among genes, neurons, and information processing as the basic building blocks of the evolutionary process, which in turn gives legitimacy to the popular cultural view of linear progress, I want to point out that Piaget's genetic epistemology, which is now one cornerstone of the constructivists' theory of learning, "views intellectual development as an interaction of an inherited genetic program with the environment"—to quote Wilson's (1978) observations about the sociobiological foundations of Piaget's thinking (pp. 66–67).

CONSTRUCTIVISM AND THE FIRING OF NEURONS

Media representations of the advantages of the information highway and the democratizing of information, along with the books now being written by scientists on how the mind works (including the nature of consciousness), suggest a shared understanding between the scientists and computer industry promoters that information is the new standard of individual and global wealth and empowerment. Although education professors and classroom teachers continue to view knowledge as constructed by individuals and groups (which is a way of thinking based on taken-for-granted liberal assumptions about how the expression of a student's spontaneous interest and exploration leads to authentic ideas and value judgments), the theoretical and ideological foundations of their position is becoming less easily distinguishable from the epistemology embedded in the popular and commercially driven discourse that equates thinking with processing data and information. Indeed, advocates of computer-mediated learning increasingly justify the enormous expenditure of money for the technology necessary for making the classroom fully (globally) connected to the information highway on the grounds that students are better able to construct ideas and solve problems when they have immediate access to the vast amounts of information that can be stored and retrieved through computer networks. In an article that appeared in *Wired*, Sherry Turkle (1996) observes that "we are moving from a modernist calculation toward a postmodern simulation, *where self is a multiple distributed system* [italics added]". She goes on to say that as students cycle through cyberspace (e.g., simulations, word processing, chat rooms, E-mail), "they become authors not only of texts but of themselves through social interaction" (p. 151). Alan C. Kay, a leader in the field of educational computing who was invited to write the article "Computers, Networks, and Education" for *Scientific American* (1991), based his arguments for computer-based learning on liberal and constructivist assumptions about the nature of individual intelligence. These assumptions are clearly reflected in his statement that

> each of us has to construct our own version of reality by main force. Literally, we make ourselves. And we are quite capable of devising new mental blocks, new ways of thinking that can enormously expand the understanding we attain. The bricks we develop become new techniques for thinking. (p. 140)

And in an article titled "Putting Computer Projects at the Heart of the Curriculum," Mike Muir (1994) makes the following constructivist argument:

> We know that students learn by constructing their own knowledge through using information in meaningful ways. This new knowledge must build directly on what each student already knows, and the students must see the connection between the new ideas and their world. Further, students need to be actively involved in their own learning and the decisions about learning. To achieve this, we decided to make computers part of the school infrastructure. (p. 30)

The blurring of lines that one might expect to exist between constructivist educators and advocates of computer-mediated learning is further reflected in how some constructivists have accepted the growing convention of treating *knowledge* and *information* as interchangeable words. Witness the following statement by Constance Kamii (1991):

> Knowledge in a narrow sense is easy to understand. It refers to specific bits of information such as the fact that Washington is the capital of the United States. . . . Knowledge in a broad sense refers to these and other systems of relationships that enable us to organize our knowledge and to interpret new information. (p. 25)

But it is not just this convergence of thinking of information as the basis of students' constructing their own knowledge that prevents constructivists from becoming effective critics either of the public discourse about computer-mediated learning for the "information age" or of the neo-Social Darwinism that is re-emerging in the guise of genetic causality. In effect, the language of constructivism fills the need for classroom teachers and professors of education to believe that their efforts contribute to individual empowerment and social progress. But it cannot serve as the basis for a fundamentally different view of intelligence. Nor can it be used to articulate the cultural and thus educational implications of the ecological crisis. This would require understanding intelligence as being culturally influenced through the multiple processes of language acquisition, as well as how our culture reproduces the earlier thought patterns and values. These patterns were, in turn, based on metaphorical constructions that included equating the exploitation of the environment with social progress.

Both the constructivist view of learning and the genetic/neuron network view of information processing share the same assumption that the individual is the basic social unit—with the scientists simply going one step further in the process of reductionist thinking by focusing on the genetic level of information coding. Constructivists might be surprised by this argument, particularly when they encounter R. C. Lewontin's (1991) summary of this new orthodoxy: "Genes make individuals, individuals have particular preferences and behaviors, the collection of preferences and behaviors makes a culture, so genes make culture" (p. 14). But they cannot deny that they have made the individual the autonomous agent of ideas and values, which they continually represent as the alternative to the existential condition of heteronomy. A second area of overlap in the thinking of constructivist educators and the genetic-evolutionary-sociobiology-oriented scientists is that they both base their thinking on the liberal view of linear progress that is furthered through some form of reflective thought (which for Wilson is the expression of "genetic fitness"). If we consider constructivist statements about students' constructing their own knowledge, the evolutionary views of Moravec (1988) and Stock (1993), the increasingly reductionist models of the mind that are emerging from cognitive neurobiologists, and the emerging field of biotechnology, we find different vocabularies for articulating the modern Western narrative of progress. The constructivists frame their view of progress in the anthropocentric rhetoric of neo-Romanticism, whereas the scientific community increasingly views the emergence of humans as more an accident of time and chemistry—thus enabling them to accept as inevitable the replacement of humans by machine forms of intelligence.

A third commonality is that the constructivist educators' emphasis on students learning to construct their own knowledge and values, and the scientists' reduction of intelligence to the firing patterns of neurons, contribute to the spread of nihilism. **Nihilism** involves the relativizing of shared cultural norms that guide how people live with each other and with the environment. The constructivists' emphasis on the individual and their assumption that change is progressive in nature lead to viewing all forms of cultural traditions as oppressive. Similarly, the scientists' use of the gene as the Rosetta stone for explaining life processes also undermines the authority of shared customs and values. Indeed, the development of the symbolic frameworks that legitimate and sustain a morally coherent commons has no special standing in the evolutionary framework that recognizes only what contributes to survival in what now represents a genetic reinterpretation of Hobbes's view of the human condition.

To reiterate a point made earlier, various learning theorists may influence a small number of graduate students and students in teacher preparation programs. They may, like Howard Gardner, even exert a wider influence that enters the public discourse (as I point out elsewhere, Gardner's theory of multiple intelligences is part of a tradition that represents intelligence as an attribute of the individual [Bowers, 1995, pp. 92–134]). Because current developmental theories continue to perpetuate the assumptions of a long tradition of psychological thought and may even share the complexity of Robert Sternberg's "triarchic theory" of human intelligence (1982), I cannot see any evidence that suggests the theories promoted by any of these professors represent a fundamentally different way of understanding the nature of intelligence or that they will supplant the popular and neurobiology-based discourses that represent thinking as information processing. I would welcome any evidence or counterarguments that would help overturn what I see as the increasing dominance of an orthodoxy that benefits economically an elite group of people and that further diverts attention from the ecological consequences of globalizing both the modern scientific paradigm and the technologically based consumer lifestyle that it helps perpetuate.

THE ECOLOGICAL CRISIS AND THE CULTURAL FOUNDATIONS OF INTELLIGENCE

Two questions should be asked about the view of intelligence now being promoted by scientists such as Crick, Damasio, and Pinker, by the proponents of computer-mediated learning, and by the constructivist learning theorists such as Kamii and Rheta De Vries: Can an individually centered view of intelligence that emphasizes the process of discovery and manipulation of information be used as the basis for a form of education that addresses the cultural challenge of living within the limits of the earth's ecosystems? Will the increasing emphasis on computer-mediated learning, and the scientific/constructionist view of intelligence on which it is based, contribute to the resurgence of neo-Social Darwinism? Social Darwinism, in this case, would serve as a meta-narrative that will be used to legitimate the loss of cultural groups that fail to conform to the evolutionary scenario envisioned in futurist thinking of scientists like Moravec and Stock (and software giants like Microsoft and Oracle).

I would like to use the first question as a reference point for explaining why intelligence needs to be understood as cultural and ecological in nature. The second question will be addressed in a more tangential manner, primarily because the tendency of scientists such as Wilson and Crick to extrapolate from studies at the molecular level to broad generalizations about the future course of humankind is based on a lack of understanding of how the deepest assumptions underlying their culture frame their notion of the evolutionary progress. Culture and ecology are integral aspects of what I call the individualizing of cultural intelligence, and understanding their role will help illuminate how the scientists quoted here fail to take account of the cultural schemata underlying their own way of thinking and to recognize that cultures based on fundamentally different mythopoetic narratives (**root metaphors**) privilege the expression of different forms of intelligence.

As I maintain in *Educating for an Ecologically Sustainable Culture* (Bowers, 1995), the paradox of the supposedly most advanced culture contributing in a vastly disproportionate way to undermining the viability of the earth's natural systems suggests that it is time to reassess the tradition of allowing scientists and neo-Romantic liberals to frame how intelligence should be understood. The basic problem is in representing intelligence as an attribute of the individual, and emphasizing the various expressions of intelligence (e.g., processing information, critical reflection, "use of these mental mechanisms in everyday life in order to attain an intelligent fit to the environment"—to quote Sternberg [1982, p. 268]), misrepresents both the culturally specific nature of intelligence and the need to assess its forms of expression in terms of moral criteria that take account of what constitutes a just and sustainable community and ecosystem relationship. This emphasis on the "processes" of intelligence has led to awarding our highest degrees to people who too often devote their thinking skills to creating technologies that introduce toxins into the environment and to persuading the public to buy more consumer goods. Our current way of thinking about intelligence also has led to the empowerment of elite groups of technologists who are working to develop smarter and more complex computer systems that will further reduce the need for human workers. The irony is that too many Americans tend to view the intelligence of these technologists as of a higher order than the intelligence of a group of elders who discuss for months how the introduction of computers into their lives will alter their basic values, beliefs, traditional ceremonies, and experience of community. In brief, the equating of intelligence with mental processes such as constructing knowledge, manipulating data, and the firing of neurons leaves us without a way of assessing whether the deep cultural schemata that are too often the unrecognized basis of thought contribute to the degradation of community life. Even teachers who introduce environmental issues into the curriculum while reinforcing the culturally specific assumption that individuals (especially in cooperative situations) construct their own sense of meaning and understanding of relationships are contributing to the double bind where, in the name of progress, individuals will act out the myth that they are the ultimate judge of how they should use their intelligence. The myth is accepted as fact because the preferred notion of intelligence does not account for the deeply rooted cultural metaphors that shape it.

For educators at all levels, from professors to elementary teachers, to begin the task of changing the myths that underlie modern culture in a way that takes account of the need to develop symbolically in directions that do not have an adverse impact on the sustaining capacities of natural systems, it will be necessary to recognize that intelligence is cultural in nature. It will also be necessary to recognize the need to develop cultural forms of intelligence that are more oriented toward nonexploitive and non-market-oriented relationships. There are still remnants of ecologically centered cultures that have developed complex forms of intelligence from which we can learn. The specific challenge is to learn from them about how to develop a more responsible and symbolically rich experience of the commons—*which is not to suggest that we should copy their traditions*. Unfortunately, these ecologically centered cultures, which might help us recognize how to save ourselves from the consequences of our own hubris, are now being threatened by the scientific, technological, and economic success of the graduates of Western universities who are using the form of intelligence that the educational process has conditioned them to accept as the highest expression of human development. Before we return to a brief discussion of how the ecological crisis can be understood as having implications for the content of the curriculum and for revising the forms of intelligence that teachers and professors reinforce in the classroom, it is necessary to lay out the evidence for understanding intelligence as cultural in cognitive style and capacity. As I have already written more extensively on this critically important issue (Bowers, 1993a, 1993b, 1995, 1997; Bowers & Flinders, 1990), I limit the discussion to a summary of the main parts of the argument.

The article by Dorothy Holland and Michael Cole, "Between Discourse and Schema: Reformulating a Cultural Historical Approach to Culture and Mind" (1995), suggests that a cultural view of mind (intelligence) can be based on the theoretical work of linguists, anthropologists, and psychologists (specifically, psychologists working in the tradition of Vygotsky and Laura) who recognized the connections between schema theory and differences in cultural epistemologies. The article represents an important summary of the scholarly work that provides a basis for understanding why thinking of intelligence as an attribute of the individual is a local myth (considering the multiplicity of cultures that have developed over the last 10,000 years) that has been universalized. I have doubts that their long march through a largely marginalized literature will lead to the scale and speed of change needed in the cultural assumptions that underlie the conceptual orthodoxies of scientists and professors of education who exert the dominant influence over the direction of educational reform. A more direct and less easily dismissed approach to demonstrating that intelligence is cultural in form and substance is to consider the connections between how the epistemological and moral orientations of a culture are encoded and reproduced through the metaphorical languages that normalize how children experience themselves and the world within the context of relationships that are largely culturally defined and linguistically reproduced.

The writings of Mark Johnson, George Lakoff, Michael Reddy, Richard Brown, and others on the metaphorical basis of the language-thought connection, which are supplemented by anthropologists such as Keith Basso, Stanley Walens, and Stephen Lansing, provide both a theoretical framework and evidence that explains how the thinking of Pinker, Moravec, Kamii, Gardner, and Sternberg (to cite a range of thinkers who start with the assumption that intelligence is an attribute of the individual) is influenced by the iconic and root metaphors that encode earlier culturally specific ways of thinking. That we think metaphorically in patterns largely prescribed by the root metaphors and meta-narratives of our culture can be seen in how the process of analogical thinking and the use of **iconic metaphors** (image words that encode the schemata of earlier analogies that prevailed over competing analogues) reproduce such historically and culturally specific root metaphors as the mechanistic view of humans and the world, change as linear and progressive, patriarchy, anthropocentrism, and the autonomous individual. I have discussed elsewhere how the mechanistic root metaphor that was the basis of the thinking of Newton, Hobbes, and other "fathers" of modern culture continues to frame how cognitive scientists understand both human and artificial intelligence. The references in the writings of Crick, Pinker, and other scientists to how the brain "functions" and to the "firing" of neurons are further examples of how this more than 300-year-old root metaphor of a mechanistic universe continues to frame current ways of thinking. We could take the root metaphor of patriarchy and trace how the process of analogical thinking over centuries in the areas of law, history, art, theology, and so forth led to language/thought patterns that reproduced this deep cultural schema as part of highly "intelligent" peoples' self-identity and natural attitude toward everyday relationships.

Insights From Non-Individualistically Centered Cultures

We can even trace how a shift in root metaphors, such as the shift from the temporal perspective of premodern Western cultures where the past was seen as providing the exemplary models for aesthetic expression and moral/conceptual authority to the modern perspective on time that places the emphasis on fostering change to ensure progress, leads to radically different analogies and to use of iconic metaphors. For example, elite groups that have a vested interest in promoting the high-status forms of knowledge associated with modernizing consumer expectations of Third World countries tend to associate words such as *tradition* and *moral authority* with being reactionary and opposed to progress. Words they take for granted include *innovation, creativity, individualism,* and *information,* which are not questioned because of the taken-for-granted status of the root metaphor that represents the temporal aspects of change as progressive in nature.

Similarly, in the segments of the language community where the root metaphor of an anthropocentric world is dominant, iconic metaphors such as "wilderness" and "nature" are understood either as in a predeveloped state or as a natural resource. Where the root metaphor of an ecology is primary, wilderness and nature have an entirely different meaning. The current debate within the environmental movement over whether ecosystems develop toward greater order and equilibrium or are characterized by disturbances and competition is really over which root metaphors will be used as a basis for understanding human/nature relationships; and the influence of chaos theory as a source of deep analogical thinking is clearly visible in the debate. As a change in root metaphors also changes the way we think about the nature of intelligence, I am proposing that a more adequate root metaphor must take into account the way the individual is nested in the symbolic systems of culture and the culture is nested in ecosystems. Thus, these fundamental relationships and sources of dependency should be foregrounded in any discussion of what constitutes intelligence.

The above examples of how historically and culturally specific root metaphors provide the cultural/conceptual/moral schemata of thought may be difficult for modern individuals to grasp, particularly when their taken-for-granted patterns of understanding individual intelligence make a historical and cultural perspective seem unnecessary—and even threatening. It may seem even more difficult to take seriously how different root metaphors and metanarratives of other cultural groups lead to profoundly different conceptual and moral schemata, including which forms of intelligence are valued within the language community. The anthropologist Dorothy Lee, for example, describes how the Wintu of northern California understand self/other relationships. Whereas our root metaphors represent individuals as being separate from what they think about and interact with, Lee (1959) observed that

> the Wintu conception of self . . . differs from our own in that it contains the total person and the activities of all its aspects, and in that it fades out gradually and without distinct demarcation. It is not clearly opposed to the other. . . . [N]either is it clearly identical with or incorporated in the other. On some occasions it participates to some extent in the other, and is of equal status to the other; where we see a one way relationship from self to the other, an assertion of the self upon the other, the Wintu see a coordinate togetherness, with, at most, a stressed point of view. (pp. 131–139)

Keith Basso (1987) describes how the Western Apache connect geographic features of the land with stories that encode the moral norms of the cultural group. As the following account demonstrates, root metaphors of the Western Apache do not represent individuals as autonomous moral agents who rely on their own power of rationality to set their moral course of action. Stories that enlighten, instruct, criticize ("shoot"), entertain, and malign are situated in different geographic contexts, with the result that hills, streams, rock formations, stands of trees, and so forth are associated with specific stories that encode the Apache moral templates for guiding behavior. Basso observes that the landscape serves to remind the Apache of the moral norms of the community. As he describes it,

> After stories and storytellers have served their purpose, features of the physical landscape take over and perpetuate it. Mountains and arroyos step in symbolically for grandmothers and uncles. Just as the latter have "stalked" delinquent individuals in the past, so too particular locations continue to "stalk" them in the present. Such surveillance is essential, Apaches maintain, because "living right" requires constant care and attention, and there is always a possibility that old stories and their initial impact, like old arrows and their wounds, will fade and disappear. . . . Geographical sites, together with the crisp mental "pictures" of them presented by their names, serve admirably in this capacity, inviting people to recall their earlier failings and encouraging them to resolve, once again, to avoid them in the future. Grandparents and uncles perish but the landscape endures, and for this the Apache are deeply grateful. "The land," Nick Thompson observes (who was Basso's informant), "looks after us. The land keeps badness away." (p. 112)

The meta-narratives of these cultures do not represent intelligence as an attribute of the individual, as is the case in modern culture. The Wintu way of representing the individual in terms of relationships that are coproduced, rather than as an autonomous individual acting on an external world, is close to Gregory Bateson's view of the individual as a participant in a larger ecology of relationships. And this cultural form of intelligence seems better suited to long-term survival within the limits of local ecosystems than our cultural emphasis on an autonomous, individualized form of intelligence where the exploitation of the environment for personal gain is often highly rewarded. Similarly, the Western Apache way of understanding that the landscape is a source of moral guidance, and thus a teacher of what constitutes moral intelligence, reflects a profoundly different ontology—that is, set of root metaphors.

ASPECTS OF INDIVIDUAL/CULTURAL INTELLIGENCE

These examples may appear to some readers to be irrelevant to the discussion of the current scientific and educational misconceptions about the connections between information and thinking. The purpose in using the Wintu and Apache ways of representing the self as part of a larger ecology of intelligence has nothing to do with the question of their ability to resist being subverted by the colonizing power of modern culture. Rather, these examples help demonstrate how different ways of understanding intelligence are embedded in the symbolic systems (e.g., metaphorical language, narratives, song, dance, technologies) used by the cultural group to renew itself in the lives of future generations. That is, the deep metaphorical foundations of a culture influence the view of intelligence encoded and reproduced in the language systems that sustain the everyday patterns of cultural life. The cultural schema that represents intelligence, creativity, and capacity to make moral judgments, as an attribute of the autonomous individual—all characteristics of the various elite groups now promoting the idea that thought is based on information and data—is simply another example of a cultural view of intelligence. It is also an example of a cultural form of intelligence that is not "intelligent" in the sense of contributing to viable relationships within human communities and between humans and the biotic community. To make this latter point somewhat more bluntly, a cultural epistemology encoded in the metaphorical constructions of a language that represents progress in terms of behaviors and technologies that serve the interests of a few by undermining the ecological well-being of current and future generations must be seen as both ignorant and immoral. Unfortunately, the individually centered view of intelligence and the myth of progress that is still used by scientists and educators to legitimate their increasingly reductionist view of intelligence prevent them from recognizing this double bind.

In previous writings, I have tried to explain the connections among three explanatory frameworks that seem especially relevant to addressing the challenges now facing educators, particularly the double bind of passing on to the next generation the conceptual and moral templates that were the basis of the Industrial Revolution. These explanatory frameworks are as follows:

1. The sociology of knowledge account of how culture is learned at a taken-for-granted level and becomes part of the intersubjective self that is the basis of thought, values, behavior, and self-identity
2. How the languages of a culture encode and reproduce past forms of metaphorical thinking (the root metaphor, analogy, and iconic metaphor connection that is part of a culture's approach to music, architecture, science, technology, education, etc.)
3. Gregory Bateson's understanding of intelligence as the unit of mind that encompasses both the "difference which makes a difference" circulating through the patterns of life that constitute an ecosystem, and the map/territory distinction that is unique to how humans participate in the large semiotic field that makes up an ecosystem

All three theory frameworks explain in different ways why the idea of the individual as a separate observer and thinker (data processor) is based on fundamental misconceptions embedded in the language at such a taken-for-granted level that the experts who think and communicate in this language unconsciously continue to perpetuate these misconceptions. These theory frameworks also provide different levels for understanding the importance of Bateson's observation that our cultural maps, which he viewed as metaphorically based, are often inadequate for understanding the territory (changes occurring in cultural-natural ecosystem relationships). The latter point is particularly well illustrated in the example of pioneers (what a loaded metaphor!) relying on the cultural maps they brought with them. They were attempting to make sense of the land and cultures they encountered here by relying on cultural maps that still encoded centuries of the troubled experience of Europe that led to the great outbound migration.

Given these previous writings, I limit my discussion to three aspects of individual/cultural intelligence that need to be taken into account in challenging the ideas that intelligence is an attribute of the individual and that information is the basis of thought. That is, a more complex view of intelligence needs to take account of what I have termed **embodied intelligence**, which includes the ways past forms of metaphorical thinking are embodied (encoded) in spoken and written language, in the layout of cities, highway systems, design of buildings, and all other material and symbolic expressions of culture. The embodied expressions of cultural intelligence can be understood as the semiotic systems that help "normalize" the taken-for-granted expectations of the cultural group in the areas of thought, values, and behaviors. The cultural message systems that reproduce past forms of metaphorically based expressions of intelligence, such as the modern glass box building that reproduced the assumptions of the Bauhaus school of architecture, the chairs and other furniture produced by Shaker crafters, the mechanistic metaphors that connect the 16th-century thinking of Johannes Kepler with contemporary scientists such as Crick and Damasio, are largely learned and experienced as part of the individual's culturally derived repertoire of taken-for-granted patterns of thinking. This form of cultural intelligence, which can be referred to as **tacit intelligence**, plays an important role in the language processes that are played out in the process of primary socialization where the taken-for-granted cultural patterns of the significant other, given the presence of certain variables, become part of the learner's taken-for-granted patterns. The shared nature of the shared tacit cultural intelligence makes the ideas of Francis Crick seem intelligent to Steven Pinker but incomprehensible to members of cultures that are ecologically centered. The third form of individual/cultural intelligence is what can be termed **intentional intelligence**. It includes explicit knowledge, as well as the conscious efforts to solve problems, make sense of relationships, think critically in ways that make the implicit explicit and problematic, recall past events, imagine future possibilities, and so forth. It is the aspect of individual/cultural intelligence that educators and learning theorists have emphasized without adequately recognizing the influence of the other two dimensions of intelligence.

Although educators should be focusing on how the embodied and tacit forms of cultural intelligence continue to reproduce the metaphorically based ways of thinking that were the basis of the Industrial Revolution, which put us on the current pathway of commodifying relationships and knowledge, they are instead increasingly being told by cognitive scientists and advocates of computer-mediated learning that access to data is the best way of involving students in "their own learning and the decisions about their learning"—to recall Muir's (1994) justification for making computers the heart of the curriculum. But the arguments for extending the use of computers into all areas of the educational process have not been accompanied by a serious discussion of the forms of cultural knowledge that are being privileged because of the epistemological orientation built into computer technology and the forms of relationships and knowledge that are being marginalized or lost altogether. This brief discussion of the cultural amplification and reduction characteristics of educational computing should be seen as another dimension of the argument against the reduction of knowledge to data and information and against treating the individual (or individuals working in groups) as the source of intelligent behavior.

How Computers Reinforce a Cartesian Form of Intelligence

Just as other forms of technology amplify and reduce certain aspects of individual/cultural experience (e.g., the telephone amplifies voice over great distance but reduces the body language and other contextual cues that are part of a more complex process of semiosis), computer-mediated thinking and communication involve complex and significant amplification and reduction patterns. Although teachers are told about the educational significance of being able to access data through the Internet, the form of intelligence encoded in the technology leads to an amplification process whereby explicit and digitalized bits of information are being represented as the basis of individual thought. At the same time, the tacit, contextualized, and analogue forms of knowledge are being marginalized. The computer further amplifies the cultural myth that language is a conduit, that it is part of a sender/receiver process of communication. This conduit view of language hides the constituting role that metaphor plays in the language and thought connection; it thus hides how language encodes and reproduces earlier forms of cultural intelligence—such as the many ways that anthropocentrism and patriarchy were passed on for countless generations as part of the taken-for-granted pattern of thinking. In addition, computers amplify the modern cultural assumption that individuals think in ways that are free of cultural influence—an assumption identified earlier as being shared by Pinker, Damasio, and Crick, as well as by constructivist educational theorists. This particular cultural amplification further reduces the ability of teachers to recognize the differences in cultural epistemologies, which seems especially important to developing multicultural curricula.

To state this amplification and reduction characteristic in terms of the double bind that most teachers do not recognize, the use of computers in multicultural classrooms reinforces a Cartesian way of thinking. One of the most important assumptions on which Cartesian thinking is based is that when individuals are thinking with data, they are free from the influence of tradition. When we consider how the computer influences students' experience of temporality (how they experience themselves in relation to the cultural way of representing the continuum of past, present, and future), we find that what is reinforced is the students' subjective experience of time—which is centered in the immediacy of what the students are experiencing and which may extend into the limited sense of the future dictated by the problem being addressed. In effect, computer-mediated thinking and communication radically marginalize the awareness of how traditions from the past are being reenacted in the present. And it makes completely irrelevant the forms of knowledge that are renewed and carried forward by elders.

Finally, computers amplify the use of language that encodes and reproduces an instrumental (and thus, anthropocentric) way of understanding the moral dimensions of human/nature relationships. Lost through computer-mediated learning are the narrativized cultural languages that used the natural world as the metaphorical basis for understanding and communicating across generations the cultural group's moral norms for governing relationships with the other inhabitants of the biome.

If we compare the cultural patterns that are amplified by this supposedly neutral technology with the patterns that are increasingly being recognized as contributing disproportionately to the ecological crisis, we come back to the question of whether the view of intelligence being promoted by the reductionist thinking scientists, computer advocates, and constructivist educators is part of the problem. Given the increasing evidence of human cultures undermining the viability of natural systems to reproduce themselves, it would seem that educators should be learning how to understand the difference between cultural forms of intelligence that are based on the hubris of technical rationality and the myth of progress, and forms of cultural intelligence that are oriented more toward renewing those aspects of the commons that have to do with community rather than markets and toward reducing the cultural demands on natural systems. Unfortunately, the elite groups that are carrying forward the tradition of an individually centered view of intelligence and that have now carried the process of reductionist thinking to the point where the nihilism of their position should be obvious are not likely to recognize how they are contributing to deepening the ecological crisis. Indeed, their maps are increasingly about neurons, the encoding characteristics of genes, and the processing of data.

References

Basso, K. H. (1987). "Stalking with stories": Names, places, and moral narratives among the Western Apache. In D. Halpern (Ed.), *On nature*. San Francisco: North Point Press.

Bowers, C. A. (1993a). *Critical essays on education, modernity, and the recovery of the ecological imperative*. New York: Teachers College Press.

Bowers, C. A. (1993b). *Education, cultural myths, and the ecological crisis: Toward deep changes*. Albany: State University of New York Press.

Bowers, C. A. (1995). *Educating for an ecologically sustainable culture: Rethinking education, creativity, intelligence, and other modern orthodoxies*. Albany: State University of New York Press.

Bowers, C. A. (1997). *The culture of denial: Why the environmental movement needs a strategy for reforming universities and public schools*. Albany: State University of New York Press.

Bowers, C. A., & Flinders, D. (1990). *Responsive teaching: An ecological approach to classroom patterns of language, culture, and thought*. New York: Teachers College Press.

Crick, F. (1994). *The astonishing hypothesis: The scientific search for the soul.* New York: Scribner's.

Damasio, A. R. (1994). *Descartes' error: Emotion, reason, and the human brain*. New York: G. P. Putnam.

de Garis, H. (1994, July 4). Wonder chips. *Business Week,* p. 88.

Ellison, L. (1994). Forward. *The commuter's guide to the information highway.* Redwood Shores, CA: Oracle.

George, T. (1995, November). Rethinking the curriculum for the digital age. *Hilltopics,* pp. 17–18.

Holland, D., & Cole, M. (1995). Between discourse and schema: Reformulating a cultural-historical approach to culture and mind. *Anthropology and Education, 26*(4), 475–489.

Kamii, C. (1991). What is constructivism? In C. Kamii, M. Manning, & G. Manning (Eds.), *Early literacy: A constructivist foundation for whole language*. Washington, DC: National Education Association.

Kay, A. C. (1991, September). Computers, networks, and education. *Scientific American,* pp. 138–148.

Lee, D. (1959). *Freedom and culture*. Upper Saddle River, NJ: Prentice Hall.

Lemonick, M. D. (1995, July 17). Glimpses of the mind. *Time,* pp. 44–52.

Lewontin, R. C. (1991). *Biology as ideology: The doctrine of DNA*. New York: Harper Perennial.

Moravec, H. (1988). *Mind children: The future of robot and human intelligence*. Cambridge, MA: Harvard University Press.

Muir, M. (1994, April). Putting computer projects at the heart of the curriculum. *Educational Leadership,* pp. 30–32.

Pinker, S. (1994). *The language instinct: How the mind creates language*. New York: Harper Perennial.

Sachs, W. (1992). *The development dictionary: A guide to knowledge as power.* Johannesburg, South Africa: Witwatersrand University Press.

Sternberg, R. J. (1982). *Handbook of human intelligence*. New York: Cambridge University Press.

Stock, G. (1993). *Metaman: The merging of humans and machines into a global superorganism.* Toronto: Doubleday Canada.

Turkle, S. (1996, January). Who am we? *Wired*, pp. 149–151.

Wilson, E. O. (1978). *On human nature*. Cambridge, MA: Harvard University Press.

BIOGRAPHY

C. A. BOWERS has taught at the University of Oregon and Portland State University and lives in Eugene, Oregon, where he writes and lectures on the cultural implications of the ecological crisis and technology. His most recent books include *Education for an Ecologically Sustainable Culture* and *The Culture of Denial: Why the Environmental Movement Needs a Strategy for Reforming Universities and Public Schools.*

3 Knowledge and Liberal Education: Representation, Postmodernism, and I-You Inclusive Knowing

Dale T. Snauwaert

Introduction

In this chapter, educational philosopher Dale Snauwaert explains how our conceptions of education are dependent on our assumptions about the nature of knowledge. It is obvious that we receive empirical information about the world through our senses, but it is far more difficult to understand exactly how what we perceive is related to what we know. This question of the relationship between the knower and the known depends on our fundamental beliefs about the nature of the world. Although such monumental considerations seem far removed from questions of curriculum and instructional methods, they are very much a matter of how we define the purposes of education itself. Our answers to these questions, even if vague and confused, undergird our actions as educators.

Snauwaert provides a historical context in which to reflect on the relationship between the way we define knowledge and understand the purposes of education. He begins with the classical Greek notion that knowledge consists of the recognition of universals in the world and takes the reader through a study of the relationship between the structures of the mind and the world through the postmodern era. At each point, he identifies the connections between these basic assumptions and the conceptualization of education.

Snauwaert's analysis leads us to question the postmodern perspective that no fixed connection exists between the structures of the mind and the structures of the world. The postmodern view is that the mind is a social construct—that it is largely shaped by social authority in power. Snauwaert suggests that this position is self-contradictory because it is predicated on the universal claim that all knowledge is relative. Complicating matters, within the postmodern perspective the most an educator can teach are methods of critical reflection to enable students to expose assumptions and hidden agendas in their own thinking and that of others.

Given these considerations, Snauwaert suggests the possibility that Martin Buber's concept of the I-You relationship can create an added and much needed dimension to human thinking. In the I-You relationship, an individual does not work from concepts, but from direct apprehension of a person, an object, and even for Buber, God. This is a relationship based on being fully present as a human being where we meet others with openness and attention. This encounter is a source of moral insight and responsibility; it is not a product of analysis, but of an immediate, profound sense of relation. The I-You relationship does not replace critical thinking, but provides a human and humane foundation for it. Snauwaert concludes that knowledge grounded in a loving encounter is a foundation for moral direction, meaning, and purpose.

—Jeffrey Kane

This chapter provides a discussion of the epistemological foundations of liberal education based on the central assumption of cognitive science: that knowledge constitutes an accurate mental representation of the external world. As Howard Gardner (1985) suggests:

> [T]he major accomplishment of cognitive science has been the clear demonstration of the validity of positing a level of mental representation: a set of constructs that can be invoked for the explanation of cognitive phenomena . . . representational assumptions and concepts are now taken for granted and permeate the cognitive sciences. (p. 383)

The *representation paradigm of knowledge* is at the core of modern philosophical rationalism and its psychological counterpart, constructivism, and it is that paradigm that lies at the foundation of the modern conception of liberal education as exposure to the formal—abstract structures and systems of representational knowledge that comprise the disciplines of knowledge. The purpose of this chapter is to (a) examine the representation paradigm and its concomitant conception of liberal education, (b) discuss the viability of the postmodern response to it, and (c) offer an alternative conception of knowledge and liberal education grounded in Martin Buber's notions of the I-You relationship and inclusive knowing. I argue that the I-You relationship is the missing dimension of an authentically humanistic liberal education and that all three modes of knowing—*representation, postmodern critical interpretation,* and *I-You inclusive knowing*—comprise different dimensions of human knowledge and a humanistic liberal education.

Modern Knowledge and Liberal Education

To understand the modern conception of knowledge and liberal education, we need to begin with the classical conceptions of knowledge and liberal education that form the foundation of the modern conception. As Paul Hirst (1973) suggests, both philosophically and historically, liberal education is "an education based fairly and squarely on the nature of knowledge itself" (p. 88). On the basis of the metaphysical and epistemological tenets of a realist theory of universals, the ancient Greeks, the founders of liberal education, believe that a fundamental and intimate symmetry exists between human consciousness and the cosmic order. For the Greeks, human consciousness is a microcosm of the universal order. From their perspective, universal patterns or archetypes exist that structure the cosmos, including the human mind; the mind and nature possess the same archetypal structure.

Given this basic structural symmetry, on the one hand, by comprehending the universal order, consciousness itself would be ordered and fulfilled in accordance with the nature of reality. On the other hand, by knowing one's self, because it was a microcosm, one could come to the knowledge of the universe, aligning one's self to its order. Hence, the cornerstone of Greek humanism and liberal education was the Socratic injunction: Know thyself. Liberal education thus was conceived as the simultaneous pursuit of self-knowledge and comprehension of the universal patterns of nature. This process of education was driven by **eros,** the cosmic impulse inherent in human consciousness toward wholeness, toward remembrance of the basic symmetry existing between consciousness and reality (Jaeger, 1953, 1965). This view is expressed in Plato's philosophy of education.

For Plato (trans. 1979), **education** is defined dialectically as the "art of turning [the power of consciousness] around in the easiest, most effective way—not of implanting sight, which it already has, but of contriving to turn the organ around to look where it should" (p. 518d). The progression in Plato's educational design, as described in *The Republic*, from gymnastics and military training to arithmetic and poetry, to harmonics and mathematics, and eventually to the dialectic, is an attempt to turn, systematically, consciousness away from the particulars of the world toward the universal Forms, which constitute the essence of those particulars. This turning from concrete, sensory experience toward abstract conceptual analysis and then to the direct apprehension of the Forms culminates in the realization of the structural symmetry existing between the mind and nature. Thus, education for Plato is a process of acquiring the capacity to apprehend directly the universal archetypes that structure the universe, the human mind, and human society. *Education* is a process whereby one directly apprehends the symmetry existing between the human mind and the universe, thereby freeing one from the slavery of passion, ignorance, and injustice.

The epistemology, ontology, and metaphysics of classical Greek philosophy was extended by the Neoplatonists and Stoics and eventually incorporated into Christianity by Augustine and then later by Aquinas. In a significant way, the symmetry between mind and nature of classical Greek philosophy was maintained in medieval Christianity. Christ represented the integration of cosmic intelligence within the human being. From this perspective, Christianity constituted the fulfillment of classical Greek philosophy (Tarnas, 1991, pp. 91–220).

The rise of modernity, however, called into question this cosmic symmetry while retaining a semblance of it, leading to a conception of liberal education based, not on the realization of structural symmetry, but on conceptual knowledge.

This questioning began in the 14th century with the nominalism of William of Ockham. Ockham's basic position is that **universals**, the belief that reality is structured by universal ideas or archetypes, are not real per se but are creations of the human mind. Universals are conceptual abstractions derived from the empirical observations of particulars in the world. Aristotle asserted that real universal patterns could be discovered through empirical observation; Ockham maintains that those patterns are not implicit in nature, but rather are projected onto nature by the mind. There is no metaphysical or ontological correspondence between the mentally constructed universal and particulars in the world. Universals, according to Ockham, are conceptual schemata through which human beings make sense of their experience, nothing more.

The 18th-century British philosopher David Hume also argues, consistent with William of Ockham's reasoning, that an individual cannot know what lies beyond sensory impression. The mind seemingly perceives relationships in the world, such as cause and effect, which imply a rational and knowable order to the world. Hume argues that the mind projects a causal set of relations onto a particular set of *random* impressions. The mind only experiences particular impressions; any seemingly inherent order or pattern is projected onto the impressions by the mind. The comprehensibility of the world is a mental construction formed out of mental habits; no pattern is implicit in the nature of reality. We are in a habit of assuming causal relations, but there is no logical certainty that these relations are, in fact, real (implicit in the nature of things). Knowledge is merely opinion based in habits of thought.

The epistemological skepticism of William of Ockham and David Hume failed, however, to capture the modern mind (in essence, these two philosophers anticipate the postmodern perspective), whose allegiance went the way of Immanuel Kant's rationalism and eventually modern cognitive psychology based on this rationalism (in the form of constructivism; Gardner, 1985). The 18th-century rationalist philosopher Immanuel Kant concurs that human beings are only capable of knowing that which is phenomenal (their own mental impressions), but he simultaneously believes that a valid and reliable knowledge of the world can be gained (e.g., Newton's physics). Kant's position is essentially that the human mind does not passively receive sense data but, based on the existence of innate categories of mind, actively structures those data. In a significant sense, we therefore can only know that which we structure by our minds. We cannot know the world in itself, but only that world constructed by our mental categories. However—and this is Kant's attempt to refute William of Ockham's and Hume's skepticism—we can know reality to the extent that it conforms to the innate categories of the mind because those categories correspond to the empirical world. Certain knowledge is possible for Kant because the a priori categories of the mind mirror the order of the world.

In other words, epistemic access to the empirical world is never direct but is always conditioned and shaped by the mind. It is only possible to know ideas, not empirical objects. Sensory perceptions are never directly received in the mind but are always processed, translated into ideas that are inevitably known in the context of other, preexisting ideas, cognitive structures, categories, schemata, and so forth. We can never, so to speak, "escape" our minds. We perceive the world through our network of prior (in Kant's case, a priori) ideas, structures, categories, and so on. Because we cannot apprehend the world directly, because we can only access our ideas about the world, knowledge and/or truth cannot be a direct representation but can be only a logically coherent relation between propositions about the world, defined in terms of the internal consistency of each proposition, the external consistency between propositions, and logically deductive relations between propositions. Knowledge is thus conceived as the formation of logically coherent theories of the world that correspond to, and thus represent, the world. The assumption here, however, is that although sensory perception is filtered and shaped through the mind, thus allowing only indirect access to the world, the structure of the mind itself corresponds to, mirrors, the nature of the world, thus allowing for accurate theoretical representation. Our minds do not deceive us but in fact allow us to comprehend an inherently comprehensible world because a symmetry remains between the mind and the empirical world.

Thus, from the modern perspective, to have a "rational" mind "implies experience structured under some form of conceptual scheme" (Hirst, 1973, p. 97). We are able to gain understanding of experience because we share a common conceptual scheme with others. Experience becomes intelligible only on the basis of the public sharing of coherent conceptual systems. From this perspective, liberal education is a process of engaging with various heretofore unknown conceptual schemata in the form of the paradigms of disciplinary knowledge. These paradigms can be conceived in terms of the basic structure of the discipline. The structure of the discipline constitutes its basic logic in terms of the questions it asks, the methods of inquiry it employs, and its standards of epistemic validity. The structure of the discipline represents an abstract, codified representation of the world. Through exposure to the structure of a variety of disciplines, one acquires the frameworks of representations that each discipline employs to make sense of the world (Bruner, 1965). This exposure expands the mind by enlarging the conceptual systems through which we can more readily understand our experience. To undergo education is then "to learn to see, to experience the world in a way otherwise unknown, and thereby to have a mind in a fuller sense" (Hirst, 1973, p. 98).

This is the essence of modern liberal education, and it is based on a particular conception of knowledge emanating from modern rationalism and cognitive psychology, what can be referred to as the **representation paradigm**. From this perspective, knowledge is a coherent symbolic representation that mirrors the structure of the empirical world. The world is conceived as the one true and real world, and the epistemological project is to map or represent it mentally in symbolic form.

THE POSTMODERN CRITIQUE

Currently, the representation paradigm is undergoing a full-scale attack by some postmodern critics. *Postmodernism* itself is an umbrella term consisting of several theoretical positions (Lechte, 1994; Tarnas, 1991). In epistemological terms, however, the **postmodern critique** constitutes a refutation of the representation paradigm. As discussed above, from the modern perspective, we can be confident that our mental representation of reality accurately corresponds to the world, for our mental categories mirror the nature of the world. That is, the world can be known with certainty because there exists a fundamental correspondence between the mind and the world.

From the perspective of postmodernism, the assumption that the mind mirrors nature is the central problem. Postmodernism agrees with the rationalist rejection of the empiricist proposition that the mind passively reflects the intrinsic order of the empirical world in favor of the view that the mind constructs that order. It rejects, however, both the assumption of classical philosophy of a basic symmetry and the modern assumption of mirroring between the mind and the world. For the postmodernist, following in essence the logic of William of Ockham and David Hume, the mind is not a microcosm of the world; it is a social construction.

The structure of the mind is not pregiven, but rather is a product of historically contingent linguistic and cultural practices. Thus, knowledge of the world is a historically contingent interpretation; there is no one indubitable understanding of the world, no one Newtonian theory that accurately represents and explains reality, and no one true reality. Rather, there are multiple worlds based on multiple interpretations, all of which are conditioned by different sociocultural and linguistic frameworks. Being historically contingent in this way, knowledge is also fundamentally linked to power. Particular understandings of reality are constructed, propagated, and maintained to preserve specific power relations (Foucault, 1974, 1977). From this perspective, no one interpretation can claim epistemic authority, but there exists a plurality of socially constructed perspectives all conditioned by language, culture, and power.

In some sense, the postmodern mind participates in the co-creation of reality. There is no external, fixed reality per se, only a reality constructed by the historically contingent mind. Because there are multiple perspectives, there is a plurality of realities, each co-created by the culturally situated, contingent individual. Multiple interpretations of reality, however, contain an epistemological injunction; they require that we engage in communities of discourse, that we enter into dialogue with each other in order to understand each other.

In addition, multiple perspectivism is bounded by what can be called **complementarity**. As we come to accept one perspective, we exclude others. As we co-create one reality, we exclude the creation of other realities. As we come to know and co-create *x*, we exclude *y*. Complementarity requires self-examination and deconstruction of tacit assumptions and ideology (political, cultural, religious); it requires entering into "critical" dialogue with others and the sociocultural world so that we come to an understanding of the source of our perspective and the possibilities that it excludes (Freire, 1973). Perhaps most important, the co-creation of one reality and the exclusion of others entails responsibility for what we know. We are responsible for our perspective and therefore for our creation of reality. This responsibility necessitates that we critically engage in discourse in order to fully understand our beliefs and their consequences.

As discussed above, the modern epistemological paradigm maintains that reality is presented to us and that the epistemological project is the accurate representation of reality. Postmodernism maintains, in contrast, that knowledge is an act of *presentation* of reality, not a representation of it; that is, in knowing we are engaged in the construction of reality. In this sense, reality isn't represented; it is *presented* in the act of knowing it. This argument rests on the notion of the social construction of knowledge and reality. However, the social construction of reality implies, from the perspective of the individual knower, a process of socialization, a process of learning—the individual acquisition of the ideational presentations of reality that the culture has constructed and/or adopted. Social construction implies that no one true reality is being represented, but rather that one reality among many possible realities is being *presented*. Through socialization, the individual acquires the presentation of reality specific to his or her language, culture, and polity. From the perspective of the individual, however, he or she is learning a presentation, and learning implies representation, not representation of Reality per se but representation of a culturally specific presentation of reality. Through socialization, the individual forms a representation of his or her cultural worldview. This claim is fundamentally different from modernism in that, instead of our mental maps accurately representing reality, they represent a socially constructed interpretation of reality. Nevertheless, the representation of cultural presentation is still a representation. Despite its attempts to refute representation, postmodernism is actually caught in a web of cultural representation. We are still caught in the cage of our mental structures, but these structures no longer have the assurance of certainty based in a correspondence with an objective reality; they are open-ended and ultimately arbitrary.

As discussed above, the modern assumption is that correspondence remains in some sense between the conceptual structure of the disciplines one learns and reality itself. Postmodernism calls this correspondence into question, however, suggesting that the conceptual structures and schemata of disciplinary knowledge do not reflect reality per se, but rather reflect power relations. That is, what the liberal disciplines constitute is ideology rather than knowledge. This conclusion calls for a radical revision of liberal education toward the development of critical rationality. Here, liberal education is not merely exposure to the structure of the disciplines—that is, exposure to codified, formal representations of the world, but a critical encounter with the disciplines in an attempt to deconstruct them, to make their representations problematic, to unmask their hidden agendas and power relations. Liberal education thus becomes an education that liberates one from the potentially oppressive power of ideology in the guise of knowledge. From this perspective, education is "liberal" in the sense that it liberates one from the illusion of ideology (Freire, 1973).

From the perspective of postmodernism, the representation paradigm leaves out an authentic, empowered subjectivity in favor of an objectified, disempowered sense of both the mind and the world; from the perspective of the representation paradigm, we are locked into, and thus determined by, a preexisting structure of the one and true reality. Postmodernism liberates the subject from this determinism, insisting that the subject is free to co-create its reality. By liberating the subject, however, postmodernism leads to a problematic and contradictory epistemological relativism. Postmodernism makes a universal claim for local knowledge; it maintains that *all* knowledge is historically contingent and therefore relative to specific sociocultural-political frameworks. Its proposition of the socially contingent nature of knowledge, however, is itself a claim that proposes to be universal—that is, true for all knowledge claims. It therefore contradicts its own precepts, in the sense that it maintains that all knowledge is socially constructed and thus not universal, but in making this claim it is itself making a universal claim about the nature of knowledge. In addition, on the basis of its own presuppositions of epistemological equality, there are no standards on which to evaluate the validity of knowledge claims. Given this epistemological relativism, one is left with political power as the determinant of knowledge, rather than any valid standard of knowledge itself. Thus, there is no truth per se, only power-based ideology. In short, the result is nihilism (Wilber, 1995).

I-You Relationships and Inclusive Knowing

The previous discussion leads to the question whether any subjective standards of knowledge can escape relativism/nihilism. Both the representation and postmodern paradigms of knowledge/ideology share commonality; they both conceive knowledge/ideology as conceptual.

The mind is by its very nature conceptual. The mind structures experience via conceptual schemata, schemata structured by language. Being conceptual, the mind, as we have discussed, can never directly apprehend the world in itself but only has epistemic access to concepts that represent or, from the postmodern perspective, present the empirical world. The conceptual nature of the mind can only allow either representation or interpretation, both indirect, mediated forms of knowing—mapmaking rather than an experience of the territory the map represents or interprets. From the level of the mind, the best that can be achieved is a representation or a socially constructed presentation of the world, not a direct apprehension of it in itself.

The epistemological validity of the representation paradigm rests upon the assumption of correspondence; however, this assumption is not self-evident. If we can never go beyond our conceptual schemata, how do we know that our conceptual schemata mirror an independent reality? We can never know with certainty that it does because we never have direct epistemic access to reality. In other words, given its own assumptions, representation is founded on an epistemologically arbitrary belief, not on knowledge per se. If the epistemological foundation of representation is recognized as arbitrary, and if we retain a conception of knowledge as conceptual, as postmodernism does, then we are led logically to epistemological relativism. There is no longer any assurance that our representations correspond to one reality per se.

As a possible resolution of this impasse, an alternative is proposed that finds its foundation, not in the conceptual mind, but in an intersubjectivity that transcends conceptual schemata. This proposition is based on Martin Buber's (1970) notion of "inclusion" inherent in the nature of I-You (Thou) relationships.

Buber maintains that there are two basic relationships: I-It and I-You. The **I-It** relationship is one where the other (the world) is objectified. One knows the other, not in its subjectivity, but as an object to be grasped, analyzed, processed, understood, ordered, coordinated, and so forth. The other becomes an object to be experienced and/or used. This is the nature of conceptual knowledge. We turn subjectivities into conceptual representations that are analyzed and logically ordered. In turning the other into a concept, we have objectified it. We have created an It and relate to it as an It arranged in a logically ordered It-world. This accounts for our experience and use of the empirical world. Conceptual representation creates an I-It relationship. We can even conceptualize parts of our own subjectivity, turning those parts into self-concepts that form our persona (Wilber, 1996). In fact, the ego as a system of self-concepts is the nature of the I in the I-It relation (Buber, 1970, pp. 111–112). The nature of conceptual knowledge and the ego is to in fact set apart, distinguish, discriminate; in I being set apart, the It-world is created, experienced, and used.

However, the I-It relation does not constitute the only form of relationship. One can relate to the other, to the world, as a You rather than as an It. This **I-You** relation constitutes a fundamentally different epistemology. The You is the essence, the unity, the presence, the mystery of the other. The You is the subjective dimension of the other; the relation to the You thus occurs intersubjectively and transsubjectively, never objectively mediated through concepts, for any conceptualization will objectify the subject, translating its essential Youness into an Itness. As Buber (1970) suggests, "the relation to You is unmediated. Nothing conceptual intervenes between I and You" (p. 62). "The You knows no system of coordinates" (p. 81). This suggests that the I-You relationship is a spiritual association in the sense that it is a communion, a meeting, an encounter between subjectivities, unmediated and direct, that is, transconceptual (p. 77).

The I-You relationship is where one meets the subjectivity, the essence of the other with one's whole being in complete openness and presence. Literally, one opens to and enters the subjectivity of the other and knows the other from the perspective of the other's subjective orientation, as well as glimpsing the mystery that is contained there as the eternal You. Thus, the relationship is both intersubjective and transsubjective; intersubjective in the sense that there is a direct meeting of subjectivities, and transsubjective in the sense that both Yous find their essence in a shared essence: both your own You and the You of the other are recognized as being grounded in the one eternal You. As Buber (1970) suggests, "the eternal You is You by its very nature" (p. 148) and "in every You we address the eternal You" (p. 150).

This is not, however, an experience of "empathy" but one of "inclusion." **Empathy** "means to transpose oneself over there and in there. Thus it means the exclusion of one's own concreteness. . . . Inclusion is the opposite of this" (Buber, 1965, p. 97). In other words, empathy is merging one's subjectivity with another, thereby losing one's own distinction as an individual. One becomes the other and in the process loses one's self. **Inclusion** "is the extension of one's own concreteness, the fulfillment of the actual situation of life, the complete presence of the reality in which one participates" (Buber, 1965, p. 97). In other words, inclusion is a meeting of subjectivities wherein individual distinction is maintained; it is an I-You relation, rather than a merger of Yous (without an I). The maintenance of the I, of individual distinction, allows one "to meet and know the other in his concrete uniqueness and not just as a content of one's experience" (Freidman, 1965, p. xv). This suggests that inclusion as the epistemological dimension of the I-You relationship is *not* conceptual, but rather a direct apprehension of the other in itself: the essence of conception is to make the other the symbolic content of one's mental experience. Here an I is not experiencing, but encountering the other in his or her concrete uniqueness as a You. The I here is not an ego, not a self-concept, but a subjectivity conscious of itself as a subject (Buber, 1970, pp. 111–112). As Buber (1970) suggests, "The person beholds his self; the ego occupies himself with his my: my manner, my race, my works" (p. 114). The mental ego cannot apprehend a You; its function is to translate and order the world into conceptual representations; its function is to make sense of the world, and in this process it creates an I-It relationship to the world. The I as self-conscious subjectivity, however, does not attempt to make sense of the world, but it "meets" and "encounters" the world. Possessing subjective self-consciousness, one is able to meet the other with complete wholeness and openness, allowing the other his or her subjectivity. This encounter is made possible by the maintenance of the I as a self-conscious subjectivity, in the sense that only a self-conscious subject can meet a subject. It is only in self-consciousness that we can be present to another and only in presence is the You revealed. Encountering the You is not a setting apart but a relation, and only subjects can relate. The emergence of an object will negate the possibility of relationship; it introduces an It that creates separation, not relation. Relationship is a spiritual association, a communion, a meeting, and an encounter of spirits in relation. However, to have a relationship, distinction of self must be maintained as well, for if distinction is lost, there is merger and hence the loss of relationship. Thus, the I-You relationship must entail self-conscious intersubjectivity. This is the only way that the You can be encountered.

Here we have a fundamentally different epistemology, one based not on representation nor its deconstruction, but one that transcends the conceptual mind and views knowledge in terms of awareness: a self-aware intersubjective encounter. This is *not* objective knowledge but intersubjective, and ultimately transsubjective, knowingness—a conscious, individuated knowledge of the subjectivity of the other. Being transconceptual, this way of knowing circumvents the problems inherent in the representation paradigm and postmodernism discussed above. By transcending conceptualization, the intersubjective encounter allows epistemic access to the reality of the other, not as an object but as a subject, for any objectification separates and thus disallows epistemic access and therefore knowledge (the reality of the other is found in his or her subjectivity). From this perspective, knowledge (as opposed to ideology) is found and founded in the realization of the I-You relationship.

As discussed above, the disciplines of knowledge constitute formal, codified systems of representation that allow, in theory, the student to interpret the experience of the world from enlarged and enriched perspectives. From the postmodern perspective, these representations are ideological, in the sense that they are social constructions based in power, and therefore demand deconstruction. From Buber's perspective, both orientations, being based in conceptual representation, address the It world and an I-It relationship to it. Through representation, the world is objectified and set apart from the I. The world becomes nothing other than our representations of it; subjectivity, its reality, is lost and thus its essential nature is lost in the very act of representation. Postmodernism enters the equation only as a deconstruction of the It-world, and when the It is deconstructed—what is left is nothingness; this is the nihilism implicit in postmodernism. What is required is not deconstruction but transformation. As Buber (1970) suggests:

> Knowledge: as he beholds what confronts him, its being is disclosed to the knower. What he beheld as present he will have to comprehend as an object, compare with objects, assign a place in an order of objects, and describe and analyze objectively; only as an It can it be absorbed into the store of knowledge. But in the act of beholding it was no thing among things, no event among events; it was present exclusively . . . and now it is locked into the It-form of conceptual knowledge. Whoever unlocks it and beholds it again as present fulfills the meaning of that act of knowledge as something that is actual and active between men. (pp. 90–91)

By meeting the It with full presence, being, and openness, the You emerges; one now enters into an I-You relationship, and

> [h]ere You appeared to man out of a deeper mystery, addressed him out of the dark, and he responded with his life. Here the word has become life and this life . . . is teaching. Thus it stands before positivity in order to teach it, not what is and not what ought to be, but how one lives in the spirit, in the countenance of the You. And that means: it stands ready to become a You for them at any time opening up the You-world. (Buber, 1970, p. 92)

Opening to the You transforms the It, to borrow Whitehead's phrase, as an "inert idea" into something real and alive, in Buber's phrase "actual." This transformative effect is the missing dimension of an authentic liberal education.

AUTHENTICALLY HUMANISTIC LIBERAL EDUCATION

For Buber (1965), what defines the educator is being conscious that he or she presents to the student "a certain selection of what is, the selection of what is 'right,' of what should be" (p. 106). The educator, by the quality of his or her being and presence, presents a version of the world to the student. In the modern and postmodern conceptions of liberal education, this is a presentation of the It-world and its deconstruction. Thus, many students experience education as dead, irrelevant, not real. They often speak of the "real world" in contrast with the inert It-world of education. In contrast with this inertness, a living situation "demands presence, responsibility; it demands You" (Buber, 1965, p. 114). By entering into an I-You relationship with students, by meeting them as subjectivities, an actual, alive world is opened to them. Being alive is contingent on having subjectivity. Death and being dead are the loss of the subjective dimension, the turning into or being inanimate, not animated by subjectivity, no longer being real.

By meeting the student as a You, what Buber calls "confidence" emerges. "Confidence means the liberating insight that there is human truth, the truth of human existence . . . he accepts the educator as a person. He feels he can trust this man . . . and so he learns to ask" (Buber, 1965, p. 106). Asking is an active, alive searching; it begins a dialogical relation, which is the essence of authentic education. By entering into an I-You relationship provided by the teacher, the student feels seen for him- or herself as a unique, worthy, real subjectivity. He or she then begins to recognize the possibility of a different world, the You-world as embodied by the teacher. As Buber (1970) suggests, "In the relationships through which we live, the innate You is realized in the You we encounter" (p. 78). Being opened to his or her own You and the possibility of a You-world, he or she becomes ready for an encounter, a meeting: He or she begins to ask. In the act of questioning grounded in the confidence of the I-You relationship provided by the teacher, the It of representational knowledge is transformed into a living encounter. The student can now enter into a living relationship with the ideas of others as alive expressions of their encounter with the world.

Buber (1970) maintains that "without It a human being cannot live. But whoever lives only with that is not human" (p. 85). The It-world and our representational knowledge of it is necessary to sustain life. Representational knowledge is also a necessary stage in our development toward inclusive knowing and I-You relationship—that is, toward the realization of our humanity. Buber maintains that our development as a human species began with a "natural association" of I-You and has evolved into a "spiritual association" (pp. 73–77). This evolution of the species mirrors the developmental pattern of the individual (Wilber, 1996). In a natural association, one has an unformed, undifferentiated relation to You. One is merged with the You without the distinction of I. This state is reflected in individual development as an infantile oceanic state of unity. What is required for (and what constitutes) growth is differentiation, a forming of an I distinct from the You. The formation of I, entailing a detachment of the I from the You, results in the formation of It and thus the loss of You. This is the development of an ego, which begins with the onset of language and culminates in late adolescence/early adulthood. The egoic I entails a setting apart and thus the creation of a representational It-world. The I has emerged as a carrier of sensations and the environment as their object, erecting "the crucial barrier between subject and object," thereby dissolving the natural association (Buber, 1970, p. 74). This dissolution is a necessary stage of development, a necessary separation that allows for the possibility of a reunification with the You without the loss of self, an individuated reunification, a relationship. Only with an I can the possibility of relationship come into existence (without an I there is merger, not relationship), and the initial formation of an I entails the formation of It. Thus, through the It, we reclaim the You, and this reclamation is a developmental process facilitated by a pedagogical I-You relationship between teacher and student.

Under the conditions of a pedagogical I-You relationship, exposure to representational knowledge is transformed into an encounter (by the teacher meeting the student as a You, confidence and asking/dialogue emerge), allowing the student to behold in the It and thus transform the It into a You, into an actual, alive knowing, a knowing that is brought to life by the meeting of subjectivities. Perhaps more important, the student develops through this experience the capacity to enter into I-You relationships. By opening to the You, not as a natural association but as a spiritual relationship, the student fulfills, to borrow Paulo Freire's phrase, his or her ontological vocation to become fully human (Freire, 1973).

As Werner Jaeger (1953) suggests, the essence of liberal education (as originally conceived by the Greeks and carried through the Renaissance and the Enlightenment) is **humanism**, the realization through education of full human potential. As Buber maintains, the It-world is necessary for life but we only find our humanity by encountering the You in ourselves, others, and Spirit. The You is our essence, and in meeting the You the humanism of liberal education is and can only be fulfilled. The I-You relationship provides both the epistemological and ontological foundation for achieving authentic knowing and thus our humanity. Liberal education must then include the You as a living encounter. The I-You pedagogical relation provides the missing dimension of liberal education as an education devoted to humanism, for "real living is meeting." In teachers meeting students and students meeting others directly and indirectly through the disciplines of knowledge, the promise of liberal education is fulfilled, transforming inert ideas and I-It relationships into living actualities.

In conclusion, the I-You conception of knowledge and liberal education is not put forth here as a replacement for modern and postmodern forms of knowledge and education. Rather, it can be maintained that each constitutes a different and valid level of human understanding. These three modes of knowing—representational, critical, and inclusive—correspond to the three ways of knowing central to the perennial philosophy: the eye of flesh, the eye of reason, and the eye of contemplation (Wilber, 1989). As Plotinus put it: "Knowledge has three degrees—opinion, science, illumination. The means or instrument of the first is sense; of the second dialectic; of the third intuition. To the last I subordinate reason. It is absolute knowledge founded on the identity of the mind knowing with the object known" (Bucke, 1969). Although critical rationality and inclusive knowing transcend representational knowledge, they also include it. The same is true for inclusive knowing both transcending and including critical rationality. Each one constitutes an advance on the other but one that includes the former level (Wilber, 1996).

From an educational perspective, human beings do engage in symbolic representation, and it is essential to learn, to understand, the fundamental structures and systems of representational knowledge as they are codified in the various disciplines and fields of knowledge and the larger culture. This is necessary for the development of a mature and healthy ego, which is linked to competent membership in a culture. Competent membership requires the acquisition of relevant representational knowledge. In addition, however, it is equally essential to acquire a critical consciousness, to be able to discern and deconstruct the ubiquitous presence of power in human affairs and knowledge—power that dehumanizes, that turns us into Its. A critical deconstruction unmasks the ultimate relativity of representational knowledge, leading to the necessity of attaining a knowledge that transcends conceptual representation, for either one is led to this deeper knowingness or one lives in the despair of nihilism. This realization of the ultimate relativity of culturally based understanding can lead to a transcendence of the egoic-I and its concomitant It perception of the world toward an opening into the You-world, into the real world of intersubjectivity and transsubjectivity; for the identification of conceptual representation as real blocks a movement into subjectivity. Thus, if you correctly perceive representational knowledge as a pure social construction, then you must conclude that what that knowledge represents is not real, and thus you are faced with the choice of living in the despair of an inauthentic reality or transcending conceptualization into the authentic reality of subjectivity. Remember: Conceptual representation creates objects both internally and externally that set one apart from the essence, the subjectivity of ourselves and others, creating objects that are not real in themselves. However, critical rationality can only proceed on the basis of a fundamental grounding in the representational systems it seeks to deconstruct. Postmodernists, such as Foucault and Derrida, do not possess only critical consciousness; they possess also a deep and comprehensive understanding of the structures and representational frameworks of the disciplines they deconstruct. Finally, human beings are not exclusively rational beings, but possess the capacity for I-You encounters and inclusive knowing, as suggested by the long and rich histories of the wisdom traditions of the world (Borchert, 1994; Bucke, 1969; Caputo, 1986; Eliade, 1972; Fox, 1980; Maslow, 1970; Stace, 1960; Underhill, 1930; Wilber, 1977, 1989, 1995). It is within human capability to transcend the conventional level of socially constructed discourse and understanding and to enter a dimension of direct knowledge. This is the pinnacle of human knowledge—in fact, the only valid form of knowledge (for only by transcending representation and encountering subjectivity is the condition of epistemic access fulfilled)—a direct meeting of the You subjectively, intersubjectively, and transsubjectively. This knowledge grounds human knowing and liberates it from nihilism. These three levels of "knowledge" comprise a comprehensive conception of human knowing and in turn an authentically humanistic liberal education.

References

Borchert, B. (1994). *Mysticism: Its history and challenge*. York Beach, ME: Samuel Weiser.

Bruner, J. (1965). *The process of education*. Cambridge, MA: Harvard University Press.

Buber, M. (1965). Introduction. In M. Friedman (Ed.), *Between man and man*. New York: Collier Books.

Buber, M. (1970). *I and thou* (W. Kaufman, Trans.). New York: Scribner's.

Bucke, R. M. (1969). *Cosmic consciousness*. New York: E. P. Dutton.

Caputo, J. (1986). *The mystical element in Heidegger's thought*. New York: Fordham University Press.

Eliade, M. (1972). *Shamanism: Archaic techniques of ecstasy*. Princeton, NJ: Princeton University Press.

Foucault, M. (1974). *The archaeology of knowledge*. London: Tavistock.

Foucault, M. (1977). *Discipline and punish: The birth of the prison*. London: Allen Lane.

Fox, M. (1980). *Breakthrough: Meister Eckhart's creation spirituality in new translation*. Garden City, NY: Doubleday.

Freire, P. (1973). *Pedagogy of the oppressed*. New York: Continuum.

Gardner, H. (1985). *The mind's new science: A history of the cognitive revolution*. New York: Basic Books.

Hirst, P. H. (1973). Liberal education and the nature of knowledge. In R. S. Peters (Ed.), *The philosophy of education* (p. 88). Oxford, UK: Oxford University Press.

Jaeger, W. (1953). *The Greeks and the education of man*. Annadale, NY: Bard College Papers.

Lechte, J. (1994). *Fifty key contemporary thinkers: From structuralism to postmodernity*. New York: Routledge.

Maslow, A. H. (1970). *Religions, values, and peak experiences*. New York: Viking Press.

Plato. (1979). *The republic* (R. Larson, Trans.). Arlington Heights, IL: Harlan Davidson.

Plotinus. (1969). Letter to Flaccus. In R. M. Bucke *Cosmic consciousness* (p. 122). New York: E. P. Dutton.

Stace, W. T. (1960). *Mysticism and philosophy*. Los Angeles: Tarcher.

Tarnas, R. (1991). *The passion of the Western mind*. New York: Ballantine Books.

Underhill, E. (1930). *Mysticism: A study in the nature and development of man's spiritual consciousness.* New York: E. P. Dutton.

Wilber, K. (1977). *The spectrum of consciousness.* Wheaton, IL: Quest.

Wilber, K. (1989). *Eye to eye.* Boston: Shambhala.

Wilber, K. (1995). *Sex, ecology, spirituality: The spirit of evolution.* Boston: Shambhala.

Wilber, K. (1996). *The Atman Project: A transpersonal view of human development.* Wheaton, IL: Quest Books.

BIOGRAPHY

DALE T. SNAUWAERT is Assistant Professor of Philosophy of Education at Adelphi University. He is interested in the relationship among knowledge, ethics, and consciousness as they pertain to educational theory.

4 Moral Outrage and Education

David E. Purpel

Introduction

Critical theorists in education such as Henry Giroux, Michael Apple, and others have provided much-needed analysis of the fundamental assumptions implicit in the structure of schools, curriculum, and knowledge. They have been able to reveal the implicit values and beliefs embedded in educational policy and practice by precise and critical analysis; they have been able to point out where stated premises and conclusions don't match. In so doing, they have been able to reveal the root metaphors that have actually served to guide thinking.

In this chapter, educational philosopher David Purpel, in essence, turns critical theory upon itself. He elaborates on the assumptions embedded in critical perspective and suggests that they are inadequate to either understand or respond to the social and cultural imperatives of our time. Purpel explains that critical rationality, born of the Enlightenment, has created a culture "cautious of generalization, suspicious of certainty, reverential of difference, and wary of affirmation." These are the characteristics of thought that not only reveal underlying assumptions but also effectively eliminate the possibility that there may be moral truths and imperatives.

Purpel maintains that we do not need more information to transform education, but rather spiritual affirmation—a recognition of, and commitment to, our moral responsibilities as human beings. He insists that we cannot reason to such insight, but rather must reason from it. Purpel, in reflecting on his own thinking and experience, turns to his own personal background as a source of inspiration. He finds in his own Judaic background a constant prophetic voice that calls for social justice, concern for others, and the transcendence of self-centered motivations. He explains that critical rationality may serve as an invaluable tool when subject to the authority of human dignity and world responsibility but that its application must be measured so as not to eliminate the possibility of mystery, wonder, and meaning in the world. No information processing, no critical analysis, can reveal the imperative to which we as educators have to respond: injustice, oppression, and indifference to human suffering. Such imperatives arise only when we as educators transcend words and pursue our ultimate spiritual commitments.

—*Jeffrey Kane*

Cultural Transformation and Education

We are asked in this volume to consider relationships among education, transformation, and information that implies good reason to believe that they are, in fact, closely connected and that we are in an era that requires social and cultural transformation. Therefore, it would seem appropriate, as we approach the end of a millennium, to consider very broadly the notion that an education rooted in Enlightenment traditions of detached, thorough, and critical reasoning and analysis is a crucial dimension of a peaceful, prosperous, and joyful society. One major goal of this century has been to enlarge and expand opportunities for formal education at all levels, a project that has shown impressive accomplishments in both scope and magnitude. It also has been a century of incredible scientific and material achievement and of enormous spiritual devastation—a century when smallpox was eliminated and genocides were perfected, when we have come to believe in the big bang theory for both the beginning and end of life, when God died a most untimely death.

In the United States in the last moments of this millennium, we still have far too many poor, far too many rich; we have far more hatred, bigotry, racism, sexism, and classism than we say we want; and we have a culture that emphasizes achievement, competition, conquest, and domination at the expense of compassion, caring community, and dignity. The abomination of homelessness persists, but it has vanished from the media and political platforms except for those that promise to shield us from the unpleasant presence of those who have no shelter. Poverty persists and increases, but instead of a discourse of poverty we have a discourse of welfare; instead of a war on poverty we have a campaign for middle-class tax relief. There is a growing gap in incomes, a widening gap of trust among racial and ethnic groups, increasing homophobia, xenophobia, and whatever phobia it is that covers fear and loathing of the other. This is a dismal record indeed for a talented and enterprising people and a shameful state of affairs for a powerful and wealthy nation that claims sacred status, one explicitly founded on the principles of liberty and justice for all.

The added shame of this situation is that our educational system has contributed to, and colluded with, much, if not all, of this. Our most powerful and influential leaders call on education to meet the demands of a cruel economy and a meritocratic culture. The great bulk of formal educational policies and practices reflect and facilitate structured inequality, rationed dignity, rationalized privilege, and self-righteous hierarchy. Moreover, much of the rhetorical justification for this violation of our commitment to a vision of liberty and justice for all comes from the ranks of the school and academy. Perhaps most disturbing of all is the realization that the movers and shakers in government, business, communications, advertising, banking, and elsewhere—that is to say, those institutions that shape our lives in critical ways—are people who almost surely have had what we have come to accept as a "good education." The very people who have brought us to our present plight are among the brightest, most articulate, most creative, most imaginative, and most reflective people in the land. It would seem that, at the very least, we need to reconsider what we mean by a "good education."

Moreover, the professional educational community has largely responded to our crises with characteristic opportunism, timidity, and accommodation, exercising their skills to meet the demands of the dominant political forces. What would seem to be required is a pedagogy of moral and spiritual transformation, but instead our profession has fashioned a pedagogy of control and standardization focused on technology, competitiveness, and materialism. Despite the overwhelming dreariness and blandness of the present professional educational discourse, however, some extremely encouraging work is being done that has great power, hope, imagination, and daring. I have in mind the work being done in what I would call a pedagogy of transformation and meaning—educational ideas directed at the search for social justice and personal meaning. Among the prominent writers in this mode are Henry Giroux, Michael Apple, Svi Shapiro, Nel Noddings, William Pinar, Ron Miller, C. A. Bowers, Jane Roland Martin, and James Moffett, all of whom address basic issues of cultural and existential meaning as the necessary framework for developing educational policies and practices. It is work that at least holds out the possibility of challenging the dominant educational discourse of achievement, competition, and standardization and of stimulating the public and the profession to reexamine the relationship between our highest aspirations and prevailing notions of schooling.

I want very much to affirm and celebrate this work even as I speak to how its very insights and analyses testify to the limitations of some of our most valued educational traditions and public schooling. What this work does in its very affirmation of the importance of serious reflection on the complexities of fundamental issues of justice and meaning is to highlight the problematics of detachment, independent thinking, and critical rationality. It must be pointed out that I am lumping together educational orientations that have important differences among them (e.g., the difference in the emphasis put on social, political, and economic concerns as opposed to writers who emphasize personal development and human growth). Among the very important connections, however, are their commitment to social and cultural transformation *and* their reliance on critical rationality, personal reflection, openness and respect for varying perspectives, and good faith dialogue. The difficulty is that this work is relatively weak when it comes to articulating and celebrating a moral and spiritual grounding that can provide meaning to the educational project and energy and hope to sustain those involved in the struggle. Intellectual insight, critical understanding, and theoretical power are surely necessary but clearly insufficient to a pedagogy of transformation because what is also needed lies in the realm of the spirit in such matters as faith, commitment, hope, passion, and devotion.

Although I am proud to be part of an intellectual and professional community and tradition that is deeply committed to the values of careful analysis, reasoned thought, and informed reflection, I increasingly find that such an orientation is by itself too weak a reed to support a response that is commensurate with the enormity of our current set of existential, social, political, economic, moral, and spiritual crises. The twin roots of this doubt are in the sense of moral outrage that I share with many people at the depth of unnecessary pain and suffering in the world and simultaneously in the absence of moral outrage of so many people. Not only do I affirm the validity of this outrage, but I consider it an absolute requisite to serious efforts at cultural and educational transformation. I also am very much aware of the problematics of a pedagogy of moral outrage, not the least of which is the psychological reality of the resistance and hostility to it when it is perceived to be guilt inductive. People simply do not want to hear constant messages of disaster, gloom, and suffering and are wont to tune out jeremiads as hysterical, if not counterproductive—the perfect defense mechanism. Those who are more inclined to confront the harshness of our times are often worried that moral outrage itself only serves to continue the cycle of hostility and divisiveness. In addition, there is the frustration that comes with the awareness of the depth, enormity, and scope of the problems that engender helplessness, if not despair. Yet it is difficult for me to see, in the absence of a passionate commitment to the plight of the suffering, how we can seriously address the really vital issues that threaten our existence as a caring people.

In addressing the matter of moral outrage, I have had to confront at least four basic questions: (a) What are the criteria for morally outrageous phenomena? (b) How do we come to internalize them? (c) What is the authority and source of these criteria? and (d) What are its problematics? I have some sense of the first issue as I affirm what I believe to be our basic human moral framework of liberation, dignity fulfillment, and peace for all. Having said that, let me quickly acknowledge that this in no way suffices as a satisfactory response. The question regarding how we come to internalize moral commitments is obviously a very complicated and controversial one, and with it comes a very strong and rich tradition of reflection and theorizing. Moreover, some very interesting and intriguing work is going on in educational theory today in this realm as reflected in the work of such people as Nel Noddings, James Moffett, and Jane Roland Martin. The harsh reality, however, is that the public schools are very far away from paying serious attention to such questions and issues largely because they do not have the political will or intellectual tradition to accept this responsibility.

Moreover, I believe it is time to question the broader notion that we can significantly affect social and cultural transformation primarily or even largely through serious study and dialogue. It is more than a little disquieting when we consider the poignant effects of critical rationality on our struggle to find meaning and create a morally sound and spiritually satisfying path to personal fulfillment, cultural richness, and social justice. This process has inevitably confronted us with enormously diverse perspectives, incredibly perplexing dilemmas, extraordinarily complex ideas, and a fathomless set of paradoxes. Because of these realities, we have learned to be cautious of generalizations, suspicious of certainty, reverential toward difference, and wary of affirmation. We have learned about the historical, political, and subjective nature of knowledge and have had to respond with critical and skeptical detachment lest we be seduced by self-serving rhetoric masked as universal truths. We have become so smart that we find it extremely difficult to believe in anything except the contingency of knowledge and the inevitability of conflict. Our critical studies have taken us to spiritual and moral inarticulateness, if not silence; our detachment has led us to the emptiness of the marginality of interested but paralyzed bystanders; and our tolerance has forced us into an unwilling consciousness of moral relativity.

Part of my skepticism is directed at the whole notion of such a thing as an educational enterprise—that is, the difficulty of the reification of education, of separating out certain processes and phenomena from a larger framework of meaning and labeling them as "educational." I have come to believe that such a reductionism blurs the intimate relationships among critical cultural, political, and social phenomena and education and to nourish a myth of an objectivity based on technical expertise. Perhaps it is time to tell ourselves that Education is an empire without clothes and that we need to return to the realms of the fully clothed.

It seems rather ludicrous to me to have this vast array of sophisticated, well-trained, and creative people called "educators" sitting around in their offices and classrooms with nothing to do except to define and solve "educational problems." Where do these educational problems come from? Do they exist as such in a conceptual vacuum, outside any larger context? Educational problems per se would seem to be of a secondary (no pun intended) nature; they necessarily arise as a consequence of other issues and concerns; for example, the efforts to teach literacy emerge from a variety of motivations: to facilitate productivity, to strengthen democracy, and to allow for personal empowerment, to name a few.

Indeed, one prime activity of educators is to determine objectives and goals in an Alice in Wonderland effort to figure out the reasons we're doing what we're doing! To me, it is quite extraordinary that we are constantly being asked to state our goals (a process, incidentally, that rarely if ever results in changing what we do). If we are uncertain about our educational goals, then how can we possibly continue to teach what we do? How could such uncertainty arise in the first place? Presumably, if we do not know our goals, then we should stop whatever we are doing and restart only when we know what the goals are. Of course, much of the goal-stating effort is largely disingenuous because, politically, it usually adds up to a post hoc justification of what we already are doing. Beyond the cynicism and ritualism, however, I believe that the impulse to ask the question of educational purpose reveals an unsettling lack of confidence in the validity of what we do and masks a deep and genuine uncertainty of our moral direction and a suspicion that we are morally and spiritually lost.

This brings me back to the third and fourth questions regarding moral outrage: What is its authority and source, and what are its problematics? My position is that, above and beyond studying educational processes, we as educators are required to wrestle with issues regarding the nature of our culture's highest aspirations and most cherished visions. To do so requires us to acknowledge the difficulties of an epistemology that focuses on observable aspects of our situation but blinds us from being in touch with its wholeness. Critical rationality is very good in taking things apart and not very good in putting things together; it can help make us smarter but not necessarily wiser; and it is infinitely better at deconstructing than it is at reconstructing.

As educators, we need to ground our work in a vision that, in some significant way, resonates with what matters most and is of the most profound nature, to matters of cosmology, religion, and spirituality. One needs to proceed from this point cautiously and carefully; figuring out what matters most and what constitutes profundity can be an extremely difficult, elusive, paradoxical, and anguishing process because we are dealing here with issues of extraordinary importance, ambiguity, and complexity.

A particularly complex and elusive dimension of this process is sorting out the role of spirituality in this quest. I share part of my own sorting-out process in the next section of this chapter. I do so, not to be merely autobiographic nor to claim that my quest has produced radically new answers to profound questions, but because I believe that the questions, processes, and insights that I came to accept are shared by many, if not most, of those interested in personal and cultural meaning and transformation. Obviously, individuals will address these issues on the basis of their own unique background, history, and orientation, and indeed I believe that the process of sharing individual quests can greatly contribute to the task of reflecting on both our differences and commonalties.

EDUCATION AND SPIRITUALITY

Although I have not resolved the issues involved with the relationship of education to matters of spirituality, passionate commitments, and ultimate concern, I have

found a source of authority that is personally satisfying and compelling. I came to a place where I realized that I would not be able to respond in depth to the question "To what should we be committed?" unless I was willing, at some basic level, to accept a starting place, a point of departure, a fundamental frame of reference, or to put it in more contemporary terms, I would need to be part of an interpretive community. At this point, I truly encountered capital M Mystery because I came to this conclusion, in part, because I realized that what I was looking for involved a process that gives life to existence; that animates, energizes, and gives direction; or as it is written, that which represents the spirits that reside within our midst. Implicit in this recognition is the realization that my commitment to social justice was not a function of the intellectual skills I had assiduously pursued but from interior sources I had thoughtlessly ignored. Perhaps this is, in part, what is meant by the term *spiritual*—literally, that which inspires and gives breath to. The first Mystery, then, has to do with the source of this energizing spirit; although I am prepared to accept, albeit gingerly and hesitantly, the importance and reality of these spirits, I remain among the baffled about what they are, where they come from, how one finds them, and what one does with them after they are found.

The second Mystery for me has to do with the reality that I find myself generally drawn to religious issues and, particularly and increasingly so, to the study of Jewish religious traditions. At first, I saw my interest as part of the way to provide further justification and validation for my work on an educational orientation that focused on equality and social justice and found powerful support for this in such traditions as the writings of the Biblical prophets. I quickly realized, however, that what was going on was more than the usual kind of academic scrambling for post hoc rationalization that passes for carefully considered inquiry. I was astonished to find, generally speaking, this material to be simultaneously familiar and fresh, old and new, accessible and remote. It was as if I was revisiting an important and suspended part of my consciousness even though I do not remember ever being in that state, at least in any systematic, thorough, or direct way. My formal religious training had been minimal, perfunctory, superficial, and banal, if not counterproductive and misleading, and yet it would seem that my work had been significantly influenced by traditions I had largely ignored and misunderstood. I still cannot fully explain why this would be so. Nor do I entirely comprehend why I am still so strongly drawn to examining Jewish sources, but I am, and I find myself relying increasingly on them for that which animates and informs my work. My reactions to these materials is varied, if not contradictory. I find much that is affirming and energizing; there is a great deal that I do not accept, much I do not even understand; some seems directly relevant to my work, and much seems quite removed from it; some of it troubles me, and all of it intrigues me.

Will Herberg points out in his book *Faith in Biblical Theology* (1976) that it is what we *remember* and what we *expect* that shapes our quest for faith. According to Herberg, "the act of faith is double: the existential affirmation of *a* history as one's redemptive history and the existential appropriation of this redemptive history as one's personal background history, and therefore in a real sense the foundation of one's existence" (pp. 40–41). Accordingly, I seek to ground my work in my hopes as they are informed by what I choose to remember and by what I want to expect. I expect and accept meaningful existence and that, as educators, we must do our work within a larger framework of meaning that which is of utmost importance to us and constitutes the substance of our very deepest commitments, those that Paul Tillich (1957) calls matters of "faith and ultimate concern." Tillich describes faith as:

> the state of being ultimately concerned: the dynamics of faith are the dynamics of man's ultimate concerns. Man . . . is concerned about many things, above all about those which condition his existence, such as food and shelter. Man in contrast to other living beings, has spiritual concerns—cognitive, aesthetic, social, political. Some of them are urgent, often extremely urgent, and each of them as well as the vital concerns can claim ultimacy for a human life or the life of a social group. If it claims ultimacy it demands the total surrender of him who accepts the claim, and it promises total fulfillment even if all other claims have to be subjected to it or rejected in its name. (p. 1)

It certainly makes sense that we determine our goals, purposes, and strategies by choosing a framework of faith and ultimate concern that is accessible and compelling to us, and it also makes sense that within this frame we are wise to study, reflect, and dialogue. Although we need not insist on linearity, however, we are still beset with the greatest of all difficulties—that of determining our faith and what constitutes matters of ultimate concern. The processes of critical rationality can operate with enormous power both within and without such frames of faith and ultimate concern, but by themselves they cannot bring us to affirm a faith or to celebrate an ultimate concern. Study, reflection, and analysis cannot be at the center of an education for meaning, although they surely can and ought to be among the inevitable and valued partners in the task of naming and acting on our faith. I believe that we are living in a time of widespread earnest and heartfelt searching for the other critical partners.

Indeed, it may be that the very human desire and impulse to seek faith and ultimate meaning is itself another critical partner. The postmodern condition is one in which we seem to seek, rather than express, faith and one that requires that we do so in order to pursue hope and sustain our struggle to create a just and loving community. Franz Rozensweig (1955), in describing the rationale for a center of adult Jewish education, said that at one time people went from the Torah into life but that now is a time when we must go "the other way round from life . . . back to the Torah" (p. 152). The modern age is one in which we encounter the world, not with faith and a sense of ultimate meaning, but with skepticism, wariness, and suspicion and convinced that we are better served by being armed with knowledge and critical rationality. This approach has certainly served many purposes well, but it has also exacerbated our alienation and anxiety, leading us to be even skeptical about our skeptical armament. Many of us indeed seek the faith and framework of meaning that can enable us to understand the evil that has befallen us and that can help sustain the impulse to resist if not overcome it and return to traditional and sacred sources like the Torah. It is one thing to study sacred traditions and sources of wisdom, however, and quite another thing to be nourished and energized by them. This

generates yet another search—the search and struggle for the disposition, accessibility, and openness to faith and the desire and willingness to be nourished by the sacred.

Abraham Heschel teaches us that we can learn to have faith only when we wonder, for only when we truly wonder we will be able to confront the awesomeness and sublimity of creation. He says in *God in Search of Man* (1955), "Mankind will not perish from want of information; but only for want of appreciation. The beginning of our happiness lies in the understanding that life without wonder is not worth living. What we lack is not a will to believe but a will to wonder" (p. 46). This wonder inevitably brings us to confronting the awesomeness of the most fundamental questions of origins, purpose, and destiny—the overwhelming and disturbing mystery of existence. Heschel says that this mystery

> is not a synonym for the unknown but rather a name for *meaning* which stands in relationship to God. . . . Ultimate meaning and ultimate wisdom are not found in the world but in God, and the only way to wisdom is through our relationship to God. That relationship is *awe. . . . The beginning of awe is wonder, and the beginning of wisdom is awe.* . . . Awe enables us to perceive in the world intimations of the divine, to sense in small things the beginning of infinite significance, to sense the ultimate in the common and the simple; to feel in the rush of the passing the stillness of the eternal. (pp. 74–75)

Faith, then, is not a function of study, not the result of research and analysis, not the culmination of reasoned reflection, but rather emerges from wonder, awe, and engagement with the infinite. Heschel (1955) is not unaware of the educational implications of such a formulation for education:

> Our systems of education stress the importance of enabling the student to exploit the power aspect of reality. To some degree, they try to develop his ability to appreciate beauty. But there is no education for the sublime. We teach the children how to measure, how to weigh! We fail to teach to revere, how to sense wonder and awe . . . the sense of the sublime, [and] the sign of the inward greatness of the human soul. (p. 36)

It seems that an alternative response to issues of ultimate meaning is to dismiss essentialist questions about the meaning of life, human nature, and the course of human destiny as naive, irrelevant, or sentimental, if not stupid and dangerous. I have chosen to speak from the perspective of traditions that assume quite the opposite—namely, that these questions are the *only* ones worth asking and, moreover, from the grounding of a tradition that takes commitments very seriously. As Rabbi Heschel (1955) has said, "Socrates taught us that a life without thinking is not worth living. Now, thinking is a noble effort, but the finest thinking may end in futility. . . . The Bible taught us that life without commitment is not worth living; that thinking without roots will bear flowers but no fruit" (p. 216).

I not only affirm traditions that recognize that as humans we are fated to create our world but also believe that, above all, we are called to create a world resonant with divine intention—a world of peace, justice, love, community, and joy for all. These are traditions that accept as givens the heights of human potential as well as the limits of human fallibilities; they posit our capacity to be generous as well as selfish; angelic as well as demonic; compassionate as well as cruel; wise as well as foolish. Such traditions revere knowledge but only as it is tempered with the wisdom that advances justice and mercy; a perspective that acknowledges the enormity of the task but recognizes human despair as sinful; and one that represents a consciousness of unmitigated outrage in the wake of cruelty and injustice but always in the faith that witness, confession, and healing offer the possibilities of transcendence and redemption. What is absolutely crucial to redemption is human responsibility and human agency because these traditions require that we act as God's agents, dedicated and committed to constructing and sustaining intentional communities based on joy, love, peace, and justice.

As educators, we should not be merely committed to education; we should instead be more deeply committed to human dignity. We should not dedicate ourselves to higher learning but to a high standard of living for all. Our responsibilities are not to select the best students but to eradicate privilege. Our commitment must not be to the market economy but to the Golden Rule. It is idolatrous to commit oneself primarily to the preservation of history, biology, or any other discipline or field when injustice, inequality, and hatred endure in the land. We need not be concerned with a decline in test scores; we need to be outraged and obsessed with an increase in unnecessary human suffering. As educators, we must not offer justice, joy, and love as rewards or luxuries, but rather affirm them as requirements for a life of meaning. Personal dignity is not something to be rationed and manipulated but cherished as inherent and inviolable.

Having access to such a tradition provides me with a framework to respond to some concerns I have expressed about moral outrage. I now have some point of reference to the question of source, criteria, and authority of moral outrage, a tradition that at least allows for an opportunity to explore, examine, and reflect. It also provides a frame for dealing with the difficulties of too much or too little outrage, as well as with its counterproductive possibilities. It surely does not provide me with answers and certainty; indeed, responding to these traditions seems often to intensify and complicate the struggle even further. What is energizing is that it involves us in a process that mandates our active and full-hearted engagement in the issues of what constitutes our sense of ultimate commitments, vows, and aspirations in a context of penultimate social danger, personal uncertainty, and human limitation.

Despite our prior commitments and vows, it is certainly true, as well as tragically unnecessary, that we have created a world in which justice, love, peace, and joy are unequally distributed; that is why it is truly a blessing when we try to reduce this inequity situation by situation, one person at a time. Our commitment, however, must extend beyond the enrichment and support of particular individuals, as worthy and commendable as that goal surely is. We must recognize that the sources of the inequality, inequity, and injustice lie not only within the souls of individuals but also within the structures of our economic, political, and cultural institutions. Our current economy requires poverty, our current culture demands elitism, and our existing political system necessitates hierarchy. Our commitments, therefore, extend to the creation of a just world beyond merely making accommodations to an unjust system; we are called to both heal the wounded *and* to create healthy environments, to respond to both the effects *and* the sources of injustice. As educators, we need to be concerned not so much with minimum scores as with minimum wages, not with classroom deportment as much as with business ethics, less with the distribution of grades than with the distribution of wealth. More accurately, we need to be mindful of the links between classroom pedagogy and social policy because of the close relationships among minimum scores, classroom deportment, the distribution of grades and minimum wages, business ethics, and the distribution of wealth.

Educational Implications

The Public Schools and Transformation

Is this an oxymoron or a cherished vision? A delusional fantasy or the stuff of dreams? Is it a useful way of distracting us from the necessity of deeper structural change or the conviction of the inevitable triumph of good sense? Much has been written and much has been expected of the possibilities of public education, and of course much has been written on how the public schools act, not as agents of liberation and enlightenment, but as engines of the dominant classes.

Public education is often asked to be an agent for social transformation, but the nature of the transformation varies in content and across time. The common schools of the 19th century endeavored with a great deal of success to transform a group of largely rural, multicultural, multilingual regions into a unified, industrial, and WASP nation. The schools of today are striving to transform us in such a way that we can accommodate to a cybernetic culture and multinational economy. It must be remembered that public schools are bureaucratic agencies of the state and are required by law to follow the policies of publicly elected officials who have total fiscal control of the schools. If transformative functions are to be assigned to the schools, the assignments will be made by those in power—that is, by the established dominant interests. In addition, we must also confront the reality of an entrenched professional bureaucracy that largely works for self-serving inertia and stasis. Although an honorable and modest history of the profession is calling for genuine social and cultural transformation, it is a story of very little impact. At the same time, it must be said that the profession has been able to make a great many technical changes (e.g., in instruction, curriculum, and assessment), but even these are usually absorbed into the basic schooling frameworks set by the dominant power structures.

However, what I believe is meant by transformation in the context of this book has to do with a fundamental change in moral and spiritual consciousness in which we reject the excesses of individualism, materialism, competitiveness, and acquisitiveness. The kind of transformation that is required is one that energizes us to pursue personal meaning, social justice, world peace, and ecological harmony. The difficulty is that those who favor this kind of transformation do not have the political clout to direct the energies of our social and cultural institutions. Hence, it is quite naive to expect that the public schools can be a primary source of such a transformation. After all, public school educators are under quite strong political, professional, and community controls that put enormous pressure, certainly not for moral and spiritual transformation, but for the intensification of our current consciousness. Most teachers are overworked and underpaid, and most come out of a tradition that stresses professionalism rather than social reform. What we will have to do is work harder to create the cultural and social conditions that will enable the public schools to do their part in changing consciousness. Schools do not exist to thwart the will of those in power, so if we want to change society, it is simply neither fair nor wise to ask the schools to be in the vanguard. This means that educators who want to work for transformation cannot limit themselves to schools, community colleges, universities, and the like but need to be involved with other and larger cultural movements.

Obviously, many forces and movements are working for the kind of transformation being described—some of them political, others economic, and others ecological. I want to speak directly to the enormous force of the current interest and involvement in spiritual matters that, until fairly recently, has been misrepresented as a rise in religious fundamentalism. A dramatic increase in religious fundamentalism has surely occurred, but a broader and more widespread phenomenon of spiritual seeking and struggling cuts across class, religions, and ideology. As I have already indicated, some of this energy has been expressed in the professional educational literature, a literature not noted for its daring. My own view is that we as educators, citizens, and humans ought to involve ourselves more directly and openly in this larger realm because it is my belief that the transformation that radical educators seek is fundamentally spiritual in nature. More particularly, I believe that we as educators can significantly contribute to the movement for transformation in two broad ways: (a) by engaging in the larger cultural struggle to affirm a spiritual basis for a vision of a just and loving community for all *and* (b) by integrating this faith and vision into our professional practices.

Ancient spiritual truths must be asserted—truths that do not constitute information but wisdom, that do not emerge from research but from the soul, and that are not matters of consensus but of affirmation. For me, it is abundantly clear that we *are* our sisters' and brothers' keepers, and we are inevitably and intimately connected with each other and with nature. It is clear to me that we suffer enormously from the loss of this truth and the resultant profound alienation. Because of this, we seek to reclaim our holiness, and in doing so we will end the isolation, suicide, murder, pillage, and pain we inflict on ourselves, each other, and the planet. Scientists, theorists, and philosophers now tell us of our intimate and inevitable interconnectedness with society, culture, history, and nature and have made it possible even for skeptics like me to approach the essence of spiritual consciousness, the belief in the oneness of being. Indeed, the question of being our brothers' and sisters' keeper becomes moot when we begin to realize that we are very likely not apart from, but a part of, our brothers and sisters.

This consciousness impels us to renew our struggle for direction, meaning, and guidance with determined intensity; Heschel (1955) says,

> Man is not the same at all times. It is only at certain moments that he becomes aware of the heart-breaking inconceivability of the world in which he lives and which he ignores. At such moments, he wonders: what is my place in the midst of the terrifying immensity of time and space? what is my task? what is my situation? (p. 130)

His own response is powerfully unequivocal:

> He who seeks an answer to the most pressing question, what is living? will find an answer in the Bible; man's destiny is to be partner rather than a master, there is a task, a law, and a way; the task is redemption, the law is to do justice, to love mercy, and the way is the secret of being *human and holy.* (p. 238)

How are the rest of us to respond to Heschel's challenging questions? Walter Brueggemann urges us to respond to such questions in a consciousness of confession and grief. *Confession* refers to a process in which we affirm our basic aspirations, hopes, visions, beliefs, and commitments, as well as to admit to our failures to act on them. This is very likely to be a matter of both celebration and grief because, as we remember our communal and personal spirits, we will undoubtedly be renewed by the energy and joy of this wisdom, and as we remember our history, we will surely be horrified and mortified by our refusal to live by them. Brueggemann makes it very clear that we cannot omit the grief process because that is a necessary part of confronting the chasms between our hopes and realities, our human responsibilities for the pain and injustice in the world, and recommitting ourselves to our cherished destinies. In his book *Hopeful Imagination* (1986), he invokes the work of the Biblical prophets as a metaphor for how we might address our current cultural and religious state, which he characterizes as a parallel exile for serious believers. In his concluding chapter, he offers three themes:

> 1. *Grief* is offered against establishment *denial and cover-up* Jeremiah regards as a lie. 2. *Holiness* is proclaimed against conventional theology that never quite faces the otherness and always hopes for and forms a *utilitarianism* that links God's holiness to some historical purpose. 3. *Memory* is asserted against *amnesia* in which nothing is noticed or critiqued and everything is absolutized in its present form. . . . *Grief* should permit newness. *Holiness* should give hope. *Memory* should allow possibility. (pp. 131–132)

It is poignantly, if not tragically, clear that much of our culture is a long way from acknowledging its responsibility for such hideous phenomena as slavery, poverty, war, racism, sexism, inequality, and hunger. This refusal to take responsibility and hence to grieve and mourn for the pain we as a community have inflicted represents to me the limitations of an education grounded primarily in critical rationality, study, and the exchange and analysis of information. Indeed, many of our most learned and reflective commentators have used their vast stores of knowledge, insight, and information to celebrate a smug and intoxicated triumphalism of capitalism, consumerism, and meritocracy, American-style. It is obviously impossible to grieve if there is no sense of significant loss or, even more strikingly, if there is a sense of significant gain! Instead of compassion for the suffering, we have learned to blame the victims or to make them invisible; many curse rather than bless the poor; and rather than seeing others as God's children, many of us see human beings through the lens of the potential customer or expendable worker. The dominant culture does not celebrate justice but competition, does not value unconditional love but grooves on conditional rewards. Its rituals are not of communal solidarity but of partisan triumphs, and its energies are not rooted in a divine impulse to seek oneness but in a frantic spirit of greed and acquisitiveness.

What I think is required for genuine transformation is an education that builds on the traditions of critical rationality by integrating them into the processes that I have been discussing in this piece—namely, awe, faith, the struggle for ultimate meaning, commitment, confession, moral outrage, and grief. In current political and cultural realities, these cannot be a significant part of the public school experience largely because they go counter to both public and professional expectations of the role of these schools. For the most part, parents want their children to succeed and look to the schools to provide them with the wherewithal to gain an edge in the struggle for privilege and advantage. Academics, for the most part, want to preserve their disciplines and areas of study, whereas school administrators are preoccupied with maintaining good will and stability. Moreover, the public schools are politically positioned to be as accommodating and acutely sensitive to community pressures as possible, effectively making them hostage to the demands of zealous and determined groups. The possibility of introducing on a widespread basis serious spiritual and moral consciousness or even dialogue to educational policy and practice is extremely remote, if for no other reason than the political clout of the Christian Right. The cliché that the public schools try to be all things to all people and consequently fail to fully satisfy anyone is basically true and must be accepted as a consequence of our political and social structures.

The daring, intriguing, and imaginative ideas of James Moffett and Nel Noddings are instructive to this issue. Moffett (1994) basically attacks our culture as bankrupt and our schools as perpetuating a ruinous consciousness and argues forcefully and courageously that only an education primarily and radically directed at personal development through various spiritual disciplines can save us from ourselves. He makes a very compelling argument for this approach, and I believe with many others that it merits serious public and professional dialogue. As attractive and creative as these ideas are, however, I would have to say sadly and ruefully that there is virtually no possibility that they will see very much of the light of day in the foreseeable future of public school practice. They are far too threatening to the dominant thrust of those who dominate public spaces.

The ideas of Noddings (1993) on teaching children to wrestle with the enduring and complex issues of fundamental belief are also quite daring for public school, although they are much less radical than those of Moffett. Noddings (1993) urges schools to provide safe and supportive opportunities to study and discuss such ideas as theodicy, immortality, the existence of God, and the nature of evil, surely a sensible and valid idea. Her plan is not, however, to make such study the focus of the curriculum but to introduce them as relevant spin-offs and dimensions of the traditional discipline-based curriculum (e.g., math, science, history, English, foreign language). She advocates that teachers commit themselves to teaching for understanding of varying beliefs; to an attitude of "pedagogical neutrality"; and to an approach that allows them to take a position, but she insists that they acknowledge and recognize differing views. All in all, I see this as a very prudent and pragmatic way for the schools to deal with such vital issues, but the relative cautiousness and lines of demarcation of her proposals only emphasize the limited range of public school possibilities. It is not an approach designed to transform the culture or to galvanize spiritual struggle, moral outrage, awe, and passionate commitment but one that hopes to stimulate students to study and reflect on the fundamental questions of existence within the traditional framework of the schools as they are. And yet, even such sensible and modest proposals are, within our current context, relatively controversial and radical with little likelihood of gaining broad support in the mainstream of educational practice. If schools are, at best, reluctant to provide for serious discussion of the most important questions of human existence, then how can we expect them to be a prime mover in the struggle for cultural and social transformation? We mustn't and shouldn't.

What Can Be Done?

Accepting the educational limitations of critical rationality for changing consciousness and the political liabilities of the public schools does not in any way mean that educators are irrelevant and marginal to the struggle for a just and loving world. It does mean that we have to reexamine the claims that we have made for enlightenment education and the public schools in the context of a commitment to social and cultural transformation. It does not mean that we should accept the anti-intellectualism that denies the undeniable and absolutely essential liberation and inspiration that can and does emerge from study, research, dialogue, understanding, and analysis. It does mean that we need to seek other sources for the energy, wisdom, and courage to sustain the struggle for meaning. It does not mean that we should cede and surrender the public schools to the forces of either blandness or zealotry; nor does it mean that we should not continue to engage in the public and professional struggle for a humane and liberating education. It does mean that we must give up the falsely reassuring and naive way we equate democratic education with public schooling.

It does mean that we as educators may have to give up some of our precious programs and pet solutions or at least be more modest about their possibilities. There is nothing particularly sacred about whole language learning or experiential learning, nothing ultimate per se in the teaching of poetry or going on field trips or even in journalizing. Indeed, it is possible to turn the teaching of imagination and critical thinking into a sacrilegious act when people use their newly augmented imagination and criticality to make a buck at the expense of others, to exploit the environment, to find tax loopholes, or to encourage teenagers to smoke. The use of portfolios may stimulate imagination; it is surely more sophisticated than conventional, reductionist assessment, and it no doubt will afford more opportunities for advancement to more people. At the same time, portfolios have been, can be, and will be used to facilitate and enhance elitism, privilege, and hierarchy. In contrast, however dubious we may be of the value of particular educational technologies, something clearly sacred and very special *is* involved in promoting human dignity and social justice and in doing so as educators.

Indeed, our deepest commitments should be the same as those of all other people: They cannot, should not, must not be anything less than those contained in our culture's highest aspirations and most cherished dreams. Our differences with other groups lie, not in the substance and nature of our commitments, but only in where and how we act on them. The struggle for creating a community of peace, love, joy, and justice must go on in every sphere, including, of course and perhaps especially, in educational institutions. We are not primarily educators; we are first of all God's agents, active partners in the covenant to create a community of peace, justice, love, and joy who, parenthetically, have decided to exercise our responsibilities to this project in places called schools and universities. Educators are called on to pursue justice, to choose life, to cherish freedom for all, and to love their neighbors as themselves, maybe more but certainly not less than anyone else. Our profession will not be ennobled by feeding the engines of material growth, personal success, intellectual mastery, or national supremacy; it is ennobled by its devotion to spiritual development, individual dignity, moral sensitivity, and universal peace.

My view is that if public school educators committed themselves to the task of participating in the continuing responsibility to create a just and loving world, the nature of their work would change dramatically and profoundly even within the context of severe restriction. It *is* possible to do at least some of what Nel Noddings suggests—that is, to engage students in serious dialogue on profound issues within the existing curriculum. It is possible to do what Jane Roland Martin (1992) suggests: create a more nourishing and loving classroom environment where students are affirmed as they thoughtfully probe their world. It is also possible to add some of the opportunities for spiritual growth that James Moffett suggests into existing classrooms. The suggestions of William Pinar (1976) about the importance of aesthetic opportunities for students to reflect on their inner lives and those of Henry Giroux (1988) that students and teachers critically examine the contradictions of their lived experiences are extremely important and doable possibilities. None of these orientations may become central to the schools, but that doesn't mean that they can't have some impact in some however modest way.

This is an era of increasing cynicism, despair, and helplessness and a time when many suggest that the best we can do is either ride out the storm or contain the damage as much as possible. Still others say that the apocalypse is now and that we should abandon ship or learn to tread water or both. I take a different view—namely, that we should renew our commitment to creating a world of peace, love, justice, and joy with greater determination, passion, and vigor precisely *because* these are such desperate times. It is surely proper to count our blessings and to affirm our vision at times of genuine cultural and social advancement, but we have an even greater responsibility to remind the community of its covenant in times of danger. This is a time when we must vigorously and passionately counteract the cynicism and despair that only deepen and extend the danger. The times call, not for capitulation or curtailment of our commitments, but for the affirmation, as Herberg (1976) suggests, of what we remember and what we expect. We ought to remember the enormous amount of unnecessary human suffering, and we ought to remember our vows to redeem that suffering with the creation of a better world. We must expect that this requires a great deal of human agency, determination, and will, and we must have faith that these efforts will ultimately succeed. We must remember the magnificent acts of courage and sacrifice that millions have offered in the struggle for a just and loving world.

Let us as educators, citizens, and human beings have faith in our ultimate commitment to the creation of a just and loving community. Easy to say, hard to do, unless we take into account our amazing human capacities and that mysterious spirit that is the source of the faith that energizes and inspires them. Each of us must search for the community of meaning that provides, protects, and enriches that source. In these communities, we can find the authority for our moral outrage and the energy to sustain the struggle to preserve the hope that is required to meet our responsibilities. Responsibility without a moral and spiritual framework becomes psychological guilt, the kind of meaningless and unrooted dis-ease that cripples people into deafness, if not hostility, to human suffering. The difficulty in recognizing, enduring, and responding appropriately to morally outrageousness is, I believe, related to spiritual alienation—that is, a failure to affirm. The reality is that we need more help than good intentions, critical rationality, and tolerance can provide in our vocation to create a just and loving community for all. We and our students need to have the faith that such additional resources are available in that realm called the spirit.

I find great consolation in what Michael Lerner said in 1994:

> The ultimate Force governing the world, the Force that has created the entirety of Being, is the energy that presses for transcendence toward a world in which all Being manifests its fullest ethical and spiritual potential, a world in which human beings recognize one another both in our particularity and in our ability to manifest ethical and spiritual possibility. That Force exercises a spiritual pull within all Being to move beyond what is to what it ought to be. . . . [T]he God of Moses is a Force that transcends all limits and makes it possible for us to do the same. This God is the Force that makes for the possibility of possibility. (p. 65)

I am further moved by what Michael Lerner's teacher, Rabbi Abraham Heschel wrote in 1951:

> Only one question . . . is worthy of supreme anxiety: How to live in a world pestered with lies and remain unpolluted, how not to be stricken with despair, not to flee but to fight and succeed in keeping the soul unsoiled and even aid in purifying the world. (p. 179)

I am deeply comforted to know that Lerner, Heschel, and I, as well as countless others across time and space, have been and will continue to be stirred by what was written in the Talmud 1,800 years ago: "The task is not ours to finish, but neither are we free to take no part in it."

SUMMARY

The focus of this chapter has not been on information nor even on education, but rather on the part that education plays in the infinitely more important issue of our moral condition. It is my view that this must be the starting point of all serious discussions of all issues of public policy, including those involving education. I share the position that we as a society have fallen tragically short of our commitment to create a just and loving community for all and, furthermore, that our educational institutions and orientations are complicit in the violation of this commitment. This failure can be seen as the triumph of a consciousness of materialism, individualism, competitiveness, and hierarchy, as well as a function of increasing cynicism, loss of energy, and rising despair.

I believe that the most powerful element that is lacking in the necessity for the kind of transformation necessary to renew our commitments is a sense of profound moral outrage. The road to moral outrage would seem not to be paved either in good intentions or in more critical rationality, sophisticated knowledge, and clever analysis. The more direct path would seem to be the one marked "spiritual" because the nature of the commitments that generate moral outrage will emerge from our most profound sense of what constitutes ultimacy. This would suggest that educators need to address seriously their own views on what is of ultimate concern in order to explore the moral and spiritual commitments that ground their educational orientations.

It is clear to me that the public schools are sharply limited in their capacity to be a major force in such a transformational process but that whatever possibilities exist should be energetically pursued. It is also clear to me that educators need to have the courage to accept the limitations of deeply cherished notions of the traditions of liberal education without in any way denying their necessity. Educators therefore need to be at once more modest and more bold; modest in their expectations of what public schools and critical rationality can do and bolder in their hopes of the possibilities of awe, faith, grief, confession, and spirit.

REFERENCES

Brueggemann, W. (1986). *Hopeful imagination*. Philadelphia: Fortress Press.

Giroux, H. (1988). *Teachers as intellectuals*. Granby, MA: Bergin & Garvey.

Herberg, W. (1976). *Faith in biblical theology*. Philadelphia: Westminster Press.

Heschel, A. (1951). *Man is not alone.* New York: Farrar, Strauss & Giroux.

Heschel, A. (1955). *God in search of man.* New York: Farrar, Strauss & Giroux.

Lerner, M. (1994). *Jewish renewal*. New York: Putnam.

Martin, J. R. (1992). *The schoolhome.* Cambridge, MA: Harvard University Press.

Moffett, J. (1994). *The universal schoolhouse.* San Francisco: Jossey-Bass.

Noddings, N. (1993). *Educating for intelligent belief or unbelief.* New York: Teachers College Press.

Pinar, W. (1976). *Toward a poor curriculum.* Dubuque, IA: Kendall-Hunt.

Rosenzweig, F. (1955). *On Jewish learning.* New York: Schocken Press.

Tillich, P. (1957). *Dynamics of faith.* New York: Harper & Row.

Biography

David Purpel is a Professor in the Department of Educational Leadership at the University of North Carolina at Greensboro. He is the author of *The Moral and Spiritual Crisis in Education* and (with Svi Shapiro) *Beyond Liberation and Excellence.*

The Legacy of Gregory Bateson: Envisioning Aesthetic Epistemologies and Praxis

Diana Muxworthy Feige

Introduction

Nothing exists in isolation. All things exist in relation. This is not to say that objects from atoms to suns occupy places relative to one another. Rather, it is to say that all things exist within, and indeed by virtue of, patterns of relationships. For example, Earth exists as part of a balanced gravitational system in which the sun, the moon, and the planets all play a role in charting its course. Were it not for the balance of these complex relationships, Earth would not exist as we know it; it would not likely allow for the creation of an oxygen-rich atmosphere or for the emergence of life as we know it, which make Earth distinctive among all the celestial bodies we now know.

This perspective, this focus on the patterns that not only run between objects but also create the conditions that give things their identity, makes all the difference in how we think about knowledge, the world, and ourselves. It constitutes a radically different foundation for understanding and for educating children so that they may learn to understand the world in terms of dynamic patterns, rather than fixed objects.

In this chapter, Diana Muxworthy Feige invites the reader to explore the meaning and educational implication of such a perspective through the epistemology of philosopher-biologist Gregory Bateson. Muxworthy Feige, following Bateson, focuses not on things in and of themselves, but on continuity amid change, on the systems that make things what they are and simultaneously allow for their evolution. She explains that symmetries weave through nature, that ratios and proportions govern the structure and form of cells, organs, organisms, and ecosystems. Although it is common to study frogs in schools by dissecting them, by cutting their tissues into finer and finer pieces for microscopic examination, Muxworthy Feige would have us understand that those cells and organs interact with one another in the life of the frog. She would have us explore the relationship between the beating of the heart and the inhalations and exhalations of the lungs. She would have us study the frog's patterns of sleeping and waking, of hunting and mating, of the cycles of a frog's life. These, in turn, would be studied in terms of the cycles of the seasons, in terms of the flora and fauna of the area, in terms of the influences of human beings on the ecosystem. Consider the meaning and implications for biological science and education of the recent discovery, made by schoolchildren, of strangely mutated frogs in a variety of regions.

The key to understanding patterns is not reduction and analysis, but a widening of perspective with an emphasis on synthesis. To perceive a pattern, an individual must exercise imagination. In this context, the imagination is not fantasy, but a disciplined, aesthetic sensibility, a level of awareness of continuity amid change.

Muxworthy Feige explains that as we teach children to view the world through reduction and analysis, we rob them of the contexts to make sense not only of things in the world but of themselves as well. We deprive them not only of the opportunity to appreciate the meaning and purpose that flow through things but also of the meaning and purpose they may find through learning in their own lives. We may think of thinking as we think of discrete objects in a lab, but we are mistaken. All things are connected within children as they are without. As children learn to think, so they establish their own patterns of relationship with the world, with themselves, and with others.

—Jeffrey Kane

Dance, dance wherever you may be
For I am the Lord of the Dance, said He.
I'll lead you all wherever you may be
I'll lead you all in the Dance, said He.

(Sung to the tune of the Shakers' "Simple Gifts")

Years ago in Puerto Rico, my uncle found his 7-year-old daughter in the backyard, digging eagerly under the bushes. He asked, "¿Pero mijita, qué buscas?" ("But child, what are you looking for?"). "El porqué del porqué, Pappi," Vivianna answered confidently ("The why of the why, Daddy"). Uncle Luis walked away befuddled. I stood in wonder.

That was it. In one brief shining moment, Vivianna had asked the most essential question. Why? Meta-why? Why do we do what we do the way we do it? Why do we think the way we do? Why so much pain? Why so much unfulfilled joy? Why so much war, so little peace? Why? Why not?

The seed was planted, and those questions have plagued me ever since. Or better yet, they have guided me. But it wasn't until my doctoral studies that I felt perhaps, just perhaps, I was getting somewhere. Not to answers, but to more useful questions. In the words of Chrissy, the lost health club devotee in *The Search for Signs of Intelligent Life in the Universe* (Wagner, 1986), "You can't expect insights, even the big ones, to suddenly make you understand everything. But I figure: Hey, it's a step if they leave you confused in a deeper way" (p. 39).

I spent those doctoral years, arduous but revelatory, poring over the work of Gregory Bateson, getting "confused in a deeper way." Bateson was a British scientist, anthropologist, philosopher born at the turn of the century, and author of, among other titles, *Steps to an Ecology of Mind* (1972) and *Mind and Nature: A Necessary Unity* (1980b). These writings are, in Clifford Geertz's (1973) sense, thick and almost impenetrable. It takes dedication to dig, as did my cousin, under them to find the beginnings of the why of the why. But once you get a glimpse of what is there, you can't let go. "Here," I recall saying to myself, "is wisdom." And I had been for too long too thirsty for wisdom.

It is a wisdom that challenges us to question our epistemological assumptions and, subsequently, to unearth the ground we walk on. It is a wisdom that invites us, not to imbibe information and perceive that cold enterprise as rigorous thinking, but rather to engage in a process of transformative inquiry. Engaging in that process, we discover patterns, connections, and meanings that otherwise remain veiled and unearthed. We enter a no-man's-land of aesthetic epistemologies and possibilities. As John Brockman, editor of *About Bateson* (1977), wrote,

> He is busy inventing something, an invention so profound that once fully pronounced, it will seem always to have been "natural." The full impact of Bateson's thinking is so radical

> that, yes, I have doubts that he fully believes in his own ideas. That is the way it has to be. He has entered no man's land. (pp. 17–18)

Educators need to pay particularly close attention because we too often reduce our task to that of deliverers of information. We reduce thinking to the gathering of information, omitting from our lessons—our often thwarted journeys with students—this process of transformative inquiry into a realm of endless patterns of patterns. Bateson (1980b) asks, "What pattern connects the crab to the lobster and the orchid to the primrose and all four of them to me?" (p. 8). That, ultimately, I propose, is the underlying question of every redeeming journey taken with students. That is the territory to be dug to find the why of the why.

What follows are clues for unearthing that epistemological—and pedagogical—territory. They are my interpretation of Bateson's provocations not only for reenvisioning what thinking can be but also for reexperiencing what that venture called education might be if only . . .

The Pattern Which Connects

We begin with a recognition that "our loss of the sense of aesthetic unity" (Bateson, 1980b, p. 21) was a serious historical epistemological mistake, that "epistemological errors are part of the machinery of the descent to hell" (Bateson, 1981, p. 348).

Quite simply, our thinking is muddled, messy. We confuse the map for the territory; separate mind and matter; objectify the irrevocably subjective; alienate and bifurcate rather than connect and choreograph. Reenvisioning science and our "habits of thought," Bateson concludes that the natural world and how we think about it should necessarily match. Biology must inform epistemology, and thus was born his lifework—as I interpret it, the preservation of the integrity (wholeness) of the natural world through a redefinition of how we come to know it.

Considering the "partiality of Occidental consciousness," this essential match is nonexistent (Lipset, 1982, p. 266). The world is round, and we go about designing curricula, reforming education, planning cities, and curing ills as though it were flat. A stagnant epistemology ossifies a dynamic world:

> It began to seem that old-fashioned and still-established ideas about epistemology, especially human epistemology, were a reflection of an obsolete physics and contrasted in a curious way with the little we seem to know about living things. It was as if members of the species, man, were supposed to be totally unique and materialistic against the background of a living universe which was generalized (rather than unique) and spiritual (rather than materialistic). (Bateson, 1980b, pp. 5–6)

> How is logic, the classical procedure for making chains of ideas, related to an outside world of things and creatures, parts and wholes? . . . How is this world of logic, which eschews "circular argument," related to a world in which circular trains of causation are the rule rather than the exception? (Bateson, 1980b, p. 21)

The operative word is *living*—"living things," a "living universe." It carries with it strong images that embrace everything from redwood forests and dolphins to elegance, sacraments, and grace. Bateson's three books—*Steps to an Ecology of Mind* (1972), *Mind and Nature: A Necessary Unity* (1980b), and *Angels Fear: Towards an Epistemology of the Sacred* (1987; essays collected and edited postmortem by Mary Catherine Bateson)—explore the meaning of what it is to be a living being in a living universe. The overarching theme is an examination of the all-important yet tragically ignored "pattern which connects":

> What pattern connects the crab to the lobster and the orchid to the primrose and all four of them to me? And me to you? And all six of us to the amoeba in one direction and to the back-ward schizophrenic in another? (Bateson, 1980b, p. 8)

It is this pattern and its hierarchical organization into ever-expanding, more complex "levels of organization" and "logical types" that "Every Schoolboy (Ought To Know)" (Bateson, 1980b, chaps. 2, 3). It is the very basis of how we learn to think and, more important, be; it is the very basis of "simple necessary truths" with which every thinking person "must make peace" (Bateson, 1980b, pp. 22, 75). Attending to this pattern, we recognize our vital connection to the primrose and each other and, in turn, inform our aesthetic and moral sensitivities; a sense of commitment and responsibility is born of an experience of union and, hence, beauty.

We don't often understand beauty in this manner because our thinking lacks clarity. Although we with our reductionist propensities tend to think of beauty as a matter of subjective opinion (in the beholder's eyes), Bateson's point is that clear thinking is a prerequisite to perceiving it. Clarity precedes beauty, or stated more precisely, they coexist in circular motion, feeding, inspiring one another. Muddle-headedness, "slovenly habits of thought" (Bateson, 1984, p. 187), is simply dangerous and unnecessary. "False premises about the natural world and the nature of action" (p. 18), lineal thinking, shortsightedness, reductionism, and oversimplification are some of the symptoms of these pernicious habits. "It is monstrous—vulgar, reductionist, sacrilegious—call it what you will," he concludes in *Mind and Nature* (1980b), "to rush in with an oversimplified question" (p. 236), "always the more beautiful answer who asks the more difficult question" (T. S. Eliot, quoted loosely in Bateson, 1980b, p. 235). The more "difficult question" is the "bigger question" (Bateson, 1980b, p. 235), asked within a wider context, incorporating more and more information. And, as his work proceeds, the questions get bigger and bigger, more and more beautiful, thus arriving "where angels fear to tread," the arena of consciousness, aesthetics, and the sacred.

Clear thinking corrects the epistemological error that blinds us from the pattern*s* that connect (the spiraling pattern of patterns of connection, the meta-pattern). Whereas we may in the past have been precise, accurate, specific in our thinking, we have not been inclusive, contextual. Our reductionist tendencies rob us of context, of seeing, perceiving, thinking of things in relation to others. There is no such thing as a thing, Bateson reminds us: "always a relationship or an infinite regress of relationships. Never a 'thing'" (G. Bateson, 1972, p. 246). Clear thinking awakens our aesthetic sensibilities and vice versa. We see Blake's "fearful symmetry"; recognize, as did the Ancient Mariner, "the biological nature of the world," releasing the Albatross that nearly drowns us (Lipset, 1982, p. 290). We grasp the whole and recognize relationships, not only atomized parts. Our historically debilitating "loss of the sense of aesthetic unity" (Bateson, 1980b, p. 19) is redeemed. Wisdom, "the knowledge of the total interactive system" (Bateson, quoted in Lipset, 1982, p. 259), is affirmed, and love, by definition, is activated:

> We can desire to become a part of something larger than ourselves because we know, in spite of the illusions of consciousness and the package of skin in which we move, that there is a sense in which this is how things really are. In love we encounter this as emotion; wisdom argues further—this is not the special experience of passion or dedication or self-sacrifice, this is how the world is made. Wisdom argues for love by acknowledging the kind of world in which that kind of love is the most basic experience. (M. C. Bateson, 1977, p. 68)

Caring, compassion—love—in this scenario is not merely a sentiment, but rather a fundamental recognition of what it is to be human. An "order of knowledge" (Bateson & Bateson, 1987, p. 197) emerges that lives in double descriptions, metaphorical thinking, and Creatural thought; a quality of thinking prevails that distinguishes between the organic (Creatura) and inorganic (Pleroma) and mentally moves accordingly. The Creatural scientist or educator or philosopher or parent is born who balances discipline and care, who can see, think, and act empathetically and rationally, scientifically and aesthetically, preserving the integrated organizational complexity of living systems. Like the gardener or woodturner, she or he knows with her or his fingers, sees with her or his hands.

Ultimately, wisdom resides in appreciating both Pleroma and Creatura, metaphor and prose, precision and imagination: "The richest knowledge of the tree includes both myth and botany. Apart from Creatura, nothing can be known; apart from Pleroma, there is nothing to know" (Bateson & Bateson, 1987, p. 200). It lives not in the naïveté of faith or the crudeness of materialism. It exists in the profound and daring recognition of "fearful symmetries," the way the world is made. It resides in a radically new way of looking, at the tree, the forest, the school, the city, Earth, you and me: "This way of looking, which sees the mental as organizational and as accessible to study, but does not reduce it to the material, allows for the development of a monistic and unified way of looking at the world" (Bateson & Bateson, 1987, p. 50).

"Cap, Why Can't We Get Them to Think Straight?"

From where I stand as the troubled, searching educator, I ask myself what all this has to do with education. I turn again to the introduction of *Mind and Nature,* where Bateson (1980b) reminds us of the "basic structures" that define our images of what

education is and can be. These epistemological foundations must be scrutinized if any substantial, fundamental educational reform is to take place. He writes pleadingly:

> This book is built on the opinion that we are parts of a living world. I have placed as epigraph at the head of this chapter a passage from Saint Augustine in which the saint's epistemology is clearly stated. Today such a statement evokes nostalgia. Most of us have lost that sense of unity of biosphere and humanity which would bind and reassure us all with an affirmation of beauty. Most of us do not believe that whatever the ups and downs of detail within our limited experience, the larger whole is primarily beautiful.
>
> We have lost the core of Christianity. We have lost Shiva, the dancer of Hinduism whose dance at the trivial level is both creation and destruction but in whole is beauty. We have lost Abraxas, the terrible and beautiful god of both day and night in Gnosticism. We have lost totemism, the sense of parallelism between man's organization and that of the animals and plants. We have lost even the Dying God.

He concludes,

> I hold to the presupposition that our loss of the sense of aesthetic unity was quite simply, an epistemological mistake. I believe that that mistake may be more serious than all the minor insanities that characterize those older epistemologies which agreed upon the fundamental unity. (pp. 18–19)

The implications for educational reform are serious. At least three pertinent themes emerge. First, epistemology is the primary agenda with which to be concerned. It needs to be made explicit and overt because it is too powerful to remain forever hidden. As James Hillman (the post-Jungian psychologist) warns, "Ideas we don't know we have, have us" (quoted in Richards, 1982, p. 4). Premises, assumptions, and epistemologies are the basis for our every activity. They guide us unwittingly in our every thought and deed: "Science, like art, religion, commerce, even sleep, is based on presuppositions" (Bateson, 1980b, p. 27).

Second, our epistemologies need realigning to reflect the internal and interactional organization of the world—that is, to reflect the pattern that connects and the hierarchical structure of its organization.

Third, and more specifically, an epistemology that attends to nature attends to the aesthetic—that is, is "responsive to the pattern which connects" (Bateson, 1980b, p. 9). It sees beauty in biology, for the communication (borrowing Paul Byers's definition of *communication* as "the process by which all the pieces of the living world find their relationships to the other pieces, to form larger wholes, and to enable the living world to grow, change, adapt, and survive" [1985a, personal copy prior to publication, p. 2]) that is biology is what is beautiful. In the aesthetic, we find our "shared biologies," for in the experience of beauty we find that "pathway in which things (cats, architecture, trees, flowers) have anything to do with one, as distinct from being 'it'" (Bateson, n.d.). It is the moment of recognition wherein we heal the "insufficient holism" (Bateson & Bateson, 1987, p. 52) and "diseased partiality of Occidental consciousness" (Lipset, 1982, p. 266). We regain the "lost core of Christianity" (Bateson, 1980b, p. 19), dance with Shiva, and rediscover our glorious "innate relatedness" (Spangler, 1978).

Working within Bateson's framework, the primary question for the educator is about perspective—finding the perspective with which to understand what education is, asking first, What do I need to know in order to know what education is? and What, then, are the premises I offer the children from which they learn to think and come to know the world? That is the first step: finding the right questions to ask, making the epistemology explicit, and examining it carefully.

Subsequently, it becomes necessary to find a perspective that affirms the inherent, aesthetic organization of the world and that nurtures, as quoted above, wisdom, "a sense of recognition of the fact of circuitry." Addressing the California Board of Regents, of which he was a member, Bateson (1980b) concludes:

> The wider perspective is *about* perspectives, and the question posed is: Do we, as a board, foster whatever will promote in students, in faculty, and around the boardroom table those wider perspectives which will bring our system back into an appropriate synchrony or harmony between rigor and imagination? As *teachers*, are we wise? (p. 248)

Do we offer students new patterns for thinking? Do we release them from the basic, false, and oversimplified premises—myths—that misguide them (e.g., in the 1960s, the "myth of 'power'"; Bateson, 1980b, p. 248)? Do we teach them that there are such things as premises—the good, the bad, and the ugly ones?

> The school system doesn't teach there's such a thing as mistakes at present, that you can be wrong, and not only that you can be wrong, you can think wrong. Your premises can be wrong. Premises aren't brought up very much. (Brand, 1975, p. 37)

Finally, do we as educators know how to think? Do we help students think? Frustrated, Bateson asks his daughter, "Cap, why can't we get them to think straight?" (Bateson, 1984, p. 187). Reflecting on his own experience as a teacher, he notes that "kids are hungry . . . for something that'll make sense" (Brand, 1975, p. 37). He recognizes that, tragically and possibly dangerously, students have stopped believing it is "possible to think, and . . . that there is anything worth caring about" (Brand, 1975, p. 33).

That, for the educator, is the essence of Bateson's foresight. Children have stopped believing that it is possible to think and care. Education, if it intends to serve humanity, must be about thinking and caring, clarity and caring:

> I don't think that caring without thinking will work in a superb civilization. Without the clarity. Without believing that clarity is possible.
>
> . . . There's a lot of hunger among the kids for clarity, and for being given permission to care. But they're liable to think that if my generation tells them that you are allowed to care, that I'm seducing them in some way. And of course they're the ones that when I make them have some clarity, they say it's a head trip. You see, there ain't such a thing as a head trip. It is a head trip if you start with the belief that the mind is separate from the body. But they are hungry. (Bateson, quoted in Brand, 1975, pp. 33–34)

Begging for clarity, Bateson continues to agonize in *Mind and Nature* (1980b). "Why," he asks, "is it that schools teach nothing of the pattern which connects" (p. 8)? Can they not see that it is inane to define what a verb is without placing it in relationship to its subject, that the sentence "'Go' is a verb" is absurd (p. 18)? Reminiscing about his own education, he adds,

> Both subjects (grammar and comparative anatomy) were tortuously unreal. We *could* have been told something about the pattern which connects: that all communication necessitates context, that without context, there is no meaning, and that contexts confer meaning because there is classification of contexts. (p. 18)

The question then posed to the educator is the "aesthetic question" (Bateson, 1980b, p. 9)—that is, again, "responsive to the pattern which connects," to meaning within a context, to the organization of the whole. Getting us—educators and students—to be clear and to "think straight" is getting us to think in a circular fashion, in spirals, to note patterns and to be continuously willing to expand the depth and breadth of the contexts ("pattern through time"; Bateson, 1980b, p. 150) in which these patterns find meaning.

Within this epistemology, the organization of the whole is most important. Meaning is found contextually and in relationship. "Things" in themselves do not have meaning; they only have meaning in the context of their relationship to other "things" and to the larger whole: "what can be studied is always a relationship or an infinite regress of relationships. Never a 'thing'" (G. Bateson, 1972, p. 246; Byers, 1985b, is also helpful in appreciating the significance of meaning-in-context).

Negation of this interconnectedness is part of the epistemological error troubling our schools. That is Bateson's thesis. What in education will "touch or teach anything of real-life importance" (Bateson, 1980b, p. 8)? What brings the children to an awareness of their relatedness, to each other, to you, and all of us to the living Earth? What pedagogically transcends the current institutionalization of mediocrity, superficiality, alienation, fear, rivalry, greed, and a strictly utilitarian and purposive ethic? As Mary Catherine (1977) elaborates,

> After all, contemporary society includes many highly institutionalized ways of functioning as a part person—of denying primary process, separating the body from the mind, emotion from reason, production from consumption, and Sunday from the rest of the week. Because our instructional systems emphasize only parts, they both strengthen those parts and also convey the metamessage that such divisions are appropriate. (p. 69)

What in education can help us feel our neighbor's pain or happiness? What in education can help us, like the farmer, empathize with the field that lies fallow (Bateson & Bateson, 1987, p. 194) and carry us past Peter Bly's dreadful apathy?

> A primrose by the river's brim
> A yellow primrose was to him;
> And it was nothing more
>
> (Wordsworth, quoted in Bateson, 1980b, p. 9)

These are the untouched questions, the avoided, neglected paramount issues in Western education. By pointing to these, Bateson is "mapping" a surface, providing an epistemological frame from which we can begin to think more usefully and holistically about education.

STORY AS METAPHOR: IDENTIFYING AN AESTHETIC, REDEMPTIVE EPISTEMOLOGY

Story is the language of the biological world. It is that "little knot or complex of that species of connectedness which we call relevance" (Bateson, 1980b, p. 14). It connects A to B and all of us to one another in the mere fact that we all participate in the telling of stories. The conch, for example, is a "whole set of stories, very beautiful stories indeed":

> This that you see is the product of a million steps, nobody knows how many steps of successive modulation in successive generations of genotype, DNA, and all that. So that's one story, because the shell has to be a kind of form that can evolve through such a series of steps. And the shell is made, just as you and I are, of repetitions of parts of parts of repetitions of repetitions of parts. If you look at the human spinal column, which is also a very beautiful thing, you'll see that no vertebra is quite like any other, but each is a sort of modulation of the previous one. This conch is what's called a right-handed spiral, the spirals are sort of pretty things too—that shape which can be increased in one direction without altering its basic proportions. So the shell has a narrative of its individual growth pickled within its geometric form as well as the story of its evolution. (Bateson & Bateson, 1987, pp. 34–35)

The conch has a story to tell, the spinal column another story, the snail another:

> And often the story about a snail or a tree is also a story about myself and at the same time a story about you. And the real trick happens when the stories are set side by side. (Bateson & Bateson, 1987, p. 35)

Then we skip levels and find a class of stories, parables, models, which "exist precisely to facilitate thought about some other matter" (Bateson & Bateson, 1987, p. 35). And then there are "the stories about the snail or tree which are also stories about you and me, in combination" (p. 35). And further yet, as much as I respond to the stories you tell me, I am also responding to the stories you don't tell me.

Stories end up being a lesson in logical types, information exchange, and communication. Whether I am reading Poe's *Annabel Lee* or examining an autumn leaf, I am experiencing the same thing, rhythm and symmetry dancing in time.

Kathryn Morton, in her article "The Story-Telling Animal" (1984), writes:

> What got people out of the trees was something besides thumbs and gadgets. What did it, I am convinced, was a warp in the simian brain that made us insatiable for patterns—patterns of sequence, of behavior, of feeling—connections, reasons, causes: stories.

Einstein had a story, and his story overturned Newton's. Bateson (1980b) adds that the redwood has a story and that it converses with our own, our external stories (behavior) matching its "internal story," processes made of the same "stuff," patterns connected to form stories (p. 14). These stories make us gloriously human:

> The first sign that a baby is going to be a human being and not a noisy pet comes when he begins naming the world and demanding the stories connect its parts. Once he knows the first of these he will instruct his teddy bear, enforce his world view on his victims in the sandlot, tell himself stories of what he is doing as he plays and forecast stories of what he will do when he grows up. He will keep track of the actions of others and relate deviations to the person in charge. He will want a story at bedtime. (Morton, 1984)

In a world that desensitizes the child, stories "instill proper sentiments" (Kilpatrick, n.d., p. 63). In a world that emphasizes the one-dimensional, autonomous individual, stories tie complex, deeply feeling protagonists to particular social traditions, loyalties, and histories. In a world that myopically promotes the development of rational, decision-making skills, stories expand the imagination, enlarging visions of what life may be.

Story is not only epistemology writ-large ("habits of the heart" à la Bellah, Madsen, Sullivan, Swidler, & Tipton, 1985; paradigms à la Kuhn, 1970) but also a specific epistemology. Not only is it paradigms for framing our deeds and decisions, but it also defines a specific paradigm. It is both the lenses and the prescription for the lenses. We act according to our story (our epistemology and paradigm), and our story is story, patterns of patterns, meta-patterns and meta-messages. We think and see in terms of stories because we are stories; epistemology and biology, again, necessarily match. Story becomes a metaphor for the immanent mind and a world organized according to the pervasive "pattern which connects." It becomes the metaphor for an aesthetic epistemology thriving in an aesthetic, ultimately unified world.

Savoring a Mindful Epistemology

Bateson's story (of story), as it evolved through the years, was specifically the organization or resonance story (transformed as the theory of logical types, information, and communication theory)—and finally the "necessary explanatory principle" of mind (G. Bateson, 1977, p. 239). It is a picture of the world that sees wholes rather than parts, a choreography of relations rather than static disparate disassociations. Where we want quick lineal resolutions to problems, causes, and effects, it sees complex loops of interrelated dynamics.

A prime example of this choreography is the household fish tank. Mary Catherine Bateson, Gregory Bateson's daughter, begins *Our Own Metaphor* (1972) by telling us of the childhood aquarium she bought with her father. In it were sand, plants, a thermostat-heater, and of course, fish. The thermostat-heater was to keep

the water at a steady temperature: When the temperature rose above a certain degree, a curved bar (made of two metals of varying thermal expansion rates) in the thermostat would switch off the heater; when the temperature fell, the now straightened bar would switch on the heater: "The effect of the rising temperature was looped back to govern the heater itself" (p. 5). A state of equilibrium (homeostasis) was constantly kept.

As it stood in front of a sunny New York City window, the aquarium, Mary Catherine Bateson (1972) remembers, had a "certain elusive self-sufficiency":

> It was the community I learned to care for, self-contained to a degree, and yet dependent on me and our household on Perry Street, so that the lives of those fish depended on the peace and continuity of our lives, just as our own peace depended on a wider political peace in those early years of the Cold War. The aquarium was a world within a world, connected to those wider systems through my capacity to understand and respond to its needs. (p. 7)

A mandala of circular relations is created in this ecosystem that adapts, changes, and resonates in spiraling "levels": The fish need the plants which need the water which needs the sunlight, and so on; and the fish need the plants which need the fish, and so on; the constancy of the water temperature (balance) is maintained by noting and adjusting to the "news of difference" (M. C. Bateson, 1977, p. 240) in temperature conditions; and between Mary Catherine, the tank, neighborhood, and nation ("networks of complex wholes"; M. C. Bateson, 1972, p. 7), the effort is being made, wittingly and unwittingly, to support a "coupling" (M. C. Bateson, 1972, p. 7) of self-corrective systems. At every level of the tank's life, a cluster of variables is actively at work. The semblance of rest and comfort exists precisely because so much activity is going on. No one variable may be understood without also taking into consideration other variables, the relationships and contexts in which their story is being written. To repeat the poet's epithet, "no man is an island"—and even islands form archipelagos.

Gregory Bateson sees swirls of information perennially being communicated in higher degrees of complexity and inclusiveness. He sees causal circuits and not straight lines; patterns, order, and differences instead of quantity, matter, and things—recognizing in this swirling perspective the art of evolution and transformation, stability and change. Causality, if such a word is ever appropriate, occurs in dances of spiral activity. The Dance of Shiva that Capra (1977) experienced is the way the world works. Difference (or "news of difference," between actual and ideal temperatures, the letter I may have written and the letter I did not write) is the information that is communicated and as such is intangible, nonmaterial, and without location in place or time. It exists in the relationship between variables, not in "the thing itself" (Kant's "Ding an Sich"), in the organization of parts, not the parts themselves. This intangibility makes it all the more beautiful.

Mind is that delicious, not so simple process that embraces these intangible differences and network relationships. It is that invisible thread that is continuously organizing the multitude of themes that create the Great Drama, the Dance of Shiva.

As Bochner (1981) concludes, "Mind is the pattern which connects" (p. 74), the story of the biological world. All is mind, for "the world is joined together in its mental aspects" (Bateson, 1980b, p. 21). The growing rose is a mind, as is the fish tank, as is the classroom, the school, as are you and I and all of us in our coexistence on this planet.

Or as Mary Catherine Bateson explains in *Our Own Metaphor* (1972), mind is a "property not just of single organisms, but of relations between them, including systems consisting of men and women, or a man and a horse, a man and a garden, or a beetle and a plant" (p. 253). To understand mind systemically is to "suggest a way of thinking which neither reduces mind to a model of billiard balls, nor sets it off in contrast to matter, but allows for a search through all orders of material complexity for forms of organization comparable to our own" (pp. 253–254). As with a resonant, systemic appreciation of love, a systemic appreciation of mind "(cuts) across the person as the locus of consciousness, and (focuses) on complexities above and below" (M. C. Bateson, 1977, p. 64). Hence, value exists not only in the persons that create a marriage but also in the marriage (the relationship) itself. The relationship has a value, a reality, and life of its own. This mindful perspective, then, very significantly, is "perhaps a basis for a new kind of respect for the structures of the world in which we live" (M. C. Bateson, 1972, p. 254).

Nature and humanity share mind, the human mind being a "manifestation of an intelligence which is immanent in nature, and which penetrates all levels" (Grof, 1981, p. 47). As such, pervasive and vital, mind is a "necessary explanatory principle" (G. Bateson, 1977, p. 239) and thus the call for *Mind and Nature, A Necessary Unity* (Bateson, 1980b). Ignoring this "necessary unity" may destroy us all.

"Bad Biology Is Bad Buddhism, Bad Zen": Deciphering Epistemological Errors

Theologians speak of knowing who God is by defining who God is not. It's called a *via negativa*, a negative theology. I would like to try the same approach in continuing to identify an epistemology that embraces mind—in other words, elaborate on this redemptive epistemology by identifying what it is not. We have just entered into Bateson's "epistemology of living things" (H. Von Foerster's term, quoted in Bochner, 1981, p. 74), the aesthetic epistemology that incorporates mind into its folds. Now I would like to turn in the direction of epistemological errors and the persistent "effort to exclude mind" (G. Bateson, 1977, p. 239).

"Epistemological errors," as quoted earlier, "are part of the machinery of the descent to hell" (Bateson, 1981, p. 348). More specifically, by excluding mind from our epistemology, we have muddled science, education, each of our opportunities to ennoble this living world. Don Quixote's Aldonza has remained Aldonza with merely passing glimpses of Dulcinea (Cervantes, trans. 1964).

The muddle is at least threefold—**dualism** (materialism and quantification), **objectivity** (alienation), and **purposiveness** (control)—each an inverse of all that is mind, **monism** (wholeness), **subjectivity** (participation), and **recursiveness** (connectedness and service).

Dualism (Materialism and Quantification)

Emily Dickinson, in one of her many melancholic moments, wrote,

> I know that He exists.
> Somewhere—in Silence—
> He has hid his rare life
> From our gross eyes.[1]

She must be thanked for her perception. It is our "gross eyes" that keep us from grasping the not immediately available patterned processes that mingle in the natural world. Dickinson described the situation poetically, and I am borrowing her poetry to describe metaphorically what academics globally are currently avidly exploring: the repercussions of a thick and hardened science (dualistic, materialistic, and quantitative), a "gross" oversimplification of the biological world (G. Bateson, 1977, p. 240).

In the recent discussions on historical paradigm shifts, the finger has been pointed at the dualism of the Newtonian/Cartesian paradigm. The paradigm, we are told, is the storm that set the avalanche in motion for reductionistic, mechanistic, and atomistic epistemologies and methodologies. Fritjof Capra (*The Turning Point,* 1983), Ilya Prigogine and Isabelle Stengers (*Order Out of Chaos,* 1984), and many others elaborate amply on the consequences of this avalanche. It is not critical here to note the details of this historical drift, but it is helpful to mention the general confusion it has created. Capra and Prigogine refer to the paradigm as an anachronism, outdated and no longer useful. Bateson concurs and adds that it is the "fundamental structure of nineteenth century science" that is "inappropriate or irrelevant to the problems confronting the biologist or behavioral scientist" (G. Bateson, 1972, p. xxi). Again, a confusion of levels is born that uses the science of the nonliving to explain the living. An inelegant match is imposed, and the epistemologies/methodologies of the physical sciences are used to explore the social sciences, to study, for example, family relationships.

The Newtonian preoccupation with mass and energy that applied the tools of a quantitative mathematics permitted the Industrial Revolution to measure, modify, and explore with a precision and rigor previously unknown to civilization. To impose

---

1. From "I Know That He Exists" (Poem 338), by E. Dickinson, in T. H. Johnson (Ed.), *The Complete Poems of Emily Dickinson,* 1960 (p. 161). Boston: Little, Brown. Reprinted with permission.

this study of an inanimate world (without evolution or adaptation) onto the study of behavior and biology (embedded in time and change) was historical madness. Rigor displaced imagination, precision displaced dynamism, and now we are in the process of reclaiming, redeeming that necessary balance:

> What we need then, is a new "paradigm"—a new vision of reality; a fundamental change in our thoughts, perceptions and values. The beginnings of this change, of the shift from the mechanistic to the holistic conception of reality, are already visible in all fields and are likely to dominate this present decade. (Capra, 1983, p. 16)

Owen Barfield, in *Saving the Appearances: A Study in Idolatry* (n.d.), carries the discussion of paradigm shifts into other intriguing arenas. To trace the relationship between the evolution of nature and consciousness, he takes us back to prehistoric times, through the Greco-Roman, medieval, and modern industrial era. He focuses on human perception and thought as they have participated with nature and God, outlining a progression from a time of "original participation" to a time of "final participation" (pp. 40–45, 133–141). By these modes, he is referring to a shift in the manner of being with nature and spirit. Historically, we have shifted from the "immediate experience" (p. 40) of phenomena wherein both phenomena and word, nature and consciousness, were indistinguishable toward a time of a human-centered participation wherein the phenomena are independent of human consciousness but involve the whole person acting intentionally, systematically, imaginatively, and spiritually. Our current task is to enter this "final participation" and "save the appearances" (comprehension of the universe) from "chaos and inanity" (p. 146). We are to save our perception from the hideous possibilities of the extremes of this condition, the idolatry of independence and separation.

The mind/body dualism stirred by the Newtonian/Cartesian paradigm is part of this senseless chaos. Stewart Brand calls it the "pathology of Cartesian mind/body dualism" (Bateson, 1976, p. 56). Bateson loathed it and organized a conference with Brand in 1976 to address its nature and disastrous implications. As Barfield points out, we may have needed to separate from the phenomena in order to study it, discover attributes we may never otherwise have known, but we need not remove ourselves so far from it that we lose touch with its vital qualities and idolize it to its own destruction. Ultimately, we must return to the phenomena with a new, enlightened mode of participation. The insistent dualism we have inherited is denying that possibility.

Bateson advises that we bid farewell to the separation between mind and matter, God and creation, and look back on it "with curiosity as a monstrous idea that nearly killed us" (1980a, pp. 5–6). It is a dualism that is "faked up" (1977, p. 247), phony, and "appetitive" (1976/1977, p. 94). It breeds far too many "false division[s]" between a "supernatural" religion and a "materialistic" science (1976, p. 56; Bateson & Bateson, 1987, pp. 50–64), epistemology and natural history, work and play, Monday and the Sabbath, science and creativity, business and home. Basically, it is unintelligible, even repulsive:

> From time to time I get complaints that my writing is dense and hard to understand. It may comfort those who find the matter hard to understand if I tell them that I have driven myself, over the years, into a "place" where conventional dualistic statements of mind-body relations—the conventional dualisms of Darwinism, psychoanalysis, and theology—are absolutely unintelligible to me. It is becoming as difficult for me to understand dualists as it is for them to understand me. And I fear that it's not going to become easier, except by those others being slowly exercised in the art of thinking along those pathways that seem to me to be straight. (G. Bateson, 1977, p. 236)

But once you have entered a "place" where conventional dualistic statements make no sense, what do you do? Where do you go? You sojourn to Oz and join people like Tolly Holt, who talked of creating a bumper sticker that read Help Stamp Out Nouns. "What has to change," he explained at the Wenner-Gren conference, "is our fascination with nouns to be replaced by a fascination with process" (M. C. Bateson, 1972, p. 63). Orientations shift, and you begin to see, like Dorothy, that you aren't in Kansas any more—that nouns, things, in and of themselves, do not exist. A noun is not just "'the name of a person, place or thing'" (Bateson, 1980b, p. 18), as we were told as children. A noun is a "thing" that has a relationship to other "things"—predicates, for instance. Without the predicate, a noun has no meaning—as Bateson quotes from *King Lear*, "'nothing will come of nothing' without information," "messages cease to be messages when nobody can understand them" (Bateson, 1980b, pp. 50–51) when they are without context. Process, information, context, and relationship in this broader perspective become the "basis for definition" (Bateson, 1980b, p. 18), explanation, and epistemology.

Materialism, the "thing"-oriented child of this dualism, subsides. You learn that it becomes an "act of faith to distrust [the] language [of materialism] and believe in monism" (G. Bateson, 1977, p. 244). You recognize, like the wise schoolboy, that the language of materialism "commonly stresses only one side of any interaction" (Bateson, 1980b, p. 67), asserting that "things" in and of themselves have qualities while forgetting that these qualities exist because of "sets of interaction in time" (Bateson, 1980b, p. 67). To say "the stone is hard," for instance, is to comment on (a) its relationship to the speaker (it resists penetration) and (b) its internal behavior (its molecular activity). Hardness is a quality that comes into being by the stone's relationship to me and its internal relationship to itself. It is the interactions that are hard; the stone itself is not hard.

This language may be "good enough for the marketplace," Bateson (1980b) continues, but is "not good enough for science and epistemology":

> It is necessary to be quite clear about the universal truth that whatever "things" may be in their pleromatic and thingish world, they can only enter the world of communication and meaning by their names, their qualities and their attributes (i.e., by reports of their internal and external relations and interactions). (pp. 67–68)

When you dare challenge this materialism, you enter, often screaming, alone and frustrated, a strange no-man's-land, an Oz without grounds:

> This means, of course, that in my mental world or universe I acknowledge no things, and, obviously, there are no things in thought . . . In thought what we have are ideas. There are no pigs, no coconut palms, no people, no books, no pins, no . . . you know? Nothing. There are only ideas of pigs and coconut palms and people and whatever. Only ideas, names, and things like that. This lands you in a world which is totally strange. I find myself running screaming from its contemplation, and essentially running back to a world of materialism, which seems to be what everybody else does, limited only by the amount of their discipline. What I feel driven to ask is, give me a pound, a little mass, a little time, a little length, some combination of these called energy. Give me power, give me all the rest of it. Give me location, for in the mental world there is no location. There is only yes and no, only ideas of ideas, only news of messages; and the news is news, essentially of differences, or difference between differences, and so on. What is perpetually happening in the works of the most learned philosophers, as well as people like myself, is a quick dash back into the idioms and styles and concepts of mechanical materialism to escape from the incredible bareness—at first appearance—of the mental world. (Bateson, 1980a, p. 6)

The irony is that the bareness belongs to materialism. By excluding the mental, spiritual characteristics of our universe, materialism excludes so much of what is necessary, beautiful, and good. By drinking its waters, we deny ourselves participation in the "ultimate unifying beauty" of the biosphere (Bateson, 1980b, p. 19). We remain forever observers and takers and never, in Barfield's sense, final participants, fully conversant with nature. We don't hear the sunrise, touch the mountain, or taste the river. We remain locked in the world of the nonliving, the "world of mindlessness" (G. Bateson, 1977, p. 239) that sees no forms, patterns, pathways, steps, and bridges; feels no rhythm, music, or dance; tells no stories; "contains no names, no classes"; and accepts "no hierarch[ies] of ideas or differences" (G. Bateson, 1977, p. 239). We remain blind to quality and enamored instead with things, and more things—quantity.

We are all familiar with the quantitative story. It's the perennial tale of wants, accounting for value in measurable amount of goods—in the words of a popular bumper sticker, "The person who has the most toys when he dies, wins." Or as Bob Marley (1976), the reggae master, sings, "In the abundance of water, the fool is thirsty."

These reminders ask the unasked question, How much gold is enough? "Simplify, Simplify, Simplify," Thoreau kept pleading, but we keep responding, "Quantify, Quantify, Quantify." Huston Smith, in *Beyond the Post-Modern Mind* (1984), writes of "number being the language of science" (p. 66) that locks the modern person into a "very restricted kind of knowing" (p. 66), a knowledge that excludes, among other things, the qualitative, participatory, and subjective dimension of life. The world of numbers is too narrow to be complete; we can count and quantify, facilitate prediction and control, but we cannot account for the immeasurable, experiential moments. As such, numbers present us with an unbalanced and falsified picture of an icy, "disqualified universe" (Lewis Mumford, quoted in Smith, 1984, p. 68).

Bateson elaborates and distinguishes between number and quantity; surely, our obsession with quantification is a problem, as Smith suggests, but it is also necessary to understand this obsession as a blindness to the (mental) value of number in the biological world.

Bateson claims that we have lost sight of some basic "truths" the Creatural world has known all along: Number is different from quantity, quantity does not determine pattern, there are no monologue values in biology, and sometimes small is beautiful (four of the "necessary truths . . . every schoolboy knows"; 1980b, pp. 53–64). Number is the script of the biological world for number is the "simplest of all patterns" (1980a, p. 8). Number is pattern and vice versa, but quantity is not pattern and vice versa. You and I, the rose and the crow, get numbers by counting or recognizing patterns; we get quantity by measuring approximations—"You can have exactly 3 tomatoes. You can never have exactly 3 gallons of water" (1980b, p. 54).

This distinction, as Bateson (1978) liked to say, is not a trivial matter; there is a "profound difference between numbers and quantity": "This difference is basic for any sort of theorizing in behavioral science, any sort of imagining of what goes on between organisms or inside as part of their processes of thought" (pp. 46, 44). "Number goes deep" (p. 45), a crow can count and remember up to seven, a rose prefers the pentad pattern for the organization of its petals . . . these are not insignificant symmetries.

Ignorant of the distinction between number and quantity, we impose quantification on a patterned world. Another preposterous mismatch. Take, for instance, the affairs of government: The government, be it in Washington or in Sacramento, national or state or university level, makes quantitative decisions (Bateson was then discussing decisions being made at the board of regents concerning the University of California's role in the production of atomic weapons). The government alters tax rates, Social Security rates, student enrollments, and so forth. But it cannot predict how these changes will affect the system because it does not know where the "weakest link" (Bateson, 1981, p. 350) in the patterning will be or how the qualitative laws (of social organization, education, foreign policy) will be affected. Every quantitative change that is made on the system puts a stress on a qualitative pattern. A mind-set that insists on thinking in terms of quantitative measures (e.g., SAT scores, letter grades) is subsequently totally unequipped to deal with qualitative affairs, educational policy—"the teaching of qualitative thought versus the teaching of quantitative thought" (Bateson, 1981, p. 350). Bateson explains this muddle in a conversation he held with Governor Jerry Brown:

> Bateson: It's one of the basic premises that no quantity ever changed a pattern, you know.
>
> Brown: I don't understand that.
>
> Bateson: Pouring money, which is quantity, into a system that has shape, will not really generate a new shape. Now you can with quantities find out what pattern is already latent. If you increase the tension on a chain, you can break it at its weakest link, and you found out where the weakest link was. But the tension didn't create the weakest link.
>
> Brown: How would you apply that to school?

> Bateson: Pouring money into them is not going to change the pattern. Therefore, something else has got to change the pattern if you are going to change the pattern. Maybe *then* money is needed, to develop a new pattern, to help it grow and all the rest of it, but the latent image that's got to be developed, whatever it is, it's got to come from somewhere else, it doesn't come from money. (Brand, 1975, p. 40)

Which brings us back to Huston Smith's more general scenario. We worship the quantitative aspect and give "minimal attention to the qualitative aspect," an error that will "inevitably land [us] in the dilemmas of our civilization," that is "the easiest way of descent to hell" (Bateson, 1981, p. 350). Our misuse of money is a prime example of this epistemological blunder. Money, Bateson insisted, is a "quantitative metaphor which does not fit the world of pattern" (p. 354). It is a fake, for in the biological world there are no monologue values, more is not necessarily better, and less is not necessarily worse. On the contrary, in the biological world, quantity has an optimum value: Beyond a certain point, a substance becomes toxic; below that certain point, it is deprived.

If only we could learn from the biosphere. If only we could respect the "rigors and rigidities," the eerie "tyranny" of the biosphere's patterns (Bateson, 1981, p. 353). Then possibly we would transform the insanity that quantifies ad infinitum and makes closets full of shoes so appetizing, military arsenals so necessary, assuming that "mutual fear breeds peace" (Bateson, quoted in Fields & Greene, 1975, p. 32). On the campuses, we could stop perpetuating a "corrupt ethic" (Bateson, 1979/1980, p. 22) that institutionalizes greed and distrust—and for the rebellious students, institutionalizes disgust and horror. Maybe then we could save the ecology of mind (the sacred) from being put on the radiator:

> There are things, you know, that give people like me the shivers. Some people will put potted plants on the radiator—and this is just bad biology. And I guess that in the end, bad biology is bad Buddhism, bad Zen, and an assault on the sacred. What we are trying to do is defend the sacred from being put on the radiator, misused in this sort of way. (Bateson, quoted in Fields & Greene, 1975, p. 26)

Objectivity (Alienation)

What difference does it make when you start seeing the world through a monistic, mindful epistemology? In Oz, again, "the word 'objective' . . . becomes quite quietly obsolete" (G. Bateson, 1977, p. 245).

Objectivity is another of those dangerous anachronisms of classical science. Smith (1984) considers it another by-product of the Promethean ethos that is hungry for power and control. It is part of the scientific desiderata that makes us miserably alienated and "denudes" the world of all that is human and real: beauty and ugliness, love and hate, passion and fulfillment, salvation and damnation (p. 84). Objectively

(and alienated), we enter the "wasteland"; subjectively (and whole), we exit and enter the "holy land" (pp. 102–107). Objectively, we work with that which is scientifically verifiable, splitting fact from value, the measurable from the immeasurable, quantity from quality, making the experiential moments "'merely subjective' projections of people's inner lives" (p. 84).

Objectivity is, in Bateson's idiom, an unwise distraction (and, remember, wisdom is a "landmark" in Bateson's story; M. C. Bateson, 1977, p. 58). As the "initial requirement" (Smith, 1984, p. 66) and gospel of modern science, it parches the soil of the disenchanted garden. The "objective people" are those outdated protagonists who use lineal models of classical science to understand the communicational, dynamic phenomena of the biological and social world. Like the fellow who wanted Picasso to draw a picture of his wife resembling her photograph, their perception is flattened, uninteresting—erroneous. They avoid thinking about anything that involves complexities, entire layers of contexts "several logical types deep" (M. C. Bateson, 1977, p. 58) and therefore cannot distinguish, for instance, among the subtleties of practice, play, and exploration, or talk about such crucial "landmarks" as love and hate.

Most significantly, and this lands us at the heart of Bateson's story, claims of objectivity deny the "necessary truth" that "we work hard to make sense, according to our epistemology, of the world which we think we see" (G. Bateson, 1977, p. 244). We work hard at mapping territories, although the map is not the territory; we work hard at wanting science to prove anything and everything, although science can only probe and show precise correspondences; we work hard at wanting to believe objectivity is possible, although all experience is subjective, and our personal contribution to our own perception is immense, "the processes of image formation [being] unconscious" (the first four of the "necessary truths . . . every schoolboy knows"; Bateson, 1980b, pp. 29–41).

Walter Lippman wrote, "We are all captives of the pictures in our head—our belief that the world we experience is the world that really exists" (quoted in Morrow, 1985, p. 17). He was complementing what Bateson was claiming: "If you continue making those kinds of errors as scientists have been doing in the past, confusing their theories with reality, one day it might happen to you that you will eat the menu instead of your meal!" (Grof, 1981, p. 37). We are better off acknowledging the menu and then tasting the dish, acknowledging the map before seeing the territory, aware that we are always perceptually playing all sorts of games. In dear Trudy's words, we are better off recognizing that "reality" is "nothin' but a collective hunch" (Wagner, 1986, p. 18).

Once we become aware of these processes, we become "in a curious way much closer to the world around [us] . . . The world is no longer 'out there' in quite the same way that it used to seem to be" (G. Bateson, 1977, p. 245). The word *objective* becomes obsolete, as does the word *subjective.* In that rare enlightening moment, we experience our own introversion, Bateson's smoke ring, "endlessly turning upon itself," making itself separate and yet of the "same substance as its 'environment'" (pp. 245–246). In that moment, we discover, or possibly rediscover, "what every human and perhaps every dog—always instinctively and unconsciously—knew: that the dualisms of mind and body, mind and matter, and of God and world are all somehow faked up" (p. 247).

We also, and this is crucial, recognize that we all are curiously responsible for the pictures; as Lippman said, we create. We begin to see what presuppositions look like and take responsibility for them. We note that there are "better and worse ways of constructing scientific theories" while also "insisting on the articulate statement of presuppositions so that they may be improved" (Bateson, 1980b, p. 29). In Mary Catherine Bateson's (1984) words,

> The intellectual task he set for himself involved challenging this whole set of assumptions [dichotomies of Western culture] and seeking for new (or very ancient) ideas that would function as true premises so that humankind in relation to nature becomes in fact a single self-correcting system, not one bound for destruction. (p. 96)

Assumptions, presuppositions, premises, fundamentals, and "necessary truths" become the repeated themes in the Bateson doomsday script. Huston Smith tells us that, as long as the "premises of material science remain unquestioned," the "learning of the imagination will remain an 'excluded knowledge'" (Kathleen Raine, quoted in Smith, 1984, p. 62). Science, if it is to be redeemed—if it is to be wise—cannot afford to exclude the workings of the imagination and "primary process computation" (M. C. Bateson, 1977, p. 72). If it is to study living systems, it must begin behaving like a living system, rather than professing pride in its intellectual objectivity: "Oh dear," said the daughter in the instinct metalogue, "those poor people. They try to study animals and they specialize in those things that they can study objectively. And they can only be objective about those things in which they themselves are the least like animals. It must be difficult for them" (M. C. Bateson, 1972, p. 48).

The problem is that it is not only difficult for them but also impossible. The daughter goes on to describe a "sort of second creature within the whole person" (M. C. Bateson, 1972, p. 48) who is not thinking holistically and instead is thinking objectively. What happens, she asks, when this second creature "looks at those parts of the person about which it is difficult for people to be objective? Does it just look? Or does it meddle?" (p. 48). It meddles and, as we are told, meddling muddles.

It muddles because it interferes with the flow of things. A peculiar kind of thinking seeps in and splits the whole into pieces. The poets and artists, Bateson tells his daughter, best understand the "effect" of this muddled meddling:

> Thought chang'd the infinite to a serpent, that which pitieth
> To a devouring flame; and man fled from its face and hid
> In forests of night: then all the eternal forests were divided
> Into earths rolling in circles of space, that like an ocean rush'd
> And overwhelmed all except this finite wall of flesh.
> Then was the serpent temple form'd, image of infinite
> Shut up in finite revolutions; and man became an Angel,
> Heaven a mighty circle turning, God a tyrant crown'd.
>
> (William Blake, quoted in G. Bateson, 1972, p. 49)

Purposiveness (Control)

The anger of the poet/scientist (Blake's and Bateson's) chimes loudly one more time. Thought has separated itself from the whole and unnecessarily disturbed the ecology of being. Thought, which is, after all, primary process, wedded to heart and intuition (see discussion in M. C. Bateson, 1977, pp. 57–73), has become the servant of a peculiar intellect. This is an intellect that objectifies, classifies, and divides the dance into an unrecognizably rigid and frigid entity. It is an intellect that is purposeful, reeking of limited consciousness. The infinite becomes finite, and God a tyrant. We, modeled in the finiteness, narrow and proud, like Job, take our intellect, our language, and our tools ("the royal road to consciousness and objectivity") and try to separate the "'helpful' things from the 'hindering' things" (G. Bateson, 1972, pp. 48–49), the useful from the non-useful.

This is the world of the "objective creature" (G. Bateson, 1972, p. 50), the scientist's disenchanted garden, full of emptiness, misused information, and shallow explanations. Take for example the anthropologists who assert "against all aesthetic sense" (Bateson, 1976/1977, pp. 94–95) that the Paleolithic frescoes helped the hunters kill the beasts. They are wrong, for they are confusing priorities, playing the objective, purposive game only too well; religion (and ritual) primarily affirmed the hunter's communion with the moon, mountains, and beasts; later it became magic, divisive, and "appetitive" (G. Bateson, 1976/1977, p. 95). The American Indian danced in honor of the rain gods, in remembrance of innate unities, then he or she danced to make it rain. Our intellect (and the language that serves it) has deceived us, and purposefulness has invaded our intentions.

Purposive consciousness becomes "almost entirely antithetical to human adaptation" (Bateson, quoted in Fields & Greene, 1975, p. 29). It becomes antithetical to all that is alive, for it imposes a skewed awareness, a constrained appreciation of the nature of aliveness, most specifically of the fluid complexities of our self-correcting world. Primarily, the argument of purpose ignores the recursiveness of nature and requires a logic that assumes that nature works in lineal cause-and-effect chains. As every schoolboy knows, "causality does not work backward" (Bateson, 1980b, p. 66), the pattern at the end of a sequence does not cause the pathway that precedes it. End does not determine purpose. *Telos,* or purpose, especially in its lineal thinking, is an incomplete explanation of causality. Like Mary Catherine's aquarium, "when causal systems become circular . . . a change in any part of the circle can be regarded as a cause for change at a later time in any variable anywhere in the circle" (Bateson, 1980b, p. 66).

In a conversation with Rick Fields and Richard Greene of *Loka: The Journal of the Naropa Institute,* Bateson outlined how this purposive lineal rationale works: Imagine a "steady state process" (Fields & Greene, 1975, p. 31) existing on a hillside of Ponderosa pines. The pines are balancing out with the deer, cactuses, prickly pears, and other living things. It is decided that a certain variable, deer scapulas, needs to be "maximized" (Fields & Greene, 1975, p. 31). The deer are killed so that the scapulas may abound. Eventually, it is recognized that the deer are becoming scarce, and the decision is then made to stop killing them. The deer feed on prickly pears, and so the supply of prickly pears is multiplied by feeding them a chemical fertilizer. Everything on that hillside is disturbed. The balance that existed is lost.

People, you and I, decided that variable D was what we wanted. We examined the immediately surrounding variables in the chain and concluded that, by maximizing these, we could achieve our goal, the maximization of D. It's the simple law of transitivity, the only one I remember from my algebra days: If "B leads to C; C leads to D; so D can be achieved by way of B and C" (G. Bateson, 1972, pp. 444–445).

The error (recall the historical "loss of the sense of aesthetic unity"; Bateson, 1980b, p. 19) is our nearsightedness. We may distinctly see what is in front of us but only vaguely, if at all, see what is beyond our immediate focus. We see part of the circle and not all of it: "Our conscious sampling of data will not disclose whole circuits but only arcs of circuits, cut off from their matrix by our selective attention" (G. Bateson, 1972, p. 445). The argument proceeds in "series of causal arrows" or it "branches in" or "branches out," neglecting all along the roundness of our world with branches and other "feedings, from other places" (Bateson, quoted in Fields & Greene, 1975, p. 31).

The circularity that maintains balances also, ironically, haunts us in our imbalances, our insistent meddling. Circles everywhere. The cycle that feeds the universe turns sour and starves it, as it ignores the treasures of a recursive, resonant system. This vicious cycle of materialism, quantification, illusive objectivity, and lineal, purposive consciousness feeds on itself, never reaching a "steady state equilibrium" (Bateson, quoted in Fields & Greene, 1975, p. 29). The logic that establishes that more of B and C will give you more of D is not only lineal but also aggressively quantitative, insatiably hungry. From this sort of argument, again, it is easy to conclude that more hours spent in school is equivalent to better schooling (better grades); more artillery necessitates more peace; and more pesticides produce better farming.

Each of the follies augments the other. Smith (1984) draws a chart and concludes that a "Promethean motivation" of control leads to a "Promethean epistemology" of empiricism, which leads to a "Promethean ontology" of naturalism, which leads to a "Promethean anthropology" of alienation (pp. 76–77, 102–103, 144). He is making an important point: A story whose characters are control, empirical proof, materialism, and alienated imbalances excludes an enormous arena of what it is to be a living being. Modernity has omitted—forgotten—something. It has forgotten "higher realms of being" (p. 72) because it has forgotten the transcendent, imaginative, intuitive, "less ephemeral. . . . more important . . . integrated, sentient and therefore more beneficent" (p. 72) dimensions of existence.

It has forgotten mind. We have forgotten mind and by so doing have run around in pernicious, messy circles that, most painfully, set us up (people and creation) as competitors in the grand market—God versus humanity, humanity versus humanity, humanity versus creation, mind versus body, spirit versus matter. Ignorant of mind, separated from one another and creation, measuring our worth in quantities, we too quickly believe that we can control the system. We become—no, I alone become—the locus of attention, getting what I want at the expense of others. By "attributing mind to the other" (M. C. Bateson, 1977, p. 67) and forgetting that we are all part of larger mind that is greater than ourselves, we fail to recognize that we "cannot do anything to the system without doing it to ourselves" (Grof, 1981, p. 49), that the attention always dwells on connections and relationships. We forget the intimacy.

Like Job, we would do well to learn some natural history:

> Knowest thou the time
> when the wild goats of the
> rock bring forth? or cans't thou
> mark when the hinds do calve?
>
> Cans't thou number the months
> that they fulfill? or knowest thou
> the time when they bring forth?
> They bow themselves, they
> bring forth their young ones, they
> cast out their sorrows.
>
> Their young ones are in good
> liking . . .
>
> (JOB 39:1–4, READ BY BATESON AT THE 1975 SAN FRANCISCO PRAYER BREAKFAST, IS, ACCORDING TO HIM, AMONG THE "MOST EXTRAORDINARY SERMON(S) EVER WRITTEN" [BATESON & BROWN, 1976, P. 84]; ALSO READ TO HIM BY MARY CATHERINE IN THE QUIET HOURS BEFORE HIS DEATH.)

ENVISIONING A MINDFUL PRAXIS: "SPRING IS LIKE A PERHAPS HAND"

Acknowledging our "necessary unity," inversely, is our ascent into a world that makes sense—redeemed, mindful, and relational, rather than bifurcated, objectified, alienated, and quantified. It is our entry into what "doing" Bateson might entail, into what a praxis founded on Bateson's pleas for epistemological redemption might look like. It is a glimpse into what, hidden in the density of Bateson's explications, we might find that serves as a frame for envisioning a mindful, aesthetically woven praxis. Following Arthur Bochner's precedent ("Bateson's Rules of Thumb"; Bochner, 1981, p. 76), I call these glimpses into a pioneering praxis "Bateson's Clues for the Wise."

These are guidelines that quickly come to mind when I think of what a redeemed thought and praxis that integrates explanation and biology might embrace. They are glimpses into what it might be like to work within Bateson's story of stories, what it might be like to "do Bateson." They also are the themes that serve as a beginning frame for visualizing what an aesthetic, mindful education might embrace. An E. E. Cummings poem, a Bateson favorite, captures the spirit of these "clues for the wise":

Spring is like a perhaps hand
(which comes carefully
out of Nowhere)arranging
a window,into which people look(while
people stare
arranging and changing placing
carefully there a strange
thing and a known thing here)and

changing everything carefully

spring is like a perhaps
Hand in a window
(carefully to
and fro moving New and
Old things,while
people stare carefully
moving a perhaps
fraction of flower here placing
an inch of air there)and

without breaking anything.[2]

Bateson's Clues for the Wise

- *Proceed tenderly.* Be gentle with living systems, serve them as well as they will undoubtedly serve you.
- *Listen to biology,* as the Ancient Mariner did and Job did not. Embrace living systems. See the sacred in the apparently ordinary, taste the beauty and power of the tiger's "fearful symmetries." Learn from the chaparral. Cultivate attentiveness.
- *Evolve, grow, change,* for these are the ways the world works. Remain forever flexible, open, awake, alert—"it's the dream afraid of waking that never takes a chance . . . the soul afraid of dying that never seems to live" (McBroom, 1979). For God's sake, never grow dull.
- *Preserve the complexity and diversity* that are necessary for the survival of all systems. Remember the story of the Indian and the explorer; treasure the contexts that give meaning to all mind. Recognize the "similarity within diversity" that inspires us to "behave as if we are parts of a single whole (M. C. Bateson, 1984, pp. 185, 231).

---

2. "Spring is like a perhaps hand," copyright 1923, 1925, 1951, 1953. © 1991 by the Trustees for the E. E. Cummings Trust. Copyright © 1976 by George James Firmage, from *Complete Poems: 1904–1962* by E. E. Cummings. Edited by George J. Firmage. Reprinted by permission of Liveright Publishing Corporation.

- *Listen to the absurd,* "[suffer] fools more gladly than . . . revisionists" (Wilder-Mott, 1981, p. 36). Invite the unpredictable; it is the "stuff" of evolution, the essence of "purpose." Avoid the "vulgarity of the fundamentalist" (Bateson, 1976/1977, p. 94), be precise without "clos[ing] off possibilities," surrendering to "dogmatic formalisms" (Bochner, 1981, p. 76). Treasure serendipity. Respect wholeness, no matter how "out of hand," wild, and inconceivable it may get. And when you keep running back screaming to grasp hold of a thing, anything, remember that that is precisely what you are doing. The thing is the illusion, however concrete and delectably comfortable it may feel. The interval is real.
- *Don't be afraid of falling in love,* but "be the wiser thereby" (M. C. Bateson, 1977, p. 72). As the Japanese say, *Kokoro. Kokoro. Kokoro*—think with your heart, feel with your intellect. Trust that "the heart has its reasons that the reason does not perceive" (Pascal, quoted in M. C. Bateson, 1977, p. 61). As Jerome Bruner (1986) writes, "perfink—perceive, feel and think at once" (p. 2). Remember that ingenuity, intuition, and imagination have a home in science. Science can be empathetic. Clarity and caring are possible and not at all necessarily exclusive of one another. They need one another: "Caring without clarity will [not] work a superb civilization" (Bateson, quoted in Brand, 1975, p. 33). Love and wisdom "in the cybernetic sense" necessitate one another: "Love can survive only if wisdom (i.e., a sense or recognition of the fact of circuitry) has an effective voice" (G. Bateson, 1972, p. 146).
- *Befriend the poet. "Think aesthetically.* Visualize, analogize, compare. Look for patterns, configurations, figures in the rug. . . . Aim for catalytic conceptualizations; warm ideas are contagious" (Bochner, 1981, p. 76). An "epistemology of living things" (Von Foerster, quoted in Bochner, 1981, p. 74) that affirms an "ultimate unifying beauty" (Bateson, 1980b, p. 19) introduces the poet to the scientist: It "makes poets of us" (M. C. Bateson, 1984, p. 185). It invites us to see the dryad in the forest, participate in the "changing face of a living lake" (M. C. Bateson, 1984, p. 231).
- *Defend the metaphor* as you defend the sacred from being put on the radiator. Cherish metaphorical thinking, for it preserves unity-in-complexity, has "multiple parts that we can use to think with" (Bateson & Bateson, 1987, p. 193). It is multiple yet whole, complex yet integrated, mirroring the relationships—the integrity—that bind and hold the multiple parts of a living system. It invites us into a world without Blake's divisive "Thought" that does not separate subjects from predicates, but rather "share[s] predicates," (Bateson, 1980a, p. 11), shares relations.

Metaphor is the world conversing, not just the poet thinking; it is not just appropriate for the lyricist, yet "inelegant in a biologist" (Bateson, 1980a, p. 9):

> And it became evident that metaphor was not just pretty poetry, it was not either good or bad logic, but was in fact the logic upon which the biological world had been built, the main characteristic and organizing glue of mental process which I have been trying to

> sketch for you in some way or another. (among Bateson's last public comments; Bateson, 1980a, p. 11)

As Capra "saw" with the Dance of Shiva, let the metaphors be. However tempting, don't "peg [them] down" (G. Bateson, 1972, p. 57).

Stop hiding the metaphors and start admitting that they are not merely "crutches to help us get up the abstract mountain," to be later discarded or disguised in "formal, logically consistent theory" (Bruner, 1986, p. 2). Darwin's notebook drawings of "randomly branching tree[s]" were not merely playful doodling (Smith, 1984, p. 146). Insight, as David Bohm wrote, "announces itself in mental images" (quoted in Smith, 1984, p. 146). As Newton and Einstein did, attend to the pictures; insight reveals itself in the most unconventional ways, not always as a "hypothesis or conclusions drawn from logical deduction" (Bohm, quoted in Smith, 1984, p. 146).

- *Converse with the universe.* It will reveal itself to you. Match explanation to this conversant universe: A science of living systems, a science soaking in stories must itself "be like a composition: aesthetically reasonable, rhythmical, qualitative" (Bochner, 1981, p. 68).
- *Proceed slowly.* Eco is impatient with impatience, and "God is not mocked" (Galatians, quoted in Bateson, 1972, p. 504). Don't rush in looking for quick answers. Often, the greater wisdom rests in finding the more useful questions. Live with a question, an agenda, a problem. "People who have ready answers," Jerry Brown tells us, "haven't heard the question" (in Brand, 1975, p. 46). Envision the circles; don't draw "sufficient conclusions from insufficient data" (Bateson, quoted in Brand, 1975, p. 46), and don't perpetuate errors by ignoring mistaken premises—"no quantity ever changed a pattern" (Bateson, quoted in Brand, 1975, p. 40). Putting more money into a flawed educational system, for instance, only perpetuates the flaw.
- *Find out what a presupposition looks like.* The schools don't teach that. Know that there are better and worse ways of thinking and that premises can be wrong. Don't eat the menu. Question so-called objectivity. Recognize the powerful, hidden premises. They can be dangerous or redemptive.
- *Feed the hungry children,* "hungry . . . for something that'll make sense" (Bateson, quoted in Brand, 1975, p. 37). They are in need of some basic premises that help them "think straight" and look responsibly toward the future. Knowledge must be "the basis of both action and ethical commitment" (M. C. Bateson, 1984, p. 230). It does not preclude love; it demands it. Love, not as naive sentiment, but as the underlying premise of "how the world is made" (M. C. Bateson, 1977, p. 68) in its interconnectedness and intimacy.
- *Be moral*—that is, recognize our interdependency. Act on this recognition, this epistemology of living, patterned evolution. Take responsibility beyond the norm of greed and alienation; "in the abundance of water, the fool is thirsty" (Marley, 1976).

- And, above all, *be.* "A scientist, after all, like a sacrament or poem, 'should not mean but be'" (Archibald MacLeish, quoted in M. C. Bateson, 1977, p. 73). Atoning ("at-ONE-ment"; Bateson, 1976/1977, p. 95) for its foolishness, a redeemed science, like Dulcinea, reaches for a more graceful name. Like spring, it is a "perhaps hand," a tender, responding lover.

IDENTIFYING AN AESTHETIC, REDEMPTIVE EDUCATION: IMPLICATIONS FOR TEACHERS

Mary Catherine Bateson, in *Angels Fear* (Bateson & Bateson, 1987), talks of "Gregory-ing" an idea. It's a form of metaphorical thinking—a way of getting inside a person and thinking with them, envisioning how that person might respond to a question or think through a problem: "The names even become verbs in mental shorthand: Can I 'Gregory' this idea" (p. 195). Empathy, as Mary Catherine Bateson suggests, becomes a discipline.

What happens, in other words, when we "Gregory" education, when we take these glimpses into his world and design an education that complements it? Not surprisingly, it is essential first to accept that "it is absolutely disastrous to carry a notion like education in a cultural system." To carry the notion around "that there is something separate called education that is going to be handled by schools and universities" is to perpetuate the errors of an already dichotomized society. To even give education a name is to "cut it off from its roots." To even conceive of education as "distinct from living and passing on living" is to condemn it. It has no choice in such partiality than to be "perfectly dull and perfectly dead" (Bateson, n.d.).

"On the whole," he adds, "Americans think of education as separate and undesirable." Most children learn that by the fourth grade, and "the smarter ones learn it by the second grade." This situation is a "very, very serious thing. . . . It is nonsense that a child doesn't want to learn. It means there is a monstrosity of some sort going on" (Bateson, n.d.). But what choice do the children have, for what is being transmitted is "nonsense," sliced and scattered bits of information that have nothing to do with one another. No one is caring for the system:

> [W]e must be concerned today because, although we can persuade our children to learn long lists of facts about the world, they don't seem to have the capacity to put them together in a single unified understanding—there is no "pattern which connects." (Bateson & Bateson, 1987, p. 196)

In Marilyn Ferguson's (1980) words, "The greatest learning disability of all may be pattern blindness—the inability to see relationships and detect meaning" (pp. 298–299).

Education, that "stuff" that goes on in schools and universities (as compared with what Bateson [n.d.] believes education "ought to mean"—the "entire machinery, system of processes . . . whereby the norms of a culture, its wisdom and follies, are transmitted through time") suffers from the addictions of the larger society. A mindless education, a "*teaching of quantitative thought,*" as compared with "*qualitative thought*" (Bateson, 1981, p. 350), insists on separating life from meaning, mind from matter, value from pattern. It reinforces the "divisive monstrosity" of the larger society, "the pathology of how we think of mind/body relations . . . and that pathology, distortion, is enormously increased obviously by the various kinds of slicing we find in education" (Bateson, n.d.). The schools emphasize only parts, they both strengthen those parts and also convey the meta-message that such divisions are appropriate (M. C. Bateson, 1977, p. 69). The "ultimate caricature" of this "divisive monstrosity" is the true-false exam in which the children are "rewarded for having broken up life into non-sensical units" (Bateson, n.d.). Schools and society feed on one another, partners in crime.

Physiology is taught in the physiology labs, botany in the botany labs, and "something you call language . . . you learn separately from grammar." And further yet, "all this slicing are ways of not only separating the subject physiology from the subject grammar, but of also separating your physiology as you live it from your grammar" (Bateson, n.d.). A tremendous intimacy is being sacrificed. Nobody is teaching the children that their physiology is their grammar, an organization of relations. They are part of a living whole, and they don't know it. The dance is not theirs to dance.

Leaves are being taught to be "flat, green things on the side of a stick," instead of being studied for what they truly are—"the leaf is that which has a baby stem in its angle, a stem is that which came from the angle of leaf" (Bateson, n.d.), and so on. The elephant's trunk, like my nose, is that which stands between two eyes which stand between two ears.

Once you begin learning, and teaching, in this way, "you move into a different world, from a thing and its name to a relationship and its name." Relational definitions become the real definitions, "simple truths" (Bateson, n.d.) we could have been taught but were not.

A lesson in anatomy becomes an entrance into a "body of relations," the "anatomical dance" that is reality. A hand is not only five fingers "outside us to grip and pick"; it is a marriage of intervals to be pictured from the inside out, with its own life and growth. The growth of a leg on a body is a "communicational necessity" to be appreciated for its evolution in a larger whole, not just for its purpose and utility. Once we start seeing in this way, we discover that not only are our individual physiologies our individual grammars, but our "shared biologies" are also a "shared grammar," a massive web of organized relations—a universal grammar, a choreographic feat. Suddenly, a "sort of life" begins to run through "what is really very formal, very structural" . . . and in many schools, very "dead in the mouth."

Suddenly, as teachers we begin to behold the other, be it the child, the plant in our botany lesson, or the dynamism of the school itself. We begin to allow living impressions of the other to stand plainly before us. The being of the school becomes as real as the being of the child. As Huston Smith (1984) suggests, educators begin to practice an education for surrender—an education that is not afraid, that embraces a "total involvement, suspension of received notion, pertinence of everything, identification, the risk of being hurt"; an education that is "reverent (allows) a choiceless letting be of what is in order that it may reveal itself in the essence of its being" (pp. 86–87).

This active participation inspires an active thinking far richer than a model of thinking as information processing. The latter is a model that robs "things" of their context and aesthetic substance. It turns the lesson, the vision of education, even the perception of who the child is into a static, falsely objectified anachronism. Instead, with an aesthetic thinking—a thinking immersed in the dynamism of the "pattern which connects"—the teacher crosses the threshold of information gathering and logical, lineal processing and penetrates past the superficial into the discovery of the laws that work within phenomena. The teacher meets the child and, in that meeting, penetrates into the core of his or her essence and needs.

The teacher breaks through facades to find essences, releasing the "fragrance of that inner attainment for the guidance and benefit of others, by expressing in the world of forms, truth, love purity and beauty" (Meher Baba, 1967, p. 110). The teacher works from essence to details, whole to parts. Everything else is nonsense. A curriculum composed, an assessment composed, instruction composed, grows out of a profound experience of this intimacy that is the fundamental reality—the "pattern which connects." Curriculum, assessment, and instruction, as one example, coexist as an ongoing choreography grounded in a vision of life—in an experience of thinking—that is seamless and passionate. Alive.

The teacher transcends the three epistemological errors and lives instead in a world of rhythm and dance. Nietzche writes, "Every day I count wasted in which there has been no dancing"; we waste the beauty we are given, the inherent recursiveness of life, and don't even mourn the tragedy of our neglect. The aesthetic teacher mourns the tragedy and immerses her- or himself in the resonance of this world. She or he plans, designs, composes instruction out of this aesthetic model of reality, knowing that rigor does not preclude creativity and vice versa. Rather, they work best together, without the analogic (flexible, open, relational) negating the digital (fixed, right or wrong). They, too, when understood across time and contextually, work best in cooperation. That is the art of education, formal and yet warm, immensely disciplined and yet beautifully fluid.

And, finally, the aesthetic teacher is attentive to form. He or she nurtures the forming process by helping "things" come into being, whether in him- or herself, the individual students, or a mound of clay. Learning is noted as a matter of calibration, organization, communication, and collaboration. Be-coming, ultimately, is the pedagogical goal.

An education for greed, alienation, and control is transformed by an education for story, aesthetic at its center, dancing rather than processing, alive rather than dead, seamless rather than fragmented. Thinking becomes an experience. Not a deed. Not a product. But an engagement, a commitment to the why of the why, to digging behind the bushes *into* the earth, *into* a realm where no such thing as a thing exists. Only "an infinite regress of relationships" (G. Bateson, 1972, p. 246).

Thinking and education enter a qualitative dimension, not a quantitative, appetitive one; mobile, not sterile; warm, not cold; graceful, not clumsy. Like the Wu Li

Master, (Zukav's [*Parabola,* 1984] dream of revisioning physics), thinking, and its partner education, dance with the student:

> The Wu Li Master does not speak of gravity until the student stands in wonder at the flower petal falling to the ground.
>
> The Wu Li Master does not teach; he "dances" with his student as he knows the universe dances with itself. (front page)

References

Barfield, O. (n.d.). *Saving the appearances: A study in idolatry*. New York: Harcourt Brace Jovanovich.

Bateson, G. (1972). *Steps to an ecology of mind*. New York: Ballantine Books.

Bateson, G. (1976, Fall). Invitational paper. Mind/Body dualism conference. *CoEvolution Quarterly*, 56–57.

Bateson, G. (1976/1977, Winter). The case against the case for mind/body dualism. *CoEvolution Quarterly*, 94–95.

Bateson, G. (1977). Afterword. In J. Brockman (Ed.), *About Bateson.* New York: E. P. Dutton.

Bateson, G. (1978, Spring). Number is different from quantity. *CoEvolution Quarterly*, 44–46.

Bateson, G. (1979/1980, Winter). Letter to the regents of the University of California. *CoEvolution Quarterly*, 22–23.

Bateson, G. (1980a). *Men are grass.* [Lindisfarne letter, tape to the Lindisfarne fellows] (M. C. Bateson, Ed.). West Stockbridge, MA: Lindisfarne Press.

Bateson, G. (1980b). *Mind and nature: A necessary unity*. New York: Bantam Books.

Bateson, G. (1981). Paradigmatic conservatism. In C. Wilder-Mott & J. H. Weakland (Eds.), *Rigor and imagination: Essays from the legacy of Gregory Bateson.* New York: Praeger.

Bateson, G. (n.d.). *Education and learning* [Lindisfarne tape IIE11]. West Stockbridge, MA: Lindisfarne Press.

Bateson, G., & Bateson, M. C. (1987). *Angels fear: Towards an epistemology of the sacred*. New York: MacMillan.

Bateson, G., & Brown, J. (1976, Spring). Prayer breakfast. *CoEvolution Quarterly*, 82–84.

Bateson, M. C. (1972). *Our own metaphor: A personal account of a conference on the effects of conscious purpose on human adaptation*. New York: Knopf.

Bateson, M. C. (1977). Daddy, can a scientist be wise? In J. Brockman (Ed.), *About Bateson.* New York: E. P. Dutton.

Bateson, M. C. (1984). *With a daughter's eye*. New York: Morrow.

Bellah, R. N., Madsen, R., Sullivan, W. M., Swidler, M., & Tipton, S. M. (1985). *Habits of the heart*. Berkeley: University of California Press.

Bochner, A. P. (1981). Forming warm ideas. In C. Wilder-Mott & J. H. Weakland (Eds.), *Rigor and imagination: Essays from the legacy of Gregory Bateson.* New York: Praeger.

Brand, S. (1975, Fall). Caring and clarity: A conversation with Gregory Bateson and Edmund G. Brown, Jr., governor of California. *CoEvolution Quarterly*, 32–47.

Brockman, J. (1977). Introduction. In J. Brockman (Ed.), *About Bateson.* New York: E. P. Dutton.

Bruner, J. (1986, April 14). Story as a way of knowing. *Brain/Mind Bulletin,* p. 2.

Byers, P. (1985a). Communication: Cooperation or negotiation? *Theory into Practice*, *24*(1), 71–76.

Byers, P. (1985b). Conversation: A context for language. *Gaikokugo Kyoiku Kiyo*, *13*, 27–40.

Capra, F. (1977). *The Tao of physics*. New York: Bantam Books.

Capra, F. (1983). *The turning point*. New York: Bantam Books.

Cervantes, M. S. (1964). *Don Quixote* (W. Starkie, Trans.). New York: New American Library.

Cummings, E. E. (1991). *Complete poems 1904–1962* (G. J. Firmage, Ed.). New York: Liveright.

Dickinson, E. (1960). I know that he exists. In *Complete poems of Emily Dickinson* (T. H. Johnson, Ed.). Boston: Little, Brown.

Ferguson, M. (1980). *The Aquarian conspiracy: Personal and social transformation in the 1980s.* Los Angeles: J. P. Tarcher.

Fields, R., & Greene, R. (1975). A conversation with Gregory Bateson. *Loka: The Journal of the Naropa Institute,* 28–34.

Geertz, C. (1973). *The interpretation of cultures*. New York: Basic Books.

Grof, S. (1981). Nature, mind, and consciousness: Gregory Bateson and the new paradigm. *Phoenix: Journal of Transpersonal Anthropology*, *5*(2), 31–72.

Kilpatrick, W. K. (n.d.) Storytelling and virtue. *Policy Review,* 60–64.

Kuhn, T. S. (1970). *The structure of scientific revolutions*. Chicago: University of Chicago Press.

Lipset, D. (1982). *Gregory Bateson: The legacy of a scientist*. Boston: Beacon Press.

Marley, B. (Producer). (1976). The rat race [Record]. New York: Warner Brothers Records.

Meher Baba. (1967). *Discourses* (Vol. 3). Walnut Creek, CA: Sufism Reoriented.

McBroom, A. (1979). The rose [Song recorded by Bette Midler]. New York: Atlantic Recording.

Morrow, L. (1985, December 2). Behind closed doors. *Time,* p. 17.

Morton, K. (1984, December 23). The story-telling animal. *New York Times Book Review.*

Parabola. (1984). In G. Zukav (Ed.), *The dancing Wu Li masters*. New York: Bantam Books.

Prigogine, I., & Stengers, I. (1984). *Order out of chaos*. New York: Bantam Books.

Richards, M. C. (1982). *Toward wholeness: Rudolf Steiner education in America*. Middletown, CT: Wesleyan University Press.

Smith, H. (1984). *Beyond the postmodern mind*. Wheaton, IL: Theosophical Publishing House.

Spangler, D. (1978). *New dimensions of consciousness* [Tape recording of a lecture given at the Symposium on the Coevolution of Science and Spirit, New York, November 17–20]. New Lebanon, NY: Sufi Order.

Wagner, J. (1986). *The search for signs of intelligent life in the universe*. New York: Harper & Row.

Wilder-Mott, C. (1981). Rigor and imagination. In C. Wilder-Mott & J. H. Weakland (Eds.), *Rigor and imagination: Essays from the legacy of Gregory Bateson*. New York: Praeger.

BIOGRAPHY

DIANA MUXWORTHY FEIGE, a native of Puerto Rico, is Director of School-Based Programs in the School of Education at Adelphi University, Garden City, New York. As both teacher and administrator, she dedicates much of her time to building stronger university-school partnerships. Her interest in the work of Gregory Bateson began while a doctoral student at Teachers College, Columbia University. With Paul Byers as mentor, she completed a doctoral thesis examining the connections between Bateson's thought and that of Rudolf Steiner and Waldorf education.

6

ARE THERE ADDITIONAL INTELLIGENCES? THE CASE FOR NATURALIST, SPIRITUAL, AND EXISTENTIAL INTELLIGENCES

INTRODUCTION

In his 1983 landmark book *Frames of Mind,* Howard Gardner introduced his theory of multiple intelligences (MI), a view of intelligence as consisting of several distinct intelligences, rather than as a singular cognitive capacity. Using eight criteria identified in this chapter and a general definition of *intelligence* as "the ability to solve problems or to fashion products that are valued in at least one culture or community," he identifies seven areas of human cognition fittingly called "intelligences." MI theory since has captured the imagination of educators and has transformed the way we understand human cognition.

At the outset, Gardner states that although he has identified seven intelligences, more might exist. With this chapter, he explores new "candidate intelligences," with some surprising results and new questions. Applying the definition above and the criteria, he suggests an eighth intelligence, the naturalist intelligence, and leaves open the possibility of one centered on matters of a spiritual nature.

The naturalist intelligence described in this chapter refers to a distinctive cognitive capacity to recognize flora and fauna. Such intelligence is not confined to things perceived visually or to natural (as opposed to human-made) objects, however. The capacity to make such distinctions seems to rest in the ability to recognize patterns in the way things are organized or function or both. (Gardner's work in developing the theory of multiple intelligences may itself serve as a highly sophisticated example of naturalist intelligence.)

The existence of naturalist intelligence not only adds to the list of intelligences but also opens significant epistemological questions. Could naturalist intelligence provide support for postcritical theories of scientific inquiry? The noted biologist-philosopher Gregory Bateson concluded that the ability to perceive patterns in nature constitutes an "intellectual aesthetic." Bateson argued (as Diana Muxworthy Feige so persuasively explains in chap. 5, this volume) that the loss of aesthetic sensibility in science has been a serious epistemological error. In a similar vein, philosopher-scientist Michael Polanyi developed the theory of personal knowledge, which based science on personal intuition and tacit skills with a vital *secondary* role for explicit observation and logic. Might these theorists be describing the role of natural intelligence in scientific inquiry? Is it possible that naturalist intelligence may play a significant role that we have yet to recognize fully or to explore?

The notion of spiritual intelligence poses significant problems relative to its content. Gardner does not address questions of metaphysics or of religious doctrine. Rather, he confines himself to the subtle and profound cognitive capacities necessary to address the ultimate issues of existence. The concept of spiritual intelligence being considered concerns how we understand ourselves in all our aspects and relations within the cosmos. Such an intelligence would describe our capacity to create an understanding or a system for understanding who we are and how we fit in the world.

In this context, Gardner's analysis of what he calls "existential intelligence" yields a moderate case for its inclusion as a new intelligence. However, its status remains vexing. Intellectual security is hard to come by where insight and delusion seem virtually indistinguishable. Perhaps Gardner here takes us to the far horizon of science—a point beyond which the scientist may not go. As Huston Smith explains, science is limited to that which is controllable, to that which may be examined through controlled experimentation. In the context of modern science, we cannot determine experimentally which, if any, spiritual propositions have any validity.

> Where naturalist intelligence suggests new possible dimensions of scientific inquiry, the very possibility of spiritual intelligence may suggest ultimate limits. Gardner does not leave us with conclusions here, but rather with a process and a near infinite set of questions. His inquiry demonstrates how we may go about discerning yet-unrecognized intelligences (if any exist) and the humility necessary to admit that we might not now or ever be able to answer all the questions we ask.
>
> —*Jeffrey Kane*

The Magic Number Seven

In *Frames of Mind*, originally published in 1983, I rejected the notion, widely held among scientists and laypersons, that human intelligence should be considered a unitary trait or ability (Gardner, 1993a). Rather, in line with theorists like L. L. Thurstone (1938) and J. P. Guilford (1967), I argued that the human intellect is best construed as at least seven relatively autonomous faculties. Only two of these faculties—*linguistic* and *logical-mathematical*—fall comfortably within the usual definitions of intelligence, and only these two lend themselves readily to testing in standardized short-answer formats. The other five faculties—*spatial, musical, bodily-kinesthetic, interpersonal,* and *intrapersonal*—in the past have either been considered talents or been deemed outside the permissible scope of human intellect.

Most previous studies of intelligence—whether of the unitary or the pluralistic stripe—have arrived at their conclusions through the scrutiny of test scores and, particularly, the examination of correlations among scores on a variety of subtests. Those who favor a unitary view see the various tests as reflections, to a greater or lesser degree, of a single underlying factor of "g" or general intelligence (Herrnstein & Murray, 1994). Those who favor a pluralistic view look at the test scores—indeed, sometimes at the very same scores—and discern instead a series of relatively independent factors organized either hierarchically or heterarchically (Gould, 1981; Sternberg, 1982).

My approach to the study of intelligence was unusual, if not unique, in that it minimized the importance of tests and of correlations among test scores. Rather, I proceeded from a definition and a set of criteria. As laid out in *Frames of Mind* and other documents of the period (Gardner, 1993b), I defined an **intelligence** as the ability to solve problems or to fashion products that are valued in at least one culture or community. I then went on to specify eight criteria for an intelligence:

1. Identifiable core operation(s)
2. Evolutionary history and evolutionary plausibility

3. Recognizable end-state and distinctive developmental trajectory
4. Existence of savants, prodigies, and other individuals distinguished by the presence or absence of specific abilities
5. Potential isolation by brain damage
6. Support from experimental psychological tasks
7. Support from psychometric findings
8. Susceptibility to encoding in a symbol system (Gardner, 1993a, chap. 4)

Although none of the candidate intelligences fulfilled all of these criteria perfectly, each of the seven intelligences itemized above satisfied the majority of the criteria.

In *Frames of Mind,* I made it clear that nothing was sacred about the list of seven intelligences. If seven did exist, I indicated, more would surely be discovered. Moreover, each of the original seven intelligences itself harbored subcomponents or constituent intelligences; it was a matter of expository convenience, rather than logical or scientific necessity, that gave rise to the original, readily described ensemble of intelligences.

Since the **theory of multiple intelligences** first gained attention, I have repeatedly been asked whether I have expanded the list of intelligences. To fob off this question, I devised the following lighthearted response: "My students have often asked me whether there is a cooking intelligence, a humor intelligence, and/or a sexual intelligence. They have concluded that I can only recognize those intelligences that I myself possess." More seriously, I have contemplated several candidate additional intelligences but until now have thought it prudent not to expand the list.

In this chapter, I consider directly the evidence for three "new" candidate intelligences: a *naturalist intelligence,* a *spiritual intelligence,* and an *existential intelligence.* As I explain below, the evidence for a naturalist intelligence is stronger and less ambiguous than the evidence for a spiritual intelligence; hence, I end up adding the naturalist intelligence to my list. The realm of the spiritual, as typically defined, does not fall comfortably under the rubric of intelligence as I construe it. Evidence for a related existential intelligence, however, is more persuasive.

In the end, whether to declare a human capacity as a "new intelligence" is a judgment call. The deeper purpose of this chapter is to explore once more how one goes about identifying an intelligence and to reveal my reservations about extending the concept in less secure directions.

THE NATURALIST INTELLIGENCE

When presenting my concept of intelligences, I generally introduce each intelligence through the vehicle of an "end-state"—a socially recognized and valued role that appears to rely heavily on a particular intellectual capacity. Thus, I designate a poet to denote linguistic intelligence, a computer scientist to indicate logical-mathematical intelligence, a salesperson or clinical psychologist to convey interpersonal intelligence, and the like.

The very term *naturalist* combines a description of the core ability with a characterization of the role that is valued in many cultures. A **naturalist** is an individual who demonstrates expertise in the recognition and classification of the numerous species—the flora and fauna—of her or his environment. Every culture places a premium on those individuals who can recognize members of a species that are especially valuable or notably dangerous and who can appropriately categorize new or unfamiliar organisms. In cultures without formal science, the naturalist is the individual most skilled in the application of the current "folk taxonomies" (Berlin, 1992); in cultures with a scientific orientation, the naturalist is a biologist who recognizes and categorizes specimens in terms of current formal taxonomies, such as those devised by Linnaeus.

In our own culture, the word *naturalist* is readily applied to those individuals whose knowledge of the living world is outstanding, such as John James Audubon, Roger Torrey Peterson, or Rachel Carson, as well as those individuals who study organisms for more theoretically oriented purposes, such as Charles Darwin, Louis Agassiz, Ernst Mayr, or E. O. Wilson. It is notable that Darwin commented he was "born a naturalist" (Browne, 1995) and that Wilson entitled his recent autobiography *Naturalist* (1994). Indeed, my recognition that such individuals could not readily be classified in terms of the seven antecedent intelligences led me to consider an additional form of intelligence.

Although one tends to think of the naturalist's abilities as being exercised chiefly with respect to plants and animals that are seen with the naked eye, I construe their scope more broadly. To begin with, there is no need to restrict the application to ordinary vision; any distinction that can be made and justified under magnification is equally valid. By the same token, species recognition by no means depends on vision; blind individuals can be extremely acute in recognizing species, and one of the leading naturalists of our time—Geermat Vermij—operates by touch (Yoon, 1995). Also, it seems reasonable to assume that the capacities of the naturalist can be brought to bear on items that are artificial. A young child who can readily discriminate plants or birds or dinosaurs from one another is presumably drawing on the same skills (or intelligence) when he or she classifies instances of the categories of sneakers, cars, sound systems, or CD jackets.

Just as recognition of tones and melodies is the core of musical intelligence, so recognition of species membership is the core of the naturalist's intelligence. It is worth noting that a full-blown naturalist goes well beyond such taxonomic capacities. Exhibiting what Wilson (1984) has termed **biophilia**, the naturalist is comfortable in the world of organisms and may well possess the talent of caring, taming, or interacting subtly with a variety of living creatures. It is also possible, though more speculative, that the pattern-recognizing talents of many artists and natural scientists are built on the fundamental perceptual skills of naturalist intelligence.

Judged in terms of the eight criteria proposed in *Frames of Mind* and listed above, the **naturalist intelligence** proves quite as firmly entrenched as the other

intelligences. There are, to begin with, the core capacities to recognize instances as members of a group (more formally, a species), to distinguish among members of species, to recognize the existence of other neighboring species, and to chart the relations, formally or informally, among the several species. Clearly, the importance of a naturalist intelligence is well established in evolutionary history, where the survival of an organism has been dependent on its ability to discriminate among quite similar species, avoiding some (predators) and ferreting out others (for prey or play). A naturalist's capacity presents itself not only in those primates that are evolutionarily closest to human beings; birds are also readily capable of discerning the differences among species of plants and animals (including ones not in their "normal" expected environment) and can even recognize members of the class of human beings from photographs (Edelman, 1995; Herrnstein & Loveland, 1964; Wasserman, 1994).

Turning to the role of the naturalist in human culture, I have already mentioned some end-states that foreground the naturalist's intelligence; it goes without saying that many other roles, as diverse as hunter, fisher, farmer, gardener, and cook, exploit this ability. Even, apparently, remote capacities, such as recognition of an automobile from the sound of the engine, or the detection of a novel pattern in the scientific laboratory, or the discernment of artistic style, may exploit mechanisms that originally evolved because of their efficacy in distinguishing between toxic and nontoxic ivies or snakes. Quite possibly, the patterns of life discerned, though put to contrasting ends, by poets and by social scientists draw as well on the naturalist intelligence.

Moreover, a scale ranging from novice to expert can be stipulated for a budding naturalist (Carey, 1985; Chi, 1981; Keil, 1994). At the early stages, no formal instruction is necessary, but entire formal fields of study, such as botany or entomology, have been constructed as a means of aiding the development and deployment of the skills of the naturalist.

An important source of information about the independence of an intelligence comes from studies that identify individuals who either excel at or lack a certain capacity, as well as neural regions that appear to subserve these capacities. Thus, the existence and independence of musical and linguistic intelligence is underscored by the identification of brain centers that mediate linguistic and musical processing, as well as individuals, ranging from prodigies to savants, who feature singular capacities that are either precocious or surprisingly lacking.

Just as most ordinary individuals readily master language at an early age, so too most youngsters are predisposed to explore the naturalist's world with some avidity. The popularity of dinosaurs among 5-year-olds is no accident! However, there is little question that certain young children stand out in terms of their early interest in the natural world and their acute capacities to identify and commit to memory many distinctions. Biographies of great biologists routinely document an early fascination with plants and animals and a drive to identify, classify, and interact with them. Such scientists as Charles Darwin, Stephen Jay Gould, and E. O. Wilson are only the most visible members of this cohort; studies of biologically oriented scientists confirm this pattern (Csikszentmihalyi, 1996; Roe, 1953; Taylor & Barron, 1963; Zuckerman,

1977). Interestingly, these patterns are not echoed in the lives of physical scientists, who are more likely to explore the behavior of invisible forces or to play with mechanical or chemical systems; nor in the biographies of social scientists, who are more likely to be engaged in verbal activities, in reading nonfiction, or in complex interactions with other persons.

Just as certain individuals appear to have gifts in the recognition of naturalistic patterns, others are impaired in this respect. The most dramatic examples occur in cases of brain damage in which individuals remain able to recognize and name inanimate objects but lose the capacity to identify and name instances of living things. This distinction has long been reported in the clinical literature (Konorski, 1967; Nielsen, 1946) and recently has been confirmed by experimental findings (Caramazza, Hillis, Leek, & Miozzo, 1994; Damasio & Damasio, 1995; Martin, Wiggs, Ungerleider, & Haxby, 1996; Warrington & Shallice, 1984).

Just which neural centers are involved in this capacity remains somewhat controversial, and, as in the case of musical aptitude, such species recognition may well be represented in different ways in different individuals, depending, for example, on whether the species are known primarily through graphic illustrations or by virtue of direct interactions with the organisms in question. Yet, because the human naturalistic capacity would appear to be closely related to that of other animals, it should be possible to confirm which brain regions are likely to be crucial in naturalistic perception. The identification of neural networks involved in particular forms of recognition—such as face or paw recognition—may provide important clues for this undertaking (Damasio, 1994; Gross, 1973).

To my knowledge, the capacity of the naturalist has not been of much interest to psychologists. Indeed, psychologists have traditionally favored artificial stimuli (e.g., geometric forms) and thus have avoided those stimuli that would be most likely to elicit more natural forms of categorization. Similarly, test makers have rarely, if ever, included items that assess skill at categorizing species membership (or other naturalist skills).

An important exception to this statement is work on categorization by Eleanor Rosch and her associates (Rosch, Mervis, Gray, Johnson, & Bayes-Braem, 1976; see also Neisser, 1976); these studies suggest the existence of special psychological mechanisms that identify "natural kinds" (e.g., birds, trees) and that organize such concepts, not in terms of lists of defining attributes, but rather by virtue of their resemblance to prototypes (how "birdlike" or "treelike" is the organism in question?). Much of children's early language learning and classification also seems to build on these natural forms of categorization, rather than on those forms that have evolved (or have been recast) to deal with human-made objects.

The final criterion for an intelligence is its susceptibility to encoding in a symbol system. The extensive linguistic and taxonomic systems that exist in every culture for the classifying of plants and animals testify to the universality of this feature. (In Western culture, we are especially indebted to Aristotle and Linnaeus.) Works of art as diverse as cave paintings, ritual dances, and choreographers' notations represent other symbolic ways of "fixing" the identifying features of phenomena of the naturalist's world. Much of religious and spiritual life, including vital rites, also draws on the natural world and attempts to capture it or to comment on it in ways valued within a culture.

This review of a candidate intelligence—in this case, naturalist intelligence—reveals a capacity that clearly merits addition to the list of the original seven. Those valued human cognitions, which I previously had to ignore or to smuggle in under spatial or logical-mathematical intelligence, deserve to be gathered together under a single, recognized rubric. Eschewing formal ceremony, I mark this acknowledgment of an eighth intelligence by a simple performative speech act. The above review serves as a reminder of the procedure by which it should be possible in the future to review and, if appropriate, include additional capacities within the family of human intelligences.

THE VARIETIES OF SPIRITUAL LIFE

The realm of the naturalist seems straightforward. In contrast, even a hesitant entry into the world of spirituality reveals a far more complex picture, one that proves by no means easy to disentangle, in the manner of an accomplished naturalist—or spiritualist!

I must begin by acknowledging that any discussion of the spirit—whether cast as a spiritual life, a spiritual capacity, a spiritual feeling, a gift for religion, mysticism, or the transcendent—is controversial within the sciences, if not throughout the academic world. Language, music, space, naturalism, even understanding of other people—all seem relatively unproblematic in contrast. Many people, including me, do not recognize the spirit as we recognize the mind and the body; many people, including me, do not grant the same ontological status to the transcendent or the spiritual as we do, say, to the mathematical or the musical.

Even those who cannot themselves identify with the spiritual realm or domain recognize its importance to most human beings; indeed, some would quip, it is *too* important. Presidents (and their spouses!) consult astrologers, rather than historians or clinicians; religions save thousands of lives, though they may also contribute to the deaths of many individuals; and books about the spirit or the soul crowd out those about memory or perception on the psychology shelves of bookstore chains. Regrettably, lack of personal belief on the part of the research community all too often results in failure to take a phenomenon seriously. We thus face an unfortunate situation: The vast majority of scholars in the cognitive and biological sciences turn away from questions of a spiritual nature, hence consigning this realm chiefly to the true believers and to the quacks (see Burkert, 1995).

Indeed, a decision on a priori grounds to eliminate spiritual intelligence from consideration is no more justifiable than a decision to admit it by fiat or on faith. And there are no easy grounds for a decision. After all, once one includes the understanding of the personal realm within a study of intelligence, such human proclivities as the spiritual must legitimately be considered. Moreover, not all intelligences deal with sheer matter in Dr. Johnson's "kick a boulder" sense; if the abstract realm of mathematics constitutes a reasonable area of intelligence (and few would challenge that judgment), then why not the abstract realm of the spiritual?

Let us assume, then, that it is reasonable at least to inquire about a possible **spiritual intelligence** or a set of spirit-related intelligences. What capacities and traits are evoked when one enters the realm of the spiritual? As an initial parsing of this area, I propose three distinct senses of spiritual. I go on to suggest that much confusion obtains when these varieties are confounded with one another and that, in terms of the current definition and criteria, only one of them can lay claim to being an intelligence.

Spiritual as Concern With Cosmic or Existential Issues

The first variety of spirituality reflects a desire to know about those experiences and cosmic entities that are not readily apprehended in a material sense but that nonetheless appear, for whatever reason, to be important to human beings. If we as humans can relate to the world of nature, we can as well relate to the world that is supernatural—to the cosmos that extends beyond what we can perceive directly, to the mystery of our own existence, and to those life-and-death experiences that transcend what we encounter on a routine basis. And, indeed, mythology, religion, and art have perennially reflected efforts on the part of humans to understand the ultimate questions, mysteries, and *meanings* of life: Who are we? Where do we come from? What does the future hold for us? Why do we exist? What is the meaning of life, of love, of tragic losses, of death? What is the nature of our relation to the wider world and to figures that lie beyond our comprehension, like our gods or our God (cf. Buber, 1970)?

Although human beings may well puzzle about these questions on their own or in informal dialogue with their neighbors, many organized systems that deal with these issues have also been constructed over the centuries. And so, in any culture, an individual may elect to adopt an already existing code or set of beliefs about these issues of ultimate concern. It is useful to distinguish between the adoption of a *traditional* version of spiritual knowledge and the *creation of a personal blend* of spiritual knowledge.

Stated in this manner, the content of spiritual knowledge may seem relatively straightforward. In practice, however, the content of the achieved knowledge may prove far more controversial. It is by no means unproblematic to state what content is, in fact, being mastered by the putatively spiritual knower—its realm, its truth value, its limitations. Indeed, in reading accounts of the spiritual realm, I am tempted to conclude that it refers, Kabbalah-like, to everything—mind, body, self, nature, the supernatural—and sometimes even to nothing! Contrast this conceptual sprawl with the domain of science or math, which seem relatively delimited and uncontroversial in contrast.

Spiritual as Achievement of a State of Being

In considering any intelligence, it is pertinent to distinguish between the two classical senses of knowing: **knowing how** and **knowing that**. For other intelligences, this distinction proves uncontroversial because the "content" of the intelligence is evident (e.g., musical patterns, spatial arrays), and it is equally clear that individuals differ in their skills or know-how in dealing with the domain.

When it comes to the realm of the spiritual, however, the two forms of knowing must be more carefully distinguished from one another. Our first sense of spiritual attempts to delineate those realms of experience, those domains of existence, that individuals seek to understand. In addition, however, many communities also recognize the existence of skills at achieving certain psychological states, undergoing certain phenomenal experiences that merit the descriptor "spiritual." Within such communities, there is reasonable consensus on possession of know-how; some individuals are simply more skilled than others at meditating, achieving trance states, envisioning the transcendent, being or getting in touch with psychic or spiritual or noetic phenomena. Indeed, specific physiological and brain states may well be correlated predictably with the achievement of such alterations of consciousness. Such cultural roles as the mystic, the yoga, and the meditator denote individuals whose ability to achieve these states—and perhaps to enable others to achieve these states—is noteworthy (Goleman, 1988).

With respect to this second variety of spirituality, one may reinvoke a distinction introduced above. It is possible to achieve a state of spirituality by following a *traditional* route—for example, by executing a set of exercises suggested by a specific priest or mystic or guru. But it is also possible to achieve such an elaborated state through a more *personalized* form of control of consciousness or through stimulation by specific substances (e.g., hallucinogenic drugs) or sensory experiences (e.g., listening to music, hiking up mountains).

A prudent observer might well concede that it is plausible to think of "a talent in achieving certain mental states" as lying within the realm of scientific analysis. Following this line of argument, one might construe the "gymnastic" aspect of controlling mental states as a subspecies of bodily-kinesthetic intelligence.

Where the believer or spokesperson for spirituality raises eyebrows is in the frequent move to the claim that spiritual concerns lead to an encounter with a Deeper Truth. It is not merely the case—as some would argue, the uncontroversial case—that individuals need to locate themselves with respect to the cosmos and to the infinitesimal, nor even that some states of consciousness are universally desirable. Rather, enthusiasts argue for the existence of a specific content—a Spiritual Truth—to which only some, or only those who have followed a certain path, can have access. And this slippery slope leads, all too often, to a belief that the world can be divided between those who qualify on some spiritual or religious or metaphysical ground and those who do not. Moreover, although one can measure the attainment of altered states of consciousness, there is no objective measure for the attainment of the State of Spiritual Truth. We have here left the realm of intelligence and moved to the spheres of dogma or doxa (Bloom, 1995).

Viewed from one perspective, these two forms of knowing—interest in a certain set of contents, and mastering the craft of altering one's consciousness—can be seen as uses of mind, whether one considers such uses to be profound or frivolous, inspired or misguided. But to many, such *cognitivization* of the spiritual proves problematic in itself. For such interested observers, the essence of spirit is seen as primarily phenomenological—the attainment of a certain state of being, what has been called a "feeling of surrender"—and not as a domain that involves any kind of cognitive problem solving or product making (Mishlove, 1994). Relatedly, spiritual concerns can be thought of as primarily emotional or affective in character—a feeling of a certain tone or intensity—and hence, again, ruled as beyond the confines of a cognitive investigation.

Spiritual as Effect on Others

Yet a third variety of the spiritual is often remarked upon. Certain individuals—Mother Theresa, Pope John XXIII, and Pablo Casals are three oft-noted examples—are considered spiritual because of the effects they apparently exert on other individuals (Storr, 1996). By their activities and, perhaps even more, by their sheer being, these individuals affect those with whom they come into contact. Knowing about Mother Theresa's life, being blessed by Pope John, or listening to Casals playing the Bach Suites causes numerous individuals to feel differently—more whole, more in touch with themselves, their God, the cosmos. And although I prefer to cite benign instances of this phenomenon, it must be conceded that Adolf Hitler and Mao Tse-tung had this effect on many of their compatriots.

All three senses of the spiritual can be aroused. In some cases, these spiritually effective figures will drive individuals toward the exploration of cosmic issues. In some cases, the spiritually effective figure will cause individuals to achieve an altered state of consciousness. Finally, in a few cases, there will be a contagion, whereby the individual affected by a spiritual individual will her- or himself, by a kind of reflected spirituality, affect yet other individuals. Indeed, many religions have spread by just such an iterative charismatic process.

The great religious leaders, like Buddha, Christ, Saint Joan, or Confucius, are often seen as having attained a level of consciousness, a connectedness to the rest of the world, a de-emphasis of self, that represents an exemplary spiritual existence. Clearly, the prospect of attaining such a state motivates millions of individuals, reflecting the spectrum of cultures, to strive to achieve a state of spirituality or to heighten the spiritual aspects of their own persons.

No doubt, certain individuals, such as those just named and others of less renown, exude a feeling of spirituality—a conviction that they are in touch with the cosmos, and a concomitant capacity to make those in their surroundings believe that they themselves have been touched, made to feel more whole, more themselves, in enhanced relation to the transcendent. Whatever the mechanism—and the term *charisma* captures much of it (Gerth & Mills, 1958)—this "contact with the spiritual" constitutes an important ingredient in conveying to individuals the goal of their quest and, perhaps equally important, how one might embark on the right pathway. But whatever intellectual powers may be reflected in the achievements of a Buddha or a Christ, it seems clear to most observers that "problem solving" or "product making" is not a felicitous description. Achievement of a certain "state of being" constitutes a more convincing description.

My brief survey confirms that the "words and the examples of the spirit" can cover a multitude of human capacities, inclinations, and achievements—at least some of which fall well outside the project of defining additional human intelligences. To begin with, my definition of intelligence has deliberately been cast in amoral terms: No intelligence is in itself moral or immoral, and any intelligence can be mobilized to prosocial or antisocial uses. Thus, it is not valid to delineate any particular form of spirituality as appropriate or inappropriate on the basis of adherence to some kind of moral code. Just as personal intelligence cannot be aligned with, or limited to, a particular political or social system, the attainment of a specific set of beliefs or a specific role within an organized religion cannot be deemed a demonstration of a particular intelligence.

By the same token, the achievement of particular phenomenal states should not qualify an individual as realizing, or failing to realize, a particular intelligence. A person may exhibit high musical or mathematical intelligence despite the absence of any reported cognitive or affective state; similarly, the claim that one "thinks mathematically" or "feels musical" has no meaning unless the individual can exhibit certain capacities to solve problems or to fashion products.

Finally, although the capacity to affect others may prove an effective means of inculcating an intelligence, it does not, strictly speaking, constitute an embodiment of an intelligence. I might be able to stimulate the development of interpersonal understanding in others simply by behaving in unpredictable or antisocial ways without myself possessing or exhibiting interpersonal intelligence. Contrarily, I might possess outstanding mathematical intelligence without the concomitant facility to aid anyone else in the mathematical sphere. My definition of intelligence is unduly stretched if it is expected to encompass an individual's effect (or lack of effect) on others.

As I reflect on the possibility of a spiritual intelligence, I am struck by the problematic nature of the "content" of spiritual intelligence: its possibly defining affective and phenomenological aspects; its often privileged but unsubstantiated claims with respect to truth value; and the fact that it may partially need to be identified by virtue of its effect on other persons.

In an attempt to deal with this important sphere of life, I find it more comfortable to talk about a potential to engage in thinking about cosmic issues that might be motivated by pain, by powerful personal or aesthetic experiences, and/or by life in a community that highlights that form of thinking and experience. I would be less than candid if I did not concede that I am also somewhat alarmed by the prospect of being assimilated to the many "crazies" and "frauds" who invoke spirituality as if it were a given or a known truth, rather than a tremendously complex phenomenon that demands careful analysis.

Still, too aggressively applied, such a critical exercise risks the premature elimination of a set of human capabilities that might benefit from consideration in terms of my theory of human intelligence. It seems more responsible to carve out that area of spirituality that seem closest "in spirit" to the other intelligences and then, in the sympathetic manner applied to naturalist intelligence, to ascertain how this candidate intelligence fares. In doing so, I think it best to lay aside the term *spiritual,* with its manifest and sometimes problematic connotations, and to speak instead of an intelligence that explores the nature of existence, in its multifarious guises. Under this new dispensation, an explicit concern with spiritual or religious matters would be one variety—often the most important variety—of an existential intelligence in operation.

EXISTENTIAL INTELLIGENCE AND THE EIGHT CRITERIA

In what follows, I focus my remarks on **existential intelligence**—a concern with "ultimate" issues. I do so because this strand of the spiritual seems the most unambiguously cognitive in nature and because it avoids those features that, according to my definition, are not germane to any consideration of intelligence. If this form qualifies, then one may legitimately speak about existential intelligence; if it does not, then further consideration of the realm of spirituality seems contraindicated.

Returning to the earlier discussion, let me begin by proposing a core ability for a candidate existential intelligence. The core ability is the capacity to locate oneself with respect to the farthest reaches of the cosmos—the infinite no less than the infinitesimal—and the related capacity to locate oneself with respect to the most existential features of the human condition: the significance of life, the meaning of death, the ultimate fate of the physical and psychological worlds, such profound experiences as love of another human being or total immersion in a work of art. Note that there is no requirement here of attaining an ultimate truth, any more than the deployer of musical intelligence must produce or prefer certain kinds of music. Rather, there exists a species potential—or capacity—to engage in transcendental concerns that can be aroused and deployed under certain circumstances.

It should be evident that this capacity has been valued in every known human culture. Cultures devise religious, mystical, or metaphysical systems for dealing with these issues, and in modern times or in secular settings, aesthetic, philosophical, and scientific works and systems also speak to this ensemble of human needs. Many of the most important and most enduring sets of symbol systems (e.g., those featured in the Catholic liturgy) represent crystallizations of key ideas and experiences that have evolved within these institutions.

Moreover, in each of these culturally devised systems, one can identify clear steps or stages of sophistication. One can be a novice in a religious system, in philosophy, or in the expressive arts; and one can advance to achieve journeyman or expert status. (In his *Journal,* the future Pope John XXIII chronicled years of painstaking training of his spiritual/existential facets [cf. Gardner, 1995, chap. 9].) The greater the premium placed by a society on a particular vehicle of existential exploration and expression, the more highly delineated are the steps en route to excellence. And there should be widespread consensus in most cases about the level of sophistication displayed by a learner, an apprentice, or a committed student. Such assessments may go well beyond the cognitive to include aspects of social, moral, or emotional existence, but that eclecticism can be equally true when one ponders the evolution of a musician, a poet, or even a scientist.

A particularly intriguing set of questions surround the identification, in the first years of life, of the future Dalai Lama (and of other lamas). If one does not believe in reincarnation, one must choose between the hypothesis that this individual is unusually gifted in the spiritual/existential sphere while a young child or that his early identification (on whatever dimension) leads to a self-fulfilling prophecy (cf. Coles, 1990). According to a recent journalistic account, a candidate lama proves his mettle by choosing correctly those articles that belonged to the recently deceased lama; success comes about because the lama can draw on memories of his earlier incarnation ("Tibetans," 1995). A more secular hypothesis is that the future lama may stand out because of his capacity to discern certain patterns in the environment—a vestige of natural, rather than supernatural, intelligence. A better marker for later existential excellence might be an early-emerging concern for cosmic issues of the sort reported in the childhoods of future religious leaders like Gandhi and of several future physicists (Csikszentmihalyi, 1996).

When one moves to the more biologically tinged facets of existential knowledge, it proves less straightforward to lay out and evaluate the evidence. Although hints of ritualistic and symbolic experiences emerge in higher primates and in the precursors of modern humans (like the Neanderthal who marks a grave with flowers), explicit existential concerns probably gain ascendancy in the Stone Age. Only at this point in evolution do human beings within a culture possess a brain capable of considering the cosmological issues central to existential intelligence. Indeed, one could go so far as to suggest that one major cognizing activity in early humans was a grappling with these existential issues and that much of early artwork, dance, myth, and drama dealt implicitly or explicitly with cosmic themes and concerns (Burkert, 1995).

Only with the advent of formal religions and with the birth of systematic philosophy did there come to exist direct linguistic-propositional accounts of the existential realm. (Myths and drama are better thought of as implicit investigations of the existential.) Like the ability to use language, **existential capacity** is a distinctive trait of humans, a domain that separates us from other species. We may link its emergence to a conscious sense of finite space and irreversible time, two promising loci for stimulating imaginative explorations of transcendental spheres, or perhaps consciousness in its fuller senses presuppose a concern with existential issues (Havelock, 1963; Jaynes, 1974).

To my knowledge, evidence with respect to the physiological concomitants of knowledge about cosmic issues is scant to nonexistent. The most suggestive evidence may come from individuals with temporal lobe epilepsy, who exhibit a predictable set of symptoms, including hyperreligiosity. Such individuals attach the greatest importance to the most minute objects and experiences, often using them as points of departure for the elaboration of extended introspective diary entries or flights of spiritual fancy (Bear, Freeman, Schiff, & Greenberg, 1985; Geschwind, 1977; La Plante, 1993). It is widely believed that certain artists, such as Vincent Van Gogh and Fyodor Dostoevsky, suffered from temporal lobe epilepsy; these creators were able to channel their symptoms and pain into effective works of art. Of course, such a disease state is not necessary for creative work, although it may incline such work toward more spiritual concerns. The contemporary Polish American author Milosz (1995) describes a poet as "the one who flies above the earth and looks at it from above but at the same time sees it in every detail" (p. 40).

I should note, parenthetically, the growing body of evidence relevant to the phenomenal aspects of spiritual/religious concerns. Relevant evidence emerges from both naturally occurring and artificially induced sources. When an individual undergoes tremendous pain—be it physical, psychic, or both—the individual feels estranged from her or his habitual world. There is acute pressure to go beyond the usual categories of experience, to focus one's attention anew (perhaps beyond bodily pain altogether), to reevaluate one's relation to the external and the psychic worlds (James, 1902; Jung, 1958). Thoughts about existential issues may well have evolved as responses to necessarily occurring pain, perhaps as a way of reducing pain or better equipping individuals to cope with it. It is thus at least imaginable that ultimate concerns have some adaptive significance (Wilson, 1975, 1978).

Not surprisingly, individuals have learned how to re-create these transcendent phenomenal experiences even in the absence of the stimulus of pain. Various drugs, ranging from the relatively benign to the unambiguously pernicious, can be ingested. Religious states may also re-create these experiences, and those mystics and gurus who can control their psychic states are able, voluntarily, to enter the realm of the transcendent. The attainment of heightened attention, as in flow states, is also within at least partial control of the experiencer (Csikszentmihalyi, 1990). Clearly, certain brain centers and neural transmitters are mobilized in these states, whether they are induced by the ingestion of substances or by a control of the will (Ornstein, 1973).

The final line of evidence, gleaned from psychological investigations, presents a mixed picture. Some inventories of personality include dimensions of religiosity or spirituality, and these instruments yield consistency in individuals' scores; indeed, even identical twins reared apart show a strong link in degree of religiosity, thereby suggesting a possible heritable component in this capacity (Bouchard, 1990). Yet, it remains unclear just what is being probed by such instruments and whether self-report is a reliable index of existential intelligence. So far as I know, no attempts have been made to relate psychometric intelligence to the capacity or inclination to activate existential intelligence, although the popularity of the movie *Forrest Gump* suggests a conviction in the folk mind that these two capacities are remote from, if not antithetical to, one another.

Perhaps surprisingly, existential intelligence scores reasonably well on the eight criteria; a stripped-down version of spiritual intelligence eliminates some of the more problematic aspects that might otherwise have invalidated the quest. Empirical psychological evidence is sparse so far but certainly does not invalidate the construct. It may seem, then, that I have backed myself into an analytic corner. If narrowly defined, that variety of spiritual intelligence here termed "existential" may well be admissible; more broadly defined, spiritual intelligence does not permit such a judgment.

A PERSONAL PERSPECTIVE ON SPIRITUAL INTELLIGENCE

Let me address this conundrum from another, more personal level. Earlier, I indicated that I feel no personal involvement in the realm of spirituality. I do not have a religious identity (although I have a cultural identity) as a Jewish person. And I am as much frightened as I am intrigued by individuals who see themselves (or who are seen by others) as spiritual individuals. I fear the strangeness of the beliefs to which they may subscribe, and I fear the influence, à la Jim Jones or David Koresh, that they may exert on others (Cohn, 1961; Storr, 1996).

Yet, in one sphere of my life, I undergo some experiences that individuals claim to have when they are engaged in spiritual matters. That is the realm of music—particularly the experiences of listening to and performing certain kinds of music. At such times, I lose track of the usual mundane concerns, alter my perceptions of space and time, and at least occasionally feel in touch with issues of cosmic import. In my own case, these issues are not readily defined in terms of natural objects (mountains, seas) or in terms of specific cosmological issues (meaning of life or death)—kinds of associations often mentioned by music lovers and by certain composers, such as Beethoven and Mahler (Rothstein, 1995). But at the very least, I feel that I am encountering the formal aspects of these realms of existence and that I am enriched, ennobled, and humbled by the encounter (Langer, 1942). I have similar, though less acute, reactions when I come into contact with certain works of visual art and architecture, with certain powerful poems and dramas. And, switching realms, I undergo some of these experiences when in contact with persons whom I love, particularly at times of marked elation or sadness.

Whether I speak here of spiritual or existential intelligences entails a semantic judgment. I could say that my musical or linguistic or artistic intelligences have been stimulated and that one consequence of this stimulation is a heightened sensitivity to issues of the cosmos—just as I might be stimulated to hurt someone or to devote my savings to a charitable cause. I could say that I am having a strong emotional reaction to a work. In such cases, I would not invoke the term *spiritual* or *existential intelligence.* But I could with equal justification decide that I am exercising my spiritual or existential intelligence, just as I would if I were working with a guru, but that in my case this form of intelligence is stimulated by intense engagements with art objects or with people whom I love. Those, in other words, are the **triggering**

events—the "affecting" objects and experiences in the world that activate an existential intelligence. Such a point of view is powerfully conveyed in a passage from Marcel Proust (1981, III):

> It is inconceivable that a piece of sculpture or a piece of music which gives us an emotion that we feel to be more exalted more pure, more true, does not correspond to some definite spiritual reality, or life would be meaningless. (pp. 380–381)

CONCLUSION: A FINAL STOCK-TAKING

In this chapter, I have considered whether there are intelligences beyond the original seven posited in *Frames of Mind*. By recognizing the "naturalist intelligence," I have answered this question in the affirmative. In the process, I have opened a Pandora's box. The number seven is no longer sacred; if there are eight intelligences, there can clearly be more.

Taking on a more vexing issue, I have considered the question of a ninth, "spiritual" or "existential intelligence." I recognized many of the problematic aspects of even considering the spiritual as eligible for inclusion in the intellect; many would object, perhaps rightly, that the spiritual is divorced from the cognitive and that to collapse these two realms involves a "category error." My analysis has suggested that it makes sense to disaggregate at least three senses of the spiritual: (a) a concern with certain cosmic contents, (b) the achievement of certain states of consciousness, and (c) the exerting of profound effects on other individuals. Through the exercise of invoking my eight criteria, I have discovered—somewhat to my surprise—that a stripped-down version of spirituality (an "existential" version, if you will) qualifies reasonably well as an intelligence.

Despite the attractiveness of a ninth intelligence, I do not intend at present to add existential intelligence to the list. I find the phenomenon perplexing enough, and the distance from the other intelligences great enough, to dictate prudence. At most, I am willing, Fellini-style, to joke about "8½ intelligences." Putting it in the vernacular, I ask readers to "stay tuned for further developments."

I close on a homiletic note. Although I am responsible for developing the idea of multiple intelligences, I cannot claim exclusive ownership of the concept. As in the case of the original list of intelligences, readers are welcome to examine my criteria and to reach their own conclusions concerning whether or not natural, spiritual, or existential intelligences "truly" qualify. I must stress the importance of honoring the set of criteria. If decisions about intelligences are to be taken seriously, then they must depend on a fair-minded examination of the available data—an undertaking that was begun in *Frames of Mind* and one that I have once again pursued here.

ACKNOWLEDGMENTS

Educating me about the dimensions of spirituality has not been an easy task. For helpful comments on earlier drafts of this chapter, I thank Thomas Armstrong, Eric Blumenson, Mihaly Csikszentmihalyi, Antonio Damasio, William Damon, Reuven Feuerstein, Daniel Goleman, Tom Hoerr, Mindy Kornhaber, Paul Kaufman, Jonathan Levy, Tanya Luhrmann, Bob Ornstein, Courtney Ross, Mark Turner, Julie Viens, Edward O. Wilson, and Ellen Winner. I owe special thanks to Jeffrey Kane, who not only commissioned this chapter but also helped me think through several major issues; I suspect that, over time, I may move closer to the position that he holds.

REFERENCES

Bear, D., Freeman, R., Schiff, D., & Greenberg, M. (1985). Interietal behavioral changes in patients with temporal lobe epilepsy. *American Psychiatric Association Annual Review, 4.*

Berlin, B. (1992). *Ethnobiological classification: Principles of categorization of plants and animals in traditional societies*. Princeton, NJ: Princeton University Press.

Bloom, H. (1995). *The Lucifer paradox*. Boston: Atlantic Monthly Press.

Bouchard, T. (1990). Sources of human psychological differences: The Minnesota study of twins reared apart. *Science, 250,* 223–228.

Browne, E. J. (1995). *Charles Darwin: A biography: Vol. 1. Voyaging*. New York: Knopf.

Buber, M. (1970). *I and thou* (3rd ed.). New York: Scribners.

Burkert, W. (1995). *Creation of the sacred: Tracks of biology in early religions*. Cambridge, MA: Harvard University Press.

Caramazza, A., Hillis, A., Leek, E. C., & Miozzo, M. (1994). The organization of lexical knowledge in the brain: Evidence from category- and modality-specific deficits. In L. Hirschfield & S. Gelman (Eds.), *Mapping the mind* (pp. 68–84). New York: Cambridge University Press.

Carey, S. (1985). *Conceptual change in childhood*. Cambridge: MIT Press.

Chi, M. (1981). Knowledge development and memory performance. In M. Friedman, J. P. Das, & N. O'Connor (Eds.), *Intelligence and learning.* New York: Plenum.

Cohn, N. (1961). *The pursuit of the millennium: Revolutionary messianism in medieval and Reformation Europe and its bearing on modern totalitarian movements* (2nd ed.). New York: Harper.

Coles, R. (1990). *The spiritual life of children*. Boston: Houghton-Mifflin.

Csikszentmihalyi, M. (1990). *Flow*. New York: HarperCollins.

Csikszentmihalyi, M. (1996). *Creativity*. New York: HarperCollins.

Damasio, A. (1994). *Descartes' error*. New York: Putnam.

Damasio, A., & Damasio, H. (1995, June). *Recent trends in cognitive neuroscience.* Lecture presented at the Center for Advanced Study in the Behavioral Sciences.

Edelman, G. M. (1995). *The wordless metaphor: Visual art and the brain.* New York: Witney Museum.

Gardner, H. (1993a). *Frames of mind (10th ed.).* New York: BasicBooks.

Gardner, H. (1993b). *Multiple intelligences: The theory in practice*. New York: BasicBooks.

Gardner, H. (1995). *Leading minds: An anatomy of leadership*. New York: BasicBooks.

Gerth, H. H., & Mills, C. W. (1958). *From Max Weber: Essays in sociology*. New York: Oxford University Press.

Geschwind, N. (1977). Behavioral change in temporal lobe epilepsy. *Archives of Neurology, 34*, 453.

Goleman, D. (1988). *The meditative mind*. New York: Putnam.

Gould, S. J. (1981). *The mismeasure of man*. New York: Norton.

Gross, C. B. (1973). Visual functions of infero-temporal cortex. In R. Jung (Ed.), *Handbook of sensory physiology* (VII/3, pp. 451–482). New York: Springer Verlag.

Guilford, J. P. (1967). *The structure of intelligence*. New York: McGraw-Hill.

Havelock, E. (1963). *Preface to Plato*. Cambridge, MA: Harvard University Press.

Herrnstein, R., & Loveland, D. (1964). Natural concepts in pigeons. *Journal of Experimental Psychology: Animal Behavior Processes, 2*, 285–302.

Herrnstein, R. J., & Murray, C. (1994). *The bell curve*. New York: Free Press.

James, W. (1902). *The varieties of religious experience*. New York: Longmans, Green.

Jaynes, J. (1974). *The origins of consciousness in the breakdown of the bicameral mind*. Boston: Houghton-Mifflin.

Jung, C. G. (1958). *Psyche and symbol*. New York: Doubleday Anchor.

Keil, F. (1994). The birth and nurturance of concepts by domains: The origins of concepts of living things. In L. Hirschfield & S. A. Gelman (Eds.), *Mapping the mind* (pp. 234–254). New York: Cambridge University Press.

Konorski, J. (1967). *Integrative activity of the brain: An interdisciplinary approach*. Chicago: University of Chicago Press.

Langer, S. (1942). *Philosophy in a new key*. Cambridge, MA: Harvard University Press.

La Plante, E. (1993). *Seized*. New York: HarperCollins.

Martin, A., Wiggs, C. L., Ungerleider, L. G., & Haxby, J. W. (1996). Neural correlates of category-specific knowledge. *Nature, 379,* 649–652.

Milosz, C. (1995, March 23). *New York Review of Books*, p. 40.

Mishlove, J. (1994). *Roots of consciousness*. Tulsa, OK: Council Oaks Books.

Neisser, U. (1976). *Cognition and reality*. San Francisco: Freeman.

Nielsen, J. (1946). *Agnosia, apraxia, and aphasia: Their value in cerebral localization*. New York: Hoeber.

Ornstein, R. (1973). *The nature of human consciousness*. San Francisco: Freeman.

Proust, M. (1981). *Remembrance of things past* (C. K. Scott Moncrieff, T. Kilmartin, & A. Mayor, Trans., Vol. 3, pp. 380–381). New York: Random House.

Roe, A. (1953). *The making of a scientist*. New York: Dodd, Mead.

Rosch, E., Mervis, C., Gray, W., Johnson, D., & Bayes-Braem, P. (1976). Basic objects in natural categories. *Cognitive Psychology, 8,* 382–439.

Rothstein, E. (1995, May 6). Mahler's eight performed "Calling out to the heavens, fortissimo" *New York Times*, p. 13.

Sternberg, R. J. (1982). *Handbook of human intelligence*. New York: Cambridge University Press.

Storr, A. (1996). *Feet of clay*. New York: Free Press.

Taylor, C., & Barron, F. (1963). *Scientific creativity: Its recognition and development*. New York: Wiley.

Thurstone, L. L. (1938). Primary mental abilities. *Psychometric Monographs, No. 1*. Chicago: University of Chicago Press.

Tibetans call boy reincarnation of No. 2 monk. (1995, May 14). *New York Times,* p. A4.

Warrington, E., & Shallice, T. (1984). Category-specific semantic impairments. *Brain, 107,* 829–854.

Wasserman, E. (1994). The conceptual abilities of pigeons. *American Scientist, 83*, 246–255.

Wilson, E. O. (1975). *Sociobiology*. Cambridge, MA: Harvard University Press.

Wilson, E. O. (1978). *On human nature*. Cambridge, MA: Harvard University Press.

Wilson, E. O. (1984). *Biophilia*. Cambridge, MA: Harvard University Press.

Wilson, E. O. (1994). *Naturalist*. Washington, DC: Island Press.

Yoon, C. K. (1995, February 7). Getting the feel of a long-ago arms race. *New York Times,* Science, B5, p. 8.

Zuckerman, H. (1977). *Scientific elites*. New York: Free Press.

BIOGRAPHY

HOWARD GARDNER is Professor of Education and Adjunct Professor of Psychology at Harvard University; Adjunct Professor of Neurology at the Boston University School of Medicine; and Codirector of Harvard Project Zero. The recipient of many honors, including a MacArthur Prize Fellowship, Gardner is the author of 15 books (the newest being *Extraordinary Minds* [1997]) and several hundred articles. In 1990, he was the first American to receive the University of Louisville's Grawemeyer Award in education. He is best known in educational circles for his *theory of multiple intelligences,* a critique of the notion that there exists but a single human intelligence that can be assessed by standard psychometric instruments. During the past decade, he and colleagues at Project Zero have been working on the design of performance-based assessments, education for understanding, and the use of multiple intelligences to achieve more personalized curriculum, instruction, and assessment. Most recently, he has been carrying out case studies of exemplary creators and leaders; he and colleagues have launched an investigation of the relationship between cutting-edge work in different domains and a sense of social responsibility.

IN PRAISE OF AMBIGUITY

MARY CATHERINE BATESON

INTRODUCTION

In this chapter, derived from a lecture, Mary Catherine Bateson brings an anthropological perspective to bear on the question, What more is there to human thinking than information processing? Her focus is on language, not as a form of symbolic representation, but as a form of communication from person to person. Although the words *communicate* and *community* are common in our everyday vocabulary, it is rare that we think of communication as a form of communion, as a foundation of community both intimate and extended.

In this context, words do not merely represent objects, events, or relationships. Beyond the explicit meanings of words, language itself creates possibilities for common ground. This potential can be understood more in a spirit of words than in their dictionary definitions. As Bateson so poignantly concludes, "Very little discussion of weather has anything to do with meteorology." There is a vital social element in language. Bateson explains that much of the meaning of language is conveyed, not through the precision of language, but through participation in its levels of ambiguity.

The ambiguity of language provides a place for the imagination to roam, to perceive patterns and relationships in the world, to find meanings in words and ideas that perhaps were never understood or even imagined when first uttered as words. Bateson, for example, explains that the Constitution of the United States, because of its ambiguity, is a living document in which we can discover new implications and achieve new understandings in the face of unprecedented questions. Understanding the Constitution requires more than a literal understanding of the words. It requires a recognition of the spirit and its role in creating community. Similarly, the words we use in everyday life are laced with ambiguity, and our capacity to understand them requires us to participate in community.

Education has long focused on "getting the right answer," acquiring given content and filling in the proper circle to demonstrate that some explicit fact has found its way into a student's head. Today, the concept of learning has expanded to include critical thinking and problem solving as desired learning outcomes. Although such levels of knowledge and thinking have undeniable value, they do convey the importance of the constant re-creation of meaning in community. We often rely on the precision of language to convey ideas, but Bateson maintains that often the process of communicating is itself the critical factor. Furthermore, the ideas conveyed often have implications discovered only as we play them out in the course of social life. Schools can serve as learning communities where children can participate in discovering the implication and meaning of ideas far beyond the choices available on a multiple-choice test.

—*Jeffrey Kane*

Ah, what a dusty answer gets the soul
When hot for certainties in this our life.

GEORGE MEREDITH, *MODERN LOVE,* L.50

If education is to prepare for life rather than mislead, it is important not to project the expectation of certainty or to promise unambiguous answers, or even the notion that the most important communication between human beings, whether in the classroom or elsewhere, is the transmission of objective information. Preparation for life is preparation for a long meander through uncertainty, for working with partial clues and rough approximations, for skillful guessing and zestful improvisation. Even those facts that seem clear and unambiguous unfold into unexpected implications—and are sometimes contradicted by new findings.

The human capacity to draw pattern from confusion underlies both empirical investigation and imaginative creation. It allows us to find our way, day by day, through an environment in which there is both constancy and variation, and over time has given us both science and astrology, different ways of seeking pattern in the stars. It is fundamental to the ability to perceive and learn and underlies ongoing adaptation most effectively if the discovery of regularity goes with flexibility about conclusions. This is especially true in a time of rapid change and cultural diversity. Patterns that once seemed clear may be blurred or reversed or overlaid with complexity; yet it is still necessary to make decisions and act upon them despite uncertainty and ambiguity.

As an anthropologist, I find that the experience of crossing from one culture into another throws me into situations where I must act on ambiguous cues (Bateson, 1994a), just as children must, just as adults must often. In the field, you feel much like a small child. You have to be willing to be incompetent, to make absurd mistakes on matters that are obvious to everyone around you. More generally, you have to tolerate a great deal of ambiguity, responding to and using words and gestures whose meanings are unclear, when the responses of others seem highly unpredictable. Much of the literature on culture contact emphasizes ways to minimize the stress this involves and to avoid dangerous or offensive errors; but there is a positive side as well to learning to live with the ambiguity.

I want to approach the issue of ambiguity through a story about the first year of my marriage, itself a cross-cultural learning experience. My husband was born in Syria and is ethnically Armenian. When I first met him, I looked up *Armenia* in an encyclopedia because the only association I had with Armenia at that time was the phrase "poor starving Armenians." Later, after reading Armenian history and studying the language (and the cuisine), I still had a lot to learn when we got married. As a new bride moving into an unfamiliar culture, I was in many ways facing it as a child must, trying to figure it out as I went along. We went to visit my husband's parents in Beirut on our honeymoon. It was the custom in this Protestant household to say grace in unison before meals, and although it is not easy to pry the words apart when everyone is speaking together and mumbling, I listened carefully and joined in. After our honeymoon, when we came back to Cambridge and set up in an apartment, this became a ritual for us as well, saying grace together in Armenian before dinner.

After a full year, I discovered that I had misconstrued the words we said every day. I had thought that the words of one line of this little prayer were "Give us your love," when in fact what the words said were "Give us contented hearts." I had been saying it wrong for a year, but the difference in pronunciation was small and nobody had noticed. When we had dinner guests, I would translate, but my husband never listened because he believed he knew what I was saying. The important thing is that my incomplete understanding was adequate for functioning, just as Ptolemaic astronomy is a pretty adequate basis for navigation.

Notice that my analysis of the words of the prayer was plausible because, as a literate adult who had grown up in a related religious culture, I know the kind of thing people are likely to pray for. If the gap of ignorance had been greater, my analysis might have been more remote. As someone pointed out, if I had thought that the words of the grace were "Give us your wheelbarrow," I might have turned to my husband and asked a question. We all share the human tendency to make sense of jumbled or incomplete information, and it is precisely when we think we understand that we *stop* asking questions.

Perhaps it was this confusion that drew my attention to that line of prayer because, for some 35 years since then, I have been trying to figure out what it would mean to have a "contented heart." The phrase has meant different things to me at different times, both a hopeless aspiration and an easy familiarity. Sometimes it means something religious; sometimes it invokes family or cultural continuity. An Armenian woman told me that as a child she had asked her mother what it meant to have a "contented heart" and had been told, "That's when your liver isn't on fire (with envy)." In fact, this little prayer keeps changing its meaning on me, no longer because of a mishearing, but because of layers of ambiguity about the nature and shared basis of contentment that I have not resolved.

Children will accept a great deal of weirdness from grown-ups, so almost anything may be plausible. Consider the example of that totem animal of all children taken to Protestant evangelical services, Gladly, a bear who happens to be cross-eyed. The child doesn't turn to the mother and say, "Why are you singing about a bear?" Indeed, the notion of happily carrying a cross constructed for death by torture is at least equally puzzling. From a child's point of view, grown-ups are quite capable of asking God for a wheelbarrow, and following that model, children feel free to ask God for tricycles and pocketknives, which is theologically equally problematic.

Once I was with Iranian friends in the holy city of Qom, when they decided to visit the shrine of Maasume, the sister of Imam Reza, which has made Qom a major pilgrimage center, exporting mullahs from its theological schools and importing the bodies of those who wish to be buried there. Although I am not a Muslim, I was veiled, so I dared to enter the shrine with my friends and sat on the carpet with my veil pulled forward while they prayed. A shabby old woman came over to me, tapping on my shoulder and mumbling, but I ignored her, and my friends tried not to giggle. After they had finished their prayers, one of them turned to me and said, in Persian, "You should ask the lady for whatever you want." I was ready to follow instructions, but for a moment I floundered in confusion: Was the old woman not a beggar as I had concluded? Or, even as a beggar, were her prayers believed to be especially efficacious? In fact, the "lady" (*banom*) in question was Maasume. But to ask a deeper question, would it be appropriate to ask Maasume for a tricycle or a pocketknife?

A relationship exists between two kinds of incomplete understanding. First, we have what seems a rather simple kind of error: I listened to the Armenian prayer and interpreted it incorrectly. The child does the same for the evangelical hymn "Gladly the Cross I'd Bear." But then we have examples, not of error in a simple sense, but of words that have a potential depth of meaning that is bound to change through the life cycle. Even when I knew who the "lady" was, even when the child grasps that a cross is to be borne, understanding remains incomplete, leaving room for growth through the ambiguity.

How often do we speak or read words that will change their meaning over time? Consider the words of wedding vows. You don't know what you're doing when you get into it, right? More important, the whole system depends on that incomplete understanding. "I do" is necessarily a dusty answer.

What is important for educators here is that the experience of participation in spite of the first kind of incomplete understanding may be supportive in the encounter with the second kind. Avoiding the first level of ambiguity with careful lesson plans may subvert a later potential for growth. What did I do with that prayer? I did what human beings always do: I was getting a muddled input that I analyzed and made sense of in a plausible kind of way that allowed me to participate and left an opening for later reflection. The capacity to participate is more important than, and often prior to, understanding.

In general, I believe, participation precedes learning, not vice versa, and ambiguity potentiates learning. This is one of the great areas where our educational systems need to be reshaped, because they tend to be based on the premise that all problems have solutions and all questions have answers, generally a single answer, that can be marked right or wrong on an exam and that school prepares the child for participation by teaching those answers. Whereas you can look at infants having conversations before they can speak a recognizable word of adult language and see that it works the other way around (Bateson, 1975). The participation precedes the knowledge.

We live in a technologically advanced mass society where numbers are more and more important. As weapons become more powerful, populations denser, and information more available, the demand for specificity and predictability increases. Nevertheless, in the back of our minds we all recognize that the imagination is nourished by vagueness and ambiguity and that human emotions do not work by the numbers. Approaching marriage with a prenuptial agreement about property has many advantages, but negotiating such an agreement does not build the relationship and may damage it. Civilization depends not only on precise technology but also on play and poetry and humor, all of them shot through with ambiguity.

At an institutional level, the effort to make behavior more and more predictable by specification and decontextualization is pervasive. Education is only one of many areas in our society that undermine the capacity to work with and tolerate ambiguity. Accountants, time and motion experts, lawyers . . . these are all devotees of disambiguation.

Sometimes, when perfect precision is not possible, choices between different kinds of ambiguity are possible. Different ways of coding measurements—digital and analog—open the door to different kinds of imprecision. With any analog instrument, a ruler, a traditional watch, a mercury thermometer, the reading of any measurement is imprecise (G. Bateson, 1972; Sebeok, 1962). Potentially, another decimal place of further precision could always be added, if the instrument were finer, but notice that the errors tend to be at the right end of the readings you record. Your error is going to be by, let us say, 1⁄100 of an inch rather than by 100 inches. The errors cluster where they matter least.

If you glance at an analog dial on a watch, which uses distances to represent the passage of time, your errors will be of that same order—"Just about quarter of 8"—not precise. If you tell time by the sun, your errors may be greater but they are of the same kind; they are "more-or-less" mistakes, the difference, say, between 2 and 3 in the afternoon, but you do know, accurately, that it is early afternoon. Similarly, a slide rule is an extraordinarily elegant analog computer that allows you to compute by adding and subtracting real lengths, always with an element of approximation. One key in using a slide rule is deciding how many places (toward the right) you can be accurate to and legitimately cite.

By contrast, in totting up a column of expenses on a calculator, if your finger does not slip, your answer is precise, but alas, you are just as likely to slip in the thousands as in the pennies. This is a characteristic of many digital processes: that errors are not sorted in terms of significance. Answers are either correct or incorrect. Thus, it is reasonable and usually sufficient to say that it is roughly half past 6, but it is not reasonable to say that your checkbook almost balances: Either it does or it doesn't, and an error of 32¢ could mask another error of $32 or $3,200. Error can occur in any digit on a display, as many people have discovered when they received erroneous bills with that kind of error.

A significant personality difference may exist between those who go digital and those who prefer the old analog watches or even stay with the sun or with the sundial, which all have a certain congruence. The kind of information that comes from a digital dial is different, and the kinds of errors you are liable to encounter are different. You always have some variation with analog readings, and you learn to accept it and take it into account. You live with an open mind about whether you and others have things exactly right. The digital reading offers the possibility of precision, but when the precision fails, you may be unprepared. Interestingly enough, the habit of reaching ballpark approximations is an important protection—for instance, in restaurants. Those who depend on digital processes tend to take numbers literally, with no sense of approximate plausibility even when they are cited by politicians.

Once upon a time, all engineers had slide rules. Now they have calculators, and so does everyone else, so few acquire the skill of managing approximations. As the world becomes more digital, the properties of digital calculations require that things be gotten right, rather than letting us, without having gotten it perfectly, ease up on precision and work with plausible approximations. This is an important and dangerous change because, in the brave new digital world, with its premium on precision, the costs of carelessness tend to be very high.

The English, rather endearingly, sometimes call computers TOMs, which stands for Totally Obedient Morons—totally obedient, but without judgment or imagination and demanding totally unambiguous commands. In conversation with human beings, especially familiar and beloved human beings, a lot of ambiguity is tolerable. I used to have conversations with my mother wherein I would say, "Look, what was the name of that woman, I remember something about sunshine and morning glories?" And she'd say to me, "Oh, yes, that was Georgianna, and she had a morning glory pattern on the curtains in her guest room when we stayed there." That is really a very effective piece of communication—the kind of communication that family members have with each other, that just gets you nowhere with a computer. It requires, besides a great deal of trust and shared experience, a pattern of heuristics, a shared pattern of search and discovery.

Human beings tend to find things because they know where to look. Well into the 1990s, the best human chess players were still able to defeat the most powerful computers. When a computer is programmed to play chess, it checks and compares thousands of alternative moves, far more than any human chess master could explore. A master chess player only thinks through a subset of the possible sequences, knowing, however, what kind of move is likely to be helpful. Skill lies in knowing which sequences to check, by a process that Herbert Simon called "selective heuristics" (1969, 1972).

Oddly enough, one advantage of not being able to check all the alternatives is that chess is endlessly fascinating and continues to be a form of play. Chess would be trivial if the players could process enough alternative sequences to make it determinate, which is why grown-ups lose interest in tic-tac-toe. Just as there is a lot of ambiguity in religion, there is also a lot of ambiguity in play.

During the campaign for the 1996 GOP presidential nomination, Steve Forbes used a television ad in which he held up a copy of the Constitution, then a copy of the Bible, and then the Federal Tax Code—a great fat manual, much longer than the Bible, whereas the Constitution is just a few pages. Forbes attributed the length of the tax code to the presence of deliberate loopholes, granted as political favors, yet all legislation today is accompanied by massive and detailed regulations designed to be fully specific and unambiguous.

The strength of the Constitution, however, is that it is, in many ways, ambiguous. We know perfectly well that we see meanings there today of which the framers were unaware. The Declaration of Independence spoke of equality, but all that the signers meant was white men over 21. Today, we mean all citizens, of whatever race or sex. Until after the Vietnam War, young men were drafted at 18 but could not vote until they were 21. They could be sent overseas to die in warfare and yet had no right to express a view. At a certain point, it dawned on the people of this country that this was out of line with the underlying wisdom of the framers, a particularly pernicious kind of taxation without representation. An evolving understanding is, in some sense, implicit in the words of the Constitution even if the people who wrote those words did not themselves fully understand them.

What would happen if we tried to draft a new Constitution today? Today's style would be to strive for something watertight, fully explicit, leaving nothing to the imagination, something that could be understood in only one way, covering every contingency. This would be an inert and tedious document, one that would not grow, one that would not encourage understanding to deepen. The words that are the most powerful for human beings are words like "Give us contented hearts," that set you wondering over decades what they might mean. In the famous Serenity Prayer used by Alcoholics Anonymous, the difference between what can be changed and what cannot is never defined, so the prayer offers, not a decision rule, but a challenge to discover new ways to adapt.

If we wanted to write a Constitution today, I very much doubt that it could be done except perhaps by a mixture of poets and biologists who understood the fact that as long as an organism is alive, the process of development and adaptation is ongoing. Similarly, we are unlikely to progress to any kind of definitive world order by legislation, by formal decision making and voting. (Bateson, 1994b). If you consider what it takes to reach a disarmament treaty, limiting just a single type of weapon, and the preoccupation with checking and double-checking and triple-checking, it becomes clear that global confederation or cooperation cannot be achieved by negotiations. This is not to say that we should not chip away at it or that it is not particularly important in some areas of trade or disarmament. Yet in such negotiations, the major casualty is trust, and every step reveals the lack of trust.

Ping-Pong, in contrast, and artistic exchange and tourism provide a way to work implicitly toward trust. Trust was generated when I sat at the table with my new in-laws, missaying a prayer but participating. Often what matters is the establishment of areas of vague agreement and nonspecific relationship that can be used as the context—the channel—for transmitting other kinds of things. Another way of saying this is that the communication that establishes relationships is, for mammals like us rather than computers, analog communication. One characteristic of the peace process in the Middle East or in the Balkans has been that whereas a few items are very clearly specified, others, such as the long-term status of Jerusalem, are left vague. This means that the process may break down at a later stage, but it allows joint participation in early stages, working side by side, rubbing along and dealing with frictions and misunderstandings, which may engender trust.

We increasingly tend to think that speech exists for the purpose of conveying unambiguous and verifiable information about some set of facts or circumstances, that speech is primarily referential. Not true. This referential function is secondary to the establishment of relationship. If we are walking down the road outside and we both simultaneously feel large drops of water on our heads and I turn to the person next to me and say, "It's raining," and she says, "Yeah, I guess it is!" am I informing her of the fact that it has begun to rain? And is she confirming this information I gave her? No! Something quite different is taking place. Our words appear to be about the rain, but they actually mean something like the following: "You and I are in the same place and are in communication with each other." I can convey an even stronger connection by rolling my eyes and saying, "Great weather!"

Vast sums are spent to increase the technical capacity to predict the weather. Whether or not it rains on a given day can affect election results and sales, power consumption and transport. But most talk about the weather is not meteorological and would be far less useful in human relations if every statement came equipped with a statistical probability. If I say, "How are you today?" am I seeking medical information? Usually not even though precise reporting and diagnosis are important in clinical practice. Even in a hospital, a patient may reply with, "Pretty good, Doc," not because he is healthy but because he likes the doctor.

I recently heard of an ethnographic paper by a Japanese graduate student asserting that when Americans ask "How are you?" they don't want the details of health and disease. Correct. But of course they do want information, usually of quite a different kind: Are you glad to see me? Are we still friends? Even, sometimes, how are you?

Well, but these are the trivial cases. The fact is that a very large proportion of our conversation has a small element of reference and verifiable fact and a large element of creating relationship, of establishing communion. When that is achieved, the rest can be vague or erroneous or self-contradictory. This kind of communication, that says, "The channel is open," is called *phatic* (Buhler, 1934; Sebeok, 1962). As soon as you start looking for it, you see it everywhere. A pilot who is coming in for a landing has her radio open to the tower, and very often the conversation seems empty for many minutes—"Ah, do you read me?" "Roger, yes I read you, yes, I hear you . . . all clear, keep on coming . . ." Why bother with that stuff? Because without it, you would not know that the radio channel was open and available for an emergency. At that point, precise information might become important.

We do all this back-and-forthing as a way of indicating that we are in touch, and it is an essential skill. If I tell you I happen to know that the mayor is having an affair with the newspaper editor, am I really giving you information about the mayor? Or am I observing something about my willingness to gossip with you? We may share disapproval, or we may share glee, and we share the satisfaction of having inside dope. You may well have heard that piece of gossip already, but there's still a gain in sharing it. Even software designers program computers to say Hello, to make the user feel comfortable, not because the computer needs it.

A great deal of discussion today asserts the loss of very basic social patterns. We wonder about the fate of the family, about community, about friendship and loyalty. Perhaps the key loss is a sense of what communication is for or about. Relationships are built through touch and tone of voice and the satisfactions of maintaining a rhythm of low-key conversation, of small talk and chitchat. We live with the vast potential of language and with a framework of science and technology that allows us to convey massive amounts of highly precise information. But all of that depends on establishing a state of connection, of context and relationship, and these are even more important for learning. The sense of connection is much more likely to be created by shared participation than by precision. The sense of being "in touch" is created by actual touch, by eye contact and tone of voice, often by reiteration of the known and familiar rather than new information. My experience with the Armenian grace taught me (or perhaps retaught me) that interaction is more important than precise translation or vocabulary. You make what sense you can out of what you hear, but communion is what matters. And when communion is important, the insistence on precision may preclude it; when lawyers get involved, goodwill erodes.

We live in a period when we find ourselves forced into distrusting others and being distrusted, into feeling that we have to document everything, make everything checkable, accurate, referential, and unambiguous. We are preoccupied in this society with disambiguation, with overspecification of all the details.

Another loss is involved in the cultural shift away from a tolerance for ambiguity, and that is the loss of imagination, a loss of potentials for development and new understanding. What if a given question has no "correct answer" but only the vague intimation of one? Playing with the question and imagining possible answers is still valuable. If you consider the value of reading a newspaper or listening to radio, as opposed to watching television, the older media required more imagination because so much less detail was provided. The process of listening or reading is much more active than the process of watching television. In the same way, educators have long advocated simple toys rather than highly specialized ones: A slightly shaped wooden block with wheels can be a racing car or a police car; a vaguely human figure can be a princess or a soldier or an infant.

It is interesting to sort out the relationship between specificity and ambiguity in the worlds of commerce. Plenty of ambiguity does appear on television, particularly in commercials that might be accused of false claims if they were too explicit, but the ambiguity is designed to lead to predictable conclusions. Many of the best creative minds in the media design commercials to be stimulating to the imagination. Perfume commercials, for instance, cannot be explicit about scent, but hint instead at possible romance, and others suggest agonies of loss and loneliness for lack of the right deodorant or detergent. At the same time, sales often depend on specification: Just as children are urged to demand specialized and detailed dolls and models, there are now as many different deodorants as there are body parts with possible odors, five or six substances to be used in sequence in hair washing, and different cleansers for every part of the bathroom or kitchen.

Religion has a curious fluctuation as well. Various examples in this chapter are drawn from religious contexts, but religious teachers are not known for tolerance of ambiguity. Consider the blood spilled and the effort poured into making religious language "unambiguous"—to be sure that all the people are thinking and believing the same thing when they say the same words. Theologians labor and bicker to put together creeds and catechisms to be absolutely unambiguous and specific and to exclude heresy. But every congregation is full of people trying to give these words their own meanings, and maybe, maybe, the words are more powerful that way, more reliable guidelines for living in a changing world.

It is important to realize that neither analog nor digital coding and neither ambiguity nor disambiguation can be separated out as reflecting a "higher" capacity. Both occur in all cultures and throughout the biological world, in different proportions. It is true that the great majority of communication systems between animals other than humans are iconic and analogic rather than digital, but if we include genetic, neurological, and hormonal communication within the organism, both kinds occur and are essential to life. In a sense, the human use of symbols, including words, that are ambiguous because they have multiple meanings, is unique, but many other organisms have some capacity to respond to ambiguous information. Huston Smith (1989, pp. 186–189) quotes Lewis Thomas (1974, p. 111) as saying, "Ambiguity seems to be an essential, indispensable element for the transfer of information from one place to another by words, where matters of real importance are concerned." Smith goes on to connect this to the need for a sense of wonder and for the willingness to accept incomplete control in order to make commitments that are necessarily open-ended.

The effort to avoid ambiguity affects education in a whole variety of ways. For years, it has been standard to design reading primers using only words that children of a given age could be expected to already know, yet the most beloved children's books are full of totally strange, unintelligible words that demand new meanings and new imaginings: "O frabjous day!" The incomplete and shifting understanding makes reading (and rereading) books of that sort an adventure, with different mental pictures for children of different ages and adults as well. Should a lesson always be unambiguous, or should there be gaps that call for imagination? Should children ever be allowed to believe that they have fully understood a poem or a Shakespeare play or that they know the "causes of the civil war"? How often, when a piece of poetry is read in school, are children told, "This is what it means." They may even be told, implicitly or explicitly, "Now you have read *Hamlet,* and this is what it means." Yet no one knows what *Hamlet* means after a high school reading; it will go on unfolding into new layers of meaning as it is read or seen on stage again and again.

This is not just a matter of Great Works from the literary canon. Nursery rhymes, proverbs, and lines from popular songs acquire meaning at every hearing. Why not play with it? We do want, I think, children to have imagination; we do want them to have a capacity to trust; we do want them to discover new meanings that we have not yet seen . . . or do we just want them to be able to reproduce what we tell them? We want them to be free to make original discoveries and to make mistakes. When people try to construct their world so that there is no ambiguity in it, whether they are theologians and inquisitors or arms control negotiators or IRS regulation writers, they are choosing an arid, rigid way of being (Alliance of Artists' Communities, 1997).

We are suffering today from several related pathologies. What is most worrying about contemporary forms of fundamentalism is the declaration that ancient religious texts—most of which were written as poetry, story, or speculation—should be read (selectively) as if they were explicit and literally true. We are running into a related pathology in debates about the interpretation of the Constitution, with "strict constructionism" emerging as a political form of fundamentalism.

All too often, major enterprises are undertaken on the premise that perfect accuracy is possible, so any error or ambiguity is culpable and opens the door to lawsuits. Yet all of measurement is subject to limitations on accuracy and diagnosis, and treatment must always contain guesswork. A shift in how we handle information phases over into a change in fundamental human relationships, in ethics, and in how we organize all of our common ventures.

Anyone who wants to be an astronaut needs to realize that, at that level of complexity, casualties are going to occur. The *Challenger* disaster was followed by an investigation to find out where the mistake was so that it could be eliminated and blame meted out. That's fine—as far as it goes—provided we don't have the illusion it will never happen again. Other disasters will occur if human beings go up in space or build nuclear reactors. Human beings are not infallible, so we should not engage in activities where error is intolerable. Yet increasingly, we are demanding absolute perfection in performances under pressure of extreme stress and complexity.

The daily papers offer multiple examples of an emerging pattern of assumptions that deny the human necessity of ambiguity. When White House counsel Vincent Foster committed suicide, it seems clear that there was a lot of dither, grief, and confusion, that his colleagues were upset and did not do everything by the book, but the confusion seems to have been human rather than malicious. If every piece of evidence brought to a court in this country were scrutinized the way the evidence in the O. J. Simpson case was, we would stop believing that any police procedure can be trusted because it is impossible to be 100% accurate. There are going to be chinks in the chain of evidence, misunderstandings, and misreportings, arising from inefficiency rather than conspiracy. Of course, police procedures need to be criticized and improved, but they will never be perfect, so we must build procedures that allow for human fallibility and still allow us to move ahead—to, as they used to say, muddle through.

One cannot defer decisions until one has found the absolutely correct answer. One must act, get involved, commit. More and more Americans fail to realize that they have to support candidates with whom they do not entirely agree, who are only partially right, and who will learn in office and change their minds. We have to vote for people who are imperfect, people with whom we disagree less than with their rivals. Indeed, any politician with whom I agreed fully would probably be a disaster for this country, and that is probably true for most of us. All our politicians are compromise figures of one sort or another. But those who stay home and do not vote are evading the moral ambiguity of having to act in the world and take positions that are not black-and-white positions.

Children need to be trained to *work with* ambiguous materials, not just reject them: to watch something, to critique it, to puzzle it out. In dealing with the media, children need to begin to be able to sort out layers of news and fantasy and to seek out the purposes and contexts, because at present, we are sitting ducks for effectively ambiguous messages! We should regard responding to ambiguity and living with it as a skill, a kind of literacy, for which we need a new word.

These are not easy concepts to express to parents, administrators, and school systems caught up in the current pathologies. In town after town, the model for improving education is writing more rules—and developing detailed curricula that will specify every minute in the student's day and every point that goes into a grade and establish clear and specific objectives for every lesson. Here the effort at disambiguation creates distrust of teachers and undermines the possibility of responding creatively in the classroom.

On the other hand, a teacher can embrace the fact that the members of a class bring with them multiple levels of understanding and will leave with multiple levels of understanding. When I was teaching in the Philippines, to a class in which the knowledge of English was very unequal, it occurred to me that I faced a choice. One could teach to the brightest and most competent students, making the others miserable and embarrassed, or one could teach to the weakest, making the brightest ones bored and frustrated. Or one could teach in such a way that students at different stages of their own learning each attended to something rather different and emerged with varying understandings. I think this is true of the best teaching and the best writing—that it uses ambiguity—and often one of the slower students absorbs some part of the more complex message that begins to make sense over time. This can only work, however, in situations where alternative understandings or partial understandings are valued and respected, where not all answers are classified as right or wrong. The kinds of differences I encountered in my Philippine classroom are characteristic of any human community; in fact, my 6-year-old daughter sometimes sat drawing in the back of the classroom and would occasionally raise her hand. Especially in situations of change or culture contact, gradients of learning run through the entire population, in addition to the differences of gender and age that guarantee different systems of meaning within families.

To prepare people to deal with cultural, religious, and racial differences, it is important to use the experience of multiple levels of understanding by such simple devices as mixing ages, instead of letting the society become increasingly age-segregated. It has struck me as one of the great ironies that we think children will learn best when they are with other children who are the same in as many ways as possible. The tolerances for ambiguity and for difference run together.

All of the different pathologies relating to intolerance of ambiguity add up to a pervasive epistemological hubris in our society. The fundamental question for education, it seems to me, is how to avoid contributing to the problem. We need to swim against this stream of disambiguation and to keep a certain balance that embraces ambiguity. Ambiguity can be uncomfortable, but children must be able to function and grow in situations where they do not know the answers, where they cannot help making some mistakes, where they must meet strangers with whom their understanding is incomplete. We need to avoid sending the message that whenever knowledge or understanding is incomplete, someone is at fault.

Above all, children need to see the world and other people, as well as works of art and ideas, as not finite in their meaning. Children need the freedom to reach the kind of misunderstanding I had of that Armenian grace originally, which permitted participation, and to move on, knowing that it is natural to go through life changing your understanding of relationships and of the world and maintaining a playful sense that it's all very serious, very positive, very beautiful.

References

Alliance of Artists' Communities. (1997). *American creativity at risk: Restoring creativity as a priority in public policy, cultural philanthropy, and education.* A report on a symposium held November 8–10, 1996, Portland, OR.

Bateson, G. (1972). Redundancy and coding. In *Steps to an ecology of mind* (pp. 411–425). New York: Ballantine.

Bateson, M. C. (1975). Mother-infant exchanges: The epigenesis of conversational interaction. In D. Aaronson & R. W. Rieber (Eds.), *Developmental psycholinguistics and communication disorders. Annals of the New York Academy of Sciences, 263,* 101–113.

Bateson, M. C. (1994a). *Peripheral visions: Learning along the way.* New York: HarperCollins.

Bateson, M. C. (1994b). Toward an ambiguous world order. In R. A. Falk, R. C. Johansen, and S. S. Kim (Eds.), *Constitutionalism and world order* (pp. 245–252). Albany: State University of New York Press.

Buhler, K. (1934). *Sprachtheorie.* Jena: Fischer.

Meredith, G. (1862). *Modern love.* London: Campbell, Thompson and McLauflin.

Sebeok, T. A. (1962). Coding in the evolution of signaling behavior. *Behavioral Science, 7,* 430–442.

Simon, H. A. (1969). *Sciences of the artificial.* Cambridge: MIT Press.

Simon, H. A. (1972). *Representation and meaning: Experiments with information processing systems* (H. Simon & L. Siklossy, Eds.). Upper Saddle River, NJ: Prentice Hall.

Smith, H. (1989). *Excluded knowledge: Beyond the Western mind-set.* Wheaton, IL: Theosophical Publications.

Thomas, L. (1974). *Lives of a cell.* Toronto: Bantam Books.

Biography

Mary Catherine Bateson is a cultural anthropologist who divides her time between teaching in Virginia and writing in New Hampshire. She is currently Clarence J. Robinson Professor in Anthropology and English at George Mason University in Fairfax, Virginia. Her books include *Our Own Metaphor: A Personal Account of a Conference on the Effects of Conscious Purpose on Human Adaptation; With a Daughter's Eye: A Memoir of Margaret Mead and Gregory Bateson; Composing a Life;* and, most recently, *Peripheral Visions: Learning Along the Way,* as well as *Angels Fear: Towards an Epistemology of the Sacred,* (with Gregory Bateson) and *Thinking AIDS* (with Richard Goldsby).

8 Understanding Ourselves: Beyond Information Explosion, Hypertext, or Mechanical Memory

Madhu Suri Prakash

Introduction

With tens of millions of bytes speeding through telephone cables and personal computers, we are apt to stand in awe of the vast amounts of data we have at our fingertips, but we have so much information, it's easy to get lost. We can get so much detail on any given topic that we tax our powers of discrimination just to keep track of what we were looking for and why. This situation is compounded by the fact that much of the information produced in academic settings is highly abstract and decontextualized.

As educational philosopher Madhu Prakash explains in this chapter, much of academic culture is concerned less with the meaning and substance of ideas than with the research processes used to generate new information. The agenda of much research is to acquire the knowledge and skill to solve problems, but the problems addressed are often abstract and removed from experience. The result is that much of what we learn neither illuminates nor responds to the immediate problems we need to face. As a consequence, students preparing for their doctorates in education often find themselves in search of a problem while experiencing very real and pressing problems in their schools and communities.

In prizing information, in seeking or demonstrating mastery of a topic, we learn to think in detached abstractions; we see concepts as transferable from one time, place, or set of people to another. Prakash's caution is that such thinking, when not grounded in richly contextualized experience of actual events and people, leaves us with intellectual castles in the air. At the same time, we can, with our citations and statistical tables, lose sight of the mystery of, and responsibility for, a single child, let alone a classroom full of them.

Prakash explains that the vast majority of us living in postindustrial cultures not only think in an abstract and decontextualized manner but also have so defined ourselves. We have abstracted our daily lives and responsibilities from people and place. Echoing Chet Bowers's (chap 2, this volume) concerns about hyperindividualization, Prakash points to the ecological and cultural crises we face because we fail to assume the tasks we are given where we live.

We need, explains Prakash, to adapt the lessons of ancient cultures to contemporary culture—to measure things by a human scale, rather than by abstractions about the economy or the planet. Drawing heavily on the work of Wendell Berry, she suggests that we need to "Think Little," that we think in terms of the place we live and the people in our local communities. In this context, she could better serve children by engaging them in sustaining local communities than in preparing for the nether world of the global economy. Prakash concludes that we as educators need to come to *ground*, to the earth, to recognize the profound problems we face in our local communities.

—Jeffrey Kane

At the beginning of the new year, Carol and I sat down to reflect on the broad goals and means of her program of doctoral studies. We started our reflections with the particular course, officially designated an "independent study," that she had signed up to do on the life and social thought of Wendell Berry.

As always, Carol had done her homework. She came well prepared for the meeting. First, she identified the books she wanted to read. Then, she formulated the broad outlines of questions she wanted to explore. Finally, those tasks admirably completed, she gazed deep into my eyes and said with her customary quiet deliberation:

"I am inundated with information. Every course that I take stuffs my head with more theories, facts, and figures. I feel completely weighed down and worn out by all this information. I find myself forgetting more than I can remember. Bombarded daily with the latest books and articles being churned out at mega-speed by the publishing industry, I can hardly think. I want to define a course of study that is different."

Different in what respect, I asked Carol. She took her time responding to my question. Although her response was slow in coming, she had no difficulty whatsoever clearly articulating the difference and departure she sought.

"I do not want to use this course to collect and process more information."

"What are you seeking from your studies?"

"Understanding."

The solidity of the word, as well as the depth of its speaker's intentions, affirmed themselves in our midst. A long and pregnant silence followed her short reply. We sat very quietly, deep in our own personal meditations on the last word Carol had just uttered, giving it such fullness of weight, a counterpoint to "the unbearable lightness of being" of the prevailing modes of studying I encounter.

Almost at the same time, we broke our long and thoughtful silence. We resumed our conversation by taking our first preliminary steps in exploring with each other some key differences that seem to us to separate human "understanding" from all the contemporary activities of academics for the production, collection, and processing of "information"—unparalleled in its profusion and prodigiousness, taking all of human history. We wondered aloud whether human understanding can ever keep abreast of this information glut.

Information or Understanding?

The vast academic literature that damns "banking education"—the depositing and withdrawing of information—is all too familiar to both of us. We have studied the philosophies of thinkers like Dewey or Friere, Illich or Wigginton, as well as dozens of other philosophers who repeatedly warn us of the burden of useless information with which modern teachers systematically burden, shackle, and oppress our students in preparing them to graduate from the educational system. Every year, millions of students graduate from this system, their heads stuffed with irrelevant texts and useless tables. That explains why they "sink" (as Dewey [1954, 1962] puts it) rather than swim in "real life"—that is, in genuinely social situations. These graduates lack the understanding needed to practice the art of living "the good life." We, their professors, fare little, if any, better than they.

Carol knows this all too clearly. She understands this at least as well as any of her professors, including me. We have nothing to teach her in this regard. Confident that she will not be scolded or punished by me for making her "professional" intentions all too clear, she has underscored from the very beginning that her educational journey is not about getting the credential required these days to become a university professor. She knows that her quest for wisdom will not be fulfilled by "banking" more and more of the information generated these days by the "educational," publishing, or data processing industries. She knows that the majority of courses in colleges and universities reduce "education" to what humans do not do as well as the latest computer and other technologies being bought and sold for storing, generating, and processing information. She knows that this variety of education mechanizes learning and reduces teachers and students alike to extensions of the machine—Ellul's technological system, efficient cogs "educated" for the smooth functioning of modern industrial societies. She knows that she does not want to become the type of professor of education who is highly "efficient" and "productive" in "manufacturing" that kind of education/knowledge.

Knowing all this and much much more, she turns to me with complete candor and humility, and declares, "There is much I do not know. There is much I do not understand. As I grow older, the 'certainties' I possessed as a younger woman disappear."

Her humility cannot be confused with passivity, for, with the forthrightness I have come to both expect and respect in her, Carol confesses her dismay with the doctoral dissertations stored in the university library. She has conducted a systematic research on them. To her, they demonstrate little more than the collection and processing of data or information, some of it supposedly "new."

"Is it possible to write a doctoral dissertation that is not an arena for exhibiting all the information one has collected and stored, for 'showing off'—that is, 'name dropping' all the authors that one has read—made respectable as a 'survey of the literature'? Am I required to have footnotes and references that exhibit all this in 'a literature review'? Would 'the educational system' accept a doctoral dissertation that reflects my quest for wisdom and understanding, as distinct from my abilities or success in storing and disseminating information?"

Neither snobbery nor cynicism taint the tone of her questions. The deep sincerity and integrity behind her questioning challenge me to plumb my own depths, seeking the same honesty, openness, candor, and "critical consciousness" with which she presents herself to me. The prevalent goals—diplomas for success and upward mobility—that motivate millions to enter and stick it out in the educational system neither brought her back to graduate school nor will "drive" her to complete her course of doctoral studies.

"The job I had as a high school teacher gave me all the income, status, or security I wanted or needed. Yet, I resigned from my tenured position. I have returned to graduate school, hoping to take time away from the classroom to deepen my understanding of what is involved in becoming educated; to appreciate what it means to be a good teacher; to address some of my confusions about what I was making my students undergo—all in the cause of 'helping' them become educated."

From the moment I was appointed her advisor, I recognized that Carol needed no preliminary course in philosophy of education to help her clarify the differences the educational system buries under the modern barrage of information—that is, the central differences that radically separate earning a credential in the field called education and becoming genuinely educated. She knows that coming to possess the former—the credential—has nothing to do with learning the art of living a generous life, a life in which she can bring joy and justice to those who suffer one or another variety of oppression, even as she fights off the shackles that have oppressed her during the course of her life—full of its own share of joys and sufferings.

"What must I know and understand in order to live a good life? What can I do to be a good mother for my daughter? A good teacher or neighbor or citizen? What is the nature of 'good work'? What is worth teaching and learning for the creation of communities that support and nurture all their members?"

At the heart of her inquiry lies Berry's fundamental question, deeply personal as well as social: "What are people for" (Berry, 1990; Prakash, 1994).

Transforming Educational Aims and Means: Moving Beyond Information Toward Understanding

In Carol's quest for wisdom, what useful or significant role can I, her academic guide and academic advisor, play? I find myself challenged as never before. Advising Carol would not be that puzzling and difficult if she, like the majority of her peers, principally sought information for a credential—the certification or the mastery of mechanics for completing her doctoral studies to acquire the official degrees needed today for becoming a "professional," a "careerist," a professor of education.

For the understanding she seeks, thumbing through the graduate studies bulletins on course offerings and graduation requirements is as useless as clicking open Windows 95 to access all the rest of the state-of-the-art information systems available at the university. All of these impressive accumulation, storage, transmission, and dissemination facilities for information have not added one whit to the increase of understanding or wisdom of modern peoples, ranking them above "traditional" or "primitive" peoples. It has taught us the skills of playing the games needed for the acquisition of credentials and career mobility.

Credentials and career mobility are not totally dismissed by Carol. They are, however, completely overshadowed by educational goals more significant for her.

What are the goals and means appropriate to education? Again and again, our regular conversations about the texts and the authors she and I continue to study together bring us to the same point: an educational quest that seeks, not to gather more information, but to achieve deeper understanding.

TO UNDERSTAND: TO STAND UNDER

To come to understand, one must literally "stand under"—humbly, fully, and deliberately conscious of one's own incompleteness, clarifies Raimundo Pannikkar. The humility he urges is reflected in the great teachers—those who, like Socrates at the end of his contemplative life, reveal the wisdom that involves knowing the extent of their ignorance, the limits of their knowledge and understanding.

In his "experiments with truth," undertaken with all the tentativeness of ignorance fully felt and experienced, Gandhi concludes the last days of his life honestly declaring:

> All that I can in true humility present to you is that truth is not to be found by anybody who has not got an abundant sense of humility. If you would swim on the bosom of the ocean of Truth, you must reduce yourself to a zero. (Gandhi, 1970, p. 74)

To be humble, one needs to stand under. This calls for overcoming the urge to stand over, in the aggressive and arrogant posture of all those individualists who seek to dominate. For centuries, humans have stood under the vast heavens, knowing the finiteness and limitations of what they were capable of understanding: conscious of their infinitesimal smallness when compared with the Great Mystery that constitutes the vastness of creation. The mysteries that give themselves up to the wondering minds of those who know that they do not know (the unknowing minds), simultaneously shroud themselves from the curious prying and poking of those whose hubris involves seeking to be gods, like Prometheus, aspiring to steal their fire.

Reminding us of the fatal flaws of our modern Promethean arrogance—at once product and producer of our modern information technologies, Ivan Illich's (1970) proposals for the "celebration of awareness" remind us of the virtues of hindsight exemplified by Prometheus's brother, Epimetheas. To understand, we must escape the traps of our mountainloads of new information; our gluttony for the forbidden apple of knowledge reflected in the World Wide Web; our Promethean lust for the fire of the gods so that we no longer are limited by "ambient temperatures" but can create the heat needed for thermodynamic efficiency (Alvares, 1992). To do this, we must learn to know and bow to our limits, acquiring the humility and hindsight of Epimethean Man.

In a similar quest for humility when faced with the grandeur and mystery of creation, Wendell Berry (1990) urges us to "Think Little," to abstain from the modern arrogance of "Thinking Big." Shy of any and all varieties of grandiose "Global Thinking," Berry reminds us that we are incapable of planetary planning. "Global thinking" is an oxymoron because we can only think about what we know, and no one can know the globe. Humbly, Berry urges us to give up the aspiration to "think globally."

Berry seeks, like Kohr, Illich, Gandhi, and the other critics of modern arrogance, the understanding that all humans must achieve to live well in their own places in such a way that we can avoid the damage we currently perpetrate on other peoples' places all over the globe. While possessing more global information than all previous generations on earth, we remain ignorant of the consequences of our smallest and most trivial actions, constituting the dailiness of our daily lives. Therefore, we do more damage to other people's places than ever before in human history, colonial or other.

All those who recognize, appreciate, and understand the global scope of this damage hope to bring us back to the "human scale." This is the scale at which human beings are capable of standing under and understanding the consequences of their choices and actions. It is the scale that we have sought to escape ever since we stole the fire of the gods, leading up to the modern expectation of escaping the finiteness of the earth to populate the other planets, the other solar systems of the endless galaxy.

When viewed from our interplanetary escapades, our own earth appears to us like a small blue bauble, as cute and little as the round ornaments we hang on our Christmas trees. That godlike perspective stirs up the sentiments to be a modern Atlas. Proponents of the human scale encourage us to leap from Epimethean hindsight, to give up our modern aspirations to be Atlas in bearing our social responsibilities, carrying the planet, as it were, on our shoulders with big talk—of global education for the global economy or of the global environmentalism being promoted today by the "big" and the "powerful" in the name of saving planet Earth.

Bringing us down from the arrogant heights of our modern Atlas's aspirations with gentle humor, Christine von Weizacker observes our hubris:

> The "Atlas Syndrome" is a frequent modern affliction that attacks pleasant, well-trained and conscientious people. They undertake to develop global knowledge and feel a global responsibility. And the more lonely they get, and the more unbearable the weight of the global problem on their shoulders, the more righteous and admirable they feel. . . . [For] Global knowledge and global responsibility are in vogue. . . . [T]hey are fashionable but impossible. (von Weizacker, 1993, p. 129)

To encourage us to resist the "Atlas Syndrome," von Weizacker (1993) urges us not to

> admire and trust the carriers of unrealistic, virtuous and virtual weights! Just imagine all the whales and elephants, ticks and fleas, baobabs and stinging nettles this person would have to carry in order to be true "Atlas" . . . then smile at this upside-down version of the world: basically we are not carriers, but rather we are being carried. So why should a per-

> son press his or her shoulders to the ground, pretend to steady the globe with supporting hands and—to make the picture perfect—stick their feet into the air, which is an airy footing indeed. And why do we revere such a clownish performance? Why not give it the laughter which is its due? Why not invite "Atlas" to get up? . . . The Non-Atlases have more versatility, the freedom to walk around, they can find good company and instead of lonely "global responsibility" they can try to discuss and decide on appropriate responsibility, which makes responses possible. (p. 129)

TO RESPOND, TO CARE, TO CELEBRATE AWARENESS ON THE HUMAN SCALE

Out in the open fields of nonmodern villages, or in the vast wilderness or plainlands not destroyed by civilization, or some distance away far from our towering skyscrapers, looking up at the unending open star-filled heavens—in such places and moments, when we stand under with wonder, we become once again capable of understanding our human limits.

Joining generations of our forgotten forebears, getting "off our horse, out of our car," descending from the modern pedestals of transcontinental or lunar flights, we can once again regain the humility needed to acknowledge the all-too-evident limits of our knowledge and power, limits on the power of our intelligence, even limits on the power of our technologies, hurtling us into that vast space, ceaselessly bombarding us with information of the solar system, nanosecond upon nanosecond.

What can we do with that ceaseless flood of information so that it serves some good—that is, starts to offer genuine service to peoples and places instead of being yet another possession that inhibits and hinders rather than empowers us to make wiser choices? Do we have an excess of the type of information that inhibits possibilities for understanding ourselves? Is our information explosion also responsible for the explosion of modern ignorance—particularly the ignorance of knowledge and skills required to live well in particular local spaces?

These questions are not being raised for mere rhetorical effect. Although some individuals may raise them for the sheer excitement of being engaged in academic vocal pyrotechnics, more and more people are, like Carol, waking up to the paralysis that accompanies the ceaseless bombardments of facts and figures that we cannot use, information that can only be stored in the mechanical memory of our machines, as useless as the grain that rots in modern storage facilities while millions die of malnutrition and starvation.

Those beginning to ask such questions see the fundamental difference between human and artificial intelligence, between human memory and mechanical/textual memory. Reflections on such differences reveal the quintessentially social nature of human memory. Computer memory, in stark contrast, can be stored in "bits" and "bytes" that are engineered and wired into individual machines, accessible to alienated, "homeless," asocial individuals.

The importance of drawing this contrast between human and computer memory has profound implications for the consideration of educational aims and means. Human memory can only be transmitted, regenerated, or kept alive through communal stories that are not frozen texts, but are continuously created and re-created, interpreted and understood in and through ongoing conversations and dialogues. These cannot flourish in impersonal settings. Human memory dies when human spaces are destroyed through processes of social engineering that inhibit face-to-face dialogue, destroying possibilities for the gaze into the eyes of the other, of I-Thou.

This occurring loss of human memory is not even being noticed by the millions still fascinated by the fabulous power of mechanical memory, which is taking over instruction and communication in modern educational institutions. Only those who can recognize their inability to keep up with the information production and accumulation of their machines, critically confronting the magic and marvels of artificial intelligence, are beginning to appreciate the experience of Frankenstein's creator. Whereas they look for ways of joining Gandhi, Mumford, Ellul, Illich, and others celebrating the "tools of conviviality" that offer escapes from the tyranny of "the technological system," others dismiss such thinkers as promoters of doomsday hysteria and hopelessness, as those seeking to return us to stone age caves and clubs, and therefore best kept out of classrooms devoted to the path of "progress" headed forward and onward toward Edens—modern or postmodern.

For those reflecting on the differences between information and understanding, between human and artificial intelligence, between organic and mechanical memory, the central challenge of the human condition in our times is how to regain the power of people that can only be exercised and celebrated through tools and technologies that allow life to be lived on the human scale. Only on this scale can ordinary people comprehend the real meaning or significance of their choices and actions. Only on this scale can we know, understand, and authentically respond to the hopes of others; to care for and comprehend ourselves; to befriend and love.

On Memory and Understanding for Making Cultural/Communal Soil

"Why I Am Not Going to Buy a Computer," like his other essays, reveals the choice of tools and technologies that Berry (1990) makes to be able to live and craft a "good life." Such a desirable life, Berry explains, demands an understanding of the place where one dwells, instead of merely residing. Underscoring the differences that separate (nonmodern/postmodern) dwellers from (modern) residents, David Orr (1992) writes:

> To a great extent, formal education now prepares its graduates to reside, not to dwell. The difference is important. The resident is a temporary and rootless occupant who mostly needs to know where the banks and stores are in order to plug in. The inhabitant

> and a particular habitat cannot be separated without doing violence to both. The sum total of violence wrought by people who do not know who they are because they do not know where they are is the global environmental crisis. To reside is to live as a transient and as a stranger to one's place, and inevitably to some part of the self. The inhabitant and the local community are parts of a system that meets real needs for food, materials, economic support, and sociability. The resident's world, on the contrary, is a complicated system that defies order, logic, and control. The inhabitant is part of a complex order that strives for harmony between human demands and ecological processes. The resident lives in a constant blizzard of possibilities engineered by other residents. The life of the inhabitant is governed by the boundaries of sufficiency, organic harmony, and by the discipline of paying attention to minute particulars. For the resident, order begins from the top and proceeds downward as law and policy. For the inhabitant, order begins with the self and proceeds outward. Knowledge for the resident is theoretical and abstract, akin to training. For inhabitants, knowledge in the art of living aims toward wholeness. Those who dwell can only be skeptical of those who talk about being global citizens before they have attended to the minute particulars of living well in their place. (pp. 102–103)

Dwelling develops understanding in and through standing under and listening respectfully and reverentially to all that our places tell us in the songs of their birds; the whisper of their breezes; the singing of their crickets; the beats of their rains; the daily stories of the people who live there with us, husbanding soils and waters, plants and trees, flora and fauna.

This knowledge and understanding of dwellers means, on the one hand, reducing our dependence on other places—places that we can neither know nor care for. It means on the other hand, strengthening our relationships with local soils and waters, with peoples and places that we can genuinely care for and be cared by (Apffel-Marglin, 1995; Rivera, 1995).

Misunderstanding him, his critics see Berry's (1990) rejection of the computer as an example of the irrationality he shares with the Luddites: those doomed to disappearing like dinosaurs, defeated by their own failure to keep abreast with the forward march of history. In addition to its irrationality, Berry's rejection is seen as proof of the parochialism or jingoism that combines small-minded attachment to local places with indifference to the plight of everything that is "out of sight, out of mind." To persuade him of his folly in not buying into all the benefits and advantages of the "computer culture," his avid critics "educate" him about all the useful information they gather through the World Wide Web or by surfing on the Internet to formulate and determine "planetary" environmental policies, beneficial not to one place but to all places.

Contemplating the promoters of planetary protection and global environmental management, Berry (1990) writes, "The heroes of abstraction keep galloping in on their white horses to save the planet—and they keep falling off in front of the grandstand" (p. 197). It is not planetary information for a manual that can save "spaceship earth," reflects Berry. "The only true and effective 'operator's manual for spaceship earth' is not a book that any human will ever write; it is hundreds of thousands of local cultures" (p. 166).

Celebrating this diversity of cultures and cultural knowledge/understanding of their places, Berry (1990) observes that it has not over centuries and still cannot be stored as mechanical memory or be learned just from books. The cultural diversity he celebrates is the knowledge, understanding, and wisdom about

> how to care for each of the planet's millions of human and natural neighborhoods, each of its millions of small pieces and parcels of land, each one of which is in some precious way different from all the others. Our understandable wish to preserve the planet must somehow be reduced to the scale of our competence—that is, to the wish to preserve all of its humble households and neighborhoods. (p. 200)

This form of preservation created by generations of dwellers past and present has been, and continues to be, done by households and communities that understand well what it means to live well in their own places, without raping or destroying other people's places. Such wisdom and knowledge do not require the information generation or storage facilities of either published texts or mechanical memory. In fact, the latter, more often than not, pose distractions and are counterproductive for engaging in the work of local culture.

To exist, continue, and regenerate itself, this culture "must exert a sort of centripetal force, holding local soil and local memory in place. Practically speaking, human society has no work more important than this" (Berry, 1990, p. 155).

Disregard for the importance of this good work, Berry (1990) observes, is leading to a "vast amnesia." This amnesia of forgetfulness cannot be compensated by the acquisition of new information. Because information newly minted or hot off the press lacks what it takes to make communal or cultural soil,

> [a]s the exposed and disregarded soil departs with the rains, so local knowledge and local memory move away to the cities or are forgotten under the influence of homogenized sales talk, entertainment, and education. This loss of local knowledge and local memory—that is, of local culture—has been ignored, or written off as one of the cheaper "prices of progress," or made the business of folklorists. . . .
>
> [W]hen a community loses its memory, its members no longer know one another. How can they know one another if they have forgotten or have never learned one another's stories? If they do not know one another's stories, how can they know whether or not to trust one another? . . . Because of a general distrust and suspicion, we not only lose one another's help and companionship, but we are all living in jeopardy of being sued. (p. 157)

Because of this amnesia, this loss of local memory, we

> feel ourselves crowded more and more into a dimensionless present, in which the past is forgotten and the future, even in our most optimistic "projections," is forbidding and fearful. Who can desire a future that is determined entirely by the purposes of the most wealthy and the most powerful, and by the capacities of machines. (p. 167)

Berry's "communal memory" is created and kept alive by local customs and traditions like "sitting till bedtime." Describing such customs and traditions in his own rural Kentucky, Berry writes:

> They told each other stories . . . that they had all heard before. Sometimes they told stories about each other, about themselves, living again in their own memories and thus keeping their memories alive. . . . [T]hey had each other, they had their local economy in which they helped each other, they had each other's comfort when they needed it, and they had their stories, their history together in that place. To have everything but money is to have much. (pp. 158–159)

Berry mourns this loss of local memory. If 1,000 computers were gifted by the federal government to his county and all their memory megabytes were filled with every detail that was ever known by the dead or dying local inhabitants of that place, it would not do a whit to ease Berry's sorrow and mourning. For those millions of megabytes of information, stored in mechanical memory, would lie dead and inert, unable to make the cultural soil that could prevent the physical soil of his county from flying away, lost.

RETURN, REMEMBRANCE, AND RE-MEMBERING

Reflecting on these ways of remembering for the re-membering that continually regenerates human communities, Berry (1990) reveals the failures of schools to help the young make and remake their own local cultural soil. Devoted to banking information for social mobility and careerism of the "itinerant professional vandal," the educational system actively destroys and displaces the teachers, curriculum, and pedagogy that for centuries have helped make, as well as remake, protect, and cherish the soil of communities.

This soil is created within the cultures that still celebrate return, remembrance, and re-membering. In contrast, modern education, wherever it is exported from the "First World," promotes the new information needed for moving and mobility. The knowledge and skills needed to make First Worlds out of underdeveloped "Third" and "Fourth Worlds" deprecates the local knowledge central to remembering and re-membering:

> The schools are no longer oriented to a cultural inheritance that it is their duty to pass on unimpaired, but to the career, which is to say the future, of the child. The orientation is thus necessarily theoretical, speculative, and mercenary. The child is not educated to return home and be of use to the place and community; he or she is educated to leave home and earn money in a provisional future that has nothing to do with place or community. (Berry, 1990, p. 163)

Although long and ancient traditions of temporary departures precede the final return of taking on mature responsibilities in local spaces, modern departures from place and community are the permanent leaving behind in search of "greener pastures"—preferably urban or suburban.

> As the children depart, generation after generation, the place loses its memory of itself, which is its history and its culture. And the local history, if it survives at all, loses its place. It does no good for historians, folklorists, and anthropologists to collect the songs and the stories and the lore that make up local culture and store them in books and archives. They cannot collect and store—because they cannot know—the pattern of reminding that can survive only in the living human community in its place. It is this pattern that is the life of local culture and that brings it usefully or pleasurably to mind. Apart from its local landmarks and occasions, the local culture may be the subject of curiosity or of study, but it is also dead.
>
> [Local culture is] the history of the use of the place and the knowledge of how the place may be lived in and used. For another, the pattern of reminding implies affection for the place and respect for it, and so, finally, the local culture will carry the knowledge of how the place may be well and lovingly used, and also the implicit command to use it only well and lovingly. (Berry, 1990, p. 163)[1]

Conclusion

These forms of reminding, knowledge, and love constitute the understanding of Carol's educational quest. This same postmodern quest is shared and pursued by millions of modern "homeless minds" looking for homes beyond the mountainloads of information—"virtual" Himalayas—accumulating around them. Looking for this understanding within these mountainloads of information is probably more impossible than looking for the needle in the proverbial haystack.

Yet, the contemporary challenge is far from hopeless. To sustain hope, it is necessary to recognize that we are voluntarily creating these Himalayas of information. Voluntarily, too, we can go beyond them in search of places where, by reacquiring the art and skills of dwelling, we also re-create the understanding that accompanies the experience of genuinely belonging to people and places. Relearning to belong requires understanding what it means to live well, rooted in our own places, with the serenity that comes with knowing one is at home once again.

1. In this chapter, excerpts from "Word and Flesh" and "The Work of Local Culture" from *What Are People For?,* by Wendell Berry, copyright © 1990 by Wendell Berry. Reprinted with permission of North Point Press, a division of Farrar, Strauss & Giroux, Inc.

REFERENCES

Alvares, C. (1992). Science. In W. Sachs (Ed.), *The development dictionary: Knowledge as power*. London: Zed Books.

Apffel-Marglin, F. (1995, Winter). Development or decolonization in the Andes? *Interculture, 28*(1).

Berry, W. (1990). "Word and flesh" and "The work of local culture." In *What are people for?* Berkeley, CA: North Point Press.

Dewey, J. (1954). *The public and its problems.* Chicago: Swallow Press.

Dewey, J. (1962). *Individualism old and new*. New York: Capricorn Books.

Gandhi, M. K. (1970). *Essential writings* (V. V. Ramana Murti, Ed.). New Delhi: Gandhi Peace Foundation.

Illich, I. (1970). The rebirth of Epimethean man. In *Deschooling society*. New York: Harper & Row.

Orr, D. (1992). *Ecological literacy: Education and the transition to a postmodern world.* Albany: State University of New York Press.

Prakash, M. (Spring, 1994). What are people for? Wendell Berry on education, ecology, and culture. *Educational Theory, 44* (2) 135–157.

Rivera, J. V. (1995, Winter). Andean peasant agriculture: Nurturing a diversity of life in the Chacra. *Interculture, 28*(1).

von Weizsacker, C. (1993). Competing notions of biodiversity. In W. Sachs (Ed.), *Global ecology: A new arena of political conflict.* London: Zed Books.

BIOGRAPHY

MADHU SURI PRAKASH is Professor of Education at Pennsylvania State University and the recipient of its prestigious Eisenhower Award for Distinguished Teaching. The author of numerous articles in *Educational Theory, Teacher's College Record, Journal of Moral Education, Philosophy of Education, Holistic Education Review,* and other professional journals, as well as books, she has recently completed two books: *Remaking the Soil of Cultures* (1997) and *Escaping Education: Living as Learning at the Grassroots* (1998).

THE MAKING OF AN INDIGENOUS TEACHER: INSIGHTS INTO THE ECOLOGY OF TEACHING

GREG CAJETE

INTRODUCTION

The great American transcendentalist Ralph Waldo Emerson suggested that if the stars were to appear one night in 1,000 years, generation upon generation would tell the story of the night a city of God shone in the sky. The fact that the stars shine nightly and that they do not evoke such wonder is less a sign of our sophistication than of our having fallen asleep. For all we have learned about the stars—their compositions, distances, and sizes—we have lost all but the slightest sense of the wild mystery of their existence itself.

The following chapter by Greg Cajete, a member of the Pueblo tribe, offers an invaluable cultural contrast to the ways of thinking so prevalent in schools throughout the postindustrial world. He explains, from the perspective of the American

Indian, that all creation, from the stars to grains of sand in the desert, is a single unfolding story. Nature is not merely a complex set of physical objects, but a divine drama in which all things play a part. All things are woven through with this larger meaning, but such meaning can neither be conveyed as information nor understood by means of critical reflection. The ever-present story of unfolding creation cannot be studied as a subject among subjects wherein all things are objects among objects.

As Cajete explains, the key to understanding is not in the training of the intellect, but in the awakening of our souls through encounters with nature. Nature, as such, is not an object or set of objects, but a source of both outer and inner sustenance. The American Indian student educated from this perspective does not learn *about* nature as much as *from* nature. He or she learns, among other things, what it is to be human, what it is to contribute to the unfolding of the world. Every lesson without is a lesson within. Education is, in essence, a process of awakening to who we are and what we are called to do. Ultimately, the goal is not self-fulfillment as much as it is fulfilling one's responsibilities in the world.

Education of this sort is dependent on a teacher who is wide awake. The teacher must be able to read the growth of the student and to recognize the inner lessons offered through experiences within a community and the larger world. These experiences include rituals, music, song, dance, sport, and a wide variety of interactions with animals, plants, and the earth itself. Everything is directed toward creating an ecology or balance of the soul. In this fashion, Cajete explains, students will learn to bring balance in their own lives and communities, as well as to establish an ecologically sound culture. The future, he concludes, will depend, not on information and information processing, but on awakened souls willing to be responsible for themselves and their parts in the unfolding of creation.

—*Jeffrey Kane*

THE TREE OF LIFE

The Indians of Mexico, as indigenous people elsewhere, venerated the physical forces of nature especially as they revealed themselves in the movement of the sun, moon, planets, and constellations. They found the cosmos imbued through and through with spirit. life, and energy. They perceived these qualities in the clouds, in the rain, in the ocean, in the earth beneath their feet, in the rocks, mountains, rivers, and springs, in the green corn they planted, and the animals and plants with whom they shared the bounty of the earth. They participated with, and at the same time wondered about, the mystery of life. As they walked this "good earth," they observed the nature and workings of earth, wind, fire, water, and spirit as these elemental forces interacted, transformed, and created the reality they knew. They watched with awe and wonder as volcanoes and great rivers shaped the land. They walked respectfully through the great jungles, upon the mountains, and in the great deserts and plains that held so many stories, so many wonders. They named the flowers, trees, and other plants, animals, rivers, lakes, and springs in accordance with the nature and qualities they perceived in them.

They reserved a special place in their imagination for the heavens. They wondered about the grand movements they witnessed in the night sky. They observed the cycles of appearance and disappearance of celestial bodies through time and space. They measured time as a function of the sacred circle of life. From their vigilant observations evolved a great calendar that embodied in thought, form, and principle the basic nature of the universe. The concept of the great calendar was predicated on an earlier myth that the sun must fight the stars from the sky every day in a never-ending cycle of the interplay of the two primordial yet complementary energies of the cosmos. They came to view the sun as a supernatural being, a great warrior. Each day, they believed, the sun fought the stars from the sky only to die at night and be reborn each new day to repeat this sacred cycle (Shearer, 1971).

This perception of these great cycles, light and dark, sun and moon, guided the mind and spirit of indigenous Mesoamerica. In the context of such a view, mythic constructs and symbolic meanings related to the birth, death, and rebirth of the sacred time of the sun as reflected in the great calendar evolved. In this richly imaginative and fertile ground of guiding stories relating the creation of the universe, the earth, and the first plants and animals, the seeds of the great Tree of Life and the story of the Great Teacher are planted.

At the core of these stories is the essence of the indigenous ecological understanding and the ideals of human intention in Mesoamerican philosophy and epistemology. In the poetic story and verse of Mesoamerican "flower and song" as explained below, the mythic origins, purpose, and vision of the great calendar, its greatest teachers, and the deepest purposes of education have been carried through the generations.

Among the Aztecs, the most recent carriers of these "flowers and songs," the deepest purpose of education was to "find one's face, find one's heart," and search for a "foundation," a truth, a support, a way of life and work through which one could most completely express one's life. This was the ideal that they sought, and toward this end they created schools called "calmecac" guided by the "tlamatinimine," the astronomer, philosopher-poets of Aztec society. In the calmecac, the tlamatinimine taught about the great calendar, medicine, astronomy, religion, mathematics, architecture, and philosophy by using the poetic chants called "flower and song." The tlamatinimine explored with their students the heavenly bodies, the cycles of space and time, the mystery of life after death, and the nature of the earth and its essential relationships. They studied man as a creator of life, as a creator of educational, ethical, legal, and aesthetic principles within the context of understanding the proper relationship between earth and sky. They explored the essence of the spiritual, communal, and personal ideals that give rise to the divine spark in the human heart and transformed man into an artist, a poet, a sage, a keeper of the great calendar or a teacher (Portillo, 1963).

Woven through the mythology of the Aztecs is the Tree of Life as a symbol, a metaphor for life, healing, vision, and transformation. The tree is symbolically interwoven with another metaphor that orients the central teachings associated with the tree. This symbol, called the *pecked cross,* the *life circle,* the *medicine wheel,* has equally deep roots in the soil of Native America. This circle of life reflects the archetypal elements of earth, wind, fire, and water. It reflects the aspects of human nature—physical, mental, spiritual, and emotional. At the center of this circle is potential realized through the interplay of volition, vision, sense of identity, values, growth, and change. The circle also reflects the four great developmental stages that give meaning and foundation to each human being through life: protection, nourishment, growth, and wholeness. These stages bring forth the key meanings and teachings behind the tree. Through an understanding of "protection" (the shade of the tree), we come to see how the earth itself and other life provide for our human life and well-being. In understanding the nature of nourishment (the fruit of the tree), we come to see what we need to grow, to live a good life. We come to understand how we are nourished through the relationships we have at all levels of our nature and from all other sources that share their "life" with us. We also come to know that as we are nourished, so must we nourish others in our turn. As a tree grows through different stages, from seed, to sapling, to mature tree, to old tree, we come to understand that growth and change are key dynamics of life in vital process. We also learn that growth and change are essentially a reflection of "self-determination," of moving toward our true potential through the trials and tribulation, through the "weather" of our lives, and then there is wholeness. This is the finding and reflection of the face, heart, and foundation through which we reflect our life as a conscious part of a greater whole, as a part of a greater life process rooted to a greater past, present, and future ecology of mind and spirit (Lane, 1984).

When we reflect in this way on the tree, we realize that this way of education is also equally tied to development of deep environmental awareness and a reaffirmation of responsibility to perpetuate the care of the earth. As Václav Havel (1995) states:

> Something Is Being Born, we are in a phase when one age is succeeding another, when everything is possible . . . The only real hope of people today is probably a renewal of our certainty that we are rooted to the earth and at the same time to the cosmos . . . it logically follows that in today's multicultural world, the truly reliable path to co-existence, to peaceful co-existence and creative cooperation, must start from what is at the root of all cultures and what lies infinitely deeper in human hearts and minds than political opinion, convictions, antipathies, or sympathies: It must be rooted in self transcendence. Transcendence as a hand reached out to those close to us, to foreigners, to the human community, to all living creatures, to nature, to the universe; transcendence as a deeply and joyously experienced need to be in harmony even with what we ourselves are not, what we do not understand, what seems distant from us in time and space, but with which we

> are nevertheless mysteriously linked because, together with us, all this constitutes a single world. Transcendence is the only real alternative to extinction. (p. 113)

The nurturing of the spirit inherent in the metaphoric symbolism of the Tree of Life is a primary focus of the indigenous teacher archetype. Cultivating and applying the teaching/learning orientation of the indigenous teacher can provide valuable lessons and insights as we attempt to produce the kinds of teachers and education capable of addressing the social, political, economic, and psychological challenges of the dangerously environmentally challenged world of the 21st century.

THE INDIGENOUS TEACHER

What are the "ecologies" of indigenous education? How does indigenous education as experienced through the stories and processes of the indigenous teacher differ from simple information processing? In part, the answer lies in an inner recognition of the ecology of the earth as it mirrors itself in the inner and outer worlds of consciousness and human perception. Implied throughout indigenous education is the understanding that there is a balance, rhythm, and universal meaning in which all play a part. The modern focus on the intellect in education and all other realms of modern society destroys this sense of connective ecology as it disconnects people from the earth and from their essential selves. Indigenous epistemological orientations are focused, not on the processing of information, but on the expression and understanding of deeper streams of meaning, form, and responsibility that underlie and otherwise guide the essential processes of all things.

Part of the process of the indigenous teacher may be defined in terms of the vital role of transferring knowledge, precepts, and understandings from one generation to the next in a given culture. There is an "ecology" to teaching and learning, of which the teacher is the facilitator and choreographer. The indigenous teacher is an archetype that has evolved into many expressions like the branches of a great tree. Today, some of these branches have been "professionalized" into a form we call "school teacher"; other branches are "counselor," "parent," "elder," "priest," "rabbi," "master artist," and so on. The metaphor of the great tree denotes the continuity of human community. In this respect, each of us is called on to fulfill some aspect of the teacher in the various kinds of roles we play throughout our lives and participation in community.

Indigenous education also recognizes a teacher of another sort—the "teacher within." This teacher is not separate from the larger world without but is united with it beyond physical boundaries. Since ancient times, indigenous teachers have pointed to the essential wisdom of the universe and the human interrelationship with the process of the dynamic unfolding of the cosmic story. Today, teachers from indigenous cultures have become spokespersons for the profound importance of recognizing the natural order of life. They also have been a consistent voice through time for the importance of the inner life of our souls as the first step in honoring our relationship with the earth and the greater cosmos. Through ritual, song, dance, meditation, art, sport, the study of various disciplines, and dozens of other vehicles, indigenous teachers have tried to awaken, challenge, nourish, and cultivate the inner manifestation of the indigenous teacher, the archetype of the teacher within, the part of human consciousness that embodies the deepest human ways of knowing and being. They realize that only by keeping the teacher within awake and engaged can there be any real hope of gaining true enlightenment. They also realize that the teacher within is a manifestation of the human soul and, as such, was deeply spiritual. If this inner teacher is not fully engaged, they know, humankind will soon forget the essential role that humans play in the natural order and in maintaining the life-sustaining web of relationships with nature and with the ecology of human community. The results of such loss of memory are war, strife, jealousy, greed, and a host of other forms of transgression toward each other, other living things, and the natural world. What kind of focus is needed, one might ask? Clues lie in the implied focus of indigenous teachers since ancient times—namely, to help integrate the power of the soul with the power of the intellect and apply it to all aspects of human and natural relationship and thereby become more fully human, more complete.

MODERN CONTEXT FOR INDIGENOUS TEACHING

Teaching and the journey of the teacher, defined here as a guiding person, are part of an ancient mythic complex with both inner-personal and outer-cultural dimensions. The journey of a teacher, as well as the act of teaching, is a very human process. Understanding and honoring the human quality of teaching is essential to creating and nourishing the deeper ecological foundation of education. An ecological process of teaching is not so much dependent on what information is being transmitted but rather on the person in whom the knowledge resides.

Great teachers of ancient times certainly earned their place as guides and leaders of their people. For American Indian peoples, the teachings and lives of tribal sages have created a foundation for the continuity of tribal culture and deep ecological understanding that many contemporary American Indians strive to attain once again. The dedication, service, and support of cultural ways of knowing of tribal elders reflected a process of development of self that few contemporary teachers are able to emulate. Why is this the case? Have we, in contemporary times, lost sight of the deeper possibilities of the teacher, just as it seems we have lost sight of the students and the deeper meanings of education?

Ancient sages often refer to the soul, teacher within, as the greatest and wisest of all teachers. Their teachings, whatever their form, refer to the journey to self-knowledge as the only true quest for teaching and learning. The most important concern of these ancient teachers was how to help others awaken to the wisdom of the soul and then learn how to apply this soulful learning to their lives and the life of the community. A goal of such ancient teachers was to come to know the "ecology of the soul." This ecology shows itself in multiple ways through art, science, architecture, and all undertakings of human beings. This ecology of the soul, and the art and craft of teaching about it, these ancient teachers had to come to know in themselves.

The soundness of the soul of a teacher is essential to establishing a firm foundation for education. Only with such a teacher can students come to have a deep sensibility for the living spirit of the earth. A few years ago, indigenous knowledge and indigenous teachers were given little credence in the realm of professional education. They were considered esoteric, primitive, academically intriguing, quaint, anything but important in the "real world." Ancient forms of teaching and learning, for the most part, were the concern of academics and those focused on alternative education or the counterculture. Only recently have ancient and traditional forms of education enjoyed the wider interest of the general public and some mainstream educators. Why?

The reason lies in the fact that the institution of modern education remains in the state of an almost hopeless crisis of vision or outright blindness. More and more, the dysfunction of schools and schooling, especially in America, is the rule rather than the exception. As is true in almost every area of modern society, the mainstream institution of education is in need of a new ecology, a new sense of purpose and meaning for education. Modern education lacks the ecological groundedness on which traditional, indigenous forms of education are predicated. As a result, indigenous cultural forms of education are attractive to those, young and old, who are searching for deeper meaning. Many moderns are starving for meaning in their education. They search desperately for a more meaningful and ecologically centered way of education. They intuitively know that academic, rationalistic education is not enough. They realize that educating their minds without the participation of body, spirit, and community, inclusive of the earth, is inadequate. Today, most teachers continue to be poorly prepared to teach toward integration of body, mind, spirit, and community. The mechanistic, technical, vocational paradigm of education that is rooted in the 17th-century Prussian military education model continues to predominate teacher education . . . in spirit and in intent, if not in content.

Although many teachers and parents are deeply concerned with the state of education, few deeply question the cosmology and mechanistic focus of modern education. Indeed, so much time, energy, money, and ego (personal, political, and otherwise) have been invested in the infrastructure of modern education that change at the level required would mean complete restructuring of all major aspects of modern education. Despite such a monumental task, the work must begin on such transformational restructuring if we are to have any hope for creating the ecologically sustainable way of life so crucial to our collective future.

The first step in such a transformation is to retrace our own stories and journeys as teachers. The teacher lives and breathes in the world and in reality is not separate from the earth. In earlier times, master teachers realized that they needed to work in concert with the earth and the inner self if their teaching was to be truly successful.

Ancient teachers understood that they achieved mastery of their art only to the extent that they were able to work in concert with the natural processes of the earth and the human soul. Teaching is not a disembodied activity; it is undertaken by a person. Preparation for teaching is not only related to acquisition of information but also includes, more fundamentally, a process of becoming. The reenchantment of teaching begins with a reawakening within each of us.

EARLY MEMORIES OF INDIGENOUS TEACHING

Telling the story of our life journeys is tracing our footsteps through the people, events, and places that have formed us. As we pause at each special memory, we realize that we have indeed been formed by our encounters with the stories of others. Telling our own stories is a way to "remember to remember" who we are and to honor the special lives that we have been given.

To remember is also a way to re-know and reclaim a part of our lives. My personal recollections of my childhood and growing up in the context of my family and community are rich with warm memories, images, and sensations.

I came to teaching as a result of encouragement from teachers whom I respected and from my mother and grandmother, all of whom passed on to me something of the reflection of the archetype of the indigenous teacher. This early encouragement, combined with my experiences of Pueblo community, set the tone for much of my work as a teacher and my quest for another deep, more authentic and transformative form of education. This forming of myself as a teacher contrasts with the receiving of information about teaching in school in that it was a gradual introduction to an ecology of relationships and being shaped by those relationships through time as a participating member of a human community in a larger community of nature.

I was raised in my grandmother's household, which included my aunts and uncles. I spent much of my time with my grandmother. Her frame of reference and values were deeply rooted in traditional Pueblo life. These values, along with my mother's caring thoughts, I now find deeply embedded in my perspective of my life and work. It is true that we are first shaped by the caring hands of our mothers.

My earliest memories are of sounds, smells, and the sensations of being wrapped up, warm, and comfortable. What I remember most about that time is always being with people, hearing talking, laughing, and singing. These are my first memories of family and community—just sounds, images, and the feeling of being safe and warm. I remember that it was a good feeling!

My grandmother was in every sense a matriarch, well known and respected in the Pueblo, as well as in nearby Hispanic villages. She was of a generation born before the turn of the century. Her world and frame of reference were therefore of old New Mexico, a time when Pueblos reflected deeper expression of community. I remember helping old people in the Pueblo plant and hoe their gardens. I remember sitting with the old ones during hot summer afternoons, eating Indian cookies and listening to all their stories.

It is interesting to think about how we seem to remember things about who we are as we are growing up. I remember going with my grandmother, when I was about 5, to visit with her friends and relatives in the Pueblo. I remember those days vividly because each visit was an adventure, a break from the usual routine. I seem to remember everything and every place we visited during that year. It was the year before I started first grade. I learned so much with my grandmother during that time before going to school.

I remember gathering plants with my grandmother and other older women around the foothills near the Pueblo. I remember playing with other children who came along with their grandmas and grandpas. I remember eating lots of watermelon and trout baked in a fire pit with wild peppermint in Santa Clara Canyon. Afterward, all the children would jump into the stream to play and try to catch tadpoles, and the old ones laughed and laughed.

I remember my grandmother telling me that all older people were my aunts and uncles, that their children were my cousins, and that I should always greet them as relatives and treat them kindly. I remember that everyone, young and old, shared food with one another. When we went to visit older people, we would take food, clothing, or some gift to give to them. We would return with fruit, vegetables, or other gifts. It was a form of reciprocal giving; that is how things got spread around. But that wasn't all; community news, tools, shinny marbles, comic books, baseball cards, and hundreds of other things got spread around too.

I remember walking or riding somewhere all of the time. I remember, when my grandmother and I would attend a feast day at a neighboring Pueblo, the kindness with which we were received, especially by the other grandmas. In these visitations, I came to know the differences between the Pueblos and other Indian peoples. I also gained a sense of the relationships within the greater Pueblo world. I felt that, indeed, we were all related. I remember times sitting with my grandmother and other people in the "saints house," a small cottonwood-leaf-lined shelter set up in the main plaza especially for Pueblo feast days. In the shelter, many people, old and young, sat praying the rosary, visiting, talking about the news of the "old days." In this way, they reaffirmed their faith in the Christian God and, simultaneously, the traditional sense of Pueblo community, values, and way of life. Pueblo life has always revolved around tradition and age-old practices. Catholicism has been given a place in the Pueblo community.

I remember watching my grandma and other women and men of the Pueblo, replastering their houses with adobe mud, laughing and working as one body. I remember my grandmother and other aunts baking bread in Pueblo ovens, and my cousins and I sneaking about trying to be the first to taste the fresh bread, pies, and cookies they left cooling near the ovens. I remember those special feasts when all my family and relatives would gather at my grandmother's home or those times she and my mother would go to other homes to help others prepare for weddings, baptisms, or some other occasion.

These things still happen in Pueblo communities today. But it is my earliest memories that still have the greatest vividness and remain within my heart. These memories are similar to those of other Pueblo people growing up at that time. Our sense of community evolves over time in sync with the changes in our lives. Yet, it is our earliest experiences that seem to form the foundation for our personal story. These early memories provide me with a sense of rootedness to place and community. I have, of course, memories of sadness and pain and of frustration with regard to my community. Yet, even these instances taught me about the true dynamics of relationship. This is what impresses me about the strength and continuity of Pueblo communities. Our grandmas and grandpas still remind us today, as they did then, to celebrate our life, be happy with what we have, care for one another, be of good thoughts and words, help each other, and share the life that we have been given. They continually remind us to be happy that we are Pueblo. In this way, Pueblo people and their communities continue to live through time and place, through their memories and their personal stories (Cajete, 1994).

This is the educational foundation that I received growing up in the context of a Pueblo family and community. It is a context in which learning and teaching happened simultaneously at many levels and in multiple ways. The process of this sort of teaching, learning, and thinking is infinitely more meaningful, complex, and subtle than the information processing characteristic of modern schooling. And therein lies the difference and conflict between indigenous education and modern schooling. Indigenous education is a process of coming to know, honor, and apply essential principles of ecological relationship in its broadest terms. It is an education that honors the continual enchantment of human relationships with each other and the natural world. It is an education for life and ensoulment.

Western Schooling

I remember the first day my mother took me to school. I cried and cried because it was such a strange place and I knew no one there. It took me a very long time to get used to school. I probably didn't say one word throughout the first grade. I really wasn't connected to education from first through the fourth grade. I was shy and quiet and usually ended up getting grouped with other Indian and Hispanic students in the lowest academic group. This was fine with me because these students were from backgrounds similar to mine and I felt comfortable with them. Despite my school, my mother was very supportive of my learning and helped me in many ways to keep up with my schoolwork.

Not until fourth grade did I somehow realize that school was a kind of game. I became connected to school once I learned the "rules of the game." I made the connection between the value placed on "making the grade" and the relative worth placed on each student, based on their achievement in school. In other words, I learned how to "compete," and I learned that I could be good at it. I excelled as a student from then on. I also had some excellent teachers who followed me from elementary through high school and cultivated my interest in art and science. By the time I was in high school, I was an honor roll student, in the college prep program, and involved with athletics, science clubs, and art. I was especially interested in art and science, which I saw as being intimately related, although in school these disciplines were widely separated. My experiences through family and community had left me with an appreciation for art and nature, so, it was quite natural for me to maintain and cultivate these interests in school. I learned very early that art is a creative process that trains mind, spirit, and perception.

The summer after I graduated from high school, I was selected to attend a summer college prep program at a prestigious eastern prep school that placed students at Harvard, Dartmouth, Princeton, Yale, and other Ivy League schools. This experience taught me several things that would later play a major role in my decision to become a teacher and greatly influence my work in Indian education. At the prep school, I was introduced to a very self-absorbed, Eurocentric social environment that did not understand or know how to respect or honor the world from which I came. I was faced with stereotypical, romanticized typecasting typical of eastern educational efforts of that time to help "the poor Indian." Intellectually, I was the equal of any other student there, but I felt alienated and lonely. Largely, the activities with which I was involved that summer were geared to fitting me to the system and providing me with the opportunities to transcend my "cultural disadvantage," which was the terminology used in those days. Several Ivy League schools offered me scholarships in an attempt to recruit me to come to their schools. Because of my feeling of cultural disconnection, however, I decided to attend a small regional New Mexico college close enough to allow me to return home often and maintain close ties to my family and community. This college also had an excellent reputation in biology. I ended up taking a double major in biology and sociology and a double minor in art and secondary education. My indigenous upbringing enabled me to perceive an ecology of process and ways of knowing the world that connected these disciplines to the greater whole.

My memories of college include the unending instances of memorization, competing for a grade, catering to the wants of the professor, study detached from experience, endless examinations, quoting ad infinitum the thoughts of others, learning about the world mediated through the eyes of others, and discussions devoid of meaningful dialogue; these are characteristics common to many of us as we recall the experience of school. Few students question whether there is not something more to education, something of deeper meaning. Most students don't question at all; they focus the all-American line "get an education, get a job."

When I entered my last semester of college and student teaching, interaction with students and the day-to-day activity of teaching submerged me in coming to terms with the system. Questions about the inherent conflict between this system and tradition, culture, and indigenous education were always in the back of my mind, but traditional education was not respected or acknowledged in mainstream teaching of science. Indigenous knowledge was an object of study and certainly not an acceptable process of learning science. Learning anything about indigenous education was the farthest thing from anyone's mind in science education then.

Toward Becoming a Teacher: A Personal Perspective

I remember my first day as a student teacher at the Institute of American Indian Art (IAIA) in Santa Fe, New Mexico. Dressed in suit and bolo-tie, I faced my class with great apprehension, wondering what in the world I had gotten myself into. That day seemed an eternity as I attempted, despite my feelings of inadequacy, to go through the motions of teaching lessons in health, biology, and physical science while under the critical observation of my supervising teacher. As days became weeks and weeks became months, I struggled through the presentation of various lessons, gaining some confidence here and there but always feeling uncomfortable and unfocused. Although these sorts of feelings are common for student teachers, my feelings of inadequacy included a deep intuitive feeling that the way I had been taught to teach science was completely unnatural to both my nature and that of the Native American students I was teaching. I felt that I was performing for an invisible inquisitor who was watching and judging my every action and word. In reality, this was my own deep conditioning to the authority of modern education revealing itself in my own wish to teach science the "right way." In turn, this internalized authority was supported by the modeling and attitude of my supervising teacher, who himself epitomized the old school of textbook science teaching and the whole worldview therein.

I can only wonder in retrospect what my students were thinking and feeling as they watched me "perform." I know that they were well versed in reading the cues of classroom and BIA schools, negotiating at least the social context of school in ways that made it at least nominally tolerable. They were, after all, quite creative, full of life and filled with the usual exuberance, curiosity, and predisposition to challenge authority of most teenagers.

I graduated from college in 1974 and began teaching biology immediately thereafter at the local high school where the teacher college was located. My first year of teaching gave me firm grounding in cross-cultural understanding and perspective. It was important for me to make learning about biology culturally meaningful for the students I was teaching. I tried lots of different approaches in my classes, looking for points of cultural connection with my students. I knew that many students had rural backgrounds similar to mine, so I used stories about the land, plants, and animals of northern New Mexico folklore for experiential lessons related to ecology. I invited local ranchers into my classes to talk about plants and to tell stories of their lives and experiences. Through this process of community-based science education, I gained a deep appreciation for the "groundedness" of New Mexico rural people in their traditions and the strength they derive from their relationship with the land. These first teaching experiences also increased my appreciation for the fact that everyone has a deeply embedded cultural base and frame of reference through which he or she learns, operates, and gains meaning.

The year following my first position at the local school near the university, I was offered a full-time teaching position at IAIA. At IAIA, I was given many opportunities to explore creatively my deepening interest in culturally based science education. During my many years of teaching at IAIA, I have been able to bring many of my ideas about teaching Indian students into being. In addition, I have been able to fine-tune my thoughts regarding the integration of culture, science, and art.

During that first year and the next few years to follow at IAIA, I began to engage in a deep, yet largely internal, debate regarding my formal training as a teacher and toward what my own experience and that of my students was moving me. At times, I would try to fit myself to the "system" as others had defined it. At other times, I would rebel. As time passed, however, my emphasis, approach, and understanding of teaching moved decidedly in the direction of culturally based education, a largely undefined and unsupported alternative in the educational world. I observed lessons in science being given by other science teachers and science education professors. They were technically sound but "sterile," as most of science education at that time. The laboratory classroom environment, the school infrastructure, and the textbooks all reflected the guiding paradigm of "normal science" and the mainstream philosophy of education.

As I worked during that first year, the realities of teaching began to unfold. The stories of students related to their struggles, aspirations, and alienation from not only science but also the whole of mainstream American education. Their stories also echoed many of my trials and tribulations as I struggled to adapt to mainstream education. It also became apparent that an introduction of Native American cultural content into the natural sciences was not only appropriate but also essential, given the characteristics of my students. For indigenous peoples, modern education continues to reflect the deeply wounding processes of colonization. Traditional forms of knowing and educating have never been given any credence in the objectified world of modern "scientifically" administered education. Like my story, the educational experiences of my students at IAIA did not revolve around abstractions, but around people, community, relationships, and nature.

The exploration of these thoughts led me to the completion of my master's degree in secondary and adult education from the University of New Mexico in 1982 and my Ph.D. from International College University Without Walls in 1986. My doctoral studies in the New Philosophy program under the auspices of International College was a true collaboration between myself and many excellent educators and creative thinkers. It went far beyond anything that I could have done or experienced in a traditional doctoral program at a mainstream university. The way this experience enriched my understanding of art, science, culturally based education, and indigenous philosophy is beyond description. My work in this program led to my writing a creative education dissertation entitled "Science and Native American Perspective: A

Culturally Based Science Education Curriculum." This work has, in turn, formed the foundation for my most recent work, *Look to the Mountain: An Ecology of Indigenous Education* (1994).

Today, I do a variety of things. I am educator, artist, consultant, and writer. I continue to listen to, and learn from, the stories of the ways people come to know their cultural selves and their relationship with the natural world. And in this listening, I hear my own story. I continue to recognize the importance of honoring the unique story and process for learning that each person and each culture has. This is why I continue to advocate for indigenous peoples and their stories as the most meaningful foundations for their educational empowerment and self-determination. And my family and community of friends continue to be great resources of strength and support for me.

My story outlines a way of perception and creative orientation as it relates to education. In my teaching, I hope to plant seeds of thought and reflection related to indigenous education and its groundedness in the basics of human nature. I believe it is a way of education pregnant with potential, not only for the transformation of contemporary Indian education but also for its profound possibilities for changing modern education as a whole. I believe that we, as Indian people, must develop the stories for a transforming vision for our future and that of our children. My story expresses some experience of being Pueblo that I have come to know. I give my story as one Indian person to other Indian persons and as an educator to other educators. I share my story as a support for the stories of Indian people and communities. I hope that my story will reaffirm theirs and empower their strength, courage, creativity, and the contributions they have made and will make in the future. For me, education is an art of process, participation, making and nurturing life-giving relationships. Learning is always a growth and life process. Learning is a reflection of our formation of "face, heart, and foundation." Pueblo elders have said, "It is good to share one's life with good thought and intention." This is not only a thought; it is also a way of standing in the world.

Defining Another Way of Teaching

Early in my own development as a teacher, I left the well-worn path of scientific/behaviorist education methodology to explore the world of alternative, culturally based education. My story is really the story of the making of an indigenous teacher and the reclaiming of an indigenous heritage of thinking, teaching, and learning. It is also about the quest to regain the indigenous voice of teaching and something of its ecology of soul.

One of the first orientations I abandoned as I struggled to create myself as a teacher was that of trying solely to achieve in terms of the system and thereby becoming numb to the real plight of students. It takes time to realize deeply the conditioning and underlying effects of modern education that is most often the result of trial and lots of error. The system of rewards for following established paths of education is enticing because they are the established roads to mainstream success. There comes a point in this sort of career path making, however, when you must make a critical choice: to become a proficient technician of modern education or to move toward the deeper realms of the art and soul of teaching.

Teaching and learning, and the cultural context or social institutions in which they may formally occur, are fundamental interactive social expressions of humans. Indigenous education began, not as an art or science, ideology or philosophy, but as a lifelong process of learning how to be in the world through experience and participation in a greater community of life. Parents and adult groups have always taught children a way of "being" in the world. The first specialized transferers of knowledge and tradition were probably shamans, whose authority for such activity was founded on personal revelation and whose primary process was that of mentoring and facilitating the learning of would-be shamans. This group of first teaching specialists later expanded to include ritual functionaries, which in turn eventually evolved to include formal educators like those in ancient Greece who were slaves and whose role was to tutor the children of their masters in the arts, sciences, oratory, philosophy, and politics.

We do not know much about those first teachers except that some of them based their teaching on personal or collective vision, the search for wisdom, self-knowledge, and understanding of the diverse ways of being human. Even then, they taught about essential understandings and practices necessary to learn one's connection to all aspects of the natural world and oneself. Yet, from those earliest expressions in the first human societies through the days of Socrates, Buddha, Jesus, and Quetzalcoatl, teaching has been an honored and transformative path, as well as a journey of trial and tribulation. The honoring of the tradition of the teacher as storyteller, transferer of knowledge, history, art, music, and dance, which embody the "soul" of a culture and people, continues in some indigenous cultures even today. In the European West, respecting and honoring the role of the sage teacher and the path of teaching began to erode during the Enlightenment and has continued to the present.

The education that we experience today has been stripped of its former dimensions and soulful meaning and deep ecological understanding in favor of the methodological application of skill development and cognitive training. The honoring of soul, creativity, spontaneity, and play have given way to an almost complete monopoly of practical skill-based knowledge designed to weed out the dreamers and to ensure the perpetuation of the modern technologically oriented world. The goal of most of modern education is to define all aspects of human teaching and learning to such a precise degree and with such technical proficiency that education can be totally controlled from entrance to exit by the vested interests of the modern industrial-technocratic-political complex. This conceptual orientation has become so much the orientation of modern education that the only real opportunity for deep holistic learning is when one exits the system intentionally or by accident or through failure.

Serious and sustained dialogue about the soulfulness of teaching and the transformative nature of learning has yet to enter the domain, the mainstream, of "professional" education. Such dialogue remains at the margins of modern education, reserved only for a few who address the humanness of education or for times of crisis and/or passing curiosity of the "alternatives" or other cultural systems of education. For the past 100 years, education in modern America has been a quest to "scientify" education. Beginning with John Dewey, this quest to become a "science" has drawn practically on social science and science in an effort to measure and "measure up." Few professional educators have a comprehensive understanding of the social cultivating dimensions of education and its essential contribution to the ecology of the soul, lest they be accused of being mystics, new agers, or spiritualists. Ancient teachers are seen to have little that could be considered a true scientifically based methodology as it is understood and practiced in modern mainstream education. Yet, they understood something of the deeper dimensions of human nature and the experiences that define the human condition. They reflected this understanding in the ways they taught and reflected on the true nature and purpose of education. Their teachings never revolved around information processing, which so limits the parameters of modern education and ensures that it never moves beyond cognitive rationalism.

The goal of the ancient teachers was to know the universal nature of the cosmos and to live from its source. For example, Vedic sages taught that the inner life of humans mirrored the inner life of nature and vice versa. Hence, they sought to resonate their inner and outer lives with that of the cosmos. Understanding the elemental forces of earth, wind, fire, water, and spirit became the foundations of the "first sciences" of medicine, architecture, and astronomy. Through such understanding, they believed, came true wisdom. Today, we call this principle "teaching the whole person," or holistic education. The ramifications of such a foundational principle applied to modern education are as profound today as they were in ancient times. Yet, at probably no other time in history have these basic principles been so poorly understood and practiced. This is perennial wisdom, a wisdom gained from long human experience of interacting with nature. This notion seems simplistic in today's world of the information highway and ultramodern technologies, but it is a wisdom born of a higher intelligence inherent in the very workings of nature. For these early teachers, human beings and all the universe possessed life; intelligence and soul were the foundations of understanding for those first teachers. This reverence for the life in all matter contrasts sharply with the Western scientific notion that matter is dead and that life as we know it is a special case, an anomaly in an otherwise lifeless universe (Chopra, 1994).

The sites for undertaking teaching about something important were therefore located in selected natural places that were conducive to connecting a student's inner reality to that of the universe. Although learning can occur anytime and in any place, ancient teachers realized that selecting the right context for "a teaching" to take place was half the job. Their perspective was that, in watching nature, we would ultimately come to truly know our own. Creating encounters with the outer environment conducive to deep understanding and facilitating the development of a receptive inner environment within the learner were always the two complementary dynamics honored within ancient teaching methods. Many ancient teachers believed that all special techniques of teaching were to no avail if the learner was not prepared to receive a teaching. If their minds and motivation were not fertile, then no amount of teaching would make a difference (Chopra, 1994).

Ancient teachers developed thousands of teaching techniques that they combined in highly creative ways, but they never forgot that the individual's own spirit would guide their real learning. Their thoughts of the ideal education was like the air; it was natural, spontaneous, original, creative, and naturally spiritual. Such natural education unfolded like play; indeed, it was a form of play. It drew its sustenance from the natural interplay of human and nature and the spirit inherent in both. It was not bounded, weighed down with dogma; it was free (Chopra, 1994)!

Reflections on the Modern View

Today's education rarely comes close to this sort of natural and inspired education. Modern American education prides itself on its practicality and attempts to teach students one part at a time, one subject at a time, one place at a time. In short, its hallmark is that of its monodimensionality and its homogenization of the learning experience. It is through and through a rationalistic process of knowing and understanding the world devoid of any real soul or passion. In fact, modern education has so defined itself as a rationalistic process that its detachment from natural human learning and knowing is invisible to its most enthusiastic practitioners. This is how narrow and misinformed modern education has become; it confuses thinking with information processing. There is no longer a sensibility for the deeper, ineffable, fundamental relational purpose for people and the whole earth. Similarly, as Oscar Kawagley (1995), Yupiaq scholar and educator, states:

> Most indigenous peoples' worldviews seek harmony and integration with all life, including the spiritual, natural and human domains. These three realms permeate traditional worldviews and all aspects of indigenous peoples' lives. Their constructed technology was mediated by nature. Their traditional education processes were carefully constructed around mythology, history, the observation of natural processes and animals' and plants' styles of survival and obtaining food, and use of natural materials to make their tools and implements, all of which was made understandable through thoughtful stories and illustrative examples. This view of the world and approach to education has been brought into jeopardy with the onslaught of Western social systems and institutionalized forms of cultural transmission. . . . The Western worldview with its aggressive educational practices and technoscience orientation has placed indigenous cultures in "harms way." These cultures have been characterized as primitive and backward and therefore wanting, are subjected to an endless stream of assimilative processes to bring their practitioners into mainstream society. The indigenous people are forced to live in a constructed and psy-

> chic world not of their making or choosing. Little is left in their lives to remind them of their indigenous culture; nor is their recognition of their indigenous consciousness and its application of intelligence, ingenuity, creativity, and inventiveness in the making of their world. (pp. 2–3)

Alternative forms of education that attempt to apply ancient principles of teaching have been considered without merit in mainstream education and, in more conservative education circles, even feared. This attitude toward alternative education continues despite the continued loss of confidence by more and more people in the current educational system and in teachers. The dysfunctional nature, extraordinary expense, and increased complexity of the educational system is becoming obvious to almost everyone who works or deals with it. Few involved with the modern institution admit to the futility of practicing education in the absence of a functionally healthy cosmology and philosophy of education. Ironically, current movements to restore an ecology lost or to find a cosmological foundation and those seeking to redefine education in ever more constrictive/mechanistic forms stem from the recognition that mainstream education is no longer serving the deeper needs of many people.

American education continues to be predominately controlled and influenced by the industrial-technocratic-political complex, the so-called mainstream. Although American Indians have become teachers, educators, or administrators in the greatest numbers in comparison with other professionals, their full participation in mainstream education has remained marginal. Modern schooling and American Indian cultural life have always remained worlds apart. The integration of Indian cultural perspectives with Western education was never considered in any serious way by earlier generations of educators, Indian and non-Indian alike. The rediscovery and integration of an American Indian perspective of education into my own work as an educator was more a result of my alienation from the guiding paradigm of Western education than of any planned response. The collective heritage of American Indians relating to traditional indigenous education is extensive. Yet, until recently, few Indian educators have been encouraged to explore this heritage. American Indian perspectives of education facilitate another core essential element of true education—that of educating the whole person. The concept of an education process that keeps people whole rather than fragmented has great appeal in our time of modern alienation and fragmented living.

Few people realize the exceptionally rich heritage of education that has come down to us from indigenous traditions around the world. Part of the reason for such a lack of awareness lies in the homogenization of the modern educational experience and its hidden curriculum of conditioning for the view that other cultural ways of knowing are somehow "less-than," primitive, inconsequential, or mere curiosity in comparison with modern education.

In very direct ways, modern schooling has perpetuated the demise of indigenous knowledge and supported our continued ecological illiteracy as writers such as David Orr (1992, 1994) and Chet Bowers (1993) have contended. According to Orr (1992),

> Schooling should not be confused with learning. . . . Schooling has to do with the ability to master basic functions that can be measured by tests. Learning has to do with matters of judgment, and with living responsibly and artfully, which cannot be measured so easily. It is possible as Walker Perry once noted, to get all A's in school and flunk life. Post-modern education has to do with the integration of schooling and active learning, a juncture that has occurred under modern conditions less often than one might suppose or wish. (p. xi)

It is time to change the role and function of schooling toward the manifestation of true ecological literacy. Let it be a kind of literacy that includes not only study and appreciation of environmentally informed historic and indigenous systems of education, but also to bring forward contemporary versions of their most important principles.

The epistemologies of indigenous people provide important models and insights into the reality of ecological sustainability and ways to create foundations for ecological literacy. These epistemologies are rooted in the long experience a people have had with their homeland. Their sense of identity as a people is so interwoven with the ecological fabric of a region that it is not too far-fetched to say that the people and their land are one ecological organism.

> Indigenous knowledge is rooted in a local culture. It is the source of community cohesion, a framework that explains the origins of things (cosmology) and provides the basis for preserving fertility, controlling pests, and conserving biological diversity and genetic variability. Knowledge is not separated from the multiple tasks of living well in a specific place over a long period of time. The crisis of sustainability has occurred only when and where this union between knowledge, livelihood, and living has been broken and knowledge is used for the single purpose of increasing productivity . . . Ecological sustainability will require a patient and systematic effort to restore and preserve traditional knowledge of the land and its functions. . . . Sustainability will not come primarily from homogenized top-down approaches but from careful adaptation of people to particular places. This is as much a process of rediscovery as it is of research. (Orr, 1992, pp. 32–33)

Because of the importance of indigenous education, as models and metaphors, windows and mirrors, to provide insight into the possible ways to reinvent a sustainable education, those ways must be seriously researched and revitalized. They are keys to educating for the kind of sustainable future that our current "way" of modern education can never hope to accomplish. Indeed, as David Orr and others contend, our education system must share in the responsibility for creating the environmental crisis that looms all around us.

As it turns out, our current system is so crisis driven that it doesn't worry about what students are learning as much as it does about what the local school board will say about student performance on the most recent battery of the SAT and ACT—the current sacred cows of school success. Environmental education is still not taken seriously by most schools, if it is taken at all. Yet, it must be understood that the environmental crisis is but one manifestation of modern society and an educational paradigm and its associated systems out of balance. The underlying cause of the crisis

arises from the narrow conception of who we are, what the earth is, and what it is to educate children so that they may live and think as human beings.

WHERE TO GO FROM HERE

When the question of how to improve the system is asked, the beginning of the answer lies in the relationship between student and teacher. As I have indicated throughout the chapter, teaching is abstract neither as content or as a process. The wisdom of indigenous educational tradition lies in the fact that it begins the actuality of our interdependence with nature and the guidance that may be provided by caring, inwardly developed people.

Some teachers have grown tired of viewing students, parents, and schools as the problem. Some have taken a proactive approach and have become determined to make the best out of every situation, even the most dysfunctional ones. This attitude seems to make a world of difference in terms of maintaining the best possible teaching/learning relationships.

Generally, the more a teacher plays the part as prescribed by the school, the greater the gap widens between themselves and students. This continues over a period of time until it becomes a them-against-us scenario played out in the context of school and classroom. Command and control then become the measure of school order, and everything else, including the cultivation of the delicate ecology of teaching and learning, becomes secondary. The attitudes, dynamics, and response that evolve as a result of such a context resemble a codependent dysfunctional relationship. Then all parties, teachers, students, administrators, parents, and community inadvertently and unconsciously conspire to perpetuate what has essentially become a dysfunctional learning context. Learning is always taking place in a school. The question is what kind of learning and toward what end. By not paying attention to this evaluation of social and communal ecology, we not only perpetuate a diseased teaching/learning relationship but also contribute in a roundabout way to the ecological crisis and dysfunction of our own social ecology. Many students come to internalize the belief that learning about "real life" happens outside the classroom and that school is just a place to put in time until they can get out and "make money." Yet, other students build a kind of "dependency psychology" in which they acquire the lack of determination to pursue anything on their own; this perception of the meaninglessness of classroom life eventually broadens to encompass all their lives. Played out in the context of the ecological, social, and cultural complexities of the 21st century, such illiteracy and lack of a grounded and sustainable worldview portends continued educational dysfunctionality of global portions. We have to question seriously not only the wisdom but also the survivability of perpetuating a sole focus as the current guiding paradigm of modern education.

If we are teachers, part of the answers to this questioning may be found in our own stories and how and why we came to be who we are, doing what we are doing.

It is essential that the relationship of our own stories as teachers and as learners with the greater story of education be understood at their deeper indigenous and ecological levels of process and being. It is also essential that the inherent wisdom of indigenous education be reintroduced into the very core of mainstream education.

The inertia of the current system of modern education is tremendous because it is so heavily "vested" at practically every level of modern society—economically, socially, politically, and cosmologically. Change comes to such a massive interconnected system in painfully slow ways. To maintain my creative sense of teaching and learning in the face of such inertia, I have developed the following criteria to guide my exploration and commitment to the teaching/learning relationship between myself and current and future students. For me, these criteria act as "prime directives" that keep me focused with regard to my role as an indigenous teacher.

- The environmental, social, and cultural crises that we face today cannot and will not be solved by the same education process that helped create them.
- Ecological sustainability implies the recovery of civic and cultural wisdom.
- Sustainability has to be a focus for the content and process of postmodern education, as well as a defining element of knowledge.
- We must teach for cultural and ecological literacy and transactional competence in working with various dimensions of the crises.
- Students must be acquainted with the deeper levels of the environmental crisis.
- We must rekindle the innate reflection of our inborn feeling of connectedness to the natural world.
- We must begin to teach for a contemporary expression of the indigenous and ecologically possible human.

FINAL THOUGHTS

A new educational consciousness must be forged that allows for the kind of teaching and learning that facilitates finding face, finding heart, and finding a foundation within the context of proper relationship with the natural world. We must reestablish the "ecology of teaching" in such a way that it allows us to explore and express our collective heritage in ecologically based ways of knowing and being. The exploration of the nature of indigenous education and its projection into a contemporary context is more than an academic exercise. It illuminates the true nature of the ecological connection of human learning and helps liberate the experience of being human and being related to nature at all levels.

Much of what today is called indigenous knowledge is really an expression of the wisdom of our inner and outer ecologies and the application of that knowledge to life and relationship. Indigenous knowledge, because it comes from the wellspring of the human soul and natural experience, is transformative in that it brings forth deep understanding. Indigenous education is about "seeking life" in all its many expressions and learning from the processes that these sorts of encounters bring. Inherent in this metaphor is the realization that everything, including teaching, writing, creating, story, art, music, and science, can be grounded in a meaningful context for deep learning about relationship. Thus, learning and teaching about any of these areas can contribute to the health and wholeness of the individual, family, and natural community. Education for wholeness is defined by this striving for a level of harmony between individuals and their world. All true education is in some way connecting as the wisdom flowing through the natural world.

Through the exploration of indigenous education, both learners and teachers can authentically participate in a creative and transformative dialogue inherently based on equality and mutual reciprocity. This way of learning, communicating, and working in relationship mirrors those ways found in nature. Teachers have significant power to determine the future of education and reorientation to the indigenous principles of relationship and responsibility for the care and healing of the earth. Part of the future of education must be rooted in the transformational revitalization of the role and archetype of "the teacher" in ourselves as teachers and the "making" of the next generation of teachers. As we collectively reflect on the metaphor of the "indigenous teacher," we must truly think about "what is education for" and about the generations of children to come who will be the affected recipients of the world that we are now creating. It is time for an authentic dialogue among teachers to begin that moves beyond simply new innovations in the technology of "information sharing." It is time to explore where we as teachers have been, where we are, and where we are going as we collectively embark on finding our way through the many paths illuminated by the dawning of a New Sun, one that, ironically, has been awaiting rediscovery. May the New Sun find us once again moving toward a sustainable and ecologically conscious future. I hope this chapter will contribute to this essential dialogue. May the Good Spirits Guide Us.

REFERENCES

Bowers, C. A. (1993). *Education, cultural myths, and the ecological crisis*. Albany: State University of New York Press.

Cajete, G. A. (1994). *Look to the mountain: An ecology of indigenous education*. Durango, CO: Kivaki Press.

Chopra, D. (1994). *Return of the Rishi* [Audiotape]. San Rafael, CA: Amber-Allen/New World Library.

Havel, V. (1995, January/February). A time for transcendence. *Utne Reader, 67,* pp. 53, 112–113. (Reprinted from [1994, September/October]. Something is being born, *New Age*

Journal). (Remarks presented by Václav Havel on July 4, 1994, at Independence Hall on the occasion of his receiving the Philadelphia Liberty Medal)

Kawagley, O. (1995). *A Yupiaq worldview*. Prospect Heights, IL: Waveland Press.

Orr, D. (1992). *Ecological literacy.* Albany: State University of New York Press.

Orr, D. (1994). *Earth in mind*. Washington, DC: Island Press.

Lane, P. (Ed.). (1984). *The sacred tree*. Commack, NY: Four Worlds Development Press.

Portillo, M. L. (1963). *Aztec thought and culture*. Norman: University of Oklahoma Press.

Shearer, T. (1971). *Lord of dawn*. Healdsburg, CA: Naturegraph.

Biography

Gregory Cajete is a Tewa Indian from Santa Clara Pueblo, New Mexico. He received his Bachelor of Arts Degree from New Mexico Highlands University, where he majored in both biology and sociology and minored in secondary education. He received his Master of Arts Degree in secondary and adult education from the University of New Mexico. He received his Ph.D. from International College in social science education with an emphasis in Native American studies. Cajete has been designated New Mexico Humanities Council Scholar in the area of ethno-botany of northern New Mexico, has been an appointed member of the New Mexico Arts Commission, and has lectured at colleges and universities nationally and in Canada, Italy, Japan, and the former Soviet Union.

Cajete has been the Dean of the Center for Research and Cultural Exchange at the Institute of American Indian Arts in Santa Fe, New Mexico. The center is an entity that Cajete conceptualized, designed, and staffed on the basis of the unique congressional mandate by which the instutute operates. He also operates a private educational consulting specializing in science, social science, and art education. He is currently Assistant Professor in the College of Education; Division of Language, Literacy, and Social Cultural Studies; University of New Mexico, Albuquerque.

10 LEARNING AS TRANSFORMATION

BOB SAMPLES

INTRODUCTION

In the days of behaviorism, *learning* was defined as an acquisition of a behavior in response to a stimulus. If a student, when asked for the sum of "2 and 2," acquired the behavior of indicating "4," she or he was said to have "learned." The information comprising knowledge in this model was always clear and distinct; correspondingly, learning was specific and measurable. Today, behavioristic theory is widely regarded as simplistic and narrow. The emphasis has shifted from sole concern for content to a recognition of thinking processes. The goal in this case is to develop the capacity to think clearly, critically, and in some cases, creatively.

Even this more contemporary model of learning has its limitations, however. A third element in the creation of knowledge is beyond specific content and thinking skills: the knower her- or himself. The learner, the person, not only processes and stores information but, to a varying extent, also engages in a process of transformation. In this notion of learning, new knowledge is given meaning in the life and mind of the learner, and the learner's life and mind take on new meaning. Learning is a form of participation in the world wherein new dimensions unfold in each. The transformation is the key to our individual and collective evolution.

In this chapter, Bob Samples introduces what may be called a transformative model of learning and of knowledge. Learning is seen as a primary force in the evolution of culture and in the process of individual human development. Samples is interested in the continuity of biological evolution and the evolution of the human mind. Building upon the theoretical work of Henryke Skolimowski, Samples maintains that biology and culture, systematic thinking and artistic and social expression, create the possibility for the "participatory mind." This framework focuses on the intuitive, personal dimensions of thinking where we learn to adapt our sensitivities and cultural gifts to participate in the creation of new insights.

The participatory mind is an essential component in driving the evolution of culture and individual human understanding. Samples suggests that it operates in accordance with the same fundamental characteristics operating in ecosystems, and he adapts them to illuminate the possibility of sustainable learning environments. Given this perspective, he stresses the comprehensive context in which the participatory mind develops. He refers to the unity and holiness of all things as "sacred," and the integrity of all things within their connectedness as "soul."

In these terms, the activity of the participatory mind in dialogue with the sacred is an opportunity for the transformation of the soul. As we learn with depth and scope, as we learn in ecologically sound educational environments, we are transformed in the process of learning. We learn to see the world differently, with new understandings, passions, and questions; we learn to see ourselves and to develop a new sense of identity and meaning. Although such profound issues rarely show themselves in daily life, they are nonetheless there in an unceasing process of evolution. Samples concludes that the course of evolution for individual children and the culture as a whole will very much depend on the types of educational environments and conditions for learning we create.

—Jeffrey Kane

At the dawn of the 20th century, classical physics, in all its certainty, failed repeatedly to explain the fundamentals of the microcosm and the macrocosm. The worlds of atoms and galaxies definitely vector to drummers different from those setting pace for a world of our size. Progress has been made because physicists, in a burst of foolhardy courage, abandoned Newtonian certainty. Quantum theory was born and is growing to maturity. Perhaps more important, ecological theory began a slow but inexorable move toward adolescence.

Analogously, we have spent much of the past century in education trying to be more certain about what constitutes learning. We have reached several plateaus of what appeared to be certainty by applying classical research methodologies, only to find our results serving exceedingly narrow perspectives. Tests, controlled experimentation, careful measurement, pre- and postexaminations, rats, cats, graduate students, and all of Skinner's pigeons have not erased the mystery of *learning*. As we draw to the close of this millennium, progress to understand learning is as much the result of changing our ways of knowing as it is about discovery born of systematic research. Classical research, like classical physics, functions best when variables are few and each can be controlled.

It is not as though we have learned nothing from these efforts. Indeed, we have. For example, we have determined that a rat is a fine research animal for cancer and a poor one for learning. Mary Catherine Bateson, in the summer 1994 issue of *Holistic Education Review,* reported her father Gregory's musings that behaviorism bases much of its stature on the results of experiments conducted with drowsy, confused, nocturnal rats being forced (for the convenience of scientists) to perform in experiments in the daytime. "They bite at night," Gregory was told. Stimulus-response theory, positive and negative reinforcement, and eventually "warm fuzzies," with its distorted view of self-esteem and self-worth, have left us yearning for depth and dignity in our quest to understand learning. An illusory quest for certainty has led us to simplistic models of learning for several decades of education in North America. The building of a worldview based on the illusion of Newtonian-bred certainty with small numbers of variables stands in sharp contrast with the complexity of our biological and ecological design.

Yet, in these new times, we seem to be the beneficiaries of a new perspective. Many have described this with the growingly tiresome phrase *new paradigm*. As "new age" as this phrase sounds, it definitely is not. Jacob Bronowski and Thomas Kuhn, whose audiences were the staid and sober community of philosopher-scholars representing classical tradition, cautioned us long ago that a new paradigm was emerging. It would not necessarily require new data, but rather would be characterized by clever and substantively different ways of recasting what we already know. Clearly, they were right. Regarding learning, that time is upon us.

In this chapter, I suggest that some key aspects of a new paradigm of learning are as follows:

1. *The Participatory Mind:* Following a path suggested by Henryk Skolimowski, we explore three models of mind that link the process of evolution as played out by universal design, to the way we choose to interact with our environment through the dual dynamics of subjectivity and objectivity, and finally to how we acknowledge our unity with all that exists.
2. *Nature, Evolution, and Learning:* We examine learning as an evolutionary component of our makeup. Seven characteristic patterns of adaptive evolutionary systems are explored in regard to learning.
3. *The Learning Soul:* In this segment, we consider an evolving perspective that blends spirituality—the quest for unity—and information, knowledge, and wisdom.
4. *Transformation:* This section provides a synthesis of the three perspectives cited above.

THE PARTICIPATORY MIND

> The sacred is surely related to the beautiful. If we could say how they are related, we could, perhaps say what the words mean.
>
> (Gregory Bateson, 1979)

Henryk Skolimowski, in his landmark book *The Participatory Mind* (1994), charts a bold new course for the philosophical perspectives of learning. His uniqueness is grounded in his belief that the human mind is an expression of the vast sweep of natural evolution. The evolutionary mind represents a unity composed of three configurations of mind: Mind I, Mind II, and Mind III. Each uses "sensitivities" that facilitate engagement and involvement between the individual learner and the world at large.

Mind I is the mind that embodies our cultural and intellectual heritage. For Western thinkers, it is the world we have abstracted into science, mathematics, philosophy, and all other organized forms of knowledge. It is characterized by the functions of the "new" brain, the neocortex, and its capacities for calculation, computation, and reductive thought. Mind II is characterized not only by the sensitivities we have chosen in the functioning of Mind I, but also *all* the sensitivities built into us by the process of evolution. Through this wider array of sensitivities, we include capacities that, by and large, we have individually and collectively chosen to allow to lie dormant and untested. Art, music, moral judgment, poetry, and love are but a few expressions of Mind II's sensitivities. Mind III is the symbiotic interrelatedness of Mind I and Mind II and the greater "reality" created by the union of the two.

The purpose of these Minds is to engage distinctive "sensitivities" with our evolutionary design and enter into a co-evolutionary relationship with self, others, and the universe. They "pay attention" to the basic sensitivities for life to go on, and they do so because they were "designed" by the universe—through the process of evolution—to do so. Karl Pribram, a noted neuroscientist, once mused in a conversation that "consciousness is what we pay attention to." It follows that if we choose to change consciousness and if we are to develop Mind III, we must learn to pay attention to different things—and that, it strikes me, is what Skolimowski's contribution is all about.

In a way, he asks us to take the version of reality that we have constructed from the limited set of sensitivities of Mind I and expand it into Mind II, with its richness of ancient sensitivities—sensitivities that have inadvertently lain dormant as we constructed the worldview of Mind I. Imagine a hunter-gatherer 20,000 years ago trying to decide whether to find food for the day or, instead, to carve the phases of the moon on a pebble that she or he carried around. Ironically, the anthropological and archaeological record *shows they did both*. Mind I has deep roots.

This proposed embracing of Mind I with Mind II in contemporary times may well be remedial—the relearning of skills of survival. This reunion will not weaken the effects of Mind I and the worldview embedded within it; rather, it represents a synergic transformation that addresses the age-old fear that reason and intuition exclude each other. Intuition is a transformed version of reason. Mind III is the manifestation of the wholeness of mind; it celebrates the merging of Mind I and Mind II with the rest of the substance of the universe.

Sensitivities of Mind II and their symbiotic relationship in Mind III are better understood if we recall the prophetic vision of psychologist Abraham Maslow. It is easy to frame the sensitivities of Skolimowski in the context of basic needs as configured by Maslow. Maslow may best be remembered in how he honored the roles of physical well-being, self-esteem, and spirituality to support the psychological integrity. The sensitivities seem to provide a more contemporary clarification of the role of the evolutionary bond between body and mind—a clarification vital to any future understanding of transformation in learning.

The role of evolution provides even more. My reading of Skolimowski suggests that Mind I established the current worldview through reflection, measurement, and calculation—a worldview that has proved to be both bane and blessing. Mind I first provides an acceptable configuration of reality and then examines the world of experience and patterns it into a cohesive expression of order consistent with that reality. The danger is high that the logic of the cohesion will become so seductive as to shut down the process of evolution. The blessing, however, is the possibility of transformation—transformation that generates Mind III—thus restoring evolution to the process.

Mind III emerges when Mind I and Mind II engage in dialogue, inviting in wider arrays of sensitivities, and begin to expand meaning and to establish new perceptions of reality. Not only are these sensitivities a *product* of the evolutionary process, but they are also a *means* for the process. Learning may be seen as the intentional engagement, exploration, and extension of the sensitivities with the three forms of Mind. As our sensitivities unfold, the more sensitive and knowing we become. Increasing the sensitivities available to us increases the richness of our reality as well.

Central to this thesis is the word *create* as used in the commentary about Mind III. Creation is a *means* rather than an *end*. Willis Harman (1995), a scholar of transformative thinking and cofounder of the Institute for Noetic Sciences, sums it up in his review of Skolimowski's book: "There is no truth or reality distinct from the mind that knows it, yet there is an absolute truth" (p. 22). A Zen koan if I ever saw one. This provocative note swirls us forward through the philosophical justification of the absolute truth, which turns out to mean that absolute truth is *participatory* truth.

Recall that I warned of the bane of the possibility of Mind II's fixity or closedness. It seems to me that we are at the juncture of a long sweep of participating in the universe with shaded vision. In ecology there exists a concept termed *ecotone*. An ecotone is that zone where ecosystems overlap. The natural stability of one system interpenetrates another, and suddenly both experience the vulnerability of newness. It is in such zones of naïveté that evolution flourishes.

The traditional philosophy of science, the foundation for old paradigm thinking, was a search for objective reality and absolute truth. It was a method of inquiry designed to discover and *fix* the laws of nature. The job of old paradigm thought is to eliminate metaphor, anchor truth, and equate discipline with predictable order. The job of new paradigm thought is to honor the integrity of precedent but to responsibly explore the "ecotones" of inquiry, those places where change is rapid and unpredictable. Clearly, contemporary astronomy and physics are stretched far beyond the limits of Newtonian vision, yet we comfortably use old paradigm principles to oversee space shuttle flights, aeronautic engineering, and the synthesis of medicines and drugs. Simply put, the foundation can no longer be seen as the temple. The job of the Mind can no longer be seen as the generator of objective closedness and "truth" as terminated, intellectual piety.

It is clear that science conducted through a participatory mind does not mean that what we perceive and conceive is subjective and therefore worthless. Rather, we have to develop high integrity and highly authentic ways of participating. This integrity and authenticity may differ in emphasis in poetry, science, mathematics, and love. Yet, what remains after participation will be a relationship with the worlds of mind, knowledge, and "reality" that has the *courage* to sustain openness and evolution. Let me offer a tongue-in-cheek example: Gravity is a force invented by physical scientists to explain the behavior of mass in the universe. Scientists confidently send rockets into complex orbits, build bridges, and design dynamic machines that honor the mathematical and physical predictions they derive. Yet, for all the complexity they seem to be able to manage, there is a deep and abiding mystery to gravity. As to what causes it, scientists postulate a massless, chargeless, so far undetected particle they call the graviton. This sounds like the troll under the bridge to me.

The certainty and concreteness of old paradigm science seem now to have been an illusion and may best be seen as a way-station en route to a participatory "truth," a destination that requires a new kind of intellectual courage. About the need for courage, let me put it this way: Classical reason requires objective detachment in reaching conclusions. Research is conducted by limiting variables and controlling those selected. One by one, factors are eliminated that do not affect the outcome. Finally, the "conclusion" is reached. Truth is wrested from mystery. But is it truth at all? Could it be that the conclusions reached are simply results that conform to the methods of reductive thought and are not "true" in a larger sense? Classical science

seeks simplicity and achieves it by taking things out of context. Contemporary science seeks relationship, connection, and simplicity. Instead, it finds complexity—discovering that as complexity increases, so too does consciousness. Comfort with complexity requires courage.

Skolimowski (1994) says it this way: "At the beginning was courage. And courage has begotten all other attributes that made us into human beings. Courage has brought about art, religion and philosophy" (p. 364). He could easily have added science, law, governance, and medicine, to name a few.

It is likely, in the evolutionary history of humans, that the Mind II sensitivities were fairly similar. Focus was on sensitivities that ensured food, water, shelter, and safety. Movement from one mind to another requires the expansion of the sensitivities. Once Mind II was established, Mind I began to open its evolutionary array, and other sensitivities presented themselves. Stress on survival likely gave way to concern about rules of conduct and governance.

The survival of our species itself is a kind of expression of success in conscious evolution. Beyond survival, the cultural mind makes choices about the rules of conduct that eventually give it form and substance. Being a member-in-good-standing of that culture requires obedience to those rules. Much of the learning in such a setting is directed at the teaching of these rules in a closed system fashion. Learning, in effect, becomes adherence to techniques for shutting down the participatory mind.

Yet, I am becoming less concerned about the note of alarm in the previous paragraph. My sense is that we are, for whatever reason, legitimizing access to information in ways never conceived of. Electronic media and technologies are democratizing access routes that would have either bewildered or amused Marshal McCluhan when he wrote his brilliant statements about the *medium being the message.* It is possible that we are becoming the evolutionary instruments of self-amplification in a way that Jerome Bruner sensed when he described the computer as a ratiocinative amplifier—an amplifier of the capacity to reason. In *On Knowing: Essays for the Left Hand* (1973), Bruner cited the historical explosions in information and assaults on worldview that accompanied the process of accessing the universe through new technologies. The microscope and telescope as amplifiers of vision, the radio as an amplifier of hearing, the whole field of remote sensing—all represent technologies that extend basic human sensory refinement. In the light of the growing list of sensitivities being explored in the culture at large, it is likely that my fears of enforced limitation and conformity are unnecessary. Yet, my apprehension about the difference between *accessing* sensibilities and *using them wisely* is one of our paramount educational concerns. The information explosion promises to deliver a severe blow to censorship of our sensitivities. Censorship is anti-evolutionary.

In a different vein, as a person who has written widely about the brain and learning, I find myself strangely exposed when I read what Skolimowski had to say about the relationship between the brain and the mind. I realize that my approach has nearly always been to describe different brain functions in the hope that such descriptions would convince teachers and parents to increase the number of options extended to children. I, like many of my colleagues, have been seduced by the notion that if we make our explanations sound objective and scientific, we can depend on the weight of the old paradigm to bring about the changes we want. This forces us to try to keep current in dozens of arenas of neural study. The task is impossible and had forced me into a defensive practice of arguing for my models of the brain, rather than speaking out in favor of learning. I have found myself seeking refuge in facts about the brain, rather than honoring the promise of mind.

Skolimowski (1994) reminds us of a simple reality, "It is a fallacy to assume that by understanding the brain we shall understand the mind. We shall understand the mind by understanding the mind" (p. 296). Learning is mind-work, not brain-work. The brain can tell us *that* we are thinking, but it cannot begin to disclose *what* we are thinking.

Some time ago, I heard a story about a preschool child who anguished her parents by insisting that she should be taught to read. Both parents resisted because neither knew how to teach reading; they didn't want to botch the job. The child persisted, and finally her nagging won out. Snuggled in her mother's lap, the momentous experience began. There was a confused pause. The child looked up at her mother and plaintively asked, "What do I read, the black or the white?"

Of course, the appropriate answer is the black. But we are deceived in believing that the answer is quite so simple. Given, the black displays the standard abstract symbols needed for writing and reading and so it becomes efficient to use them in conventional ways. Yet, what is lost? Why have the Chinese chosen to display their letters in vertical columns for their reading? What is the purpose of Hebrew script being read from right to left? Why does Japanese have two families of text, *katakana* and *kanji*? All of these systems work for those who use them, and each possesses a rationale somewhere in history that justifies the logic and truth of the offering. Obviously, the participatory mind can participate in different ways.

I wonder, as I explore the consequences of the participatory mind, whether I can comfortably live with the loss of certainty. I wonder whether this way of thinking is new or represents a re-union with things we have forgotten as a species? I occasionally wonder whether the distances I create between myself and those who have chosen different beliefs is the basis for my bigotry, fear, and insecurity. Collectively, can the ways we think be ultimately the causes of war and violence? If the way I think teaches me to detach and see separateness rather than unity and wholeness, will I ever gain the courage to accept the responsibility to *belong* to experience? "Children are our hope," Skolimowski (1994) claims. "For them, magic is natural. They co-create effortlessly with the universe" (p. 296). Their minds participate naturally.

NATURE, EVOLUTION, AND LEARNING

Evolution is learning—learning is evolution. Erich Jantsch, a polymath who once directed the Center for Research in Management at the University of California at Berkeley, explored the foundations of management for several decades, seeking first to determine the historical variety of management systems and second to determine the characteristics of long-term success in such systems. As a result of his study, he became convinced that long-term success in management was best expressed by organic evolution and best supervised by nature. No human system of management could even begin to match nature's amazing record.

Here is an explanation for starting an essay on education with comments about management. Jantsch's first cut at the historical models of management took him, not surprisingly, from contemporary corporate approaches across time into the medieval domains of organized religion and from there into whatever could be disclosed by the earliest records of written history. What he found were variations of control for short-term gain. Surely, there were exceptions. Some institutions satisfied their vision of long-term management with promises of eternal life after death. Others, managing toward their dreams of a distant future, anchored their approaches in conquest and rapacious dedication to war-acquired territory. Neither of these examples, eternal life and conquest of the world, are really long term in the same way that Jantsch saw the workings of organic evolution.

Evolution is, for the most part, sternly inclusive. It plays the game so that the game can continue. There is no winning, no losing, only continuous transformation. It is clear that those organisms not suited for any stage of the process often disappear or adapt. The conditions that nurtured extinction and adaptation gave Charles Darwin and, even more so, his disciples the opportunity to tout the "law of blood and fang." The vividness of the metaphor of endless competition unfortunately caught the imagination of succeeding generations. We are just beginning to amend its wrong-headed influence in the realm of education and management, as well as other sectors of social commerce. We benefit by viewing evolution as a long-term process, rather than a short-term one. Yet, impatience, embedded in the human lifespan (60–100 years), seems to coerce us into short-term perspectives. To understand evolution, transformation, and continuity, we must nurture our perspectives of the long-term and widen the scope of what we consider.

Diversity

Contemporary scientists argue whether evolution produces diversity or diversity sustains evolution. Either way, diversity must be sufficient to nourish certain evolutionary processes. Shortly after its formation, Earth was a starkly sterile place. Now, scientists estimate more than 30 million species in residence. Moreover, they estimate 10 million organic molecules and 1 trillion polymers—all are grist for more species. Without diversity, novelty diminishes and evolution most likely slows down. In natural systems, diversity nurtures continuity and survival. Specialization acts to reduce organic flexibility and fluency. If sudden changes in context occur, specialists are more likely than generalists to risk extinction.

Within the realm of education, diversity is characterized by experiences that increase, rather than limit, student options. Attention to multiple intelligences, learning modalities, learning styles, cooperative learning, and creativity increases diversity because these support widely different experiences in instruction and performance.

It is not enough to offer diversity in content if the ways of processing the content are all the same.

Diversity increases the potential for educational success as surely as it favors evolutionary survival.

Optimization

The processes that exchange matter and energy are conservative in natural systems. This conservatism is analogous to savings accounts of matter and energy. Nature is not a spendthrift; instead, it uses resources without extravagance. "Less is more" is a way of thinking about this criterion. When organisms "feed," they consume what is necessary and little more. Studies abound telling of human intervention in optimal settings with the intent to get more efficiency out of the systems' natural processes. Disaster usually follows. For example, when the U.S. Corps of Engineers straightened the meandering course of the Kissimmee River to increase the flow rate to Lake Okeechobee, more water was deemed "better." A disaster was created. The languid meanders moved slowly enough to provide the time to be able to break down the dissolved fertilizers and nutrients carried by the river to the lake. The "higher efficiency" river dumped the concentrated nutrients in the lake, which biotically "died" from an overdose. Now, the same federal agency is "re-meandering" the river much to its original form.

Embedded in the ethic that *more is better* is a view of schooling in which wisdom is linked to the number of courses taken and credit hours passed. School policy establishes the required courses and enforces student involvement in them. At the same time, teachers often carry their own version of maximization to extremes with their requirements for homework. Homework is often seen as the way to "get more of the student's time," with time being the "resource." In nature, healthy systems always have an energy base on which to fall back. It is not unlike a savings account and can be thought of in that way. Optimization, then, is characterized by a surplus in regard to the use of available resources. Maximization is characterized by the use of most, if not all, of a given resource.

Optimization means striking a balance between the student's experience with the skills and content of a discipline so that she or he also feels fulfillment in the arenas of emotion and feeling, as well as in content. Maximization is usually framed in content terms only. Overemphasized content, as repeated practice, spawns burnout.

Cooperation

Cooperation, until recently, has seldom been seen as a major component of evolution in natural systems. As mentioned earlier, this has been the result of wrong-headed application by Darwin's followers and their infatuation with competition as a driving force in evolution. Contemporary biologists have put to bed the notion that competition drives natural selection.

It rests with those of us who are concerned with education to address the negative role that competition plays in learning. When competition becomes institutionalized in our thinking, we inadvertently create an infrastructure of adversarial aggression. The literatures of education and psychology are replete with the negative effects of such practices; an example is Alfie Kohn's book *No Contest* (1986). Competition creates adversity, and adversity limits the perceptual and conceptual options of the learner. As is well known, the practices of cooperative learning have become popular during the last decade. These are noteworthy additions to school experience—yet a note of caution. Cooperation toward achieving only reductive content and reductive thinking skills does little to increase the evolutionary ways of thinking embedded in cooperation as a life-skill. Cooperation must not be seen as a more pleasant technique for revisiting old paradigm thought, but rather as a commitment to expanding new paradigm thought.

> *Cooperation is the spawning ground for civility. Educators must not only invest in providing the skills of cooperation in school experience but commit to the emerging worldview of cooperation as well.*

Self-Regulation

In natural systems, self-regulation may well be the quintessential characteristic of the origin and continuity of life. As was clear in the example of the Kissimmee River, human intervention in natural systems is inevitably aimed at some form of control. When that control countermands self-regulation, matter and energy do not flow as they once did; self-regulation is interfered with. Erich Jantsch, in his landmark book *The Self-Organizing Universe* (1980), explores our world from molecule to galaxy, citing the patterns of self-regulation found in all corners of creation.

Some educators persuasively argue that the ultimate goal for education may be to develop the capacity for self-regulated learning in students—a capacity that ensures lifelong learning. Many disagree, claiming that self-regulation and the self-reliance it produces is anticommunity. They claim that self-regulation builds a cavalier kind of individualism. I totally disagree. Community is benefited by whole, self-reliant individuals committing to the collective well-being of society. Hollow humans, those without self-regulation, are job security for despots. They wander through life, looking for opportunities to exploit or be exploited.

Self-regulating humans are not automatically exploitative. The image of them as "rugged individualists" who become self-centered and selfish is flawed. Rather, it is important to consider that self-regulation fosters an intrinsic wholeness that diminishes the need for exploitative dependence on outside sources. Rather than dependency, self-regulation nurtures what some call a benign interdependence or, as I prefer, interrelatedness.

Self-regulation is a basic ingredient of lifelong learning. Many critics of such approaches want desperately to restrict the child's mind so as to create a society in which control rests in the hands of a chosen few. Religious extremists demonstrate this well. The absence of choice ensures that what students learn is how willingly they submit to coercion. Students must learn to manage their own pursuit of knowledge beyond the vicarious world of the text and the tube.

Self-regulation is the skill of autonomous learning. Without it, students become dependent on, and manipulated by, outside influences. They become a response awaiting a stimulus.

Change

Change is continuous in natural systems as it is in cultural systems. However, much cultural energy is devoted to the prevention of change. In nature, the exchange of matter and energy characterizes change; without it, there would be neither life nor evolution. Change originates from the inside of every organism and also impinges from the environment. From genetics to avalanches, nature embraces all of the options for change. In the natural world, excluding humankind, few organisms do little to prevent change. Instead, they have perfected how to respond to changes emerging in their environment. Responding to emergent change is a basic skill of evolution.

One view of school holds that it is the institution that ensures the students will learn the values that characterize their society and culture. This suggests at the outset that schools are conservative and tend to preserve traditions. Most arguments about schooling revolve around what kinds of changes the students are expected to experience and who should cause them. Self-regulation, discussed above, encourages students to learn the skills of responding to change that emerges from the system. Yet, schools are formal instruments of society. Their uneasiness about self-regulation is predictable. Schools bear much of the responsibility for changing students into viable citizens. Schools most often do this by controlling the experiences that students are permitted to have. In effect, schools impose their version of "frozen" change on the curriculum. The curriculum often becomes a closed system of experience where change is not permitted. In such a setting, how do students learn the necessary skills of responding to changes that are imposed on them? Further, how do they learn to respond to a complex world in which the only certainty is continuous change? Much of schooling is about how to *prevent* change, rather than how to *respond to* change.

Strangely, educators are quick to acknowledge that change is continuous. Yet, when pressure exists in their "ecosystem," they most often *return to the basics* in one form or another. This is maladaptive change—a hardening of the categories, if you will. Conservatism of this sort is all too reflexive and is erroneously seen as an expression of evolution when it is, in fact, devolution. We think we know how to impose change for the better, but we have little evidence that we know how to read changes that emerge from the interaction of systems with each other. Yet, in support of teaching life-skills, the capacity to recognize and respond to emergent change is vital. In a world where change is universal, any educated person must possess the skill and the courage to follow the unknown.

> *True leaders in scholarship, as well as in citizenship, are adept at recognizing and responding to change. Imposed change can be seen to foster discipline and preserve tradition. Responding to emergent change provides the skills of evolutionary continuity.*

Connectedness

Natural systems have no nonconnection; all parts are, in reality, elements of a seamless unity. In nature, plants, animals, and rocks do not classify themselves into hierarchical taxonomic systems. This is the task of humans choosing reductivism. It is for human convenience that objects and processes in the natural world are named, classified, and put into some kind of abstract order. A major difficulty with naming and classifying comes from our tendency to act as though the object named *is* what it is named and the act of naming is the true expression of wisdom. We end up believing in the map, rather than in the territory.

Reductive separation is at the very heart of old paradigm thinking approaches and is the dominant mental exercise in schooling. When students are asked repeatedly to differentiate, separate, and categorize, they build a reflex toward reductivism. Because we have exposed students to this reductive tendency, few seem to have developed the perception and conception needed to recognize the interrelatedness and connectedness that characterize ecological approaches. Nearly always, nonconnectedness establishes the foundation of our view of intelligence. Questions involving specified differences, comparisons, and taxonomic schemes characterize the soul of contemporary curriculum. Students skilled in reductive approaches commonly score high on standardized measures of intelligence. Indeed, IQ is derived from dominantly reductive approaches.

> *What is missing from our formal schooling and training is the capacity to reconnect what we have reductively separated back into cohesive wholeness. Unless we reunite the messages of reductivism into an ecology of unity, we risk ignoring the basis for global understanding.*

Niche

Niche, ecologically speaking, is the way an organism earns a living. In healthy evolving systems, all of the "living" an organism does is what is necessary for it to stay in the game. The game is evolution. As we look at healthy, diverse, interconnected ecosystems, we find that they persist if they benefit each other in relationship. When they do not benefit each other, then self-regulating changes take place. These changes involve all parts of the system and continue until a dynamic balance is restored.

In many current educational practices, much energy is being spent to support reductive separation. We see students separated from each other and isolated on the basis of specific characteristics. It may be ability grouping, remediation, second language; the list goes on. Such efforts result in a kind of homogenization. Narrow sets of rules provide the map that leads us to "success." These rules apply at the level of the individual (the lesson), at the level of the class (the lesson plan), and at the level of the institution (the curriculum). Testing and evaluation drive the whole process. We propose here a broadening of the rules so as to fit the notion of the ecosystem. In natural systems, a niche is created by the response each organism has to the common input of the whole ecosystem. Simultaneously, the individual tacitly contributes back to the whole the consequences of the role it plays. The others respond.

> *In natural systems, evolution flows on information—the total information flow in the system. Information in systemic terms possesses far broader meaning than in usual use. From particle to particle, molecule to molecule, person to person, and galaxy to galaxy, the metaphor of information exchange guides the flow of matter, energy, and life. Each niche contributes to the flow of information; none are exempt.*

Conclusion

The outcomes of these ecological attributes are, in a sense, spiritual. Note here that I chose the word *spiritual* to represent a manifestation of unity, the kind of unity inherent in a worldview that embraces, rather than divides and separates. Old paradigm thought separates spirit from nature; new paradigm thought unites them. Gregory Bateson sensed this when he titled his most popular book *Mind and Nature: A Necessary Unity* (1979). This exploration of ways of "reading" the grammar of that unity is intended to provide us with the reflex to see that all members of an evolving system are equal in their contribution to the whole.

In schooling, if we truly create a worldview that embraces these seven qualities of evolving systems, we must step beyond the domination of basic skills and reductive thought as being the single goal of contemporary education. We must step away from the history of American educational practice and honor the demands of the complex world that has emerged as the ultimate classroom. It is likely that emerging technologies will provide powerful avenues for learning basic skills prior to school and through the first few years in school. In addition, the arts will likely flourish in curricula that honor holism and synthesis, as well as reductive thinking. The metaphoric mind will grow to be an equal partner of rational thought.

The purpose of this section is to familiarize the reader with a selected list of seven conditions to look for and support in the classroom. If these qualities are present in the surroundings of learning, then it is likely a new awareness will emerge about learning. Perhaps student and teacher alike will come to cherish diversity and benefit from its presence. It may be that adjustments need to take place in the pace of learning as we seek optimal rather than maximal. Imagine cooperation running rampant in the school and spilling over into the lifestyles of all present. If we look around tomorrow's classroom, might we not see evidence for self-regulation in all quarters and recognize the seeds of lifelong learning? Change can become a welcome ally for growth, rather than a threat to traditional stability. Can we learn again, as have many primal people on our planet, that all things are connected and inextricably related? Is it possible that we can begin to see worth in all things and respect each organism and its niche? Such is the dream.

The Learning Soul

The human soul is the sacred connection to all life and the world that sustains it, to our membership in the human family, and within the spirit of our personhood. Fulfilling this sacred connection is the promise of evolution. Rare, in educational settings, are conversations about the sacred and the soul. Somehow, these words—*sacred* and *soul*—seem to have slipped into a domain of timidity and fear for many educators, a domain reflexively called up in religious terms. The timidity and fear shore up our confusion about which is church and which is state. Best stay out of the fray, an action that stokes our growing paranoia of religious zealotry. All this brings about a clarification of the definition of these words as I will use them.

> *Sacred* is the innate tendency to experience the world *whole*. It expresses a reverential oneness, a unity among all things.
>
> *Soul* is a sacred connection between all things. In the living world, this is expressed through our connection to all life and the world that supports it.

Aware of the traditional meaning of these words, I ask the reader to indulge in the liberty I take in emphasizing the reverential rather than the religious. This holds true for both *sacred* and *soul.* My motivation is simple: I am not sophisticated enough to use these words in a way that would embrace all the religious persuasions of my readers. Rather than err by supporting such tacit censorship, I choose to use these words in this historically limited manner. Be sure, however, that they honestly represent my argument in how I use them.

Shakespeare recognized this oneness of the sacred when he said, "One touch of nature and all life is kin." E. O. Wilson (1984) more recently has called this connection to nature "biophylia." He defines *biophylia* as the innate interest and fascination we have with other forms of life. As one reads Wilson, it is not long before the connections he defines are seen to be imbued with the sacred and soulfully connected to a kind of unity that his work as a student of ecosystems requires. Countless other scholars recognize the sense of unity in fields as disparate as anthropology and art, astronomy and economics. In fact, all that is required is the way of seeing the world expressed in the first part of this chapter.

Soul: A Clarification

Soul is the sacred connection between all things. It invokes the possibility for a state of grace to exist within our inner and outer unities. Its most conspicuous form connects us to life and the living—from amoeba to senator, virus to nightingale. It belongs as well to what we casually call "inanimate." It is expressed in the rhythms of clouds and stratospheric storms. It is found in crystalline caverns and on the faces of jewels. Rules that are scarcely understood sculpt matter into perfect repetition of structure and form and, as far as we know, everywhere in the universe. Stars, like mountains, are born, live, and die in patterns moving back and forth across the boundaries of time and space.

As deep as these cosmic mysteries are, an even more inconceivable gift is to be ours. In the most fragile domain of all, in a thin layer across Earth's surface, is that condition, that miracle we call life. Frail cells, made up of the same stuff of rocks, air, and seawater, gather together in astonishing format. Alive—sensing, feeling, reproducing—*living!* I posit three attributes of soul for this journey: natural soul, cultural soul, and personal soul.

Natural Soul

The first, the *natural soul,* is the molecular and genetic expression of eons of success in carrying forth the continuity of life. All living things possess this quality of soul. Although the final gift of my genetic journey has made me human, other living things have achieved their own sacred terminus. In humans, soul is manifested by the way we express the gifts of our natural destiny through conduct that is honoring to ourselves, our physical world, and other forms of life. We, as physical beings, are the substance of natural soul; we have been configured by the journey of all life in this world in which we live.

Cultural Soul

A second form of soul exists alongside the design of nature. It is the soul embedded in culture. Our tribal traditions, our ethnic roots, and our social community create favored ways of conducting ourselves that reflect how we have chosen to express our natural gifts. When this conduct celebrates compassion, empathy, and wholeness, it is soulful within the domain of culture. No culture has exclusive claim on this attribute of soul. Each culture has crafted, to the best of its ability, a version of soul

dedicated to moral and ethical expectations. In this cultural world, a context, a pattern through time, is based not on our evolutionary journey but rather on our social and cultural history. It is an expression of the path our various cultures choose to follow in determining how we get along with each other in civic and social terms.

Personal Soul

The third form of soul belongs to each of us personally. It is defined by the consequences of the choices we make as individuals. Its main attribute is will. Whereas nature's soul is expressed through our connection with the life process and all living things, and cultural soul is manifested in the human community, the soul of self is both within and apart from both of these. The soul of self is reflected in the personal choices we make attempting to live our lives in grace. Grace in the personal soul is expressed by being responsible to the legacy and continuity of nature and the natural soul. In addition, culture is honored by making responsible personal choices about how to extend the integrity of community through the commitment of our personal soul. The power of the personal soul is expressed when it embraces both the natural and the cultural soul through its own free choice and commitment.

Our natural soul is fashioned by nature, and our cultural soul is fashioned by how we greet each other as humans. Nature's script is evolution, humankind's script is relationship, and a person's script is choice. Nature's stories are told in silence; culture's stories are told in language, law, and power. The person's story is told in choice and action. Soul belongs to nature, culture, and self. Its greatest challenges rest in the world of culture because cultures have used their language, law, and power to create the illusion of an exclusive soul. Whereas nature blesses an inclusive vision of soul, culture supports the illusion of exclusivity. Those who claim that soul is the life force within us are only partly right. Nature's gift of life is also an obligation that falls upon the soul of self. Because life itself does not determine how it is to be lived, the individual soul must mediate between the gifts of nature and the demands of culture. Choices must be made that craft equity and honor in the trinity of soul.

Learning and Soul

Learning can provide a deeper sense of unity with everything, or it can create the illusion of separation and exclusivity. As I explore learning, I am clearly biased toward a vision of unity and wholeness. Just as I prefer the wholeness embedded in soul, I believe the wholeness that unites a learner with all that exists is the legacy of the natural soul. The cognitive, affective, and psychomotor; intellect, emotion, and feelings; mind, spirit, and body—all in reality are one.

Learning *is* evolution and evolution *is* learning.

The gift and challenge that we humans have been given is to continue the legacy of evolution by returning the various exclusivities of the cultural versions of soul to a rightful unity with our natural heritage. Culture has never been an evolutionary invention ordained to separate itself from nature. Rather, it rightfully embraces it. Learning is a natural expression of unity; we must restore that unity to education through soulfulness.

Sometimes we will look at this process from within our personal perspective, and other times we must step outside and see through the will of nature. We must always realize that when we contrive such a separation, we are doing it for some convenience. In truth, we and nature are always one in the fullest sense. Learning through the three realms of soul reunites us with our evolutionary design and balances our inner wisdom with that wisdom that surrounds us.

If we look only at ourselves, it is clear that learning *is* evolution. If we look at the world that surrounds us, then it is more appropriate to say that evolution *is* learning. The immensity of the outside world can and does occasionally baffle us with its complex stories. The learning that we are striving to bring into balance is a balance born of *many* realms—the inner and the outer, the human and the natural. When the integrity of our inner world is in balance and synchronous with the outer world, we partially achieve the realm of what Robert Sardello (1992) calls "soul." *Soul* is the quality of life that graces our inner and outer unity and makes us one. Cognitive, affective, and psychomotor; reason, emotion, and feeling; mind, spirit, and body—all blend in a holy alliance of unity striving for completeness.

TRANSFORMATION

David Hawkins once told me that the potter is as transformed by the clay as the clay by the potter. In 1972, when George Leonard introduced the word *transformation,* the title of his landmark book, to the educational community, it was a shocking concept to many. I recall a meeting at which a school superintendent shouted as he stalked out of the auditorium, "Heresy!" George, who had given a keynote address, found out quickly that "learning" was acceptable but "transformation" was not. Learning, at that time, was rooted in behaviorism. Thus, learning was seen by most as a change in behavior. Those who welcomed Leonard's courage were reinforced by the broader scope of the word *transformation.* I, at that time, was a member of a growing group that saw learning as a change in motivation as well. We willingly welcomed a wider array of sensitivities into the arena. These were not cordial times for increasing the scope of learning as educators, by and large, were narrowing the scope of exploration.

Behaviorism loomed in instructional technologies. Funding sources, and the academic community of scholars who oversaw the training of teachers, chose to define professionalism as the adherence to a version of education that enforced the ways and means for controlled change. Educational practice was clearly old paradigm and far narrower than the design of the human mind. The only haven for supporting the concept of transformation was in the rhetoric of the so-called new age, busy inventing itself in the early 1970s. Currently, anything that smacks of transformation in education is a visible target for religious, political, and philosophical extremists.

Much has changed since that time, and much has not. *Learning* is what we do in school, but *transformation* is not. Whatever we mean by learning is still thought of in terms of what we have offered in schools for more than a century: basic skills, content disciplines, competitive athletics, and a familiar litany of extracurricular activities. Learning is welcome within these boundaries. Yet, transformation packs a sinister and unsettling side. It is summed up by a colleague who said, speaking for a hypothetical parent, "School should teach kids how to read a word, spell a word, and know a word's meaning; what we don't want is for kids to mess with changing what a word means!" Metaphor is still banished.

In a school district in the western United States, the student body recently revolted when the school board closed all extracurricular clubs rather than allow a proposed club for lesbians and gays. These youths rushed from their secondary school to civic offices with their protest. The students were clear that their actions were not in support of the ethos of the proposed club; they were concerned that options for learning were being stripped away from their lives. To my knowledge, the school had never been involved with *radical* behavior of this sort.

I have no doubt that these students had been exposed to concepts such as values, civil disobedience, and democracy. They had "learned" them in the abstract, safe ways common to contemporary schooling. Yet, their learning became transformed when it became the core of an experience that required them to embark on a clearly unfamiliar course of action. At the end of this excursion into democracy, not only were the students changed but the concept of democracy itself had changed in each student's mind as well. A tragic note: During the protest march, one student was killed by an automobile. The concept of democracy suddenly embraced another transforming idea: People can die protecting democracy. It is ironic that we ignore the spirit of transformation that lies at the heart of democracy.

The participatory mind, as envisioned by Skolimowski, was drawn into action by the students' sense that justice was being violated. They had skills and knowledge that they had learned in school, and the courage to put that learning to work in the world outside their school. It was as though they had found archival shards of a dormant mosaic and suddenly reassembled them into this transformative moment. Previously abstract information was transformed in a new and more authentic context. The difference was in the students' exhibiting the courage to choose to act and bring life to their own learning. They transformed that learning into something they had never experienced before that was deeply and profoundly connected to their own life experience.

I am not proposing that Civil Disobedience 101 become a graduation requirement. I am suggesting that the curriculum be sown with the seeds of potentially transformative experiences—experiences that transform the learner, the content, and the context in which education takes place.

This brings us to three offerings embedded in this chapter: participatory learning, natural systems, and learning as a soulful activity.

The Participatory Mind and Learning

Mind engages with experience. The students described above have been long taught that what they learned in school is important; and it is. Yet, just as a responsible curriculum teaches about democracy, schools must also allow the students to experience participatory democracy.

Objective reality is fallacious. It is a closed system descriptor in a world where the human mind actively participates in determining reality. If the mind finds the concept of objective reality useful, it will find and preserve a niche for it—knowing that other niches serve the mind as well. The participatory mind also requires a home for *subjective* reality, *reverential* reality, and *spiritual* reality, to cite a few. Each gift of the participatory mind embraces the context of unity while simultaneously honoring the reductive parts. Ideally, the participatory mind teaches us the reflex to embrace the experiences of learning and transformation. It makes our minds integral to the enterprise.

Nature and Learning

The seven characteristics of healthy, evolving ecosystems represent a mind-set, a worldview, a way of perceiving and conceiving experience. They offer us a way of regenerating our capacity to see the rhythmic patterns inherent in the natural world. These are offered so that, at the very least, teachers or parents might bring to children a tacit respect for these ways of engaging in life. We want to restore ways of knowing that serve the long run—the capacity to adapt and remain resilient in the shadowy, unfamiliar, changing world the future promises. Evolution may be learning, but it is also transformation.

The Soul and Learning

Transformation is also an expression of soulful celebration. Soul expressed through our natural design is a celebration of life. Soul expressed through our genetically encoded tendency to affiliate is a celebration of community and culture. Soul expressed through our autonomous personal choices is a celebration of willful courage and non-exploitative self-hood. As we acknowledge and honor the sacred lessons taught by natural systems, culture and community, and our own courage to choose, we have the possibility of living lives of transformation. Our "map" to this celebration is inscribed in our genetic code. It realizes a heritage seldom considered. We are *designed* to transform.

Students in an information age, possessing participatory minds, cannot be constrained by shibboleths and hypocrisy. If they are to believe that what they are taught is worthwhile, they must be given the power to transform. Without practice, transformation is reduced to the trivial and superficial. Electronic consciousness democratizes information. Students using history texts that are 10 years out of date can call

up the Library of Congress and explore yesterday's *Congressional Record* and today's committee meeting schedules. They can see firsthand what Congress is doing in the name of democracy. It isn't pornography and terrorism that many fear on the Internet; it is that students will find out that *truth* is participatory.

Our cultural makeup represents the accumulated efforts emerging from personal choices made in the history of our culture. Today, we are born into cultural heritages that are thousands of years old. Clearly, some cultural practices are dysfunctional. We are faced with the task of making the choices that will transform dysfunctional cultural choices into those that favor sustainable life on our planet. We must make choices that consciously include nature, culture, and self. We are kindling the courage to do so. God, territory, profit, and skin color cannot be sustained as valid reasons for war, genocide, environmental degradation, and terrorism.

Learning is transformation personalized. Evolution is transformation contextualized. We are designed to experience both.

References

Augros, R., & Stanciu, G. (1987). *The new biology.* Boston: Shambhala.

Bateson, G. (1979). *Mind and nature: A necessary unity*. New York: E. P. Dutton.

Bateson, M. C. (1994, Summer). Learning as coming home. *Holistic Education Review,* 21–28.

Bruner, J. (1973). *On knowing: Essays for the left hand.* Cambridge, MA: Belcap Press of Harvard University Press.

Harman, W. (1995, Autumn). *Noetic Sciences Review*.

Jantsch, E. (1980). *The self-organizing universe*. New York: Pergamon.

Kohn, A. (1986). *No contest.* Boston: Houghton Mifflin.

Leonard, G. (1972). *The transformation*. New York: Delacourt.

Sardello, R. (1992). *Facing the world with soul*. Hudson, NY: Lindisfarne.

Skolimowski, H. (1994). *The Participatory mind*. London: Penguin Books.

Wilson, E. O. (1984). *Biophylia*. Cambridge, MA: Harvard University Press.

Suggested Readings

Cajete, G. (1994). *Look to the mountain: An ecology of indigenous education*. Durango, CO: Kivaki Press.

Capra, F. (1982). *The turning point*. New York: Simon & Schuster.

Charles, C. (1995). *Creating community within environment education* (Proceedings of North American Association for Environmental Education).

Csiksentmihalyi, M. (1993). *The evolving self*. New York: HarperCollins.

Darling, D. (1995). *Soul search.* New York: Villard Books.

Kauffman, S. (1995). *At home in the universe*. New York: Oxford University Press.

Kormondy, E. (1984). *Concepts of ecology.* Upper Saddle River, NJ: Prentice Hall.

Laslo, E. (1987). *Evolution: The grand synthesis*. Boston: Shambhala.

Lovelock, J. E. (1979). *Gaia: A new look at life on Earth*. New York: Oxford University Press.

Maturana, H., & Varela, F. J. (1987). *The tree of knowledge: The biological roots of human understanding.* Boston: Shambhala.

McClaren, M., Samples, B., & Hammond, B. (1995). *Connections: The living planet*. Scarborough, Ontario: Ginn/Prentice Hall.

Roszak, T. (1992). *The voice of the Earth*. New York: Simon & Schuster.

Samples, B. (1981). *Mind of our mother*. Reading, MA: Addison-Wesley.

Samples, B. (1993). *The metaphoric mind* (2nd ed.). Torrance, CA: Jalmar Press.

Sheldrake, R. (1991). *The rebirth of nature*. New York: Bantam Books.

BIOGRAPHY

BOB SAMPLES has authored or coauthored nearly two dozen books, including the classic *The Metaphoric Mind.* He has published more than 100 articles in journals, magazines, and collected works. He was the recipient of the Educational Press Award for Excellence in 1978. He and his wife designed and edited *Windstar Journal* for several years. More recently, they collaborated as coordinators of the first instructional edition of the Globe Program, Vice President Gore's initiative to have schools assist scientists in making crucial environmental measurements.

Samples currently serves on the board of trustees of the Sol y Sombra Foundation and serves as Adjunct Faculty and Adviser for the Center for the Study of Community. His current investigations include his continuing work in brain-mind function and biologically based conceptual models.

11 Education and the Soul

John P. Miller

Introduction

Much of contemporary educational policy and practice has its foundation in economic interests and concerns. The result is that we, as educators, can sometimes lose sight of children as persons. Corporate interests see children as a means to an economic end, and the public seems to rest comfortably with the idea so long as their children have an increased probability of getting good jobs.

In this chapter, educational philosopher John Miller suggests that we need to remember who, indeed, we are educating. Miller believes that the American transcendentalists, and particularly Ralph Waldo Emerson, were on the mark when they referred to the human soul. Today, the term is considered rather quaint at best, but Miller understands it as the very essence of our being. It is at once the center of our individuality and what unites all of us. The soul is foreign to most contemporary educational discourse because it is not something one can isolate or investigate. It cannot be abstracted from experience, but engaged only as we become inwardly awake. The soul is perceptible only as we leave theories and objectives at the doorstep.

As difficult as it is to be awake to the soul, it is just that easy to be well informed, critically minded, and asleep. Although new technologies offer previously unimagined power and information, they may also deflect our consideration of the larger questions of who we are, what we are doing, and why. We are moving headlong into the expanded use of information technologies in schools, with the principle reason being that the "information age" requires personnel with technological skills. Although it may (or may not) be true that the workplace of the future will require such sophistication (technology becomes more user-friendly as it develops), the argument does not follow that teaching children to meet the requirements of the technological future in any way serves their educational interests. They might be far better served, practically and soulfully, by teaching them to approach the world with wonder and a sense of reverence. Even though such dispositions may seem cognitively superfluous, Miller contends that they are the foundation of all wisdom.

Education that nourishes the soul involves more than emotion; it develops in the learner a creative, disciplined quality of mind. Soulful education, as Miller describes it in this chapter, integrates three core ideas. The inner life is developed through nurturing the imagination, creatively working through the arts and sustaining a direct, intuitive relationship with the environment. In this regard, Miller remains consistent with his transcendentalist roots and echoes the educational emphasis of the American Indian perspective elaborated by Gregory Cajete (chap. 9, this volume). The function of the imagination is not to create fantasies, but to discover the patterns weaving through the world. The arts do not simply offer catharsis, but access to dimensions of our souls that we might not otherwise recognize. Nature study is not simply the study of ecosystems, but the doorway to perceiving ourselves enmeshed into the creative flow of the world.

Soulful education, because it does not remain within the confines of logical empirical science, depends on living people. Its lessons cannot be found in books, computer programs, or floppy disks; they are not reducible to information that in some way may be processed.

—*Jeffrey Kane*

The 20th century has not been good for the soul. Through horrendous wars, holocaust, violence, and environmental degradation, life itself seems to have lost its vital essence. In particular, a mechanized approach to living has contributed to the loss of soul. We have adopted a machine-like approach to living, and the "bottom line" dominates our lives. In education, we constantly hear the mantra of how education must make a nation, any nation, globally competitive. Thus, the schools' main role is to produce consumers and producers. We rarely hear from a government official that education might help in the development of human beings and the human spirit.

Our language is also filled with mechanistic metaphors. For example, in Ontario, the Royal Commission on Learning released a major report in January 1995. At the end of report, the commission made its recommendations and said the province should focus on "four engines of change."[1] The metaphor of engine again arises from our machine-like approach to education. Our language betrays us.

Without soul, our society seems to lack a basic vitality or energy. Except for the energy in consuming and producing, the way many people feel is summed up by a cover of *Newsweek* that showed a man's tired face with the title: "Exhausted." People on the streets, on the subways, and in the shopping malls often look exhausted, disgruntled, or angry. As result, people seek fulfillment in alcohol, drugs, food, work, and a variety of other addictions. The pace of life itself is soulless. We all seem in a mad rush to acquire and consume, with little time for simple pleasures. We are not satisfied with just feeling fresh air on our cheeks or watching children at play. We crave possessions and entertainment, and we seem never to get enough.

The machine has been a principal metaphor for the last 300 years. In 1747, the French philosopher Julien de La Mettrie declared, "Let us then conclude boldly that man is a machine, and that the whole universe consists only of a single substance [matter] subjected to different modifications" (cited in Shlain, 1991, p. 85). Today, efficiency and numbers rule. Business for years was run by management by objectives (MBO), whereas educators developed behavioral objectives. It is possible to view outcomes-based education as another machine-like approach to education with the emphasis on production and results, rather than on the process of learning.

We are told now that we live in the information age, in which the computer is the prototype for most activity. Computer-based models are used to construct and shape reality. Children seem to see the world only through computer games, television, and videos. In most rural cultures, children and adolescents develop a relationship to the natural world; for example, in indigenous cultures the vision quest is

1. The four engines of change are (a) a new kind of school-community alliance, (b) early childhood education, (c) teachers, and (d) information technology.

based in nature. In the 19th century, Emerson complained at the beginning of his first book, *Nature*, that humans had lost their original relationship to the universe. If this was true in the 19th century, I wonder what Emerson would say today when the media and institutions determine our reality and industrialization seems bent on destroying the natural world (Jones, 1966, p. 27). Clearly, when we have lost our original relationship to the universe, we have also lost soul.

In fact, we have tended to see the universe and the earth as inanimate and without purpose. Again, La Mettrie, in the 18th century, saw everything, including the human being, as soulless:

> The term "soul" is therefore an empty one, to which nobody attaches any conception, and which an enlightened man should employ solely to refer to those parts of our bodies which do the thinking. Given only a source of motion, animated bodies will possess all they require in order to move feel, think, repent—in brief, in order to *behave*, alike in the physical realm and in the moral realm which depends on it. (cited in Shlain, 1991, p. 84f)

Matthew Fox (1994) has discussed some essential elements of the machine worldview. For example, the earth is seen as inert, and events are seen as determined. The universe itself is seen as a machine, and all experience is secularized; from this perspective, we look to the earth for resources. Scientific materialism predominates, with an emphasis on objectivity, rationality, and efficiency. Society reflects a bias toward a masculine worldview with hierarchical organizations. Fox concludes, "Souls have shrunk terribly due to this machine cosmology" (p. 259).

Education has also adopted the machine metaphor. Schools can be likened to factories. Like the assembly line, students sit in rows where they learn how to conform to expectations set by business and government. The product is success on a standardized test whose results are often compared with those from other schools or even from other countries. Results on these tests are compared to economic data between these countries, and various attributions are made regarding how the education system relates to economic productivity. Despite supposed reforms in education, students often fill out worksheets and memorize textbooks. With the emphasis on textbooks and tests, little room is left for soul in our schools. Although most subjects have a soulful quality, the arts, which in many ways are the most conducive to the soul's development, are often made a marginal part of the education program and are sometimes removed entirely from the curriculum.

Education has often been made to conform to "scientific principles." In the 1920s, Franklin Bobbitt thought that the "backward" institution of education could be improved by employing the "scientific management" techniques used in industry. Bobbitt (1912) argued, "Education is a shaping process as much as the manufacture of steel rails" (p. 11). He compared the process of teaching to making industrial products; therefore, in his opinion, education had to focus on creating a product—the student's mind—which should be shaped according to uniform standards. Development and introduction of appropriate standards were needed. In fact, Bobbitt suggested that business and industry set these standards for education. Tanner and Tanner (1980) contend that "the trend of education catering to the demands of business has been a continuing trend in American education" (p. 329). An example of this phenomenon in recent times can be found in the 1960s, when school systems turned to businesses to develop "performance contracts" to improve pupil performance in the schools. Today, various school districts, such as Hartford and Baltimore, are turning their schools over to private industry.

Other examples of mechanization of the curriculum include outcomes-based education, which is currently in favor in North America. For example, in Ontario, the curriculum policy for Grades 1 to 9, entitled *The Common Curriculum,* is an outcomes-based document. Hundreds of outcomes are listed that teachers must achieve in four main areas: (a) the arts, (b) language, (c) mathematics, science, and technology, and (d) personal and social studies (Self and Society). I believe that outcomes-based education is based on a false premise in that all students are expected to achieve all of these outcomes. Supposedly, students can achieve the outcomes at different rates and in different ways, but what about unexpected outcomes? Is human behavior really so predictable as outcomes-based advocates argue? Some of the most powerful moments in teaching and learning are the spontaneous moments of insight that are beyond any system or set of specific expectations. In short, outcomes-based education has no balance between the planned and the spontaneous. Spontaneity is essential to the realization of soul.

The accountability movement is another example of mechanization in the curriculum. Teachers are expected to be constantly testing students so that the public is satisfied with what is going on in the classrooms. Unfortunately, the tests focus on a very limited portion of the curriculum and ignore the important areas, such as personal and social development. These tests tend to stress information that will soon be forgotten by the student. The student begins to see school as a game in which succeeding is based on passing tests that seem to have no relevance to anything except what we might call useless knowledge. When school is seen as a game, vitality is lacking. Classrooms become lifeless places where students focus on achievement in a narrow and competitive manner. A curriculum of meaningless tests is another example of education without soul.

The results of all this are summarized by Robert Sardello (1992):

> Education instead has become an institution whose purpose in the modern world is not to make culture, not to serve the living cosmos, but to harness humankind to the dead forces of materialism. Education as we know it, from preschool through graduate school, damages the soul. (p. 50)

We can reclaim our souls. Instead of denying and oppressing the soul, we can learn to let the soul manifest itself in the world. Instead of confining the soul, we can learn to celebrate soul. By reclaiming soul, we find that the classroom or any educational encounter takes on a new vitality and purpose. Students and teachers no longer go through the motions, but instead feel alive and nourished in what they do. In a word, learning becomes soulful.

THE NATURE OF THE SOUL

Before discussing education and how it can be more soulful, I think it is important to discuss the nature of the soul.

1. Soul is not an entity or thing, but animating energy or process. Consider Emerson's (1990) definition:

> All goes to show that the soul in man is not an organ, but animates and exercises all the organs; is not a function, like the power of memory, of calculation, of comparison, but uses these as hands and feet; is not a faculty, but a light; is not the intellect and the will, but the master of the intellect and the will; is the background of our being, in which they lie,—an immensity not possessed and that cannot be possessed. (p. 174)

As a source of energy, we can sometimes feel the soul expand. A beautiful piece of music can make our souls feel expansive; likewise, in a threatening or fearful situation, we can feel our souls contract or shrink. A soulful curriculum would provide a nourishing environment for the soul's expansion and animation.

We can recognize soul in people when we see their eyes light up, when their speech is animated, when their bodies move with grace and energy. Sophia Hawthorne saw this quality in Emerson as he walked the streets of Concord:

> It became one of my happiest experiences to pass Emerson upon the street. . . . I realized that he always had something to smile FOR, if not to smile AT; and that a cheerful countenance is heroic. By and by I learned that he always could find something to smile at also; for he tells us, "The best of all jokes is the sympathetic contemplation of things." (Holmes, 1885/1980 pp. 238–239)

Soulful energy is not just energy, but loving energy. I will have more to say about this shortly.

2. In the soul lie our deepest feelings and longings. When we realize these longings and are able to manifest and work with them, we begin to feel deeply fulfilled. In part, we can see life's journey as an attempt to discover and realize these deep longings. One of our deepest longings is to find soulful work. Fox (1994) states,

> Our souls, that is, our awareness and our passions, our ecstasies and our pain are not tidy and small. We, like the rest of the universe, are expanding and are great in size—"magnanimous," Thomas Aquinas calls us, which means literally, "large souled." There is great dignity to our being, great dignity to our work of exploring that inner being and expressing it. (p. 129)

I believe that much of career education is misguided because often career is viewed as some sort of rational choice. Rationality is part of the process, but the soul gradually finds its way in the world and attunes itself to what it feels its life work might be. This often happens through fits and starts because the individual may not

find his or her life-fulfilling work until midlife or even later. Thomas Moore (1992) comments,

> We like to think that we have chosen our work, but it could be more accurate to say that our work has found us. Most people can tell fate-filled stories of how they happen to be in their current "occupation." These stories tell how the work came to occupy them, to take residence. Work is a vocation: we are called to it. . . . finding the right work is like discovering your own soul in the world. (pp. 272–273, 279)

3. The soul seeks love. With regard to love, the soul seeks union with other souls (e.g., soulmate). This can take the form of romantic love, love of kin, universal love, or love of the divine.

Romantic love in our culture has been trivialized through soap operas and Harlequin romances or is the target of cynicism. Yet, romantic love can teach us a great deal. When we fall in love, we see the angelic nature of the beloved. Some say this is a romantic illusion, but perhaps we see the other's true nature—that is, the person's divinity. Through love, the soul touches the eternal, the divine. Through wisdom and loving kindness, we can begin to see the angelic nature not only in our beloved but in all beings. We attempt to connect to this inner core of goodness and decency in others.

This is what Nelson Mandela recognized during his 27 years in prison. Although his guards could often be cruel and unfeeling, suddenly he would see an act of kindness that would reveal the gentler side of the person. Mandela (1994) comments:

> I always knew that deep down in every human heart, there is mercy and generosity. No one is born hating another person because of the color of his skin, or his background, or his religion. People must learn to hate, and if they can learn to hate, they can be taught to love, for love comes more naturally to the human heart than its opposite. Even in the grimmest times in prison, when my comrades and I were pushed to our limits, I would see a glimmer of humanity in one of the guards, perhaps just for a second, but it was enough to reassure me and keep me going. Man's goodness is a flame that can be hidden but never extinguished. (p. 542)

The loving soul attempts to express its joy through music and song. Sardello (1992) comments:

> Soul learning does not consist of the internalization of knowledge, the determination of right meaning, the achievement of accuracy, but is to be found in what sounds right. That the soul sings was understood by the ancient psychology of the soul of the world—the singing of soul was known as the music of the spheres. (p. 63)

The world could use more singing souls. The loving/singing soul feels attunement with the Tao, or the flow of the universe.

Love also motivates us to help make the world a more beautiful place. Theodore Roszak (1992) states that ecologists are motivated by love for the planet and its beauty, rather than by guilt. Action motivated by guilt, no matter how valid, can produce more guilt.

4. The soul dwells in paradox and does not approach life in a linear manner. Although the soul seeks the light of love, it also has its shadow side. We know the phrase "dark night of the soul" as the soul must deal with loss, grief, and pain, which are an inevitable part of life. If the soul tries to ignore pain, such as the loss of a loved one, then important soul work is being ignored. In North America, we are not comfortable with pain, and we usually seek relief in alcohol, food, television, movies, and even fundamentalism. Yet, the cost to our souls is enormous because the soul seeks to be in touch with the basic realities of life, which include suffering and death as much as love and joy.

Thus, we must give room for the way of the soul. By listening to the soul, we can be sensitive to its ways and needs. One way that we can listen to the soul is through contemplation. Robert Sardello (1995) suggests that soul logic "synthesizes rather than analyzes" (p. xx). According to Sardello, unlike cognitive logic, which seeks the right answer, soul logic seeks the healthy answer, which serves the whole being. Sardello states, "Illness occurs when something partial is taken to be the whole" (p. xx).

Fragmented approaches to reasoning have been at the root of much sickness and alienation in our culture. Because we have either refused or been unable to see the interdependence of things, social alienation and environmental decay have occurred.

The soul can spend long periods incubating over a problem or conflict. On the surface, nothing appears to be happening in relation to the resolution of the problem, but the soul often does not conform to our expectations of time. It has its own timetable. Eventually, however, if allowed to work in its own way, the soul will find a solution.

Contemplation and soulful knowing are characterized by non-duality. We become that which we contemplate. Consider Emerson's view of contemplation:

> We live on different planes or platforms. There is an external life, which is educated at school, taught to read, write, cipher and trade; taught to grasp all the boy can get, urging him to put himself forward, to make himself useful and agreeable in the world, to ride, run, argue and contend, unfold his talents, shine, conquer and possess.
>
> But the inner life sits at home, and does not learn to do things nor values these feats at all. 'Tis quiet, wise perception. It loves truth, because it is itself real; it loves right, it knows nothing else; but it makes no progress; was as wise in our first memory of it as now; is just the same now in maturity and hereafter in age, as it was in youth. We have grown to manhood and womanhood; we have powers, connection, children, reputations, professions: this makes no account of them all. It lives in the great present; it makes the present great. This tranquil, well founded, wide-seeing soul is no express-rider, no attorney, no magistrate: it lies in the sun and broods on the world. (cited in Geldard, 1993, p. 172)

Contemplation, which is the soul's main form of learning and knowing, is hardly ever encouraged in education. Instead, we are taught to find the right answer or develop the right argument. By ignoring or denying contemplation, the soul is also denied. The soul hides while our minds analyze, memorize, and categorize.

SOULFUL LEARNING

I believe that it is possible to have soulful learning in our schools. Education then becomes vital and alive. Soulful learning involves both inner and outer work. With regard to inner work, I agree with Matthew Fox (1994) that "we need a massive investment of talent and discipline in our inner lives" (p. 22). Education has virtually ignored the inner life of students and teachers, but I believe that it is possible to develop for the inner life a curriculum that includes guided imagery, meditation, dreamwork, and journal writing. The arts are essential to soulful learning as all the arts can provide nourishment for the soul. Finally, studying the earth in a way that acknowledges its sacred qualities can also help the soul, particularly linking the soul with the Earth soul, or **Gaia**.

A Curriculum for the Inner Life

The inner life of the student can be stimulated and nourished in several ways. I believe that, with television and videos, today's children have little opportunity to use their imaginations. When I was growing up, I listened to stories on the radio, and I remember going to my room and listening to it sometimes with the lights turned out. As a story was told, I would create pictures in my own mind. Before the radio, storytelling occurred around the hearth or campfire, and the story would also call on our imaginations. Today, very little calls on our imaginations. Instead, images from television and magazines have taken over our consciousness.

Guided imagery, or visualization, is one tool that can activate the inner life of the student. **Guided imagery** is simply picturing an object or set of events in the mind's eye. I will describe a few ways that visualization can be used in a soulful manner. One way is simply to have students close their eyes and imagine a story as it is being read or told. This can be done in language arts or even history as students can see themselves as people in a certain historical period or event. In science, students can also visualize activities, such as the water cycle, after they have studied the cycle. By visualizing becoming the water and going through evaporation and condensation, the students connect their inner life with abstract subject matter. One of the most creative ways of using guided imagery is to have students visualize a set of events (e.g., going underwater or into space) and then write stories about what they saw. They can also draw pictures. Many visualizations use symbols from nature, such as the sun, mountains, and water, to help in the process of personal integration and nourishment of the soul.

Meditation is not used as frequently as visualization, but I believe that it can have a role in the curriculum. The noted philosopher and novelist Iris Murdoch (1992) wrote, "Teach meditation in schools" so that students can learn to quiet their own minds (p. 337). Gina Levete (1995), associated with the Interlink Trust in England, has written a document entitled "Presenting the Case of Meditation in Primary and

Secondary Schools." By encouraging students to sit quietly, they gain access to their inner lives and begin to see their own thoughts. Some forms of meditation, such as the loving-kindness meditation, encourage the development of compassion for all beings on the planet. Meditation can nourish the students' souls and their relationship with other forms of life.

Another tool that can be used is dreamwork. A graduate student (Quattrocchi, 1995) has written a thesis on how she used dreamwork at the secondary level. She had students keep journals about their dreams over the course of a year. She found that, by working with the dreams, the students gained nourishing insights. All the students who participated in her study commented positively about the experience, and some indicated that the dreamwork had enhanced their creativity.

Another part of a curriculum for the inner life is keeping a journal. Journal writing is already included in the curriculum of many schools, particularly those approaching language instruction through whole language. Here I am suggesting that students keep private journals in which they record their deepest feelings and desires. A **journal** for a writing class is usually some sort of reflective diary that contains ideas that can lead to further writing or the completion of an essay. Alternatively, the students can keep "soul journals," wherein the students explore their deepest feelings. Of course, these journals are not for public viewing.

The Arts

The arts can provide extensive nourishment for the soul. One of the arts, music, was at one time specifically designed for the soul's development. Pythagoras believed that music could heal the soul and even align the soul with the cosmos itself so that the soul was in harmony with the music of the spheres. Plato continued this theme, as James (1993) summarizes:

> Yet for the present purpose, the important point, setting aside all ethical considerations, is that for Plato, and thus for the Western intellectual tradition that was to follow, music was the key to the human soul, the most potent instrument available to man for enlightenment. (p. 59)

Unfortunately, music and the other arts are relegated to the fringe of the school curriculum. Unless specialists teach the arts, the regular classroom teacher avoids them. Here is where **Waldorf education** has so much to offer the public school, and particularly how we train teachers. Waldorf teacher training is suffused with arts so that eventually the new Waldorf teacher is not afraid to present his or her art on the chalkboard. In most Waldorf classrooms, the teacher has drawn some beautiful picture related to the main theme being studied. More important, the teacher brings an artistic sense to everything he or she does. Richards (1980) makes this point:

> It is an intuitive seeing, which comes about as a result of exercising and experiencing one's physical senses imaginatively, wholeheartedly, and whole soulfully. This is why artis-

tic practice is so important in all learning and education. This is why neglect of the artist in each person is so impoverishing to society. Without this spiritual sense organ, this way of seeing the formative forces at work in a physical process, we are blind and duped by appearances. (p. 73)

Earth Connections

Another approach that could be helpful to the soul is to awaken our connection to the earth and its processes. Some forms of environmental education can be helpful here, particularly those described in the *Holistic Education Review* ("Ecology and Education," 1993; "Environmental Education," 1989). These programs not only focus on recycling cans and bottles but also bring students to the outdoors where they can become ecologically literate. They can learn to answer questions such as the following:

1. What soil series are you standing on?
2. When was the last time a fire burned your area?
3. Name five native edible plants in your region and their seasons of availability.
4. From what direction do winter storms generally come in your region?
5. Where does your garbage go?
6. How long is the growing season where you live?
7. Name five grasses in your area. Are any of them native?
8. Name five resident and five migratory birds in your area.
9. What primary geological event or processes influenced the land from where you live?
10. What species have become extinct in your area?
11. What are the major plant associations in your region?

(*Co-Evolution Quarterly*, 1981–2, p. 1)

Another helpful approach is to read indigenous peoples' literature about the earth. A particularly good collection of such literature can be found in *Earth Prayers From Around the World.* One example from the collection (Roberts & Amidon, 1991, p. 95):

Grandfather,
Look at our brokenness.

We know that in all creation
Only the human family
Has strayed from the Sacred Way.

We know that we are the ones
Who are divided
And we are the ones

Who must come back together
To walk in the Sacred Way.

Grandfather,
Sacred One,
Teach us love, compassion, and honor
That we may heal the Earth
And heal each other.

Finally, the students can study *The Universe Story* (Swimme & Berry, 1992) to gain a deep sense of awe and reverence for the universe itself. As we awaken our relationship with the universe and the Earth, the soul gains a sense of wholeness and connectedness; it gains a sense of place.

The Soulful Teacher

Although I have mentioned certain subjects and approaches that help nurture the soul, I believe that any subject can be taught soulfully. If the teacher brings his or her own soul to the classroom, then the subject being taught takes on a vital energy. In the soulful teacher's class, the students can sense the teacher's commitment to learning.

Two qualities that the soulful teacher can usually bring to the classroom are presence and caring. **Presence** arises from mindfulness, wherein the teacher is capable of listening deeply. In my own work at the Ontario Institute for Studies in Education/UofT, I encourage teachers to bring **mindfulness**, or moment-to-moment awareness, to the classroom and their interactions with students. Below is a statement by one teacher able to bring this awareness to the classrooms.

> As a teacher, I have become more aware of my students and their feelings in the class. Instead of rushing through the day's events I take the time to enjoy our day's experiences and opportune moments. The students have commented that I seem happier. I do tend to laugh more and I think it is because I am more aware, alert and "present," instead of thinking about what I still need to do. (Miller, 1995, p. 22)

Closely related to presence is **caring.** The caring teacher relates the subject to the needs and interests of the students. Nel Noddings (1984), who has written extensively about caring, suggests that when this happens, the student "may respond by free, vigorous, and happy immersion in his own projects" (p. 181). When the teacher demonstrates caring, community can develop in the classroom. Marcia Umland, an elementary school teacher, talks about how this can happen:

> When I wanted to spend all that time with those little people in class, I found that the intimacy I had shared with my peers in college in the sixties was carried over into my classroom. I cared about the students and couldn't stand to sit in the teachers' lounge where they were gossiping about their students . . .

> I get exhausted, but not burned out. Sometimes I'm dropping my dream for a day or two, but most days I'm on, and stunned by the kids. Lately I've realized that in setting up in a classroom at last I've given myself permission to form a society I'd like to live in. (Macrorie, 1984, pp. 155–161)

I think it is important that teachers nurture their own souls through meditation practice. Since 1998, I have made meditation a requirement in the courses I teach at the graduate level. Most of my students are experienced teachers. More than 600 students have been exposed to the practice in the course, and the vast majority find the practice an important, and often vital, process in the nourishment of their own souls. Again, I cite the comments from one of these teachers:

> My meditation practice this summer has reconnected me to the importance of resting in "that place" so that my spirit can be renourished to continue with hope and joy. Certainly, as teachers, our students crave connection with the best of our spirits. "Connectedness" is what they crave. Connectedness is what we all crave, really! Through meditation, I have been able to reconnect with the life within me. I know that continued practice will enable me to replenish my soul so that what once was the "drain" of teaching will become life-giving. (Miller, 1995, p. 22)

The time has come for soulful learning. We have had enough of machine-like approaches to education that deaden the human spirit. Current trends of outcomes-based education and accountability drain the vitality from our classrooms. The pressure for quantifying all learning without concern for quality represses the student's soul. Instead, we can learn to bring onto the earth an education of deep joy wherein the soul once again learns to sing. Soulful learning nurtures the inner life of the student and connects it to the outer life and the environment. It acknowledges and gives priority to the human spirit, rather than simply producing individuals who can "compete in the global economy." Restoring the soul to education is not a new vision. It is a vision articulated by the Greeks and various indigenous peoples for centuries. It is found in Taoism and the in the teachings of Christ and the Buddha. Why should we aspire to less than our ancestors? Education has lost its way; we need to look to the soul to recover and remember our "original relationship to the universe."

REFERENCES

Bobbitt, F. (1912). Elimination of waste in education. *Elementary School Teacher, 12,* 269.

Co-Evolution Quarterly. (1981–2, Winter). *32.*

Ecology and education in a purposeful world. (1993, Autumn). *Holistic Education Review,* 6(3), 2–55.

Emerson, R. W. (1990). *Ralph Waldo Emerson: Selected essays, lectures, and poems* (R. D. Richardson, Jr., Ed.). New York: Bantam Books.

Environmental education: A sense of wonder. (1989, Fall). *Holistic Education Review, 2*(3), 32-62.

Fox, M. (1994). *The reinvention of work: A new vision of livelihood for our time*. New York: HarperCollins.

Geldard, R. (1993). *The esoteric Emerson: The spiritual teachings of Ralph Waldo Emerson*. Hudson, NY: Lindisfarne Press.

Holmes, O. W. (1980). *Ralph Waldo Emerson*. Boston: Houghton Mifflin. (Original work published 1885)

James, J. (1993). *The music of the spheres: Music, science, and the natural order of the universe*. New York: Grove Press.

Jones, H. M. (Ed.). (1996). *Emerson on education.* New York: Teachers College Press.

Levete, G. (1995). *Presenting the case for meditation in primary and secondary schools*. London: Interlink Trust.

Macrorie, K. (1984). *Twenty teachers*. New York: Oxford University Press.

Mandela, N. (1994). *Long walk to freedom*. Boston: Little, Brown.

Miller, J. P. (1995, Fall). Meditating teachers. *Inquiring Mind, 12*(1), 19-22.

Moore, T. (1992). *Care of the soul: A guide for cultivating depth and sacredness in everyday life*. New York: Walker.

Murdoch, I. (1992). *Metaphysics as a guide to morals.* London: Chatto & Windus.

Noddings, N. (1984). *Caring: A feminine approach to ethics and moral education*. Berkeley: University of California Press.

Quattrocchi, M. (1995). *Dreamwork in secondary schools: Its educational value and personal significance.* Unpublished doctoral dissertation, University of Toronto.

Richards, M. V. (1980). *Toward wholeness: Rudolf Steiner education in America.* Middletown, CT: Wesleyan University Press.

Roberts, E., & Amidon, E. (1991). *Earth prayers from around the world: 365 prayers, poems, and invocations for honoring the earth.* New York: HarperCollins.

Roszak, T. (1992). *The voice of the earth*. New York: Simon & Schuster.

Royal Commission on Learning. (1995). *For the love of learning*. Toronto: Queen's Printer.

Sardello, R. (1992). *Facing the world with soul*. Hudson, NY: Lindisfarne Press.

Sardello, R. (1995). *Love and the soul: Creating a future for earth*. New York: HarperCollins.

Shlain, L. (1991). *Art and physics: Parallel visions in space, time, and light*. New York: William Morrow.

Swimme, B., & Berry, T. (1992). *The universe story*. New York: HarperCollins.

Tanner, D., & Tanner, L. N. (1980). *Curriculum development: Theory into practices.* New York: Macmillan.

Biography

John P. (Jack) Miller has worked in the area of humanistic/holistic education for approximately 25 years. He is the author or coauthor of several books, including *Humanizing the Classroom* (1976), *The Compassionate Teacher* (1981), and *The Holistic Curriculum* (1988/1986). Two of his works have been translated into Japanese, and he has worked with educators in Japan since 1994 to assist in the development of holistic education there. Miller is Professor of Curriculum at the Ontario Institute for Studies in Education/University of Toronto. At OISE/UOT, he is coordinator of a program in Holistic and Aesthetic Education.

12 Care of the Senses: A Neglected Dimension of Education

Robert Sardello and Cheryl Sanders

INTRODUCTION

In this chapter, psychologist Robert Sardello and counselor Cheryl Sanders present a radically different view of the human being—more specifically, the human senses—than is common in Western science. Basing their work on the psychology of C. G. Jung and Rudolf Steiner, as well as the phenomenological method of philosopher Maurice Merleau-Ponty, they begin with the understanding that we are both physical and spiritual beings and that these two aspects of our being are interwoven in our physical bodies. In this context, the body has both physical and spiritual dimensions, and the senses are not limited only to the role of conveying information about the physical world. The senses also orient us spiritually. They have a complex existential function that gives us a distinctive sense of ourselves.

Sardello and Sanders challenge the notion of human thinking as a form of information processing by focusing on the word *human.* They do not accept the term as given or as a matter of philosophical speculation. For them, the question of human thinking requires that we address our spiritual nature as we live in our bodies and the world. This is not an abstract task; it requires that we observe the profound and subtle ways we live in the world and make *sense* of the world and ourselves.

Sardello and Sanders focus their attention on the senses—once again, not only physically but spiritually as well. Given this perspective, they introduce and describe the role of 12 rather than 5 senses. Some senses correspond to the sense organs of our bodies; others are more phenomenal in nature. The latter are subtle and best introduced in terms of phenomena we experience. Thankfully, the authors offer specific and ample examples. The picture of the human being and of the senses challenges some of our most basic assumptions. It may also stir us to consider how it is that so many Americans hold spiritual beliefs and see the body in completely mechanical terms. Are we still caught in Cartesian dualism? If so, how shall we make our way out? Is the belief in the spiritual a myth that should and will fade as our scientific understanding grows (as cognitive neuropsychologists conclude)? Is it possible that we need to heighten our vision to address the spiritual, rather than to insist it conform to our current ways of thinking?

—*Jeffrey Kane*

For the past several decades, the ideas and philosophy surrounding education and educational practice have centered much more on how to teach what to teach than on who was being taught. It has been an assumption that the child must be brought into some enlightened state by being made to know through the accumulation of information. Education is not merely being influenced by a heightened need for information; the transfer of information has emerged as the central purpose for education itself. Our rational educational goals, which influence local schools more than ever before, are composed of nothing more than statistical measures of test scores. Learning has become equated with information known, rather than with the one who knows. This is an entirely materialistic stance not only in relation to education but more especially to the human being.

In this move away from education as an unfolding of the individual, our imagination is no longer compelled to the picture of the human being as the central idea of the enterprise. We have forgotten that we are creating our very social reality with this activity and that we are a society of individual people, not of information containers. The earlier we attempt to educate the child into the realm of thinking information, the more we cut off the possibility to quicken individual creativity and the capacity for imaginal thought. In large measure, concentration on what is to be learned rather than on who is learning relies on neglecting what most immediately presents itself to any teacher: The teacher stands before 30 or 40 embodied human beings, each of whom is actively engaged in dynamic, ongoing, sensory involvement with the surrounding world. If the senses are effectively cut off from consideration as important to education, if the epistemology of learning does not take into account the preconceptual domain of the living body as the nexus of inner awareness and action in the world, there is no possibility of educating toward a harmonious relation between the individual and the wider world.

In this chapter, we try to recover the neglected dimension of human sensing as integral to education by proposing the importance of a mindful study of the body in its living relationship with the world. Our approach is based on a synthesis of three streams of modern psychology: (a) existential-phenomenological psychology (Abram, 1996; van den Berg, 1972), (b) Jung's archetypal psychology of the soul (1964, 1968), and (c) the psychological contributions found in the spiritual science of Rudolf Steiner, the founder of Waldorf education (1966, 1972, 1974, 1981, 1983, 1988).

Existential-phenomenological psychology contributes an all-important method of describing the human being as what Maurice Merleau-Ponty (1962, 1964), a significant philosopher in this tradition, calls the "body-subject." By this term, he conveys an understanding of the human body as that mysterious and multifaceted phenomenon that always accompanies one's awareness and, indeed, seems to be the very location of one's awareness, both of oneself and of the world. His vivid descriptions of the life of embodiment cut through the legacy of Cartesian dualism, which still unknowingly guides much of educational thought that approaches the mind as if it were not embodied and behavior as if it had no mind.

Jung's psychology, which he also calls "a phenomenology of soul life," contributes two important premises followed in this chapter. First, he teaches us to value the inner life and gives a method for doing so by his descriptions of soul, which include far more than subjective awareness. Further, he does not divide soul from the body; he sees soul life as a continuum, a spectrum, ranging from instinct to archetype. Second, Jung provides a sensibility for the pathological; if we read his work carefully, we develop a capacity of knowing when soul is dangerously out of balance (Hillman, 1979).

Rudolf Steiner figures centrally in this chapter as the individual who for the first time describes not 5, but 12 senses (see also Konig, 1960, 1984; Soesman, n.d.). He presents these descriptions in numerous places but always as brief indications, which we have developed much more extensively in this chapter. Steiner also gives, through his Spiritual Science, understanding of the human being as a being of body, soul, and spirit, and that understanding also guides the present work.

Although these three streams of work form the basis of what follows, we do not explicate phenomenology, soul psychology, or spiritual science. Rather, we show

how a convergence of these three points of view enables us at least to begin paying attention to sensory phenomena and then to seek ways of caring for the senses in the work of education. We do not propose a new program, but rather hope to open the way for research and observation, which must begin, however, with coming to our own senses.

THE 12 SENSES AND THEIR RELEVANCE TO EDUCATION

The 12 senses are the basis through which we are able to enter the world and participate with the unfolding marvels that are its wonder. We are immersed every moment in sensory delights and distractions, horrors and ordinariness. The young child is awash in the seeming arbitrariness of innumerable sensory stimulants and possibilities for stimulation or soothing resting places. To begin to understand the nature of the sea of sensoriness in which we swim, the senses must be taken out of their usual nexus of interrelation and interdependence and viewed individually in their uniqueness and as unique phenomena.

For those in education, the theoretical ideas about thinking and the education of thinking are not rooted in the actuality of life; they do not account for the fact that we currently live in sensory chaos. Without a capacity to recognize the sensory world in which we are cast, we have no proper medium in which to develop thinking in healthy directions because the body is always disturbed and we express ourselves through our bodies first. In today's world, sensory life is culturally disordered, and we seek more and more avenues for intensifying physical awareness, whether through drugs, food, exercise, television, or any other of the myriad addictions that increase in relevance daily.

The senses become disordered when too much of a simulated world is inserted between our bodies and the surrounding world (Sardello, 1992, 1995). Through the senses, we open to the wide expanses of the world, from what is at hand to the outer reaches of the cosmos, and gradually discover ourselves as citizens of the Earth. Our senses are very disordered in the present because the surrounding world has been largely replaced by a simulated world—a world of humanly constructed objects of every type imaginable, which changes our experience from that of sensing the fullness of the world to being overwhelmed by sensory objects that capture our awareness. If our senses do not give us the true qualities of the outer world, we become surrounded by wholly mechanical representations of the world.

It is not possible, however, to be in the world without being a part of everything that makes the world what it is. The response is not to seek isolation out of fear, but rather to reimagine education as facilitating a move to balance. Trying to ensure a balance in the sensory world, of the mediated with the natural, the simulated with the immediate, is an education of the whole human being. One essential task for educators is to recognize that the senses, and therefore perceptions and experiences, are disrupted and will continue to be disrupted by the simulated world of technology, science, and economic pursuit. Balance in and of the senses, and the subsequent freedom of thought and actions, can be consciously sought and taught, but it cannot occur naturally. As more people live in areas of high population and as technical devices of every sort intervene in our sensory contact with the world, we will need to become trained in the art of living in our senses, whereas information of knowing *about* the senses will serve us poorly.

The Order of the Twelve Senses

The senses can be more deeply understood when they are approached somewhat in an order given by their characteristics. The senses are in three groupings, with four senses clustering in each of the three groups. First come the senses through which we experience our own embodiment, or corporeality: touch, balance, movement, and life. Second are the senses through which we experience the outer world surrounding our bodies: smell, taste, vision, and warmth. Third are the senses through which we experience the life of the spirit in the world and others around us: hearing, speech, thought, and the "I."

The Four Corporeal Senses

Beginning with the senses through which we experience the corporeality of the human body, we recognize that sensing our own bodily life is absolutely crucial. If these senses are seriously disrupted, we are numb to bodily feeling, or the immediate feeling of being alive. Although the word *feeling* does signify that the feeling of the body correlates to the emotional feeling life as well, the description of these senses will be from the body's perspective. Each of the four corporeal senses gives us the feeling of life in different aspects. The healthy operation of these senses is responsible for the right working of the will. By *will,* we mean the capacity to meet the world, to encounter it out of the individual forces of bodily life, to move out into the world to find our place, but in such a manner that we respond to what the world presents, not merely what we want to get from it.

The Sense of Touch

The whole of the body is the organ for the **sense of touch**. When the sense of touch functions in a healthy way in our contact with the surrounding world, we feel an instinctual sense of a divine quality, as being a part of everything that surrounds us. The sense of touch gives us a feeling of the interior liveliness of our own bodies. To the sense of touch, the outer world is not given to us in a way that we can know the particularities of each thing we touch. When we touch something or are touched by something or someone, we come up against a resistance. The outer thing cannot be known by touch alone; vision, movement, and other senses are needed for this. We come up against the world as something other than our bodies; that feels very mysterious, as if we have come up against a very great mystery. If we are not touched, the liveliness of our own bodies is dimmed.

The Sense of Balance

The **sense of balance**, centered in the inner ear, senses the relationship between the earth's gravity and the body. When the sense of balance functions in a healthy way, we are able not only to stand straight and upright but also to move around in the world without it "swaying" or our becoming dizzy. This indicates that we have a point of reference in relation to the world and ourselves. We also feel a subtler feeling: inner calm and security. With the sense of balance, we are able to take our place in the world as human beings between the sky above and the earth below, what is before us and behind us, and what is to either side of us.

In the current world, much throws us off balance. The extreme instance, when, for example, we have an inner ear infection, is vertigo. But much subtler states of vertigo occur. When balance is not quite perfected, not fine-tuned, so to say, vertigo feels more like a vague sense of about-to-be-swallowed-up-by-the-surrounding-world. It is as if the ground could at any minute part and we could fall in.

The Sense of Movement

The **sense of movement** senses whether we are still or in movement. We feel the movements of our bodies primarily by means of the muscular system. This system senses not only the larger movements of our body, such as that of our arms and legs, or the feeling of our necks when we move our heads, but also much subtler movements, such as the movement of the eyes and the fingers and toes and the movement of our chests and bellies when we breathe. When the sense of movement functions properly, we experience a bodily sense of being free. This feeling is quite remarkable. We get a feeling for this quality when we step outside in the sunshine and stretch or feel as if we would like to run in the wind.

In the current world, the sense of movement is either too cramped or becomes too muscle bound. Sitting all day long, being carried from place to place in a car or a bus, makes us feel cramped, not only in our muscles but also in our life. We also ask children, from day care through college, to sit quietly and engage in an abnormal lack of activity, an engagement with information that does not move them inwardly. We replace the inner movement of imagination and wonder with empty entertainment and stimulation to "hold" their attention. The inner sense of movement dims, and we feel more as if we are lugging our bodies around. The ways we try to balance the feeling of being cramped—through going to the gym and working out on the exercise machines, jogging, playing such games as football or basketball—do not result in a healthy sense of movement either. We may feel a tingling in our muscles and get a temporary high from the increase in blood circulation, but it is more like a momentary breaking through the barrier of confinement, which does not, however, give us the ongoing corporeal feeling of freedom.

The Life Sense

The **life sense** senses the interior conditions of the organs of the body. When the organs of the body are in harmony, each with the other, we sense a feeling of bodily ease. When one or more organs of the body are understimulated or overtaxed, we feel states of pain or discomfort, or a general feeling of uneasiness, or we feel tired, "run down," depressed, hungry, or thirsty. The life sense can become very confused. We can feel tired when we are not, if all our time is spent in "brain work"; we can feel hungry or thirsty when we are not, by being stimulated by advertising or becoming accustomed to food inundated with sugar; or we can be constantly nervous, which can be confused with being thirsty or hungry all the time; so can being bored. When the life sense is disrupted, one main symptom is a vague sense of fear. With this vague sense of fear comes the impulse to fix what is wrong. But what is wrong is not evident in the absence of somatic illness.

Disruptions of the Corporeal Senses

In the area of the corporeal senses, disruptions have monumentally destructive effects, most especially in the realms of education and children. What does it mean for such a seemingly simple and fundamental sense as the sense of touch to be disrupted in a small child or a child of school age? The disruption of the sense of touch begins in our culture at birth, with the life-saving miracles of disinfectable plastic everything and the enormously convenient and time-saving, as well as always sterile, disposable diapers made of papery, absorbent, but drying stuff. And then, of course, all furniture, toys, life-saving car seats, and life-enhancing bouncers, strollers, baby backpacks, playpens, and beds are constructed for the easy cleaning and disinfecting, fire-retardant, and drool-absorbent qualities most required for today's modern baby. Everything the newborn touches and that touches her or him is manufactured and simulated. Despite all the arguments for the wonders of these items, what does it mean that so little that touches the newborn is natural, alive, imbued with natural warmth? What dims in a person as a result of the world she or he encounters from birth?

If touch introduces us to the mystery of the other and reflects back a sense for the mystery within the unknown border of ourselves, touch is also the origin of a bodily perspective for any feeling we have for the mystery of what is not us, what is perhaps called spiritual, or even divine. Touch allows us to develop capacities for a sense of boundaries but introduces us to the boundary as worlds of possibilities for discovery. Boundaries in and of themselves offer a moral signature, a place that one crosses with care and respect. The disruption of the sense of touch creates the breakdown of the capacity to experience the other as mystery. The other becomes merely object, perhaps plastic or paper, or utilitarian, able to be used to fulfill impulses, drives, or desires. Possibilities for aggression against the other magnifies, or withdrawal from the other is necessary to create safety for my own personal boundary.

Equally disastrous is the disruption of the sense of balance. In children, the sense of balance is assumed to be in place once they stand alone. After this milestone in development is reached, the child will begin to speak and, within a year or less, start referring to her- or himself as "I." Standing upright is the fundamental gesture of the human being and the foundation for the capacity to refer to ourselves with this unique pronoun. Maintaining our equilibrium, our balance, is the bodily gesture of the "I." When I stand up and feel dizzy, or when I enter a room and am overwhelmed by the presence of someone I honor, or when I look out over the Grand Canyon, I can lose my equilibrium and become dizzy. Also, driving over a small but steep hill too quickly, running in circles as part of a game, or riding an amusement park ride can cause me to lose my equilibrium for a moment. I return to my inner sense of balance when I regain my focus and connect with a focal point in my immediate surrounding (through vision) or fill the space around me, whether it be the Grand Canyon or the night sky, with my own presence in it. When I do this, I am no longer dizzy and have experienced the world holding me up, so to speak, by giving me myself back.

But what if we never are sure of a point of reference through a disruption of the sense of balance? And what would cause such a disruption? When the "I" is always a little uncertain, a little undermined, we do not experience the possibility for a feeling of freedom. Freedom here is not political, but more the quality of being myself in the midst of millions of other selves and freely being able to mingle in and among others without losing my balance and maybe becoming someone else. When balance is disrupted and the "I" is under attack, however, it is not a feeling that is experienced. For example, some children are always trying to compensate for what they experience as an unstable environment by moving around. A lot. And if the room does not keep still, abstract symbols and pictures on papers do not stay still either and, in fact, may add to the nauseousness by wavering counter to the room. Moving becomes an inner compulsion to stay in some relationship to the outer turmoil, and so children move to keep from being overwhelmed by the world. In how many cases could this be what is referred to as attention deficit disorder? This condition is considered epidemic in our schools, and yet this may be simply the response of the "I" under attack by the modern world. We respond to the cry with diagnosis, medication, or behavior modification. Balance and the sense of the free, human "I" are undermined.

But that is not all that is lost. The sense of balance is the basis for our capacity to trust. When we can stand firmly in and for the self and move into the world without the loss of the self, we develop an inner assurance about the world that participates with us in maintaining our own equilibrium; we develop trust. With the "I" under attack and the sense of balance so often in jeopardy, very little trust emerges from the educational experience. If the world is never to be trusted, we perpetuate the frenzy to stay ahead of the dizzying world and are denied the possibility to find a still point for reflection, contemplation, rest, restoring inner balance.

Movement as a sense is quite amazing. It not only tells me that I am choosing to move from here to there, but also that the world is moving around me and in relationship to me. In young children and especially infants, movement is choreographed in relation to the sounds in the environment. Research has shown that the normal newborn moves in coordination with the sounds of the mother's voice. The activity of movement is even subtler than just the voluntary muscles in response to stimuli. Our eyes move in relation to the things around us and inform our bodies how to move. The larynx moves in response to the voice of the other, and our muscles move in relation to the object. For example, to open a door, my body must have a plan to get to the door and turn the door knob before I set out to do so; otherwise, I might not actually arrive at the door. This little plan is not just about me, but is in cooperation with the door. The door draws me to it, directs my movement, as it were, to it. The plan is fulfilled when I open the door. Our sense of movement is the bodily sense that gives us an inner feeling of purpose, of destiny. The sense of purpose fulfilled by the most insignificant of our movements is also there in the overriding gesture of life itself, as if we know where we are going and how to go about getting there. This phenomenon is given when we encounter something and feel, "Yes, I know this," or, "I know I've met this person before."

The nature of movement that involves a plan to fulfill a purpose is the aspect that needs most careful attention in education. To read or write, spell, or do math problems requires a certain quality of movement—a healthy sense of movement. Should one's sense of movement be disrupted in subtle ways, what must the all-important school task of reading or writing become? When we learn to read, the letters must each be looked at individually, usually speaking their sounds aloud one at a time. Slowly, we begin to put sounds together and meet the next letter with recognition. Soon, we skim through the letter part and experience the whole word and then the whole of the sentence in the activity of reading. This is accomplished through movement across and down the page. These are extremely fine-tuned movements. When the sense of movement is disrupted, the subtle demands on the sense itself become impossible. We perceive this attack and disruption of the sense of movement as all forms of dyslexia. We treat this disruption by mechanical remediation and never recognize the qualities of the sense of movement that are not able to be expressed.

The sense of movement is disrupted by our very ability to learn by imitation and move in relation to the world into which we are born. For example, if all we hear all day from birth are the mechanical, electronic sounds of television and stereo, this will inflict a certain character on the way we move. In addition, if we are shuttled about in cars, buses, subways; carried, pushed, and hauled in and out of mechanical conveyances; taken to malls, grocery stores, and downtown where people are rushing and hurrying about much like automobiles driving on a highway, our initial experience of movement is that this is something mechanical, which we imitate deeply with the first forays we take into being part of the world. We move like machines.

The next step is that today's children are learning to move in relation to the instantaneousness of the computer and will be at even more of a disadvantage in relation to the movement of the written word because this new technology will most likely bring about deeper disruption to the sense of movement. Because, with the computer, we can present enormously diverse elements of information and pictures, programming at the keyboard the presence of the whole world, we misrepresent, to the literal quality of the child's mind, where the world is and how it moves. Telling a young child (under age 7–9) that it is "just" television, a movie, or a computer game or program does not eliminate from the imaging capacity of the child's mind the images that move as electronic impulses. Because a young child learns through imitation and because that imitation includes the very deepest aspects of the world around her or him, that which is presented via electronic mechanisms will be reflected in the way the child grows into the body.

To bring balance back into movements of the body and compensate for the young child's exposure to electronic media, one could lie on the grass and watch the movements of clouds or the flow of a brook over rocks. One could also walk in a quiet, secluded spot, away from traffic, and feel the reality of the body in movement in relation to the stillness of the surroundings. We may need to become much more creative and diverse in the kinds of games and play we teach children because, since the advent of television, children are losing the natural ability to invent and play their own games and activities. This ability may decline even further as children at earlier and earlier ages are presented with computers as teachers. Watch for an increase in individuals with dyslexia of all kinds.

The life sense is perhaps under the greatest attack of all the corporeal senses because it is the sense in which we are most unconscious. Whereas balance is experienced when we are comfortable in our bodies, the life sense is experienced when we are most uncomfortable. When the inner organs come into some imbalance or are attacked by some outer organism, when we feel ill or succumb to a virus or stub a toe in the dark, we are aware of our bodies in a different way and seek assistance to recover the ability to live in our bodies unconsciously. Pain gives us an acute presence of our bodies and makes us attend to them. When we are in pain, we are conscious of our life sense.

But now we see that the life sense can show us at least part of the reason disruptions in society are so prevalent. When discomfort and annoying symptoms arise, we react in absolute horror at the idea of being indisposed, missing work or school, or feeling bad for more than a few hours. Addictive behavior is, in part, the consequence of the cultural expectation of immediate alleviation of any uncomfortable consciousness of the body. In addition to the abhorrence of uncomfortable physical sensations of the body, we experience an unwillingness to be presented with the intrusions of emotional and psychological discomforts. Both physical and psychological pain can be enormously important teachers, guiding us toward significant life changes. When the life sense is manipulated, controlled, and tyrannized by forms of medicine and therapy that too easily and quickly dull the pain, we live in a social reality that promotes addictions of all sorts and the propensity to senseless and unconscious aggression.

But the life sense is also disrupted in other areas. In our time, life is dictated by the clock, and we are socially conditioned to respond according to the dictate of the hour of the day. But, as we once were more governed by the "schedule," we are now becoming more and more governed by the "program" of the computer. When we succumbed to "scheduled" life, we left natural time and entered the tempo of the clock, living at a pace mechanically derived from the fragmentation of clock time. Natural time eludes us now, and we fantasize about returning to its comforting flow. The time of play and picnics, love and reunion, work and sleep, and bath and stories restores the life sense. This time was supplanted by deadlines and meetings, workouts and working lunches, falling asleep over work, and the dash for the commute. Now we enter the even more futile and crazed tempo of e-mail and cell phones, fast food and faster faxes, and multiple, instantaneous meetings and mergers. We move at computer time and, as such, are always thrown off balance by the instantaneousness with which everything can happen, with nothing touching us, nor we it. The space in which life occurs is the time of duration. Duration, once so integral a part of our sense of living, now is cut off from what we think to be "life." Life as duration offers itself to be touched and relished. Duration has been lost for the sake of the tempo in which we think we are supposed to exist but know to be hollow.

The life sense also makes it possible to develop the capacity of compassion. Knowing when one is well or ill involves more than knowing about one's own body. Illness itself teaches compassion for others, but if discomfort has always been numbed, the necessary ground for feeling the suffering of others will be absent. Valuing the experience of illness does not preclude recovery from it, but it does allow that the illness itself has more to offer than the personal discomfort accompanying the disease. Thus, more evolves from it than the negative reaction I have to being the one who is sick. The disruption of the life sense, experienced as the need to diminish all pain, gives rise to "victim consciousness" and "entitlement," rather than develops capacities of being the comforter of others.

From a phenomenological approach, it becomes evident that these four senses alone have a tremendous impact on the education of children and that ignoring the development of the senses leads to perilous consequences in society. Attending to the unfolding of the corporeal senses in education could bring about a revolutionary new approach to who is being taught and to how to teach the individual to become a free and truly "human" being.

The Middle, or World, Senses

Whereas the corporeal senses are the basis of will, the **middle**, or world, **senses** are the basis of the feeling life. The term *world* is used because this middle grouping of senses have to do with the communion of the body with the world. These senses are smell, taste, vision, and warmth. When these senses are dulled or disrupted, the overall result is a dulling in the feeling realm for the world. We then become tremendously interested in feelings but take them to be entirely our own inner states. We try to make ourselves feel by all sorts of psychological therapies or stimulants of all kinds, not realizing that the fundamental problem lies in the fact that we have lost intimate relationship with the outer world.

The word *feeling* means "touch." Touch has a dual direction. On the one hand, feeling means to touch inwardly. Feeling is to be touched inwardly by the world. On the other hand, feeling also implies a movement outward; our soul, or feeling life, moves outward into the world to make connection with it. The four world senses all have this characteristic, each in different ways, of drawing the world into ourselves and going out to meet the world through soul.

The Sense of Smell

With the **sense of smell**, the exchange between our bodily beings and the world occurs through the element of air. Odors work through the air element to bring the world into our bodies. Some specific aspects of feeling life are related to this sense and to the gesture of bringing the world into the body. We cannot open and close our noses as we do our eyes or our mouths; through smell, we remain open and vulnerable to the world. One of the most uncomfortable aspects of having a cold is not being able to smell. Smell gives us the most intimate feeling of the world. The world surrounding the body comes into the interior of the body and is there met by the soul, where we have an experience of the substance of the world in an inner way. We experience many different odors. The tendency is to lose ourselves in smell; smell permeates us. If you smell a rose, it is experienced everywhere in the body. The smell takes over, and it takes a while to recover from the moment of becoming a rose.

A very specific feeling quality of the world is given through smell. Picture smelling a rose. Then picture smelling a rotten egg. The first smells good; the second smells bad. We might be able to find a more refined language to express the difference, but it would still have these two qualities. It is quite amazing that qualities of smell are felt in this way, that the substance of the world reveals itself in these two ways. To speak of one thing smelling good and another thing smelling bad is neither an intellectual judgment nor a conclusion that we make. It is the given nature of the smells. The immediately given qualities of the world are experienced at a bodily level. The sense of smell experienced does sense "this smells good or this smells bad." Smell is experienced as moral qualities. Not moral as in morality and judgment. The most basic feeling we have is moral feeling. Smell give us the bodily basis for moral judgment, although it is not in itself moral judgment. Even as adults, we retain something of the connection between smell and moral qualities. We speak of something "smelling fishy" or "being left with a bad smell," or we say "something is rotten in Denmark." Caustic soap, for example, smells bad, but it may be very good for certain things. One does not judge on the basis of the smell, but the smell gives us the fundamental gesture of good or bad.

But what happens when odor becomes manipulated? For example, suppose a very caustic soap is permeated with the smell of lavender. Right at the level of the body, we are introduced to cover-ups. Right at the level of the body, we are given a kind of life instruction that says we can make things appear however we want them to appear. What things are, does not matter. Perhaps the capacity of lying is instilled long before we know anything about moral choices.

Care for the sense of smell has to do with becoming conscious that, in our time, smell must be experienced metaphorically. Caustic soap pervaded with the odor of lavender smells *like* lavender. A lavender flower smells lavender, not *like* lavender. We often take literally the smell of something and think that it is that thing. For example, an orange smells orange, but shampoo made to smell orange smells *like* an orange. In thinking we are smelling orange when we smell shampoo made to smell like orange, our rational intellect is deceived, and we do not think, "This only smells like orange but it really is shampoo," we just think, "This is orange shampoo." Things really cannot be made to smell other than they are; they can only be made to smell as if they were something other than they are. This metaphorical activity is very interesting. The rational intellect cannot think metaphorically. *A* cannot at the same time be *B* for the intellect. But imagination can and does combine things that do not rationally belong together. The suggestion here is that the healing of the disordered smell world has to do with the development of the capacity of imagination. If caustic soap smells *like* lavender, that also means it does *not* smell like lavender. The caustic smell cannot be completely covered, and if it is, the odor of lavender is so strong that no lavender ever smelled that particular way.

For children, smell can be especially confusing. We place tremendous expectation on young children by our assumption that smell functions automatically and that very little ever needs to be addressed in the education of smells. In addition, by only addressing smell as one of the "five" senses, we assume no connection between what we smell and how our feelings evolve. Education should not be taken as literal in the realm of the senses but should approach the child in the realm of imagination.

The Sense of Taste

The **sense of taste** could well be called the cultural sense. How we make things in the world depends a great deal on taste. It is not by accident that the word *taste* refers to the experience of flavors in the mouth and also to a primary characteristic of culture. But the most basic quality of taste, the one that really defines the value of taste in the bodily realm, is almost completely lost. Thus, we also are tremendously confused because of the fragmentation of our culture and have great difficulty determining the nature of our own culture. We certainly have great diversity in the sense of taste, and diversity is also important to culture. But there is something even more important. When we taste something, regardless of the particular flavor, we have the capacity of tasting whether what we are eating is wholesome or unwholesome, healthful or unhealthful. This is an actual quality of taste, but it is nearly completely lost as a tasting capacity. Thus (in a cultural context), the question whether what we make in the world is healthful, not only for us but also for others and for the rest of the earth, either is not taken into account or is terribly confused.

The word *taste* comes from Middle English *tasten,* which means "to examine," "to test," "to sample" (Ackerman, 1990). Taste is a transition zone between our bodies and the world. We are sampling or testing the world to find out what it is like in all its variety. Just imagine all the things people eat. The earth offers about 20,000 edible plants alone. And besides the foods we are accustomed to in our culture, other cultures value tastes such as that of rodents, grasshoppers, snakes, kangaroos, snails, bats, turtles, or piranhas.

We are most sensitive to bitter tastes. The taste buds can detect bitterness if it exists in the ratio of 1 part in 2,000,000. We can detect something sour in the ratio of 1 part in 130,000; something salty, 1 part in 400; and something sweet, 1 part in 200. Different parts of the tongue detect these tastes: sweet things at the tip; bitter things at the back; sour things at the sides; and salty taste over the surface, but mainly up front. There are revealing metaphors here. Salty taste enhances any taste because it is all over the surface. The taste of salt is also right up front, easily recognizable. Bitterness runs deep. Sweet is the first introduction; sour comes at you from the sides. Because bitter and sour are the most sensitive aspects of taste, it would seem that these aspects of the world are what we are really meant to come to terms with. It is most interesting, then, that we cover them over mainly by adding sugar to practically everything. Salt also becomes a covering once it goes beyond the limit of enhancing. Thus, we get a picture that, in the current world, the sensitivity of taste has been reversed. We thus imagine the world as if it should be all sweetness; but once the body has taken in so much sweet flavor, that is the way the body approaches the world—not being sweet but expecting everything to be sweet. In contrast, we can imagine that if we were more in touch with bitterness and sourness, we would come to realize that the quality of sweetness in something has to be developed out of our own inner soul forces.

Taste is more active than smell. We are always open to smell. We have to open our mouths to taste. And we have to be active to taste—chewing, dissolving, and swallowing. In addition, we have to add something to the world of taste: saliva. More will is involved in tasting. We actively engage the substance of the world. Sweetening works against the will element of engaging the world. Sugar is ego food; it strokes us and makes us feel good, and with sweet things the tendency is just to take them in and then want more and more. Bitterness, in contrast, strengthens the development of the will. Sour awakens the will, and salt keeps taste alert; it brings taste to consciousness. These are the activities of taste in the context of the soul. To take them prescriptively ("I'll feed my child bitter food so that she will have a strong will") is too literal and could contribute to the further disruption of the sense of taste. More important for healing the sense of taste is the eating of natural, unadulterated food (no preservatives or additives) in a quiet, calm setting.

Taste has now become part of the world of virtual reality. Artificial flavors were invented in the early 19th century, but not until the 1960s did they become prevalent. The cultural history of tastes probably follows much the same pattern as that of odors. Virtually the whole spectrum of food flavors has been artificially constructed. The majority of food on the supermarket shelf has some form of artificial flavor. Sugar dominates. It is now possible to create a virtual chicken. Manufacturers can mold a chicken shape from vegetable protein and then add imitation chicken breast flavor, chicken fat flavor, chicken skin flavor, and basic chicken flavor. These are all chemical flavorings, known as *flavoromatics.* This virtual chicken would, of course, taste *like* chicken. Hundreds of flavors are involved with chicken. Only a few of these are artificially developed, but these are heightened while the other, subtler flavors are allowed to drop away. It would seem that the soul effect of simplifying taste in such a manner would be that we would also lose the capacity to perceive the subtle and complex aspects of life. Again, the metaphorical, imaginative capacity needs to be developed in order not to be taken over by virtual food and, in its wake, virtual values of every sort that define our culture.

The concepts of "family values," "ethical values," "economic values," and "political values" of all sorts are the cultural abstraction of the sense of taste. As such, education of "values" can be theoretically applied to educational curriculum with no sense of the true nature of the value ever being conveyed. Virtual chicken is now taken to the national debate over values!

The Sense of Vision

The **sense of vision**, sight, is the primary sense through which we feel. The blind person notwithstanding, the predominate sense through which we relate to the world is vision. But we usually only look at one side of vision. This one side is that the eye, the organ of sight, is quite literally an extension of the brain out to the surface of the body. When the optometrist looks into our eyes, he is actually looking directly at the brain. The corporeal senses are all transformations of the skin, and through them we commune with the "flesh" of the world. But with the eye, the tendency is to have an intellectual view of the world.

Vision has many more mysteries than the tendency to see all the world intellectually. When we look at one color for a time and then close our eyes, we see the opposite color. This happens only with the sense of vision. When we taste something bitter, the opposite, sweet, does not complement it. The miracle of vision is that the eye complements harmoniously what is missing. This means that the soul is quite close to the surface with vision because the complementary color we experience is the activity of the soul filling in what is missing. Whereas such phenomena are often described in terms of the "bleaching" of the receptors in the ball wall of the eye, physiological functions are an expression of the relation of the higher aspects of being to the physical world. Yes, the nerves act in a given way, but they do so with reference to purposes quite beyond physiological function itself.

Vision apprehends only two things: shapes and colors. The apprehension of shape is closely related to the eye-brain connection, but the apprehension of color is not an intellectual experience; it is an emotional one. With color, the basic quality of mood of soul is expressed in relation with the world. Further, color in the world expresses something of the inner qualities of outer things of the world. The colors of the autumn leaves do not just create a mood in us; they are a mood of the world, its inner, soul quality at the time of autumn. The mood of the world is quite different in the summer, with all the green; quite different in spring, with the blossoming of all kinds of colors; and different still in winter, when things turn toward being gray and white. With color, nature displays her inner workings to the outer world (Steiner, 1982).

Color is a bodily basis for feeling. One can then wonder what happens to feelings when one works 8 or more hours a day in an office building in which the predominate shade is white (which is not a color). What happens when the cinema comes along and Technicolor, color television, magazine graphics, and Polaroid snapshots are introduced? These extraordinary inventions give us colors that are not at all like the colors we encounter in the world, but more like paints that have been splashed over scenery, revealing only surfaces. Behind the surface, there is no soul, no life of feeling and relationship, no possibility of reflection and contemplation, but only decoration, stimulation, expectation of reaction. On the surface the color is too vivid, too colored, too perfectly simulated, rather than the play of light and shadow creating color. The colors are used for effect, hitting you over the head with emotion versus creating a mood, setting a backdrop, or inviting one to participate. Too much exposure to this type of thing, and we begin to experience the world as painted, rather than as full of colors that are every moment coming into being, changing, disappearing, and reappearing.

Colors play. Paint covers. When I look out my window every evening at the sunset, the purple and red and orange and blue and gray of the sky change from one second to the next. It is a wonderful experience of how color is every moment creating. The world of color has an unmistakable spiritual dimension that is lost with surfaces that look painted.

The difference between color expressing the inner, soul qualities of the world and artificial color has yet another dimension. We look at colored surfaces. We become involved in the world of color. This means we become involved in the world as color because the eye is the sense organ that actually contains all the other sense capacities. Vision encompasses all the other senses. That is why we can speak of all the other senses through metaphors that are basically visual. We cannot speak of the eye by means of smell, but we can talk about smell by means of vision. If I say that odor comes into the nose, carried by the air, you will notice that you have a visual picture of this process. The eye is connected with most of the other senses. For example, the capacity of balance also works through the eye. We partly keep our balance through the eye. Four muscles move the eye up and down, right and left; other muscles make possible a rotary movement of the eye. These play into the sense of balance and also very much into the sense of movement. We also see sweet colors, dirty colors, as well as warm and cool colors. The eye is the all-encompassing sense organ and, as such, is often the tyrannical source of overcompensation of the disruptions in other, subtler senses, such as balance and movement (Aeppli, n.d.).

In education, the care for the sense of vision has to do with learning to pay attention to the play of color, primarily in the natural world. As children live more and more in a totally simulated environment, the attention to the natural world tends to become dramatically decreased. (This is somewhat relative, of course; that is, if you live on the plains of Wyoming versus the suburbs or any city, the child's experience of the world as given is different but the value of the simulated object versus the natural world may remain the same, canceling out the quality of the difference.) Thus, we see that seeing, vision, as a sense is not just whether it functions adequately or not, a matter of periodic check-ups, but the activity of seeing and, thus, of feeling can be enhanced, manipulated, repressed, or totally distorted. We must learn to see with its attendant moods, and as such, seeing sensitively can be taught. A curriculum for seeing is rather like religious education and therefore must be taken on with great care and concern for values and conscience.

The Warmth Sense

In this grouping of the senses through which the body comes into communion with the world, one final sense gets very little attention. Science is aware of this sense but has done little to investigate it, and when it has, the results have been varied and unclear. This sense is the **warmth sense**, or the temperature sense. We sense the difference between the warmth of our bodies and the warmth or coldness of things outside our bodies. This sensing has nothing to do with absolute temperature. For example, here is a common experiment: Take three bowls of water. Fill one with ice water, one with hot water, and one with lukewarm water. Put your left hand into the bowl of ice water for 5 minutes, and at the same time put your right hand into the hot water for the same amount of time. Then put both hands into the bowl of lukewarm water. To the left hand, the lukewarm water will feel hot; and to the right, the lukewarm water will feel cold. The lukewarm water, measured by a thermometer, is a given temperature, but we feel it differently with each hand. This is a good way to get a sense of the warmth sense. Something has to happen between our bodies and the world for us to experience temperature. A flow must occur. When heat flows from the body into the outer world, the experience is one of coldness. The flow of warmth away from the body is coldness. When we grasp a hot object, heat flows from the object into us and we feel warmth. This description is simple physics. But the question remains, where does the experience come from?

The flow of warmth away from the body is a contraction of the soul. The soul reaches out to the world, and when it receives nothing back, this is the experience of coldness. The warmth sense is the bodily basis for a similar dimension in our relationships with others. On the one hand, when we reach out to someone and receive nothing back, we also experience coldness, although here it is much more a pure soul experience. But a person can leave you cold, and that coldness is felt in the body, almost like temperature. On the other hand, when we open ourselves to the world and do receive something back, we feel warmth; it is similar with our relationships with other persons. From the viewpoint of the soul, the warmth sense has to do with our interest in the world. It has to do with that ongoing flow between ourselves and the world and between the world and us.

In the educational setting, we see more and more reliance on technological equipment to stimulate and entertain children and therefore keep their attention. When "attention" is held to be mere stimulation of nerve impulses, a deep mistrust of feeling develops. Stimulation becomes necessary to feel warmth, or aliveness, at the expense of relationship and trust in other human beings. Computers, films, television, and so on take the place of the warmth of human exchange and presence, and a capacity to give of one's self to another cannot develop. The warmth sense is even more basic than vision; in a way, it is the basis of the four world senses, for if there is not interest in the world, the other three are already dulled.

Healing the Four Senses of the World

To summarize the four senses called "world" senses: With the sense of smell, the exchange between our bodily being and the world occurs through the element of air. Odors work through the air element to bring the world into our bodies. With the sense of taste, the exchange between our bodies and the world occurs in the element of water. A substance is brought into the mouth, where it is dissolved in the fluid of saliva. In the case of vision, the exchange occurs between our soul and the soul of the world. Color, for example, is not just on the surface of things, but expresses the inner qualities of the outer world. This is an element of earth. And in the sense of warmth, flow is required between our bodies and the world. Warmth or coldness relies on the flow of heat. The flow is related to the element of fire.

This alchemical imagination of the world senses shows their relationship with the world, based on the four primary elements of earth, air, fire, and water. The reason for introducing such an alchemical image is to bring out that a creative process occurs in the sensing of the outer world. It is not just a matter of receiving impressions of an already fixed and completed world. For the world to be there, as experience, we have to be creatively involved with the world and it with us; sensing here is creation happening. The alchemists understood the responsibility of being involved in creation in this way through the senses. If the world senses are dulled, especially in education, the ongoing creation in this way through the senses is hindered. Proper care, even education, of the world senses is to take up the responsibility of being involved in creation, not just using and consuming it for our purposes.

Indications for Educating the Four World Senses

A few comments have been made concerning how to go about strengthening each of the four world senses. Part of the difficulty with these senses is that the sense organs for each of these senses are different. That means it is possible for each of these senses to be dulled one by one in the conditions of the current world. There must be a way that these senses do not become rigidly separated, because if they do, the feeling life, even if it exists, is dismembered. The care of these senses can be best attended by means of the art of painting. Painting is not at all simply something visual. It is a way of working in a disciplined way in the realm of feeling, of keeping feeling whole. When one is working with red, blue, purple, yellow, any color, there is also a subtle sense of taste, a soul-like quality that has to do with taste. So, with painting, vision and taste are brought into an ongoing relation. Working artistically with color also brings vision into ongoing relation with the sense of warmth. When we say red is hot and blue is cool, there is a real basis for this in the color. And each stimulates smell in a subtle way having nothing to do with the overt smell of the paint. Great care must be taken in painting, however, that also respects the age and experience of the child in school. For example, painting with light and watery watercolor paint, as opposed to the heavy and dense oil or even water-based acrylics, better serves young children.

The emphasis here is that artistic work is not an arbitrary idea related to education, but rather is an absolute necessity, particularly for children, whose senses are still more lively than those of adults. Artistic work is a necessity if the four middle senses are not to become too separated. Art is not a frivolous extra in school; it is crucial as forming the basis for a healthy feeling life.

But not just adding art to the curriculum for children is needed. Teachers would also need to begin to paint to bring balance and healing into their own sense lives. For the adult, also spending time with good paintings, developing a real relationship with them, can be healing for the four world senses. Here, it is important to stay away from interpreters of art, from historians of art, and from critics of art because, most often, these disciplines take us away from the immediate sense experience of art. They tend to teach us to look away or to look at, rather than to become involved in, the immediate sensed experience with art.

The Higher, or Community, Senses

Only one of the higher senses, as explicated by Rudolf Steiner, is recognized as a sense at all. This is the sense of hearing. The other three are the word or speech sense, the thought sense, and the ego sense (Steiner, 1996). Disorders of the sense life that we have spoken of so far most likely could not be balanced only through the suggestions made. A new liveliness, spirit, vigor, and interest in and for the senses can come about through learning to experience the community, or relational, senses. Even these senses, however, are greatly subjected to being dulled, more so because they are not even recognized. Once they are, and paid attention to by adults, sensing in these realms goes a long way toward healing all the senses. The communal senses have to do with sensing qualities of other human beings. They could also be called the interrelational senses. The first of these senses, *hearing,* is more of a transitional sense between the world senses and the communal senses. The *language sense* is the bodily capacity to sense the speaking of another person. The *thought sense* concerns the capacity to perceive bodily that another person is engaged in thinking, although it does not include directly perceiving the thought content. The *sense of the "I,"* or individuality, involves developing the capacity to sense the particular quality of the other that is one's own, unique, individual being. Part of the work in considering these senses is to begin to observe and see whether you can actually experience them.

Each of the communal senses correlates with one of the corporeal senses. The sense of touch correlates with the sense of the "I"; the life sense, with the thought sense; balance, with hearing; and movement, with the speech sense. Because of the particular polarities between the corporeal and communal senses, healing and balancing of the corporeal senses can be approached through the development of the higher senses. But this healing takes place through relationships. When, even if but for a few moments, I can experience in a direct, bodily manner something of the true individuality of another person, that sensing acts on the other as a kind of spiritual touch, and the person feels more at home with his or her body. When I attend to another person in such a manner as to sense his or her engagement in creative thinking, that can be healing to the life sense of the other person. When I truly listen to another person, such hearing also acts to bring alignment of balance, and when I pay intimate attention to the speech of another, that sensory attention also acts to bring the sense of movement of that person into equilibrium. Care of the communal senses is the responsibility of all adults who interact with children, especially in schools. The adult must seek the development of these senses and bring them to bear on who they are as teachers and what they do in teaching.

The Sense of Hearing

Let us now consider each of the community senses. The **sense of hearing**, as a higher sense, involves becoming conscious of the two sides of hearing: (a) that it gives us the inner qualities of the outer world and (b) that it gives us, through the body, an earthly experience of the spiritual nature of another person. Hearing a bell, a siren, or the wind blowing through the trees is something quite different from hearing the voice of another person. Hearing the sounds of the world gives us a sense of the inner qualities of things, but hearing another person gives us an immediate sense of the inner soul life of the person. We hear fear or desire or need or intimacy.

The sacred quality of hearing is disrupted by electronic intervention in the current world—not only recording, amplification, and digitizing but also the intervention of the telephone, wherein voice is separated from bodily presence and human gesture. As with all the other senses, none of these things is bad or wrong or to be completely avoided. We must become conscious of what they do, however, and always make sure that balance is provided—real music, real conversation, real speaking, real hearing, and real listening.

The Speech Sense

The **speech sense** is not just knowing I am or another is speaking, but is the specific capacity to sense the word, even in an unknown foreign language, as human language. The language spoken may have a musical quality to it, but we recognize the words and must quiet the words in us to hear the words of another. The hearing of the spoken words of another is possible because we follow the movements of the other's larynx with our own as that person speaks. We "speak" with the other. But this is an inner gesture, and our outer speaking must be silenced to hear the other. As such, to hear language, we must deliberately quiet ourselves and our movement to be present to the other's speech. Very often, when we do not put ourselves aside in this way, we really do not hear what another person is saying. Because we know words and their meanings, we think we know what the person is saying, but we do not. We only hear what we already think. Hearing language is a highly spiritual act. We have to hold our own personalities in abeyance to hear another's speech. We

have to sacrifice what we are feeling and thinking, our judgment, and become present to the language itself.

When I listen to someone speak, my larynx is also moving. So, listening is also always speaking, but it is speaking what the person speaking to me is speaking. We typically are not aware of this. Heard language crosses over into speaking language. This is a helpful image because it shows how intimate language really is. When language is conceived of only as a means of communication, we have a theory of language that leaves us lonely. From the point of view of communication, language does not convey anything of the person, but only what the person communicates. But through understanding something of the language sense, we see that language is not communication, but communion.

Beyond hearing language and the sensory capacity to recognize language, we have the sensory capacity to understand what is said through language. To understand meaning, language itself becomes transparent. The concepts we understand are not identical with the language we speak. Language passes on an idea, but never completely. When we have an idea, it is often terribly difficult to find just the right words to express it. When we do find the right words, they are never quite adequate. Not really having said what we meant, or not being able to express what we really meant to this particular person, or not being able to put into words what we are thinking is an experience we have all had from time to time. The thought sense, however, moves the other way. Through this sense, we perceive first that someone else is thinking and immediately sense, usually through language, the meaning of what the person is thinking. To understand someone, language has to be erased. I do not pay attention to the words, but rather what is meant by the words. The ideas conveyed by language are silent.

The Thought Sense

The **thought sense** perceives the thinking of another person; through this sense, we are able to understand another person. To perceive the thought of another, a particular kind of attention is involved. To be an attentive listener, I must develop the capacity of hearing, of language, and of having true ideas, not simply taking up those used by others. If I have not developed these capacities, I cannot truly understand the other person. But I also cannot understand the other person if I am occupied with my own ideas. I have to have the capacity, at the moment of listening, to extinguish my own thinking and put the thinking of the other person in its place. The thought sense requires selflessness.

The thought sense has two main disorders. The first is that it may not develop, particularly in a world in which information is mistaken to be thought. To develop this sense and the other communal senses as well, the individual must be willing to remain childlike until the end of life. The best teachers we always remember were not the ones who were trying to teach us something, which is nothing more than indoctrination. The best teachers were those who were willing to stand up in front of class and think. Observing this happen was the greatest inspiration. We observed wonder, curiosity, interest, experimentation, openness—all very childlike qualities. The second disorder lies in the tendency to develop the capacity of thinking in egotistical ways. Thinking, when it is valued at all, tends to be promoted only for what it can do for us. It may mean we can enjoy the act of thinking, read important books, or enter a professional field. Almost never is it considered the necessary preparation for being able to be selflessly present to others.

The Sense of the "I," or Individuality

The **sense of the "I,"** or individuality, does not refer to experiencing ourselves as individuals, but rather to experiencing another person as an individual. Sensing the individuality of another person is a spiritual act, occurring through the body. The sense organ for sensing individuality is the whole of the human body and is actually most related to touch. The mark of sensing individuality is most often strife, much more so than harmonious acceptance. When I perceive something of the individuality of another, a struggle is likely to occur. As long as I hear what I like or want to hear, nothing within me is challenged and nothing truly new comes through. To become aware of this sense requires meeting one's own fears—of being challenged, of not knowing, of being permeated with the mysterious nature of another person. We have to understand that we are basically afraid of the unknown, be in others or in ourselves. This fear is quite healthy because it prompts the development of spiritual courage. Of course, strife can be purely a clash of egotism with egotism. The experience of strife is quite different from a battle of egos, however. It is to perceive another as completely other, not like me nor anyone I know. This can be a painful experience, perhaps one in which we feel diminished, but also a moment of enormous respect. A feeling of the sacred center of the being of the other person develops. For this reason, the sense of individuality is quite confused in our time. It is a sense that is in the process of developing and easily goes unnoticed.

Every form of mass movement works against the sense of the "I." A tremendously powerful leveling process operates in our culture; everyone is supposed to be like everyone else. The whole of our current educational system is based, however innocuously conceived, on this premise. It is the basis for the indoctrination that we all receive, whether in public or private school, to become a member of this society. In addition, the people who are outstanding (meaning simply that they stand out, not that they are somehow "greater")—politicians, entertainers, or sports heroes—present us with images or packages of themselves, not with their actual selves. This sense is very difficult to care for in our self-indulgent culture. Especially with the disruptions of the corporeal sense—in particular, in people who have experienced harm through abuse—an understandable need to feel the self in a bodily way emerges. But this diminishes the capacity to truly experience the other because we have so little of ourselves and, therefore, little capacity for self-sacrifice. The care and development of this sense requires awakening to a sense of true service, which in itself requires purification of the soul.

How education proceeds from this point will transform society or send it plummeting back into the savagery of the Dark Ages. True education recognizes the whole human being to be educated. The debate and debacle of "theories of education, learning thinking, information processing, and systems of information retrieval" are relevant to computer programming, not to the education of human beings. We need to realize that the human being and mechanically derived systems meant to describe the human being are not even remotely the same thing. The higher, or community, senses, when actually experienced, verify this unbridgeable difference. Care of the language sense, the thought sense, and the sense of individuality requires a special sort of attention because these three communal, or interrelational, senses are not yet completely developed in our time; they are still in the process of becoming an integral part of our being in humanity as a whole, and they develop in the individual throughout life.

The greatest hindrance to developing the interrelational senses throughout life is actually brought about by corporeal sense disturbances that occur very early in life. If the corporeal senses are disordered, the relational senses cannot develop. The sense organs for the corporeal senses are the body as a whole even though sensing may take particular bodily pathways. The sense organs for relational senses are also the whole body. Thus, an intimate connection exists between these higher senses and the lower ones. Besides the overall relation, there is the particular relationship between these two domains of sensing. The movement, balance, touch, and life senses are all quite integral to the early years of education and, as such, could be profoundly nurtured in the formative, first years of school, when the will of the individual is most in need of developing with inner strength. The senses of smell, taste, vision, and warmth, as the foundation for the life of feeling, could be addressed through the imagination and development of true artistic capacity in the middle years of education, giving the world individuals with conscience and true depth of feeling for the earth and all who live here. From this solid basis, the capacity for true, living thinking could develop, blossoming from the unfolding of the senses of hearing, speech, thought, and "I," creating a true culture, a world unimaginable to the technical imagination bent on making us all efficient processing devices.

References

Abram, D. (1996). *The spell of the sensuous.* New York: Pantheon Books.

Ackerman, D. (1990). *A natural history of the senses.* New York: Random House.

Aeppli, W. (n.d.). *The care and development of the human senses.* Forest Row, UK: Steiner Schools Fellowship.

Hillman, J. (1979). *Re-visioning psychology.* New York: Harper & Row.

Jung, C. (1964). *Civilization in transition* (Collected works. Vol. 10). Princeton, NJ: Princeton University Press.

Jung, C. (1968). *The structure and dynamics of the psyche* (Collected works, Vol. 8). Princeton, NJ: Princeton University Press.

Konig, K. (1960). *The circle of the twelve senses.* Lecture given at the Waldorf Institute, Spring Valley, NY.

Konig, K. (1984). *The first three years of the child.* Hudson, NY: Anthroposophic Press.

Merleau-Ponty, M. (1962). *Phenomenology of perception.* London: Routledge & Kegan Paul.

Merleau-Ponty, M. (1964). *The primacy of perception.* Evanston, IL: Northwestern University Press.

Sardello, R. (1992). *Facing the world with soul.* New York: HarperCollins.

Sardello, R. (1995). *Love and the soul: Creating a future for Earth.* New York: HarperCollins.

Soesman, A. (n.d.). *The twelve senses* (J. Cornelis, Trans.). Forest Row, UK: Hawthorn Press.

Steiner, R. (1966). *Study of man.* London: Rudolf Steiner Press.

Steiner, R. (1972). *Creative education.* London: Rudolf Steiner Press.

Steiner, R. (1974). *The kingdom of childhood.* London: Rudolf Steiner Press.

Steiner, R. (1981). *A modern art of education.* London: Rudolf Steiner Press.

Steiner, R. (1982). *Colour.* London: Rudolf Steiner Press.

Steiner, R. (1983). *Deeper insights into education.* Hudson, NY: Anthroposophic Press.

Steiner, R. (1988). *The child's changing consciousness and Waldorf education.* Hudson, NY: Anthroposophic Press.

Steiner, R. (1996). *Anthroposophy: A fragment.* Hudson, NY: Anthroposophic Press.

van den Berg, J. (1972). *A different existence: Principles of phenomenological psychology.* Pittsburgh: Duquesne University Press.

Biographies

Robert Sardell, Ph.D., is cofounder of the School of Spiritual Psychology, based in Great Barrington, Massachusetts; a faculty member of the Dallas Institute of Humanities and Culture; and a faculty member of the Chalice of Repose Project, Missoula, Montana, a training program for caring for the dying through sacred music. He is former Chair of the Department of Psychology, University of Dallas; former Director, Institute of Philosophic Studies, University of Dallas; and a practicing psychotherapist for more than 20 years, working in Jungian and archetypal psychology. He also developed a spiritual psychology based in Jung and Rudolf Steiner. He is the author of *Facing the World With Soul; Love and the Soul: Creating a Future for Earth;* and *Freeing the Soul From Fear;* editor of *The Angels;* coeditor of *Stirrings of Culture;* and author of more than 100 articles.

CHERYL SANDERS, M.S., is a cofounder of the School of Spiritual Psychology and an addiction counselor and teacher, having worked in public agencies and private practice for 18 years. She cofounded a program in perinatal intervention at Parkland Hospital, Dallas, and conducts workshops on forming community coalitions for women and minority groups for health and human services. She also conducts workshops for faculties and parents dealing with teaching about abuse, violence, and addictive behaviors.

13 From Cognitive Learning to Creative Thinking

Joan Almon

INTRODUCTION

This chapter challenges readers to view human thinking from a spiritual perspective. Joan Almon, an early childhood educator, introduces the idea that thinking need not be a product of abstraction, but rather an immediate form of engagement not only that provides us with information but also for the transformation and development of ourselves as human beings. It is commonplace to see thinking as the manipulation of facts and figures to solve practical or theoretical problems. Almon, however, contends that thinking can begin in the early childhood years as a form of imaginative engagement that not only matures in time to abstract concepts and critical thinking skills but also provides a foundation for healthy human development.

Almon offers a spiritual perspective on child development and human cognition based on the work of Austrian philosopher/scientist Rudolph Steiner. Steiner maintains that the physical world we see is a product of creative spiritual forces. He sees both spiritual dimensions in the world and in us as human beings. His philosophy is at the pedagogical core of the international Waldorf school movement, the world's largest nonsectarian school initiative now including more than 600 independent schools.

Almon maintains that the first task in encouraging the healthy development of children is to have them imaginatively interact with the world through play, story, and artistic activity. These experiences, she explains, are essential to nurturing the creative forces at work not only in the growth of the intellect but also in the healthy development of children's bodies. From this perspective, it is essential to delay the kind of abstract reasoning that one usually associates with formal academic learning. Such abstraction serves only to separate the child from the world, to make the world a separate object, rather than a place first and foremost where a child may find him- or herself at home.

Almon, following Steiner, suggests that we can best serve the cognitive development of children by recognizing that thinking evolves metamorphically. More specifically, she explains that as children grow, they pass through a variety of distinctive stages of development that have their own unique balances of imagination and intellect. Furthermore, each phase of childhood creates an opportunity for children to grow in terms of their capacities to think, feel, and act in the world.

In these contexts, the author maintains that human thinking can become far more than information processing. It can become a form of spiritual nourishment and insight, a source of wisdom beyond practical knowledge. Almon concludes that such heightened capacities for thinking are necessary to recognize and respond to the challenges that face us individually and culturally, spiritually and practically.

—*Jeffrey Kane*

Humanity as a whole stands on a threshold where thinking can unfold and find a new relationship to soul and spirit or else become smaller and narrower to fit itself into the convention of standardized tests, news bits, computer programs, and the like. The first path can lead to creative renewal for the individual and society, whereas the second generally leads to a narrowing of human capacity and resulting illness. Good intentions alone do not enable humanity to claim the full scope of being human or the full range of thinking. Basic steps of development lead to creative thinking, and they need to be recognized and nurtured at home and in school. At the moment, most families and teachers wish to advance thinking by teaching academic subjects as early as possible. One result, however, is a growing strain on the nervous system of children, which has profound effects on development right into adulthood. The spark of individuality that lies at the heart of each child is hindered from growing freely, and in adulthood one is less able to find the wellsprings of individual creativity and growth. It is not too late, however, to reverse the trends of contemporary education and allow the minds of children to develop in a focused but creative manner. Currently, American education is oriented toward making computers the new foundation of all education, from early childhood onward. One could still learn from the mistakes of the past 20 years, however, and establish a developmentally sound and healthy basis for education. Just as the educational decisions of the 1970s had a tremendous impact—mostly negative—on a whole generation of children, leading to the current crisis in education, so the decisions of the next few years will shape the experiences of the next generation of children. We have only a small window of time to consider creative and healthy alternatives to technologically driven education.

Human beings are gifted with tremendous capacities. From theoretical physics to filling out tax forms, our mental abilities cover a very wide range. At the same time, we have a broad array of artistic and social capacities, and our physical skills vary from participating in energetic sports to creating the finest handwork. Each other animal species is quite narrow in its range of capacity, whereas human beings are incredibly diverse. Yet, if we look at much of education in the United States today, we might conclude that the only aspects of the human being worth developing are a narrow range of mental abilities and a wide range of athletic skills. Artistic subjects are dropped from the curriculum as soon as school budgets grow tight, and handwork, gardening, or other physical activities besides sports have generally not been included for decades. More and more, the emphasis is on a very narrow form of thinking that enables one to do well on standardized tests and to communicate at the simplest levels. One frequently hears high school teachers and college professors complain that something has gone wrong with our young people, for they can no longer think. At the very time when modern problems require a tremendous breadth of understanding as well as depth of insight, human thinking is tending to become narrower and more superficial. What is happening?

If we look at the changing patterns of the United States and other industrialized countries during the past 200 years, it is not hard to trace the major shifts from a largely agrarian society to the factories of the industrial revolution and onward to modern times. Today, factories are still present but are much less visible, and the focus is on computer-related work. Cities today are considered on the cutting edge if they have research parks and Silicon Valley-type corridors developing on their outskirts. Along with this shift in the workplace, a shift has occurred in the way society has come to value thinking. Recognizing the importance of thinking in modern life, society has allowed it to become the primary focus for evaluating children, their placement in school, and their long-term direction for higher education and work.

Yet, without a deep understanding of thinking, one overlooks its profound nature and its importance to the soul and spiritual life of the individual. Thinking is more than a tool for our practical work life. It is a source of tremendous creativity and renewal. Thinking can be filled with light and illuminate the darkness. It can sprout wings and soar and look at the world from a vantage point different from the one we can manage when we are enmeshed in daily affairs.

Unfortunately, the trend is to allow thinking to become narrow enough to fit into standardized tests or to be suited for computer usage. One needs to broaden the perspective, as many educators are attempting, so that thinking can fully awaken in its abstract and philosophical forms during adolescence, the time when such thinking ripens, along with the awakening of a deep idealism. If thinking is to become fully awakened in adolescence, then children need a foundation of creative engagement in early childhood and an imaginative and artistic experience of education in the elementary school years. Such creative activity involves the whole child, physically and spiritually. Too often, educators think that the path to creative thinking rests upon creative problem solving, which is primarily an intellectual activity and does not nourish young children. Instead, it strains their nervous systems.

In contrast with education that awakens early intellectualism, one can create an education that fosters children's play and their love of stories, songs, and verses. Through such activities, the imagination is stirred and the creative forces are allowed to flow. As a teacher, one sees that the children who have strong capacities for creative play also tend to have greater vitality and health. When fantasy play and imagination are not cultivated in children, humanity runs the risk of continuously reenacting Adam and Eve's plight in the Garden of Eden. We eat from the Tree of Knowledge but are banned from eating from the Tree of Life. Without life, however, the fruits of knowledge turn bitter.

Humanity stands at a threshold today, where it needs not only rational thinking but also thinking that is full of life and that supports the spiritual and soul growth of each individual. We are at a point where thinking can either blossom into new and very fruitful directions that are intimately bound with inner growth or shrivel and become a source of illness in our bodies. When we look at young people today, we see both tendencies. The generation under 30 is a remarkable group. Their minds are very open, and their capacity for soul-spiritual awareness is profound, yet they are showing increasing signs of illnesses connected to nervousness and stress. Such illnesses, in part, can be related to the overstimulated, over-awakened state in which society, families, and schools keep them from early childhood onward. In this chapter we explore the modern problems afflicting children, as well as the healthy development of creative thinking.

The Problem

The contemporary shift toward a society focused on computers has led to the growing alarm of many parents, who fear that their children will not be ready for the world of the next century. Perhaps they feel like strangers in a world for which no one prepared them. At any rate, they place an inordinate emphasis on their children needing to learn academic and computer skills at a very young age. Computers in nursery schools are increasingly common. One mother at a conference on computers and young children expressed her concern when she stood up and said with fear in her voice, "If my 3-year-old does not learn to use a computer, he will never get a job at age 18." No one thought to point out to her that the bright men and women who developed the computer industry, both its hardware and its software, had grown up without computers in their homes or schools.

With a strong background in creative thinking and a strong individuality that accompanies it, one can learn computer usage in high school or college with relative ease. Before that, one needs a creative experience of learning that enhances the sense of self as a unique individual capable of creative thinking. In the introduction to his book *Computer Power and Human Reason*, Joseph Weizenbaum (1976), a well-known professor of computer science at Massachusetts Institute of Technology, points to the relation of science and creativity as a basic idea of life: "That science is creative, that the creative act in science is equivalent to the creative act in art, that creation springs only from autonomous individuals, is such a simple, and one might think, obvious idea" (p. 2). Later in the book, he points out how the absence of this creative autonomy in the individual leads to a feeling of powerlessness and of subservience. One feels like a robot, and even those at the very top of the governmental power structure express the feeling of powerlessness and of being a "slave" to the dictates of a computer.

> Technological inevitability can thus be seen to be a mere element of a much larger syndrome. Science promised man power. But as so often happens when people are seduced by promises of power, the price exacted in advance and all along the path, and the price actually paid, is servitude and impotence. Power is nothing if it is not the power to choose. (p. 259)

When one asks early childhood educators why they are placing such emphasis on early academics and computer usage even though many acknowledge that it is not in the child's best interest from a developmental point of view, they shrug their shoulders, look somewhat shamefaced, and say they have no choice because the parents are demanding it. Many parents take their cues from the educators, and when they see workbooks, learning centers, and computers in every nursery and kindergarten, they feel no need to question their own feeling that their children must begin early if they are to succeed. The one supports the other with an ironic twist. The whole process was described in the following way by a mother of young children:

> She was moving to a new community and was looking at various schools while deciding into which neighborhood she would move. She was given school tours by principals who all stressed the advanced learning opportunities being given to young children in their schools. When she sat down with them in conversation and explained that she was not concerned about early academics but wanted her child to have a creative and wholesome beginning to life, the tenor of the conversation changed abruptly. The principals spoke in

more personal tones and said they agreed with her wholeheartedly but could no longer offer such an education, for most parents would not accept it. The push was too strong toward intellectual education and computer usage. They had to comply with the demands of the parents.

I experienced a similar catch-22 on a trip to Russia in the late 1970s. America was already deeply committed to early academics at the kindergarten level, and one reason for instigating early academics was the fear that arose when *Sputnik* was launched. America was shocked that Russia was in the lead in space and began looking for ways to catch up. By the early 1970s, the answer seemed to be early academics. In my naïveté as a new teacher, I had assumed that someone had gone to Russia, studied early childhood education there, and replicated it in the United States. Therefore, on a trip to Russia, I asked whether I could visit a kindergarten to see the latest in their early childhood ideas. I was taken to a lovely kindergarten/day care that was full of toys and had a playful atmosphere. No printed words or numbers were to be seen. Because toys had essentially disappeared from American kindergartens by that time, I was thoroughly puzzled. In conversation with the director, a dynamic Russian woman who appeared to be an excellent educator, I was astonished when my translator explained that the director was apologizing for how backward her kindergarten must appear to me. She knew that American kindergartens were very advanced, and she hoped that Russia could soon catch up with us. I tried to explain through the translator that America had been trying to catch up with Russia and had made a huge mistake in early childhood education. I begged her not to follow our lead in the matter. Unfortunately, this was too much for my very able translator, who was sure she was misunderstanding me. Indeed, it must have sounded utterly ridiculous to her. No amount of explaining on my part seemed to help, and she simply refused to translate. Years later, when she visited me and saw my kindergarten, full of simple materials with which children could play in the most creative ways, she was better able to understand what I had tried to communicate on that day.

One could be amused by such tales of modern absurdities were it not for the price that children are paying today. It is no longer simply an academic question of one type of schooling over another, but of the health and well-being of children. Children in the technologically advanced countries are beginning to show signs of serious stress and nervousness, and, in part, this is related to the intense pressure being put on their nervous systems at a very young age. In the United States, for instance, the number of children with a diagnosis of attention deficit disorder (ADD) or ADD combined with hyperactivity is growing rapidly. The drug Ritalin is often being prescribed for such children. Statistics vary but range from 1 million to 1.5 million children in the United States now receiving Ritalin. These numbers have risen about 2.5 times since 1990 (*Good Housekeeping,* 1996, p. 66; *Mental Health Weekly,* 1996, p. 6). Whereas some children genuinely need help because of constitutional problems in the nervous system, many others appear to need help primarily because they cannot accommodate to current educational practices. These include developmentally inappropriate demands on the nervous system, such as the requirement to concentrate on academic subjects in the preschool when the child's constitution is geared for learning through self-directed, creative play. An article in the *Houston Chronicle* (1996, p. 1) indicated that one reason for the great increase in Ritalin usage is the pressure on schools and parents for academic performance. The implications of Ritalin usage are cause for genuine concern and serious study. Currently, it is a medication given primarily to middle-class and upper-class children to help them excel academically, in sports, and in other realms of life. Efforts are also underway through the National Institute of Mental Health to identify potentially violent youths and to medicate them with Ritalin and other drugs from childhood on. These efforts were fought by Dr. Peter R. Breggin and Ginger Ross Breggin and are reported in their book *The War Against Children* (n.d.).

In Germany, where the problems of children seem less severe than in the United States, concern over new health problems is nevertheless growing. At the Center for Children and Youth at the University of Bielefeld, researchers have identified a new body of illnesses common to children in technologically developed countries. Unlike the fever and highly contagious illnesses of old, the newer diseases are primarily associated with the nervous and respiratory systems. They include nervousness, stress, and hyperactivity but also significant increases in allergies, asthma, skin disorders, sleep disorders, and eating disorders.

These modern trends are a double tragedy, for they afflict a generation of children who appear to be especially open and concerned about helping the Earth and all who live on it. This is admittedly a fairly subjective view, but it is echoed by many teachers who speak of their students having a profound sensitivity to the world around them while suffering greatly at the hands of modern society. One indication of the nature of this young generation is the amount of social concern and volunteerism one finds on college campuses. Not since the 1960s has one seen this amount of social interest among college students, many of whom give many hours of their time to ecological organizations or to those working with the poor.

During the past 10 years, one has also noticed another shift in the awareness of children and youths: A growing number are choosing to be vegetarians on their own at a young age. Ten years ago, teenagers made this choice; then, a growing number of 5-year-olds of my acquaintance announced themselves to be vegetarians, often saying that they did not want to kill animals. One class teacher in England said that when his current seventh-grade class began first grade, fully half of them were vegetarians by their own choice. This generation seems to have a deep concern for the Earth and its well-being, a concern that is much needed if we are to find ways to heal the Earth and to overcome the ravages of pollution. As one 6-year-old boy said to me from the depths of his heart, "You know, I just love this Earth. I just love it. I love the stones and the plants and the animals, but especially the animals." Then in a more childlike tone he said, "When I grow up, I am going to work in the zoo!"

One wishes to protect this generation with their deep social concerns, but instead one sees them growing more and more nervous, frightened, and insecure. This modern phenomenon may be understood in different ways, but one way is to look at the tremendous emphasis being placed on thinking and the stimulation of the brain and nervous system at a young age. In the normal course of development, mental growth in early childhood comes about through children's play, which includes the unconscious imitation of adults. Through play, children are continually learning about life; indeed, they are trying life on and making it their own. For young children, learning is not only a mental activity but is also very much a physical activity and an emotional one. Today's emphasis on cognitive learning at a young age tends to isolate thinking from feeling and willing and places much strain on the nervous system. In extreme cases, illness sets in. In most children today, one sees a one-sidedness: The brain and nervous system are very awake, whereas the social realm, along with artistic creativity, remains undeveloped.

In addition to learning cognitive skills at a very young age, today's children are asked to integrate far more sense impressions than were children of 50 or 100 years ago. Readers need only think of all the pictures that flash before them from the television screen or the rapidly changing scenery outside a car window. In earlier times when one walked or was conveyed by a horse, the scenery changed at a much slower rate. One cannot return to olden times, but one does need to understand the demands placed on children's nervous systems by the tremendous number of sense impressions they are exposed to and are asked to integrate. For many, it is an impossible task that leaves their nervous systems exhausted.

Such exhaustion has short-term and long-term consequences for children. As described before, modern children are apt to be nervous, to have very short attention spans, sometimes coupled with hyperactive behavior, and to suffer increasingly from allergies that can affect the behavior of the children profoundly. This new syndrome of illnesses is sometimes called the **new morbidity** and "reflects the changing nature of pediatric practice as it shifts away from traditional medical illnesses toward those with a greater psychosocial component." Thus states an article in the *American Journal of Public Health* (Newacheck, Budetti, & Halfon, 1986, p. 183). The article identifies the new major health problems among children as including learning difficulties and school problems, allergies, and speech and vision problems, and the coping and adjusting problems of adolescents. It is not always clear whether these illnesses are increasing as rapidly as they seem to be or whether they are more prominent now that other illnesses have been reduced. In either case, teachers report anecdotally seeing a rapid increase in these ailments, including allergies in children, which can have a profound effect on children's behavior.

I recall one 6-year-old in my kindergarten who had several food allergies and as a result he was on a very strict diet. I met him only after he was on his special diet and found it hard to integrate the stories I heard of his wild behavior the previous year with the relatively calm child I knew. One day, however, he came to the kindergarten in a very agitated state. Several times during the morning, he grew frustrated over seemingly small problems and would throw himself down on the floor, weeping and kicking. He used all his self-control not to attack other children, but by the end of the morning we were all exhausted. At noon, I told his mother about his difficult morning, and she went home and checked a new cereal box she had opened that morning. It was the same brand he had been eating for some time, but she now saw that one ingredient had changed. He was allergic to the new ingredient, and the extreme behavior of the morning was a result of his allergy. The next morning, he ate a different cereal and was fine again. I have seen a similar pattern with many other children, and this link between allergy and hyperactive or aggressive behavior has been explored by some physicians (Crook & Stevens, 1987; Feingold, 1974). When Dr. William G. Crook, for example, published data from a 5-year clinical study of 182 hyperactive children seen between 1973 and 1978, he reported, "Three out of four of the parents found that hyperactivity was related to one or more foods the child was eating" (Crook & Stevens, 1987). In general, such work has not been well received, yet my experience and that of other teachers indicate that many behavior problems in children today could be lessened through more attention to diet and allergies.

What comes first—an overactive nervous system or an allergic sensitivity to the foods and substances of the environment? In many cases, it is difficult to say, for the two often go together. They are part of a picture that something is going wrong with children today, and it is a problem that society is reluctant to recognize or address. To do so would mean looking at the human being in a much broader way and to explore again the nature of thinking. Is it a process only of the nervous system, or is it a creative deed that arises from all facets of the human being?

We are fortunate that the current generation of children and young adults is a particularly strong one from a soul and spiritual point of view. It is as if humanity is being given a warning signal. This generation, which has been subjected to an unprecedented attack on the nervous system, is feeling the impact physically, but many are still surviving with a certain wholeness and integrity. If the trends continue, however, and even become accelerated through computer-oriented education, then this generation will raise the next generation with even more extreme conditions. Then the impact of a one-sided, overactive nervous system will make itself felt more fully. It will become increasingly difficult to turn the tide toward wholeness and health. It is not too late to change directions and allow thinking to develop in a healthier manner. To do so, however, one needs an understanding of how thinking develops in a creative and healthy way, as well as models of what actually works in child rearing and education. Many educators have developed cogent ideas in this regard or are working on new approaches in the classroom. My own background, however, is in Waldorf education, which brings together insights into the development of all facets of the human being, including thinking, along with methods of education that have evolved during 75 years for children of all ages. In this context, I would like to introduce the approach of Waldorf education to creative thinking, which brings health and renewal in its wake, rather than a tendency toward nervousness and illness.

DEVELOPMENT OF CREATIVE THINKING

The first Waldorf school was founded in 1919 in Stuttgart, Germany. Rudolf Steiner (1861–1925) was a philosopher, a lecturer, and an educator and a man of deep insight into the spiritual nature of the human being. His insights imbue his work not only in education but also in curative education, medicine, agriculture, the arts, and many other fields. His overall philosophy, **anthroposophy**, pertains to the spiritual wisdom (*sophia*) of the human being (*anthropos*). Already at the turn of the century, Steiner began to describe ways that education could help children grow into strong individuals with a concern for the world around them. In April 1919, workers of the Waldorf Astoria Cigarette Factory in Stuttgart heard Steiner lecture on ideas for social renewal, including new approaches to education. They were stirred by the possibilities of how education could allow one's unique individuality to blossom, rather than to be suppressed for sake of society or the workplace. The next day, they asked him to open a school for their children. With the support of Emil Molt, the factory's owner and Steiner's longtime friend, a school was opened 5 months later, with several hundred children in eight classes. Within the next 5 years, a high school was added, and in 1926 a kindergarten opened. In all, about 900 children were then enrolled. That original school continues to play a strong and active role in the Waldorf movement and has worked to encourage a growing association among the 600 schools founded since that time in about 50 countries.

Before opening the first school, Rudolf Steiner selected the teachers from a circle of very capable individuals who had been studying and working with him for some years. Together, they had explored the nature of spirit and matter and the way they interpenetrate each other with the human being serving as a bridge between the two. Steiner then introduced them to his insights on child development and education in three lectures per day during a 3-week period.

Like all forms of modern education, **Waldorf education**—also known as Rudolf Steiner education—places much emphasis on thinking, on helping students awaken to as full a consciousness as possible of themselves and of the world around them. In doing so, however, it does not pull thinking away from life. It does not isolate it as an abstract act separate from feeling and willing. It views all three—thinking, feeling, and willing—as essential if human beings are to reach their full potential. A mental genius lacking the warmth of feeling and the fire of will is a cold human being. Ideas born out of coldness, without the warmth of soul or the fire of spirit to enliven them, carry a deathlike impulse in them and can do tremendous harm to the individual and to society. Gone are the days when one could argue that all scientific advances are positive simply because they bring greater knowledge. Such thinking was destroyed by the atomic bomb, which showed clearly that some forms of thinking were now so advanced that the results could bring tremendous destruction if not checked by compassion for humanity and for the earth. For each new advance in thinking, comparable advances must take place in human feeling, as well as in moral development. Rudolf Steiner (1994) expressed a similar thought in terms of spiritual advancement: "*For each single step that you take in seeking knowledge of hidden truths, you must take three steps in perfecting your character toward the good* [italics added]" (p. 62). Otherwise, the temptations to misuse knowledge are enormous.

In one form of thinking, ideas awaken and become ideals that stir the soul and guide humanity toward life and renewal. Rudolf Steiner (1994) described this process in the following way: "*Every idea that does not become an ideal for you kills a force in your soul, but every idea that becomes an ideal for you creates forces of life within you* [italics added]" (p. 25). These are living ideas and come forth when life-filled, creative thinking is allowed to ripen into idealism. Such ideas arise when willing, feeling, and thinking have been helped to develop in age-appropriate ways. Said differently, living thinking arises when body, soul, and spirit are allowed to interpenetrate and fructify one another. To think the world anew requires the wholehearted participation of the thinker.

Rudolf Steiner was concerned that thinking be alive and at the same time practical, both for the benefit of the individual and for the world at large. He emphasized the importance of learning and thinking as social deeds:

> *Every insight that you seek only to enrich your own store of learning and to accumulate treasure for yourself alone leads you from your path, but every insight that you seek in order to become more mature on the path of the ennoblement of humanity and world evolution brings you a step forward* [italics added]. (1994, pp. 24–25)

Rudolf Steiner, as well as John Dewey and Maria Montessori, emphasized that thinking must become practical, but for him it was a path of life set against a background of the deepest human strivings for soul/spiritual growth and transformation both in the personal and social realms.

In looking at the problems of modern society such as poverty, racism, and environmental decay, one sees that new forms of thinking are urgently needed. To think through a problem in new ways is much more than a mental exercise. It can carry a force of untold good that brings new healing and renewal in its wake. I am reminded of a story about Anwar Sadat, president of Egypt from 1970 to 1981, whose efforts toward peace in the Middle East were remarkable. When asked what had led him to reach out to Israel and begin conversations after years of isolation and silence, he said that following a talk in Egypt about the Middle East situation, a young bearded man stood and asked: Have you ever gone to Israel and simply talked with the Israelis? Sadat realized that he never had tried such a simple and direct method, and the more he thought about it the more he believed that he needed to try. His resulting conversations with Menachim Begin led to the Camp David peace accords and the first lasting peace in the postwar Middle East. One cannot underestimate the power of a new idea when it resonates through the mature-feeling life and is brought into concrete action. It can become a powerful tool for social healing. For this reason, the developed feeling life with a strong sense of social morality is greatly needed if thinking is to be of positive use to humanity.

Such thinking requires years to develop, and the school years are crucial in laying a foundation. A living, creative thinking is not merely taught; it is cultivated and nurtured through several phases. One phase leads to the next, but not primarily through a pattern of linear development. Rather, life-filled, creative thinking develops through a series of transformational growth steps, wherein one capacity after another seems to go to sleep like the caterpillar in the cocoon, only to emerge later in a new and more advanced form. When one knows the patterns, one watches with wonder as fantasy play awakens in the 3-year-old, develops fully, and begins to go to sleep in the 6-year-old. Then *imagination* emerges, the schoolchild's capacity to learn all about the world by forming inner images that are filled with feeling. In puberty, this ability, too, fades away, in preparation for the birth of thinking, which enables the adolescent to experience life in new ways through the mind. Unfortunately, today's children are being asked to think analytically from a very young age, and by the time they reach adolescence they have lost their interest in such thinking. Rather than feel new frontiers open in the mind, they react with boredom and seek their new experiences through the body with early sexual relations or altered states of consciousness brought about by drugs or alcohol. Where the mind is actually blossoming and growing, however, it usually calls the adolescent back from such harmful diversions, and such students are less likely to be caught in a downward spiraling direction. Through the opening of their minds and the development of thinking, they find that they can soar and can explore all the worlds they can think of.

Waldorf education takes these phases of development into account as it creates schools that begin with the nursery/kindergarten and go through high school. The kindergartens are radically different from the grades, which again are significantly different from the high school. Each is created to support the inner capacities of the students, yet the three work together to form a whole education. Rudolf Steiner was very insistent that all three levels of education be present in a Waldorf school. In the early years of the first school, when it was not yet possible to have a kindergarten because of lack of space and money, he is quoted as emphatically stating to the teachers, "We need kindergartens! We need kindergartens!"

THE "I" AND THE GROWING CHILD

One central pillar of Waldorf education is the threefold picture of the human being and how the development of thinking, feeling, and willing can be supported through a healthy education. Steiner also stressed the importance of **the "I,"** or the essence of each student coming to birth so that the individual could blossom and grow. Without the development of one's own unique "I," one cannot grow into a free and independent human being who can carry out one's tasks on the earth. An intimate relationship exists between the incarnation, or birth, of the individuality and the development of thinking, feeling, and willing. This connection is evident already in the first 3 years of life. In the 1st year, the child intently works on the will and mastery of the limbs, which results in his or her being able to stand erect and walk around age 1. In the 2nd year, the child works equally hard on acquiring the basics of language and developing verbal communication, and in the 3rd year, verbal thinking begins. Although all of these develop further in the years to come, a moment of climax also occurs as the child begins to call herself "I" around age 3. No longer does she say, "Susie wants milk" or "Me wants milk." Now, she says "I," and one senses that she really means it.

I recall one child I knew well telling me just before his third birthday that when he turned age 3, he was moving to a new house. He spoke so convincingly that I believed him and asked his parents about their upcoming move. They looked baffled and said they had no plans to move. I realized, then, that this was the way he perceived the great changes that happen around age 3. He was moving from one house to another. He was preparing for this birth of his individuality and was beginning to call himself "I." This is a profound moment in a human being's development, and as we move into the new house of our own "I," a veil is drawn over our earlier state. Very few people can remember events from the time before their third birthday. As little Michael said, we lived in a different house then, and it is very hard to go back to it.

Although the 3-year-old's experience of "I" is very important, it is still occurring on a small scale. No one holds a 3-year-old responsible for his or her actions in the way one does a 21-year-old who has experienced the more mature birth of the "I" or individuality. What precedes this greater birth is a pattern very similar to that of the first 3 years. During the first 7 years, the child learns primarily through the will. The young child is nearly always in motion. Arms and legs build and create, and through such playful activities the major lessons of life are learned. I once heard of a humorous study in which professional football players followed 3-year-olds for a day. By the end of the day, the football players were exhausted and the children were still feeling very energetic. This is not surprising to those who know little children and the enormous energy they have for movement and activity. In the next 7 years, the child lives less in the limbs and more in the rhythmic system, physically composed of lungs, heart, and circulatory system. Now the whole realm of feeling and imagination develop, and pulse and breathing grow more stable. This is the age when children traditionally played rhythmic games such as rope jumping to verses or throwing a ball against a wall, with verses such as "A: My name is Anna, and I come from Alabama." Such games are rarely played by the intellectually advanced children of today, although they are of great benefit in bringing health back to the overstimulated child.

Between ages 14 and 21, the child moves from the middle realm into the head, and thinking becomes much more active. Now comes the development of abstract thinking and the capacity to form independent judgments. These ages are not to be considered an exact picture of each child's development. Rather, they are an archetypal picture that allows for much individual variation. At the end of this process, however, is the greater birth of the "I," or individuality. Now the young adult becomes responsible for his or her behavior and life situation. This was a traditional age of coming to maturity, and as in the first 3 years, it follows after the development of will, feelings, and thinking. It is an important part of the whole picture, for if thinking is stressed too greatly at too young an age, the threefold development is disturbed. The incarnation of individuality is often hampered, and one is less strong in one's own self and less free to make decisions and to follow one's own path of life. This loss of freedom is probably the most tragic outcome of hurrying our children, for such hurrying interferes with the very essence of evolving into a unique human being. The result is a huge personal and social loss. In democratic nations, one goal of education is to foster the growth of free individuals, yet if contemporary education leads to a stunted experience of the "I," it is not well suited for democratic life. One could understand the "hurried child syndrome" in totalitarian regimes but not in active democracies. The individual and the society are paying far too high a price for the premature development of a narrow band of thinking. For a short-term gain, one suffers tremendous losses.

THE THREEFOLD HUMAN BEING

Without taking feeling and willing into account, there is no way that thinking can have a living, creative quality. It will inevitably be one-sided and rather dry. To say that someone lives in an "ivory tower" captures this one-sided experience of living only in the thinking, isolated from the other realities of life. One-sidedness can also develop in the realm of feeling, as is evident in the image of the artist living in a garret, full of passion and feeling, but with little energy for mental activity or for practical life. The image of one-sided will is the athlete who is all brawn and no brain, befuddled by thinking, uninterested in feeling or the arts, but a powerhouse on the sports field. One has to be careful with such images and not confuse them with real people, who always carry some of each quality, even if it is a very small amount. Yet, behind these stereotypes is a picture of the threefold human being, cut apart and divided, but nevertheless threefold in nature.

In the threefold picture, thinking, feeling, and willing are each related to corresponding organs and systems of the human body. Thinking is most associated with the brain and nervous system, feeling with the rhythmic system of heart and lungs, and willing with the movement of the limbs but also with the forces of the digestive system. A polarity exists between the head with its cool, contained forces and the limbs, radiating out in straight lines full of warmth and motion. The limbs must be in motion to do their work, whereas the head needs to be at rest to perform well. One Waldorf teacher, wishing to make this point to his seventh-grade students in an anatomy lesson, had them walk around the room, imitating chickens with their heads in movement. In the midst of this, he called out a simple multiplication problem that they had done many times. None could think of the answer until they held their heads still.

Another polarity exists between the head and limbs and pertains to consciousness. We can observe our thinking and become conscious of it, but the will is a mysterious force that lies below the realm of consciousness. Likewise, with the digestive system. If we are conscious of it, it is usually because we are suffering from indigestion. Usually, we are very unconscious of its activity. Between the two extremes of the head and the limbs is the rhythmic life of the heart and the lungs, which provides a harmonious balance.

With this overview of the threefold development of the child in the background, we can fill in the picture of the willing, feeling, and thinking. One sees the will developing strongly already in the 1st year of life as the child begins to master his body in preparation for walking. A wonderful example of this was little Gordon, whose family stayed with us for a month when he was 6 months old. He was at the stage of trying to turn over from his back to his stomach and would happily spend hours each day lying on his back flinging his arm over his chest, trying to build the momentum to turn himself over. I would return from school each day and refresh myself by sitting in the living room and watching him. It was amazing how often he would try and be undaunted by what we would consider failure. He was at last rewarded by the strength and coordination to turn himself over. After repeating that deed several times, he was ready to master the next movement.

No one, I hope, would be so heartless as to set such a task for a baby, but from deep within the child is a knowledge of what must be accomplished and the wherewithal to do it. The role of the adult in all this is to set the example of being an upright human being who can walk, use language, and think. Without such examples, children falter in their own development, but with such examples and their own powerful urge to imitate, they move through an amazing amount of learning on their own. This holds true throughout the first 6 or 7 years while imitation is still a strong force in the child. Gordon's determination to master a new skill was echoed for me by another child, Ivana. When she was 4, she told me that she could tie her shoes. I probably looked doubtful, for often children of that age think they can tie but can only do the first step. Tying bows is a complex task that usually is not mastered until age 6 or 7. Sensing my doubts, she promptly sat down on the floor and displayed a perfect ability at tying her shoes. I was stunned and later asked her mother how this had developed. She laughed and said that all weekend Ivana pretended to be going to a birthday party. She took scraps of paper and bits of yarn and tied dozens of packages, working hard on the bows. By the end of the weekend, she had taught herself how to tie bows.

Beginnings of Creative Thinking

Ivana's experience is a picture of will at work. No one could demand such concentration and activity from a 4-year-old, but left to herself she will call forth the determination and will to master a difficult task. It is also a picture of the power of play. Once fantasy play begins for the preschooler, she will frequently embed her learning situations within the context of creative play. This capacity for fantasy play is a fascinating dimension of the child between ages 3 and 6, and it is important to note that fantasy is born around the same time as thinking begins in the child, between ages 2 and 3. Until then, children are essentially realists. They will take on a task like Gordon out of the sheer pleasure of doing it, or in play they will handle objects or bang on them but without a story context for their play. Once fantasy is born, make-believe situations begin to fill their play.

One can see the birth of fantasy when playing with young children in a sand area. If you hand a 2-year-old a dish of sand and say, "Here's a birthday cake for you," you must be very careful, for the child is very apt to eat it. He takes you quite literally. If you give the same birthday cake to a 3-year-old, she may look at you and say, "It's make-believe, right?" Fantasy is present, but the child is learning to move back and forth between earthly reality and make-believe realms. Give the cake to the 4-year-old, and there is no problem. She will typically accept it with joy, place sticks in it for candles, decorate it with leaves and flowers, and call her friends over for a birthday party. Fantasy is in full flow. It is a wonderful, magical capacity for turning one thing into another and for allowing one play situation after another to arise. I could write chapters just on the different fantasy play situations that the children in my kindergarten classes created over the years. Basic motifs repeated themselves but with infinite variations. The child's mind is incredibly fertile between ages 3 and 6, and it is just in these years that thinking begins. Anyone who thinks that thinking is a rational and linear process in the human being has not watched a child at play. Thinking and fantasy begin around the same time in children, and their complementary nature is one of the strongest indications I know that thinking in the human being is meant to be a powerful, creative force full of life. It is one of the added tragedies of our times that more and more children enter our kindergartens unable to play. They are pulled up into their heads, full of bits and pieces of knowledge but unable to come down into their limbs to feel life and actually play. Waldorf kindergarten teachers throughout North America are asking themselves how they can help children play again. The inability to play is one of the early signs that a child's thinking is becoming too dried out and that too many demands are being made on the nervous system.

The young child's play is such an important element in the development of human thinking that it deserves deep exploration. Only a few aspects of it can be mentioned here. Ashley Montagu, a well-known anthropologist, understood the connection between the fantasy play of the child and the creative thinking of the adult and speaks of it in his book *Growing Young* (1983):

> The imaginativeness of much of children's play, whether alone or with others, whether of the "let's pretend" variety or some other, is in the direct line of ascent to the scientist's "as if" fiction, "let's pretend." The scientist says to himself, "Let me treat this 'as if' it worked this way, and we'll see what happens." He may do this entirely in his head or try it mathematically on paper or physically in the laboratory. What he is doing is using his imagination in much the same way the child does. The truth is that the highest praise one can bestow on a scientist is not to say of him that he is a fact-grubber but that he is a man of imagination.
>
> And what is imagination really? It is play—playing with ideas. (pp. 156–157)

The connection between play and thinking is a powerful one and was illustrated for me by a child named Keenan. One day, he was building a car with a wooden board and log stumps turned on their sides for wheels. It is not difficult to make such a car, and my kindergarten children did it often, but on this day Keenan wanted to find a way to steer it. He had a basket of ropes and tried in every way he could think of to attach the ropes and get the car to turn corners. For 45 minutes, he worked intently on this, ignoring his friend Stephen, who repeatedly came and asked him to play with him in a different part of the room. It was easy to picture Keenan as a scientist in the laboratory. He was intent and concentrated and deeply immersed in 6-year-old experimentation in the form of play. After exhausting every possibility, Keenan gave a little shrug, dropped the ropes, and went off to play with Stephen. He was not visibly disappointed. He had experimented and learned it was not possible. Later, he could learn that he needed an axle, steering rod, and a few other things to steer such a car.

A sequel to this play situation occurred a month later. I had been churning some butter and was at the stage of paddling it to remove the thin, milky part. The butter was turning a golden yellow. Keenan was by my side, watching all of this intently. "Why," he asked, "is the butter yellow? When you put the cream in, it was white." "Yes," I said, "I've often noticed that the white cream turns yellow, but I don't know why." Keenan was clearly not content to leave the matter in this unresolved way. He stood by my side, deep in thought. One could almost feel the ideas going through his head. At last, he said, "I know why. You see the cream came from a cow, and the cow eats grass, which is green. Green is made up of blue and yellow, and that is where the yellow comes from." I found it a remarkable piece of thinking from a boy just turning 7, but I was even more amazed sometime later to learn that he had been correct in his thinking. Grass contains carotene, the same substance that makes carrots orange. In the summer, when cows eat grass, their butter turns a golden summery yellow. In the winter, when they eat hay, the butter stays white. Farm women traditionally added a bit of carrot coloring to the winter butter to give it a sunny look.

Consequences and Possibilities

The body of research about play and its importance in the development of thinking, as well as other faculties in children, is growing. Some of the best research I know was done by Sara Smilansky of Israel, who studied children's play in her country and in the United States. She differentiated different levels of play, from the simple manipulative play wherein objects are handled but no fantasy-filled stories are told to the highest level. This sociodramatic play occurs when children play together for an extended time (30 minutes or more) with simple props, playing out a fantasy situation. Having developed a measuring instrument for observing children and rating their capacity for such play, she and her coworkers found the following: Those children who scored highest on play, displaying a strong capacity for sociodramatic play, were also noted for making greater gains than other children in several areas. The chart of gains found by Smilansky is shown in the following box (Smilansky, 1990, p. 35):

Gains in Cognitive-Creative Activities

Better verbalization
Richer vocabulary
Higher language comprehension
Higher language level
Better problem-solving strategies
More curiosity
Better ability to take on the perspective of another
Higher intellectual competence
Performance of more conservation tasks
More innovation
More imaginativeness
Longer attention span
Greater concentration ability

Gains in Socioemotional Activities

More playing with peers
More group activity
Better peer cooperation
Reduced aggression
Better ability to take on the perspective of others
More empathy
Better control of impulsive actions
Better prediction of others' preferences and desires
Better emotional and social adjustment

Another study that should be cited here took place in Germany 20 years ago. German educators were being swept away with an enthusiasm for early academics like their American counterparts; however, several professors conceived of a study to compare children from 50 play-oriented kindergartens with those from 50 academic-oriented kindergartens. The children were followed through fourth grade, and the results were startling and conclusive. Children from play-oriented kindergartens excelled over the others in every area studied. They did better in terms of physical development, emotional and social development, and mental development. The results were so strong that German kindergartens returned to a play approach more or less en masse (*Der Spiegel*, 1981). In the United States, no comparable study was done, and for 20 years and more, children have been subjected to academic-oriented programs beginning at age 5 and younger. If play is valued at all, it is as a means of learning academics. Otherwise, it is considered a waste of time.

If the academic approach to preschool were successful, one would certainly see the results by now. Children should be learning more, with a higher degree of thinking and better test scores. I know of no indicators showing such gains but many indicators showing a decrease in children's well-being. Articles are frequently written about declining test scores, and Jane Healy, in her book *Endangered Minds* (n.d.), points out that some of the tests themselves have been rewritten to make them easier. Thus, if one compared today's results with earlier results, the decline would be even more noticeable.

The education of children is another of life's modern dilemmas that calls for deep moral insight, as well as rational consideration. We now know that it is possible to teach many young children to read, write, and master other cognitive tasks at a young age. We are faced with the moral question whether it is the right thing to do. Since 1945, humanity has again and again faced this type of question. When we developed the atomic bomb and realized what an incredibly destructive force it was, we passed a watershed. Prior to this discovery, we had the impression that we should pursue all avenues of scientific exploration and follow them to their logical limits. But we began to see how destructive such knowledge could be. In regard to the bomb, we could keep going, or we could hold back. This is the dilemma of the modern human being. In one field after another, our enthusiasm is ignited with new possibilities. We then see the destructive side and have to make the decision, sometimes quite painfully, to hold back and not proceed. To continue in the current direction in education by placing so much strain on the nervous system of the young child not only endangers the health of the child but also makes thinking a much more difficult task. When thinking is narrowed and separated from the life forces of creativity, something shrivels in the individual. The "I" cannot come fully to birth and find the means of unfolding itself. It is blocked and hampered, and a deep frustration is felt by the individual. The loss is enormous, both for the individual and for society.

As a closing image, I would like to share a story told to me by a mother of a little boy. When she was pregnant with him, she had a vivid dream. In the dream was a golden child, radiating light and bringing tremendous joy into the world. She watched the child growing older in the dream, and his strength and radiance grew greater. Then, at age 6, she saw him being placed into a box, and the golden light was cut off. She awoke deeply shaken and was determined to find a way to educate her child without placing him in a box or cutting off the essence of his creative being.

All children are like the child in her dream, and all need to be educated in such a way that the spirit within them can grow and infuse every aspect of self, including, and perhaps most especially, thinking. Human thinking is capable of blossoming into new dimensions of soul and spiritual life that bring new meaning to life and that enable one to become a creator in the deepest ways.

If throughout childhood, thinking, feeling, and willing are allowed to develop in a healthy manner and if the individuality can incarnate and take hold of this threefold nature, then in the adult years the individual can transform the basic capacities into greater capacities of soul and spirit. This is a path of inner development that is possible for the contemporary human being precisely because thinking is as developed today as it is. Modern human beings are capable of profound inner development, and without such growth they often feel as if they are living in a box. Rudolf Steiner describes a modern path of development in many of his books and lectures. He opens one of his basic books, *How to Know Higher Worlds* (1994), by saying, "There slumber in every human being faculties by means of which a knowledge of higher worlds can be attained" (p. 13). He names these higher faculties—imagination, inspiration, and intuition—and they arise as the adult "I" works on the basic capacities of thinking, feeling, and willing and transforms them in such ways that higher faculties are awakened. With the modern tendency to divert the development of thinking, feeling, and willing, this matured adult process becomes much more difficult, if not impossible. Then the deep decisions that each adult must make about life and individual destiny become extraordinarily difficult. The inner freedom of the human being is endangered, which has profound consequences for both the individual and society.

This is the struggle facing humanity today. The question stands before us whether the individual can blossom into the fullness of becoming human or whether through fear and misguided judgment we will opt for something much less. With each decision we make regarding the education of thinking, we pave a road that leads humanity in one direction or the other.

REFERENCES

Breggin, P. R. & Breggin, G. R. (n.d.). *The war against children*. New York: St. Martin's Press.

Crook, W. G., & Stevens, L. J. (1987). *Solving the puzzle of your hard-to-raise child.* Jackson, TN: Professional Books.

Der Spiegel (German news magazine). (1981, December 14).

Feingold, B. F. (1974). *Why your child is hyperactive*. New York: Random House.

Healy, J. (n.d.). *Endangered minds*. New York: Simon & Schuster.

Good Housekeeping. (1996). *222*(5), 66.

Houston Chronicle (2-star edition). (1996, May 19). p. 1.

Mental Health Weekly. (1996). *6*(10), 6.

Montagu, A. (1983). *Growing young*. New York: McGraw-Hill.

Newacheck, P. W., Budetti, P. P., & Halfon, N. (1986). Trends in activity-limiting chronic conditions among children. *American Journal of Public Health, 76*(2).

Smilansky, S. (1990). Sociodramatic play: Its relevance to behavior and achievement in school. In E. Klugman & S. Smilansky (Eds.), *Children's play and learning.* New York: Teachers College Press.

Steiner, R. (1994). *How to know higher worlds*. Hudson, NY: Anthroposophic Press.

Weizenbaum, J. (1976). *Computer power and human reason*. New York: W. H. Freeman.

Biography

Joan Almon graduated from the University of Michigan with a major in sociology in the mid-1960s. In 1971, she helped friends open an alternative kindergarten in Baltimore. Within a few months, she learned of Waldorf education, and as she brought each new idea and practice into the kindergarten, the children lit up with a deep inner flame. Their response convinced her that she needed to look more deeply into this education. It has been 25 years, and she is not yet at the end of that journey. The children and the education continually reveal new depths of life that bring renewal in their wake.

Almon has taken many courses in Waldorf education and other aspects of education, many at the master's level, but without receiving a formal graduate degree. Only in recent years could one obtain a master's degree in Waldorf education, but during these years, her life was been too full of teaching adults, working with children, writing articles, and traveling to kindergartens around the world for her to sit still for formal study.

Recent authored articles include "Educating for Thinking: The Waldorf Approach," *Revision, 15*(2), Fall 1992; "Waldorf Education and the Social Demands of the 1990s," *Holistic Education Review, 6*(4), Winter 1993; "The Child: Play and Development of the Young Child," *Renewal: A Journal for Waldorf Education, 2*(1); and "The Needs of the Children in the 1990s: Nurturing the Creative Spirit," *Holistic Education, 7*(4), Winter 1994. She has been editor of the *Waldorf Kindergarten Newsletter* in North America since 1983 and editor of several of its publications.

Since 1983, Almon has been Chair of Waldorf Kindergarten Association of North America; since 1985, a board member of the International Waldorf Kindergarten Association, based in Stuttgart, Germany; since 1989, a consultant and part-time teacher in Waldorf kindergartens and teacher training seminars in North America, Asia, South Africa, and Europe; and since 1993, a member of the council and leadership group of the Anthroposophical Society in America.

14 AUTHENTIC CURRICULUM

DAVID SOBEL

INTRODUCTION

There is a time in education when all plans and theories recede into the background. There is a time when the student encounters something that we intend to teach. The question is, What will happen at this horizon where student and world meet? Will the world reveal itself? Will the student find new patterns of coherence or new mysteries? Or will the world remain opaque—described by teachers and books in repeatable words and numbers powerless to reveal anything new? Does the student achieve insight or simply acquire information?

Ironically, the difference between the two is hard to see. Students in the elementary grades often respond to the explicit curriculum excitedly and acquire information and skills dutifully even if what they learn makes the world no more comprehensible or meaningful. Natural curiosity, playful exuberance, and encouraging teachers can go a long way before the ultimate disappointment of learning matures into cynicism. At the secondary and collegiate levels, competition frequently serves as motivation. Thoroughly acculturated into an information processing educational paradigm, students no longer look to their studies for insight or illumination. Frequently, students work hard and acquire all the academic content necessary even as it remains detached and unassimilated. They may learn to answer questions and logically process abstractions without the expectation that the results should necessarily make sense in the "real world."

In this chapter, David Sobel, speaking as a parent, teacher, and college educator, offers an alternative approach to education in which learning is both cognitive and affective. Sobel combines progressive tradition, Piagetian learning theory, and holistic educational perspective in what he calls the "authentic curriculum." This concept of the curriculum is centered on children's interests but is not indulgent of them. It begins with an appreciation of the wonder, awe, and fascination that are often part of childhood but often out of place at school. Sobel's aim is to build moments of such involvement into extended explorations of the world. He suggests that teachers be prepared to seize these moments where they may be developed into educationally substantive experiences. Such experiences would not provide information about something, but an experience of it—an encounter with something real and meaningful, rather than a mastery of an abstraction.

Sobel maintains that these moments of mystery and excitement are part of the magic of childhood, of the search to understand how the world is put together and where we fit in the puzzle. There is no separation of the cognitive and affective aspects of being. The task of the teacher is to work at the horizon where children engage the world so that a child is both informed and inwardly nourished by the encounter.

—*Jeffrey Kane*

Parents are always asking me where they should send their children to school. I have served on two local school boards, and I cofounded a small, independent early childhood center in the region. As a professor of education, I have been in most public and independent schools in Vermont, Massachusetts, and New Hampshire within an hour of Keene, New Hampshire, so I have a pretty good comparative sense of what's happening in schools. But when I get a call from a mother who is relocating from Indianapolis and wants to know which school district is best so that she can look for a rental in that town, I still have trouble making a recommendation.

If it was Bill Bennett on the phone, past secretary of education and proponent of a national curriculum model based on the concept of academic excellence, I wouldn't have any problem. New Hampshire prides itself on the success of its public school students. Despite minimal funding from the state, New Hampshire students have some of the highest SAT scores in the country, and the high school graduation rate is respectable as well. Many public schools in my district are friendly, efficient, and successful at producing children who are good readers, know their math facts, and are good at Trivial Pursuits. Although many New Hampshire schools are moving toward a more holistic and developmental pedagogy, many are still based on the concept of learning as information gathering. These schools treat children like empty vessels and fill them to overflowing with state capitals, grammar rules, and the beginning and ending dates of numerous wars. Although many parents are less clear than Mr. Bennett, they know that they want more than the gas station ("Fill her up!") model of education. They want imagination, musical competence, a sense of purpose, and environmental literacy. They want their children to develop social responsibility and to take charge of their own learning. They want their children to think like artists and entrepreneurs, not like computers.

For parents with this mind-set, I suggest a guiding maxim: "Make your school decision on the basis of least damage, rather than on the assumption of greatest benefit." A focus on greatest benefit seduces parents into thinking quantitatively; they look for schools with high test scores, more minutes of homework, a greater variety of extracurricular offerings, and more emphasis on skills. A focus on least damage encourages parents to assess schools more qualitatively and from a preservation of childhood perspective. What's the culture and climate of the school like? Are children encouraged to think and feel, rather than just to memorize? Do children and teachers seem happy? Do children have the time and space to be children? Are there displays of children's artwork, productions of children's music and drama? I encourage parents to look for a school that feels like a studio or a workshop, rather than like an office or a library. And I advocate for the controversial, nonacademic position that it's more important for children to be happy than smart in elementary school.

Of course, what we all want is for our children to be happy and smart, full of life and full of facts, and some schools manage to achieve this balance. But John Burroughs wisely cautioned, *"Knowledge without love will not stick. But if love comes first, knowledge is sure to follow."* If schools emphasize the acquisition of information without the context of a love of learning, knowledge will not stick. So what's a parent to do? To help parents with their decision making, I often describe the process that my wife and I have gone through in deciding where our children should go to school. My approach in this chapter is to elucidate my thinking about "the something more" that many parents want for their children in school and then to portray an approach to learning, the practice of "authentic curriculum," that maximizes the likelihood of the integration of love and knowledge.

CHOOSING SCHOOLS

Three years ago, when we had to make the school decision for our children, we had three prominent choices. We could send them to the nearby public school in the rural town where we live; to one of two Waldorf schools, both within a half hour of our home; or to the Greenfield Center School, an independent progressive school about an hour south of our home. All of these are fine schools, and I feel proud that graduates from my program teach in each of them. But the conceptions of thinking and learning that inspire the teachers and that shape instructional decisions are quite different in each case. Articulating these conceptions to ourselves helped my wife and me make our decision.

The local public school in our town is the pride of many parents, and as an elected school board member I have been dedicated to helping it flourish. The facility is spacious and well cared for, the student to teacher ratio is 15:1, our per-pupil expenditure is the highest in the county, and the teachers are dedicated. In the past few years, we have eliminated the art and music teachers who came once a week and have implemented an integrated art and music program that melds with the classroom curriculum. We have multiage family groupings so that children stay with the same teacher for up to 3 years, a conflict mediation and resolution program, computers in every classroom, and school drama productions that involve everyone in the school. Despite all these desirable aspects, an underlying tone makes me hesitate. When push comes to shove, the emphasis is sometimes too much on reading and mathematics skills and covering the curriculum. The California Achievement Tests and the new state assessments in all of the core subject areas shape the curriculum. Grades loom large as motivators, and my daughter's best friend who lives next door gets $5 for each A on her report card.

To understand the tyranny of curriculum that causes me concern, consider this vignette: I was surprised a few years ago to learn that the first- through third-grade class was studying the solar system. I have always been puzzled about the curricular commitment to studying the solar system. Who decided it was so important? Studying the solar system is almost always the same and always too abstract. Barely anything you can do is tangible and hands-on with the solar system; very few teachers actually do night sessions so that children could at least look at the planets and the moon. So, instead, everyone makes scale models of all the planets, and very few children actually gain any understanding. I can tolerate the study of the solar system in the upper elementary grades because it jibes with a developmental interest in exploration and outer space, but its presence in the early grades seems frivolous to me. When I asked the teacher why she was doing it, she said, "It's in the district science curriculum; I have to teach it."

Regardless of my concerns, the first-grade daughter of family friends loved the unit and, after the unit, could breezily recite the order of the planets from the sun out to Pluto. On her way to a winter vacation with her parents, however, Monica wanted to know, "Mommy, which planet is Mexico on?" This is an illustrative example of what Howard Gardner might call knowing without understanding. The ability to recite the names of the planets doesn't mean that Monica had a grasp of planetary geography or that she had developed any sense of scale or even wonder. Curriculum that emphasizes learning names and that sacrifices understanding leads to knowledge that does not stick. We're creating a nation of Teflon minds with here today, gone tomorrow memories. The emphasis on content without understanding at this school made us somewhat hesitant about sending our children here.

Waldorf schools are based on the philosophy of Rudolf Steiner, a German scientist and visionary whose work has spawned new approaches to medicine, agriculture, the arts, and education. Although much of the philosophy is rather esoteric, many salient features of the classroom practice are very appealing. Waldorf classrooms are filled with poetry, song, movement, and the arts. Didactic instruction in writing and math are downplayed in the early elementary grades, with much more emphasis put on reading and math emerging out of stories and drawing and painting. In optimal situations, the class teacher stays with her class from first through eighth grade and therefore develops a deep sense of each person and the personal themes and circumstances at work for each child. The class teacher is mainly responsible for the main lesson, and then the children also have teachers for woodworking, handicrafts, games, music, and other special subjects.

Festivals play a significant role in the structure of the school year and serve to create a close community of parents, teachers, and students that has a tangible presence in children's lives. The Michealmas Festival at the autumnal equinox includes children's games, a humorous theater production by the teachers, and a stone soup feast. At Halloween, parents and teachers create a magical mystery candlelit tour around a woodland pond. The ambiance is charmingly spooky, rather than the normal frightening and grotesque haunted houses that are now so common. At the winter solstice, an Advent celebration elegantly re-creates the movement from the deep darkness of December to the rebirth of light in March. The emphasis in these celebrations and in the classroom is to preserve the "magical thinking" of childhood, to let fantasy and imagination thrive as the foundation for academic learning. It is the teachers' first priority to create consciously a holding environment that is secure and aesthetic.

Because it felt like this school had the right emphasis on love as a foundation for knowledge, we decided to place our children in this school. And although it has been a mostly satisfying experience, we still have some concerns. The children spontaneously break into song frequently, and we have been thrilled by our children's skill in knitting, painting, and recitation. But we have been a taken aback on occasion by their comments that school is boring; my third-grade daughter often feels unchallenged by the curriculum. And during a study of the creation story from the Old Testament, my daughter commented at dinner one night, "I don't agree with what my teacher is saying. First, there's not just one God, there are many gods, and they are both men and women. And second, it's not just God that's alive, everything is alive and has a little bit of God inside it." When I asked whether they got to talk about different ideas about God in the classroom, she said. "No, our teacher just tells the story and we have to tell it back." So, although I appreciate all that the school is trying to do, I am often frustrated by the nonconstructivist orientation of the teachers. Their mind-set is that too much thinking and logic and debate is not healthy for young children and that this kind of cognitive enterprise should wait. Even though I agree in principle, I have much more of an incrementalist inclination and want to support speculative thinking when it genuinely emerges in the classroom.

The local public school seems to put too much emphasis on information processing and skill development without sufficient context. The results can be an alienation from learning and too much stress on children. At the Waldorf school, the emphasis on imagination and affective comfort can get overdone and become a bit boring and lacking in cognitive challenge. Thoreau talked about seeing sand castles in the air and building foundations underneath them. To me, it feels like the public school helps children build foundations without seeing castles and the Waldorf school helps children see castles but I wonder whether foundations are being built. Are both possible?

The Greenfield Center School is an independent progressive school in Greenfield, Massachusetts. Drawing inspiration from developmentalists such as Arnold Gesell and Jean Piaget, and educational philosophers like John Dewey, Maria Montessori, and Friedrich Froebel, the teachers have created a school that both honors the unique capacities of childhood and puts appropriate emphasis on cognitive growth. If it weren't so far away, this would be the first choice for my children.

The classrooms at the school always feel like well-kept art studios to me. It's evident, from the work that is aesthetically displayed around the room, that children are in the midst of serious scientific, artistic, and literary construction. The language curriculum emphasizes children's writing, and the mathematics curriculum is based on using concrete materials to solve real problems. The social studies curriculum builds on the understanding of the expanding horizons of childhood and requires children progressively to build models of the school, the neighborhood, the town, and then the region throughout the elementary grades. There's a serious commitment to ethical standards in the renowned "social curriculum" that the school espouses and a comprehensive commitment to child-centered environmental education. In this atmosphere of infectious energy, children appear to be both happy and studious.

In a recent book, Bob Strachota (1996), a second-grade teacher at the school, describes his approach:

> A seven year old once said to me, *"I like the way you teach soccer. You're always in the middle, but not in the way."* He had captured what I try to do in all my teaching. I want to inspire the children I teach to be passionate about untangling the mysteries of numbers and spiders and history, and also to care deeply about sorting through the problems of how to be fair and kind. I know, however, that the children are the only ones who can create their understanding of how the world works and of how to do the right thing. So while I put myself in the middle of their efforts, I also try not to be in the way.

Two things feel important about this statement of core values. First, I like Strachota's concerns with the children being passionate about knowledge and caring deeply about being kind and fair. He seems to have a sense of balance about love and knowledge. Second, I like his notion of being in the middle but not in the way. He recognizes that the teacher must be a guiding force but that the children have to do the work. He wants children to take charge of their own learning within a context of ethical principles. One of the most important tools in Strachota's (1996) technique is his use of real questions:

> I've come to define a real question as one which engages the teacher and the learner in exploring the mysteries of the universe, rather than one which engages the learner in exploring the mysteries of what the teacher wants her to say or know or do. If my class is rowdy at a transition, I can ask the children how they should move in the room; or I can explore with them how we could wait peacefully and use energy at the same time. The latter question engages the mind and passion of the class and the teacher. It helps us both to wonder about the space between what we know and what we don't know; it helps the children take charge and invent. Using real questions as the core of my teaching I am continually fascinated by the dilemmas of life and am able to offer them to my students as intriguing and meaty problems.

Strachota seems to have his finger on the pulse of what makes for inspired teaching and learning. The "something more" that we're looking for in schools emerges when teachers engage children in real fascinations and real problems. Computers, and children who are programmed as if they were computers, are good at answering questions. But they're not good at asking questions. And it's the ability to ask questions and pursue answers with verve that we want to cultivate in schools.

Real Questions

At dinner the other night, my 9-year-old asked a real question: "Where exactly is heaven? Do planes fly through it?" she puzzled, and then with hardly a breath, continued, "And, is there just one heaven, or is there a heaven for each planet?" I suspect that these questions don't usually come up in the conventional study of the solar system. If they did, they would probably get tossed aside as inappropriate and irrelevant. Teachers aren't supposed to talk about things like heaven, and pursuing children's ideas about a question like this would take time away from learning the names of the moons of Jupiter. But perhaps this would be a great way to get children interested in discussing the layers of the atmosphere and figuring out whether heaven is in the troposphere or the stratosphere or whether it's a place that we can't see but we know exists, like the land of dreams.

For the 4 months of my sabbatical a few years ago, my children attended a well-respected bilingual school in Costa Rica. The children were stressed out by the placement test, the first test that either of them had ever taken, and they were initially taken aback by the serious emphasis on skills at the school. Their days were filled with learning math facts, grammar, and handwriting. And they didn't have many conversations about the location of heaven. But my daughter learned about a year's worth of math in a month, her reading improved in leaps and bounds, and she loved the school. My son's numbers and letters became legible for the first time. They both enjoyed gaining the facts and skills that hadn't been emphasized in their prior learning. And although my wife and I were thrilled with their substantial learning, we wouldn't want them in a school like that all the time.

What many of us want is a school where the curriculum respects both the inner and the outer lives of children. This approach can be found in both public and independent schools, but it is constantly under assault by advocates of curricular consistency and standardization. If we learn to recognize what we want, then we can be effective advocates for a well-balanced approach to schooling.

AUTHENTIC CURRICULUM

All the current rumblings about a national curriculum in the United States make me nervous. Nervous because I have watched the national curriculum developments in England over the past 5 years and have listened to teachers describe the things that have been lost as a result. Nervous because the actuality of a national curriculum threatens to contradict many of the good developments that are emerging in the name of site-based management and teacher ownership of the curriculum here in the United States. I am also concerned because we already appear to have a de facto national curriculum. An examination of curricular scope and sequence charts from the major elementary reading and mathematics textbook series or the curriculum guides from one school district to another shows a wide congruence about national expectations of skill development at different ages. There's as much difference between Addison-Wesley, Scott Foresman, and Macmillan as there is between Coca-Cola, Pepsi Cola, and Royal Crown Cola. They're all bubbly, sweet, and not very nourishing.

The situation in England is particularly disheartening because, to my mind, many British teachers and small primary schools have carried the banner of what I want to call *authentic curriculum* for the past 30 years. **Authentic curriculum** refers to the curriculum that springs forth from the genuine, unmediated individual and developmental fascinations of children and teachers. In a talk to a group of British teachers in 1969, David Hawkins described one source of authentic curriculum:

> Everyone knows that the best times in teaching have always been the consequences of some little accident that happened to direct attention in some new way, to revitalize an old interest which has died out or to create a brand new interest that you hadn't had any notion about how to introduce. Suddenly there it is. The bird flies in the window and that's the miracle you needed. (Hawkins, 1973)

British teachers have been masters at dealing with the "bird in the window." Responsive to the shell that Fiona brings in after holidays or to the news story that connects with yesterday's classroom event or to just the right book that fits with Roger and Ben's construction in the block area, British teachers have created and shaped curriculum out of the unique chemistry of the individuals and events in their classrooms. As the national curriculum implementation has proceeded in England, it's been discouraging to hear teachers comment that these special, idiosyncratic projects and pursuits are gradually being elbowed aside or not allowed to grow and flourish because of the pressure to cover all the mandated material. "There's just no time nowadays," they complain. This righteous and compelling demand for curricular comprehensiveness and consistency extirpates local color and character in classrooms. It's like the homogenization of the American commercial landscape by fast-food restaurants or the decimation of traditional cultural practices with the arrival of television and a market economy.

I have always heard that you can walk into any second-grade classroom in France and the children will be working on the same pages in the workbook whether you're in Paris or Lyon or Marseilles. This seems like the fulfillment of the national curriculum dream. To me, it's a nightmare. Rather, I have always said that a diagnostic feature of a good classroom is that you can walk in and see something happening that you've never seen before. The intersection of 20 children's concerns and interests, the teacher's passion, the cultural milieu, and the prescribed curriculum in all its permutations and combinations should generate some new species of curricular flowers. Maybe not every day, but at least once every few months. If this isn't happening, the magic and mystery of learning, of knowledge unfolding, isn't present. Its preservation is as important as the protection of rain forests in Costa Rica and dwarf wedge mussels in southern New Hampshire.

From the Inside Out

Is authentic curriculum a new idea? Do we really need a new term to describe something that's been around for a long time? Certainly, many competing terms exist that seem to describe the same approaches. There's *integrated curriculum*, *developmentally appropriate curriculum*, *thematic* or *project-centered curriculum*, as well as *informal education* and that old bugaboo *open education*. Authentic curriculum certainly overlaps with all of these but is not synonymous with any of them.

The term *authentic curriculum* has emerged out of our work in the Education Department at Antioch New England Graduate School. In preparing my comments in summer 1989 for our annual first community meeting with new students in the Integrated Day Program, I realized I wanted to talk, in specific terms, about what the faculty believed in. I wanted to go beyond the grand, eloquent ringing phrases about honoring individual development and social responsibility or about the symbiotic *I-*

Thou-It relationship among the child, the teacher, and the curriculum. I wanted to model the phenomenological honoring of particularity in describing actual nitty-gritty examples of good curricular practice in classrooms. The examples in my head all had an insistent, self-affirming quality about them—like the seemingly fragile plant that pushes its way up through the asphalt. The movement quality originated down deep and then came up and out.

My wife, an expressive arts therapist, was at that time involved in the practice of a new hybrid form of choreography and therapy. She described it as movement from the inside out, where the individual meditates or quiets herself and allows movement to emerge. As opposed to head-down movement, thinking about the movement, and then instructing the body to perform, the idea was to eliminate the mind as source and let the body stir within and the movement to follow. After a movement session, the mind then became active, looking at the movement patterns and images and reflecting on their significance. This methodology is described as **authentic movement**, and I realized it conveyed the same dynamic principles that I wanted to convey about curriculum.

As I had prepared my comments the night before the meeting, I was not able to share, or reality-check, my thinking with my colleagues. Instead, after I introduced the term and shared my examples, I asked my colleagues whether they had similar illustrative examples. Without hesitation, everyone shared poignant portraits of similar kinds of classroom work, some of which I share below. Since coined, the phrase has started to stand on its on. It has carved a niche in our semantic universe, and we are constantly on the lookout for living and breathing examples of authentic curriculum. This sense of *rightness* or *fittedness* that we feel supports our conviction that we are describing a distinct species of classroom practice. Certainly, it's been seen before, but because it looks like other similar species and occurs infrequently, it's never been taxonomically differentiated. Before it falls before the chainsaws of curriculum reform, I want to try to qualify and describe it.

The term *authentic* in this application predates both the notion of *authentic assessment* and the use of *authentic learning* as a theme for the April 1993 issue of *Educational Leadership*. All three usages bear much in common, but I think it's important to distinguish between the quality of authenticity as implied by the advocates of authentic assessment and the quality of authenticity in curriculum as we have described it in the Education Department at Antioch New England.

What's taught in schools is often different from what's assessed. Hence, the objective of authentic assessment is to bridge this discrepancy by bringing the assessment in line with the true goals of the curriculum, or to bring internal consistency or coherence to the curriculum/assessment cycle. But the goals of the curriculum and the assessment are generally determined by administration and teachers and reside mostly in the objective external world, apart from the inner lives of children.

Authentic curriculum, on the other hand, refers more to the process of movement from the inside out, taking curriculum impulses from inside the child and bringing them out into the light of day, in the classroom. It implies a necessary connection between the subjective, inner lives of children and the objective, external

world of schooling. Froebel, the 19th-century creator of the kindergarten, suggested an analogous kind of pedagogical dynamic when he said, "For the purpose of teaching and instruction is to bring ever more out of man rather than to put more and more into him" (1885/1970).

A Living, Breathing Example

Time to get specific. The following narrative is adapted from a journal entry written more than 20 years ago when I was teaching a group of first graders at the Harrisville School in Harrisville, New Hampshire. It is useful here as a springboard for a discussion of the salient attributes of authentic curriculum.

Let the Floodwaters Go **28 April 1973**

The ever-present spring drizzle had stopped just a few minutes before, so I decided to let the children go outside for recess. Granted they were going to get their feet wet, but it had been raining for too many days to keep them inside again. The air was beginning to freshen, the new leaves glistened and the nerve-wracking black flies were still holed up enough to make it a beautiful, though gray, morning. Brian and Chip gravitated to the waterworks area and began to create two dams, one above the other. This area is created where a small drain pipe empties out from underground onto a muddy hillside, and a child-sized rivulet courses down the hill, begging to be shaped. Regularly, two or three boys would play in this area, but soon a dozen different boys had converged and a massive project began to take form.

The cooperation was admirable. Somehow, all the boys seemed to parcel themselves out into specific roles. Some tended the upper dam, some the lower one. There were channelizers, and two boys in charge of controlling the flow of water from the pipe. Then there were the mud and clay collectors preparing the materials for the dam tenders. It suggested many images of beavers and bees. The fascinating aspect was that no one was in charge. There were many conflicting ideas, lots of arguments about whether to heighten this dam, deepen this pool, when to let the water out of the pipe, but they were all worked out without a hitch. Everyone was caught up in the building, the mud and the clay, the flow of the water, the necessity to keep the dam strong. Frequently someone would warn, *"Ten minutes till the flood!"*

I let things go way past the end of recess, not wanting to intercede, but then finally told them that they'd have to bring things to an end. The consensus was to break down the dams. *"Let the floodwaters go! Let the floodwaters go!"* they chanted spontaneously. The dams were burst one after the other and the water poured down the hillside to everyone's great delight. I reminded everyone to wash, remove their muddy shoes and come to the rug for discussion. Chip, who had been a clay preparer, wanted to save some of the clay, so we set it aside to see what would happen to it.

My initial plan for discussion was to draw a large, collective map of the whole project. I thought we would talk about trapping the water, how the water got from one place to another, other ways of making the system bigger, adding more channels, more dams, etc. I was interested to see how much they could move from their kinesthetic involvement in the mud and water to a two-dimensional representation. Then after creating the map, I planned to send them back to change the dam system the next day.

I started by asking some questions about the source of the water, calling only on those with raised hands in order to organize their enthusiasm. When I asked about how they made the water run faster, Peter explained, *"By holding it back by damming it."* This led us into talking about dam construction. It seemed the significant problem with the dams was that if you didn't keep repairing them, *"the water would seep through little holes in the bottom of the dam, holes you can't see, and then the holes get bigger and more water comes through,"* Brian summarized. He explained with a lot of gestures, one hand showing the dam and wiggling fingers on the other hand showing the trickling water.

About this point, I abandoned the map idea and started asking about the differences between clay and mud as building materials, a difference they had introduced. Chip said, *"Clay is better. It's stickier and it holds together more."* At this point I pulled out Chip's clay and Mary, my assistant, went to get some potting soil. I thought we'd see about the differences between clay and dirt. I made a ball of clay and a ball of mud and asked the children what would happen if I put my finger in them both. Most agreed I would make a hole in both. When I stuck my finger in the clay one, it stayed together while the dirt one fell apart. But at their urging, I made the dirt one wetter and after two more trials the dirt/mud ball stayed together too. *"Is clay just wet dirt?"* I queried. I then made another ball of each and put them in water and we watched the dirt one disintegrate while the clay one held together. *"Are clay and dirt different other than just being wetter or drier than each other?"* We set aside a ball of clay and a ball of mud to see what happened, and since we'd been at this for close to a half hour, we broke for lunch.

During the next 2 weeks, we went off in a variety of directions. Some of the boys returned to the waterworks area and continued to build new structures, modify their dam-building techniques, and add more technology. One of the morning options became doing experiments with clay and mud to see which was stronger. I showed one group how to make miniature bricks; they modified the procedure, made a lot of them, and then started building miniature houses with the bricks. Later on, this branched off into building structures with stones and concrete. From the brick building activities we got into a series of discussions about the best way to build tall walls with building blocks. We built one wall with the blocks on top of each other and another wall with the blocks overlapping each other. We then devised a way to standardize a sideways glancing blow to see which wall was stronger. The lessons from these discussions got applied to both their constructions with the unit blocks and in the bridge they built from the large blocks that spanned the hallway and connected two rooms together.

Another group became involved in modeling with the clay that we collected from the clay deposits outside. One morning, discussion focused on the differences between the potter's clay that we had in the school and the natural clay we found outside. Michael's parents, both professional potters, came and did some handbuilding activities with these children.

That one vibrant damming experience and the discussion that followed resonated throughout the curriculum for the rest of the school year.

Defining the Ecology

Understand that, in my 4 years of working with children at the Harrisville School, no more than a dozen of these truly captivating involvements turned into potent curriculum. The rest of the time, we all went about the business of good education, holding to the daily rhythms, doing reading, writing, math, and theme work while we prepared and tried to lay the groundwork for the outbreak of authentic curriculum. Hawkins (1973) says,

> We all know that we can't succeed at it all the time or sometimes not even very often but we all also know that when it does happen it's worth a great deal because in fact far more is learned under those conditions than under conditions of routine presentation of subject matter.

What are some of the sources, the spawning grounds, of authentic curriculum? Many are embedded in the dam-building account. I will first try to isolate them and then describe them in greater depth with diverse examples.

Play

Children's play is often the fertile soil in which authentic curriculum takes root. If there are no times and places for children to play, and this applies throughout the elementary years, it will be very difficult for curricular impulses to emerge. Anticipating that the children were going to get very wet and muddy, it would have been reasonable for me to forbid their waterplay and attenuate the whole activity. Or sensing the possibilities, I could have interceded early on and directed it toward my own ends. By staying out of it, a wave of energy emerged that sustained the children's involvement.

Individual Fascination

Although the waterworks example doesn't illustrate this in a striking fashion, individual fascination is often a crucial starting point. Authentic curriculum often emerges out of just one child's deep, persistent interest and fascination with something. It's like the dog that won't let go of the bone. In this case, Chip was one of the instigators. He could always be counted on to immerse himself in messy, shapable projects, but his role in this capacity was fleeting on this occasion. Sometimes, one child labors on by himself for a long time before things start to snowball.

Group Chemistry

The group that got involved in the waterworks project was in no way a happy, cooperative group. Squabbles and fights were regular occurrences. They often wanted nothing to do with each other. But the spontaneous colleagueship and cooperation that emerged during this activity was a striking example of the kind of rapture that characterizes curriculum at its best. It's similar to the spell that good storytellers are able to cast over an audience. Each child involved is buoyed up by each other child's involvement. My recognition that they were all riding this same wave of momentum was the reason I relaxed the recess boundaries and let it flow as long as seemed possible.

Serendipity

Although sensitive teachers are able to set the stage for authentic curriculum, it often emerges out of the blue. Water issued forth from the drainpipe only when there was lots of groundwater. Our appearance on the playground soon after it had been raining for many days meant an unusually good flow of water that day. Had we skipped going out that day, the whole sequence of events might never have happened. The whimsical nature of when the curriculum muse will appear makes it hard to stick always to lesson plans.

Teacher Capitalization

It would have been easy for me either to ignore the whole activity when we went back inside or to persist with my mapping idea. The first alternative would have squandered the rich curricular potential; the second would have very possibly squashed the children's interest. In providing the opportunity for them to share their excitement and discuss their discoveries, I nudged their investment up to the next quantum level. Hawkins (1973) says,

> This is again something very different from the stereotype of the permissive classroom because what's involved all along is a teacher who is making *educational capital* out of the interests and choices of children and out of the accidents that happen along the way, as well as out of his own cleverly designed scheme for getting something new into focus.

The Collective Unconscious

When I was 7 years old, my favorite activity was stream damming. Children around the world share this fascination of making small worlds, shaping the forces of nature in miniature, or as Edith Cobb (1959) says, "making a world to find a place to discover a self." The making of small worlds is one of the deep themes of childhood, the kind of thing that good teachers know you can make "educational capital" out of on a regular basis. The strange fascination with dinosaurs in first grade and horses for fourth-grade girls are other examples of oddly persistent and widespread, deep themes. Although it's valuable to speculate about the psychological rationale for these themes at different ages, it's more important just to recognize that they exist and try to use them in planning the curriculum.

Certainly, these features overlap, and it is likely that they contradict each other, but when enough of them are present, the possibility of authentic curriculum making an appearance is heightened.

Taxonomic Differentiation

Let me place authentic curriculum within the context of other approaches to curriculum. First, I don't want my advocacy of authentic curriculum to be confused with support for a laissez-faire, free school approach that lets the children do what they want to do. Although a certain openness and responsiveness to children are necessary to prepare the conditions, a prominent role is played by the teacher in shaping what happens. It's like the martial arts principle of taking your opponent's force and using it to accomplish your ends.

Maya Apelman, in her article "On Reading John Dewey Today" (1975), summarizes nicely my own general convictions about the role of the teacher vis-à-vis the curriculum:

> Dewey said that advocates of what had come to be known as the "child-centered curriculum" tended to abdicate their responsibility as adults whose wider knowledge and experience should facilitate the child's entry into the world of people and things, of the present and the past. Today the same tendency exists among some teachers. Many of the young "anti-establishment" people who go into elementary school teaching refuse to assume the responsibility and authority which must be a part of any mature person's functioning. "There is no point in . . . being more mature, " Dewey wrote, "if instead of using his greater insight to help organize the conditions of the experience of the immature, he throws away his insight."

In contrast, teachers held captive by mandated curricular programs enforced by rigid testing schedules certainly won't be inclined to abandon the district guidelines to do clay modeling when the children are supposed to have 30 sight words by Christmas. Joel Greenberg (1977) captures this ethos nicely in critiquing school districts' love affair with packaged curriculum and planning initiatives:

> The package reduces the teacher to the role of disseminator of specialized, research materials and to the role of transmitter of programmed, planned ways of using these materials. While they may originally have been born of the observed needs of children, they are disseminated wholesale. . . . Even what is called "individualized instruction" is commonly doled out this way, the concept having been diluted to "type of individual" or, more simply, to rate of instruction with identical material.

What we are seeking, in terms of informed curricular practice, is the artistry of balancing the need for curriculum structure and objectives and an openness about how to achieve the objectives. In addition, the objectives need to be stated in such a way so that they don't imply an inflexible time structure, creating the need to cover all the material, so that when fortuitous serendipity strikes, it can be attended to and not ignored. Hawkins (1973) clarifies that Dewey was a strong advocate of this perspective:

> Dewey, for example, is very strong in asserting that the Experimental School, which he ran for a time, had a definite curriculum and there was no freedom to depart from this curriculum. This was imposed: it was a pattern which could be argued about, it wasn't sacrosanct, but at any given time there was a curriculum and everybody understood what it was. Within this, the teachers were enormously free to pursue these general subject-matter situations in any way they wanted to and it was quite clear also, to many of them at least, that an important group involved in making those decisions was the children themselves.
>
> If you read some of the accounts of what some teachers and some children in that school did, you can see that they were having a great good time making their way through some aspect of the curriculum but diverging all over the place. They were diverging into other areas which were also on the curriculum and nobody regarded it as a waste of time, therefore, if in the process of studying some primitive society they got heavily involved in the craft of pottery, because that was also part of the curriculum.

Thus, authentic curriculum is most likely to crop up in a classroom where the teacher manages that delicate balance between what Whitehead (1913/1967) called "the rhythmic claims of freedom and discipline." Much good practice exists in today's schools that illustrates this artistry, but let me try to define how authentic curriculum is either a subspecies or perhaps an emergent species distinct from other popular progressive approaches to curriculum.

Developmentally Appropriate Curriculum

Much of the valuable curriculum innovation of the past 20 years has come about through an application of Piaget's work and a recognition of the organic learning processes in childhood. Originated in England as the language experience approach to reading, *whole language* and *the writing process* have revolutionized and humanized reading and writing instruction in many American schools. The Nuffield Mathematics Project, which came out of British primary education, was translated and made more accessible in the *Math Their Way* and *Math: A Way of Thinking* books and approaches. The British MacDonald 5/13 Science curriculum series is still one of just a few science curriculum projects to tie program objectives to Piagetian stages, rather than to specify content objectives by grade level as is done in the vast majority of American science curricula.

Although I am a devout supporter of all these curriculum initiatives, it seems important to note that the major emphasis has been on children's cognitive development in each of these innovations. With subtle accuracy, each of these curriculum approaches has articulated stages of cognitive development and keyed instructional approaches to the unfolding process of logical thinking. What's missing, however, is a sense of affective development, a recognition of the developmental themes that dominate in children's inner lives. Erik Erikson, Robert Kegan, Howard Gardner, Joseph Chilton Pearce, and Rudolf Steiner are a few of the developmental theorists who have charted the inner lives of children, but very little of this understanding makes an impact on curriculum planning.

Many teachers intuitively migrate toward topics of native interest to children, but few can articulate the deep, developmental rationale for why children are intrigued. There is little sense of the connection, for instance, among children's natural interest in geographic exploration, of exploring the boundaries of their immediate world around ages 9 and 10, and the appropriateness of studying the Explorers in fifth grade. The Waldorf schools' curriculum, based on the writings of Rudolf Steiner, is one of the few models of curricular topics chosen because of the fittedness with the development of the inner life of the child.

Authentic curriculum is distinct from developmentally appropriate curriculum in tapping into the affective and emotional lives of children. I certainly am not advocating for one to the exclusion of the other; rather, I am suggesting a potential basis for curriculum planning other than just cognitive stages of development. Sylvia Ashton-Warner's (1963) "key word" approach is a good example of an instructional approach based on emotional, rather than cognitive, realities. Her use of individualized sight words for beginning reading, different for each child, chosen on the basis of which words were most laden with strong feeling for the individual, is a good example of authentic curriculum.

Integrated and/or Thematic Curriculum

Whitehead's mandate that we "eradicate the fatal disconnection of subjects which kills the vitality of our modern curriculum" (1913/1967) has been taken to heart by those educators who advocate integrating the language, math, science, and social studies curriculum areas through themes and projects. Dorothy Paul, describing the myriad examples of environmental education work done in her British classroom, says:

> By the middle of the autumn term in 1969, most of the children were working on environmental materials they had brought into the room. They often described their work in prose or poetry, thus bringing together many of the traditional disciplines such as reading, history, geography and, of course, writing. Many of the things that were going on in the classroom tended to erode boundaries between disciplines. Nothing eroded them faster than the stream table. (Paull & Paull, 1972)

Integrated curriculum strives to contextualize learning, to encourage children to see the connections between home life and school learning, to provide situations in which mathematics needs to be done to solve a real problem. But in the name of integrated curriculum, the same exclusion of the children can happen. Teachers dutifully plan integrated themes that require writing and math problems and appropriate science experiments all related to preparing food for the harvest supper, but in their haste to do everything, serendipity is prohibited.

In their book *Yesterday I Found* (1972), Dorothy and John Paull describe two curriculum projects with 9- to 11-year-olds: one on bones, the other on mold. Dorothy explains that the bones project began when, without any forethought, she brought some X-ray plates into the classroom and they were discovered by some students. What emerged was a project, at first anchored by one child's interest, that involved a variety of drawing, reading, skeleton reconstruction, owl pellet dissection, and art projects that persisted on and off for many months.

In contrast, Dorothy and John did extensive preparation in the form of background reading, materials preparation, and trial experiments before introducing the mold project (as in molds and fungi) into the classroom. Soon after the project began, the children's interest waned and the whole thing was abandoned. John Paull theorizes about why the project didn't work:

> It seems that I made the error of taking the fun of full investigation out of the hands of the children and the teacher. I designed the containers, I read all the exciting books. For me this was a rich learning experience that developed when the Elementary Science Study booklet aroused my curiosity. I made the mistake of assuming that the children and teacher would react as I did. The episode showed me clearly the difficulties of "packaging" an idea away from the context of the classroom it will be worked out in.
> (Paull & Paull, 1972)

As well-intended as some curriculum planning is, integrated or not, the proof of the pudding is in the individual interests and the group chemistry of each individual class. One year, the unit on bones might captivate a group of fourth-grade children for 6 weeks; the next year, with a different group of fourth graders, it might be ho-hum and things will be done by the end of the 2nd week.

The clue to authentic curriculum is recognizing the innumerable variables at work in determining whether something will catch fire or not. To allocate and allot specific time blocks for all the units of study during the course of an academic year ahead of time is asking for trouble. There must be space for the spontaneous fruiting of some unplanned-for project and for the abandonment of a well-planned unit that has worked in the past. This is not, however, an argument for not planning. Louis Pasteur said, "Spontaneity favors the prepared mind." The better prepared you are, the more likely it is that the bird will show up in the window at just the right moment.

It is also important to place the notion of authentic curriculum within the current context of holistic education. **Holistic education**, as distinct from progressive education or open education, recognizes the spiritual interests and pursuits of the child as a valid component of the child's education. The spiritual life of the child can be supported by providing time and space for meditation in schools, recognizing the equal strengths of verbal and logical left hemispheric thinking, as well as spatial and intuitive right hemispheric thinking, entertaining the notion that there may be higher beings, one God or many gods, that affect or shape our lives. These considerations suggest that we need to structure time and procedures in schools for engaging in artistic practices, for emptying the mind of linear thought, for guided imagery, for communion with nature. In turn, these practices support authentic curriculum in that they invite inspiration, encourage the muse to make an appearance, and allow for the genuine interests of an individual or group to rise to the surface. The result is a curriculum project rooted in the unique qualities of the group, historical moment, and place.

Back to the Classroom

Let us move back into the landscape to explore some tangible examples of authentic curriculum at different grade levels and emerging from different sources.

The Loch Ness Monster Project

The Loch Ness Monster Project emerged out of the cultivated interest and fascination of one child. Kelly, a third grader in Jane Miller's vertically grouped first- through third-grade classroom at the Harrisville School, was constantly intrigued with the Loch Ness monster. She brought in newspaper articles, she got books out of the library, and she talked about it at morning meeting. Miller supported the interest, encouraging her to pull together whatever information she could find into a report. Working at the school at the time was an artist-in-residence doing a variety of projects with children. Miller hitched him up with Kelly, and the result was a simple animated film describing the various hypotheses about the size and origins of the Loch Ness monster.

Kelly then thought that maybe she'd like to make a model of the serpent, not just a model out of Plasticine, but a life-size model. Because the consensus of all the scientific estimates was that the monster was 50 ft long, this presented a bit of a problem. But Miller forged ahead. The school maintenance workers had just finished painting the school and had a few spare days. Miller enlisted their help in making a wooden frame that they covered with chicken wire, but they decided to compromise on size and make it a half-scale model—only 25 ft long. Now everyone got involved. All the children in the class helped cover it with a skin of polyethylene plastic; make the eyes, nose, and mouth; paint scales on the sides; and generally make it into a fearsome-looking monster.

Speculating on what should happen next, Miller and the artist-in-residence decided that they should surreptitiously slip it into the local mill pond, under cover of darkness, and send press releases to the local papers, indicating that because Nessie was so tired of being harried by scientists in Loch Ness, she had decided to relocate to Harrisville, New Hampshire. The children helped to work out the details of the story.

A local reporter and photographer showed up the next day to take pictures, interview Kelly, and write the story. The Associated Press wire service picked up the story, and the whole curriculum project was described on front pages around the country. Within a few days, copies of the article from the *Jacksonville Herald,* the *Phoenix Sun Times,* the *Tacoma Daily News,* and a myriad other places arrived at the school, sent unsolicited by tickled readers. They all said approximately the same thing: "It's great to read this kind of good news in the paper. Keep up the good work. We thought you'd like to know your story made it all the way here."

Miller capitalized on the opportunity. She posted a large map of the United States in the classroom, identified the location of all the places from which the class had received letters, and they were off on a United States geography unit. Some of the children sent thank you notes, others decided to research other scientific mysteries, and Kelly was a little overwhelmed by all the attention.

This no doubt is one of those once-in-a-blue-moon examples. Like the little acorn that grows into the stately oak, it's important to recognize that, for every acorn that makes it, another 999 never germinate but rot, are eaten by squirrels, or grow to saplings before they're shaded out by other trees. But the experience of just one of these kinds of curriculum projects during a school year can have an indelible effect on the attitude toward learning of a whole class. Note how significantly the teacher's initiative and willingness to support the individual's fascination provided the impetus for each significant jump in scale and commitment along the way. Also note that the presence of the artist-in-residence and the availability and willingness of the maintenance staff at just the right moments made this possible. Finally, recognize the collective unconscious fascination with monsters and mysteries, the creatures in the deeps, the shadow or dark side. Many children pursue understanding creatures like Nessie as a way of dealing with, taking hold of, their unnamable fears, their fear of the dark, their fear of the dark side of themselves. The curriculum can provide vehicles for children to give shape to their fears and gain cognitive skills in the process.

Becoming Birds

For 2 years in the mid 1970s, I worked with Follow Thru teachers in the Brattleboro, Vermont, public schools during their School Outdoors week. First through third graders came to the summer camp setting at Camp Waubenong to participate in environmental education activities. As a staff, we were committed to not lapsing into conventionalized naming and preaching activities, so we brainstormed how to overcome these barriers.

On the one hand, I have always been resistant to bird curricula with children. Part of this stems from my own childhood sense that watching and naming birds was dumb. Somehow, it never appealed to me until I was in my early 20s. I dislike ardent bird watchers and environmentalists who try to foist their newfound enthusiasms on unsuspecting 6- and 7-year-olds. On the other hand, birds are fascinating and beautiful creatures, and some children are entranced by them. We initiated our curriculum planning by agreeing that we were not going to start our work with birds with the children by getting them to identify birds by seeing glimpses of them and then looking them up in books. Rather, we speculated, what is it about birds that appeals to children? It was immediately apparent that the sources of intrigue were (a) they fly and (b) they make nests. Using the developmental principle that children like to become things, rather than to objectify them in early childhood, we came up with our plan.

We gathered a bunch of large refrigerator boxes, cut them into sheets, and had the children lie down on top of them with their arms outstretched. We traced around the children, but instead of following the bottom part of the arm and the upper torso, we drew a straight line from their wrists to their waists and then down on both sides to about the knees. The children then stood up, cut out the shape, and voila!—an individualized set of wings. We strapped them on to each child, made it clear that they were not to try these out by jumping off roofs, and they were off. A leader and a flock of six to eight birds leaped into action, flying through the forest, exploring life as birds. We made it to the meadow where hay had been cut recently and said, "If we're birds, we need nests." And so we made child-sized nests.

The next day, we said, "We've been thinking. You make great birds, but we noticed that you're all brown, and the birds we see around here, well, some of them are brown, but some of them have lots of colors. What are some of the color patterns on birds?" Children described some birds they had seen, we didn't emphasize names, and then we pulled out the paints so that they could paint their wings. More bird games followed. About the next day, children started to notice the birds around the camp. "Hey, that's the same bird as me, that's the color pattern on my wings." Then the bird books came out. Soon we had children poring over bird books, trying to identify what kinds of birds they were and to learn what they ate. Because we had started at their level of developmental fascination, had engaged their empathy through participating in bird consciousness, they were now ready to objectify and enter the more cognitive realm.

In my course Cognitive Development and Learning Theory at Antioch New England, I encourage graduate students to do research with children. My objective is to try to help prospective teachers get inside the child's world to see how they think and feel and to understand their distinctive developmental ways of organizing the world. One recent project emerged out of a student's childhood memory of thinking she could fly and wanting to try it out when she was a child. She wondered: Do all children go through a stage when they think they can fly? Is there a specific age when children are intrigued with this idea? Although she only interviewed 25 children, her findings were intriguing.

Children start to wonder about flying around age 4. By age 5, they start to wish they could fly, and they start to jump off hummocks and branches to see if anything happens. Many are convinced that if they flap their arms furiously, they stay in the air just a bit longer than if they don't flap. By 6 or 7, children want to try it out more seriously. This is when children make wings, climb up on the roof, cast fate to the wind, and sometimes break a leg. By 7 or 8, they realize they probably can't fly (except in their dreams), and the interest appears to fade, except for those who go on to be hang-gliders and pilots. The lesson here is that the birds curriculum that we generated tapped into this fairly age-specific fascination with flying. By starting with our perception of children's affective or thematic concerns, we found an avenue of access that brought them into the subject matter. This kind of planning can increase the likelihood of authentic curriculum.

Smuggling Gold

Literature-based reading programs often engage students in personal reflection, discussion, integrated reading, and writing, but teachers rarely take the next steps to extend the themes of a book through dramatic simulation. The following account is drawn from an unpublished paper by Dan Maravell (1991), who completed his graduate internship in teaching in Paula Denton's fifth-grade classroom at the Greenfield Center School in Greenfield, Massachusetts. It illustrates the potential value of addressing the deep themes of secrecy, intrigue, and adventure that emerge strongly in 10-, 11-, and 12-year-old children.

In looking for books to help students make sense of their potential role in the Persian Gulf War in 1991, Denton and Maravell chose two books about the Nazi invasion of Europe during World War II. Maravell's group chose to read *Snow Treasure* (McSwigan, 1984), a true story about how the Norwegians smuggled their national treasury of gold bullion out of the country and into the United States for safekeeping. Moved from the capital, the gold was hidden in a snow cave near the coast in preparation for it to be moved through the town and down a steep road to a fishing boat hidden at the end of a fjord. The stickiest part of the plan proved to be getting the gold out of the woods and down to the edge of the fjord because the Germans occupied the base of the fjord and guarded the length of the road. The solution was to have school children smuggle the gold on their sleds, making runs right through the ranks of the Nazi guards. Over the course of 6 weeks, 38 children managed to complete this incredibly risky task.

In consulting with Maravell about how to take this study into children's lives, I suggested that we consider the 10-year-olds' fascination with intrigue and personal challenge. How could we translate the challenge into the classroom? Could he somehow set up an activity that would engage the students in the emotional tension and personal riskiness of the story? Following my lead, Maravell got his reading group together and formed a secret Defense Club, just as the children in the story had done.

> My six students and I met out on the landing in the middle of the attic stairs for our next reading period and talked about what we could smuggle, and how it could work. We decided to do bricks and that we had to hide them in the classroom without anyone else knowing, not even Paula, the teacher.
>
> One student said that we needed to make a pact to secrecy, to never tell, even if caught and tortured, and we were about to swear to it, hands joined in the center, when another student ran into the room and came back with a wooden sword. We all had to "swear on the old Norse sword," grasping it all together exactly as the children had done in the book. (Maravell, 1991)

Maravell brought the bricks, all wrapped in silver foil, to school in his truck. From there, it was completely up to the students to move the "gold." Maravell appointed one student to be in charge of the Defense Club, just as Uncle Victor, the fisherman, had done in the story. For their first hop, the students decided to move the gold from the truck into the downstairs kitchen.

> We were checking out various cabinets and around the frig when a Nazi spy, one of the office staff, came into our midst. She wanted to hang out, say hello, be friendly. The kids were squirming. A couple of foil wrapped bricks had been set down in plain view on the counter. "What have you got there," she queried? "Oh, we're planning a party and we made some zucchini bread. It turned out pretty good." Four of the students were in the corner, bricks still up their jackets, and they had to move nonchalantly out of the way so the staff person could get into the frig. Finally she departed. (Maravell, 1991)

From here, the children worked in pairs or alone to get the bricks into a seldom-used fabric drawer in the back of the classroom. Numerous problems had to be solved. When the smugglers stayed inside at recess, they were frustrated to find other students who also wanted to stay inside. Some students moved the bricks from the kitchen to way stations closer to the classroom to take advantage of windows of opportunity when the classroom was empty for a few moments. When one student wanted to hide a brick in the chair, instead of in the fabric drawer, Maravell refused to settle the conflict and made the students resolve it themselves. At the end of the study of the book, which also included a short play and the creation of a newspaper, the students unveiled their accomplishment, much to the amazement of their colleagues and the classroom teacher. Although there had been many close calls, they had pulled it off without a hitch.

The smuggling activity served as the bridge between the Norwegian children and the students in Maravell's classroom. Bonded together by a shared adventure, the students could empathize with the anxiety, fear, ambivalence, and pride that the Norwegian children experienced. The emotional connectedness carried the students into full involvement with the historical facts and problematic issues of war. And it helped the students understand how children in Kuwait and Iraq must have been feeling at that same moment as war raged around them. By finding the connection between the book and fifth graders' personal fascinations, Maravell opened an avenue into living history and literature. This search for the particularities of connectedness among teacher, student, and curriculum makes for genuine authentic curriculum.

And So Forth

It has been hard to choose the most illustrative examples of authentic curriculum. There is the sixth-grade teacher in Shutesbury, Massachusetts, who starts the school year by taking his students caving. This initiates a semester-long study of underground geography whereby the students study spelunking, draw three-dimensional cave maps, collect rocks, and learn geology. By Christmastime, a jewelry-making station is set up in the classroom. Students tumble rough semiprecious stones until they're polished and then mount them to make earrings, necklaces, and bracelets that are sold at the Christmas fair. In simulation of age-old rites of passage, the teacher has taken his students through an initiation by taking them down into the earth to find the rough forms of their new selves. These rough selves are polished symbolically into gems, transformed into something of value. The curriculum integrates academic and archtypical themes in an artful fashion.

Or the third-grade teacher in Keene, New Hampshire, who not only read *Paddle to the Sea* to her class but also had each child make a handmade boat, just like the boat made by the young boy in the story, with instructions to the finder carved indelibly into each boat. The third graders then walked to the Old Stone Arch bridge over the Ashuelot River and ceremoniously launched their boats into the ocean-bound current. The craftsmanship of each boat was testimony to the fact the boat building connected each child to the story and to the geography that the boat was about the explore. The boat was an embodiment of the developmental fascination, ascendant at 8 and 9 years of age, with pushing back the boundaries of the known world. These children wanted to know what was beyond their neighborhood, how streams and rivers connected, and where the path led; this curriculum was one small way of addressing those questions. Authentic curriculum assembles the world as it unfolds the self.

CHAOS THEORY IN THE CLASSROOM

Some of the current initiatives in the national curriculum arena actually preserve the possibility of authentic curriculum flourishing in classrooms. The National Council of Teachers of Mathematics has produced a set of standards and curriculum guidelines that sets out the content, skills, and pedagogy that it advocates for mathematics instruction in schools. These guidelines, however, "do not contain the content specificity that is common in the national curricula of other countries . . . and they leave states, districts, schools and teachers enormous room for unique local interpretations" (Smith, O'Day, & Cohen, 1990). Knowing that they have a specific destination, teachers are empowered to take curriculum into their own hands and get to the destination by whichever route they choose. Thus, it is possible to take side trips and respond to the serendipitous bird in the window when it shows up.

But most national curriculum initiatives are not so broad minded. They tend toward content and method specificity and will enforce their rigid prescriptions with national testing schemes. The mind-set is mechanistic, simplistic, and based on an information processing paradigm. If we can control input and demand adherence to standards, then we can guarantee improved output. But classrooms are not like factories, and children are not like workers, and the predictive science models of Newtonian physics may no longer be the appropriate metaphoric source for thinking about education.

I have been searching the literature of *chaos theory* for new metaphors, new ways of thinking about curriculum dynamics in the classroom. Rather than assume that classrooms behave like clockwork, let us consider that they work like weather systems, one system that chaos scientists have been working to understand. Weather systems have classically eluded long-range predictability because they are multivariable systems with a "sensitive dependence on initial conditions" (Gleick, 1987). With so many interacting variables, slight changes at some distant point can make a major impact in how weather systems will evolve. That is why an ironclad forecast for beautiful weekend weather on Thursday can turn into intermittent showers by Saturday morning.

Classrooms have the same kinds of dynamics. When you factor in 20 different personalities, unexpected fights in the hallway, canceled band practices, the unexpected birth of baby gerbils, and eight students absent because of the flu, it's hard to guarantee that your weekly curriculum plans written on Sunday evening will bear much resemblance to the classroom state of affairs on Thursday. It is feasible to stay on track, but sometimes only at the expense of numerous missed possibilities. Certainly, teachers need a clear vision of what's appropriate and useful and make choices about the potential productivity of any tangent. But everyone acknowledges that curriculum becomes intriguing, alive, and compelling when something out of the blue captures the imagination of a group of children. Chaos theory suggests that we should recognize the inherent unpredictability of the behavior of such a complex system as a school classroom.

Authentic Schools

In an article entitled "What Should Schools Teach?" Vito Perrone (1988) explores this question of mandating uniformity of content in schools. Professing serious concerns about specifying which facts children should know at the end of which grade, Perrone describes a school in Revere, Massachusetts, where the principal of an all-White school discovered that 100 Cambodian children would be moving to the town during the next school year. When the children arrived in school, they were met with outstretched hands of welcome and friendship.

> The principal and teachers made a decision that it was critical for everyone in the school—children, teachers, custodians, secretaries, lunch workers—to know who these Cambodian children were, where they came from, and why they were coming to Revere. Getting ready for the Cambodian children became the curriculum for the next four months—the reading, social studies, language arts, science, and arts program. It was real, and, as a result it was vital. Those in the school community learned how to speak to the Cambodian children and also gained considerable knowledge about their cultural patterns as well as their suffering. As part of their preparation, those in the school learned about prejudice and the harm that prejudice brings to persons who are different.

Responding to the bird in the window, this school diverged from the habitual curricular mind-set and responded to the unique particularities of its own culture and community.

Submitting to the mind-set that children's brains are like computers just waiting to be programmed will turn our attention away from the local contexts that give meaning to learning. Curriculum as software means that the same program can be downloaded into children's minds at the same time anywhere in the country. But what's relevant to third graders' lives in Montpelier, Vermont, in January will in some ways be different from what's significant for third graders in Tempe, Arizona. The pending change in moose hunting laws in southwestern New Hampshire during 1995 created the opportunity for a rich and complex study and final town meeting simulation in the South Meadow Middle School that year. No prepackaged curriculum existed that was relevant; it had to emerge out of the particularities of the moment. And the immediacy of the problem gave meaning to the learning.

The mind-set of learning as information processing neglects the role that "meaningfulness" plays in significant learning. Necessity is the mother of invention; inflexible programming is the mother of boredom. Honoring the specific ecology of the life of an individual student, classroom, or school can be the basis for the outbreak of authentic curriculum. As with all endangered species, we need to learn to identify the habitats in which authentic curriculum thrives and protect them from the bulldozers of homogenization. Think of it as our contribution to biodiversity.

References

Apelman, M. (1975). On reading John Dewey today. *Outlook: The Journal of the Mountain View Center, 17,* 18-28.

Ashton-Warner, S. (1963). *Teacher*. New York: Simon & Schuster.

Cobb, E. (1959). The ecology of imagination in childhood. *Daedalus, 88*(3), 537-548.

Froebel, F. (1970). *The education of man* (W. N. Hailman, Trans.). New York: Augustus M. Kelley. (Original work published 1885)

Gleick, J. (1987). *Chaos: Making a new science.* New York: Viking Press.

Greenberg, J. (1977). Engineered education. *Outlook, The Journal of the Mountain View Center, 23,* 10-21.

Hawkins, D. (1973). How to plan for spontaneity. In C. Silberman (Ed.), *The open classroom reader.* New York: Random House.

Maravell, D. (1991). *Notes on a problem-solving activity in a literature study.* Unpublished paper, Antioch New England Graduate School, Keene, NH.

McSwigan, M. (1984). *Snow treasure.* New York: Scholastic.

Paull, D., & Paull, J. (1972). *Yesterday I found.* Boulder, CO: Mountain View Center for Environmental Education.

Perrone, V. (1988). What should schools teach? Issues of process and content. *Insights Into Open Education, 21*(4), 2-9.

Smith, M. S., O'Day, J., & Cohen, D. K. (1990). National curriculum: American style. *American Educator, 14*(4), 10-17.

Strachota, B. (1996). *On their side: Helping children take charge of their learning.* Greenfield, MA: Northeast Foundation for Children.

Whitehead, A. N. (1967). *The aims of education*. New York: Free Press. (Original work published 1913)

Biography

David Sobel, M.Ed., is Director of Teacher Certification Programs in the Education Department at Antioch New England Graduate School. Prior to 1997, he served as Chair of the department for 12 years. He was one of the founders of the Harrisville Children's Center, has served on the boards of public and private schools, and is currently a member of the editorial board of *Holistic Education Review.* His published books include *Children's Special Places, Beyond Ecophobia: Reclaiming the Heart in Nature Education;* and *Mapmaking With Children: Sense of Place Education for the Elementary Years.* His articles examine the relationship among child development, authentic curriculum, and environmental education. He was the recipient of a 1991 Education Press Award.

Sobel's exploration and documentation of the natural interests of children are the foundation for much of his work. He has served as a consultant with school districts, nature centers, and the National Park Service to assist educators with curriculum development and program planning from a learner-centered perspective. He is particularly interested in fostering developmentally appropriate science, social studies, and environmental education.

15 EVOLUTION, TECHNOLOGY, AND ROMANCE

KIERAN EGAN

INTRODUCTION

The Swiss developmentalist Jean Piaget theorized that human beings proceed through a variety of fixed cognitive stages, each with its own particular assumptions about the world and intellectual processes. The Soviet psychologist Lev Vygotsky maintained that cognitive development was shaped by sociocultural influences. In this context, the "modes of understanding" that an individual uses to make sense of the world are very much dependent on the particular cognitive tools made available.

In this chapter, Kieran Egan explains that each linguistic skill we acquire, aside from extending our mastery of language, creates a new dimension of mind, an extension of ourselves. Thus, as cultures and individuals acquire new linguistic skills, a corresponding development takes place in the way we collectively and individually think.

Building on the epistemological insights of philosopher/scientist Michael Polanyi, Egan explains that we incorporate new cognitive tools into our frame of reference so that they give us new capacities (e.g., the ability to code and decode written symbols) to see new and varied dimensions of the world. In short, newly acquired cognitive skills create new stages of development with unique characteristics and modes of thought.

In this chapter, Egan focuses on the development of the romantic mode of understanding attendant to the development of written literacy skills. Such cognitive development is clearly evident in early Greek literature and upper elementary school children. In both cases, written literacy opens the possibility of exploring what is "actually going on in the world" without bowing to the mystery of the gods or boxing the possibility of mystery in a rationalist framework. With written language, the possibility opens to create accurate records and accounts that nonetheless reflect a highly personal frame of reference. In the romantic mode of understanding, objects and events are interpreted within narratives driven by emotion, where the limits of possibility are always under stress. The romantic mode of understanding employs a framework of personal metaphor, rather than rational processes, to make sense of the world.

The key here is to see the romantic mode, not as a belief system or set of concepts, but as an active orientation of mind. It is an effective orientation where everything is experienced in terms of personal meanings. A romantic mode of understanding is so woven through with emotions that they shape meaning. Egan's thesis is that the emergence of written literacy does not merely create a new capacity for transmitting, receiving, storing, and processing information, but rather creates an affective/cognitive basis for understanding. It allows one, literally, to feel one's way through ideas. In reflecting on this capacity to see with our hearts and heads, we may find clues to restoring a needed balance in our own cognition.

—*Jeffrey Kane*

During the mid-Pleistocene era, dramatic evolutionary changes in the brain, larynx, pharynx, and jaw of our ancestors supported language development, which in turn supported unique forms of cultural life and the uniqueness of human childhood in the animal world. As a result of these evolutionary changes, human children today are born with a peculiar sensitivity to language—attending to the distinctive rhythms of their mother-tongue even in the womb and demonstrating, within days of birth, preferential attention to it over other languages (cf. Pinker, 1994). Within the first few years of life, children learn language with remarkable ease and speed; of the indeterminate range of human languages, they become expert users of one or two. Similarly, we are genetically predisposed to learn very quickly the norms and conventional beliefs of one particular society among the indeterminate range of possible societies and to become in some significant degree affectively committed to one set of norms and beliefs. Because language supported new and complex kinds of societies, humans who could retain some general learning capacity throughout life, providing flexibility in learning additional skills and adapting to changing conditions, enjoyed an evolutionary advantage. So today, after the very rapid learning of language and social norms closes down around 6 or 7 years, we retain, even if with diminishing effectiveness as we age, a general capacity that permits further, though more laborious, learning.

Early learning of language and of beliefs about the natural and social worlds is robust and lays down a network of presuppositions that are thereafter rarely changed. Whatever we pick up thereafter by using our general learning capacity is relatively laboriously gained and fragile (e.g., see Gardner, 1991, for a discussion of the resulting problems for education). The complexity of the mental operations required for language use, along with the relative flexibility of our general learning capacity, has enabled humans to adapt their environments for symbolic communication in a variety of ways. Among the recent and most influential symbolic technologies is writing.

It is clear that humans do not simply devise and use even the simplest tool for a limited particular purpose and leave it at that—as many animals do. One peculiar feature of brains evolved such that they manage language is that they, as it were, expand into the tools they use, incorporating them in a curious way, creating a tacit mental dimension that includes the tool as part of our sensorium (Polanyi, 1967). So, to use one of Polanyi's examples, when poking in the dark at some rocks, we do not construct in our minds what we actually feel, which is the impression the stick makes against our hand, but we rather expand into the stick and "feel" its tip poking around at the rocks. We expand mentally into our tools so that they are not simply used for the purpose for which we invented them, but become a part of our minds and allow us to enlarge the purposes we can form with their addition to our potential. One of the most fruitful tools in this regard has been literacy. Invented to keep simple records, it has transformed our lives. I want first to consider some effects of our incorporation of this tool into our minds, or of our minds expanding into this tool.

Some rather energetic discussions about literacy and its social and psychological effects have taken place during the past quarter century. Although I do not entirely ignore these, I want to look at a level of literacy's influence that has not, as far as I am aware, been much considered. I try to show that one result of our incorporating the technology of literacy is a somewhat distinctive kind of understanding that seems best called *romance.*

What kind of category is a "kind of understanding"? It comes from extending Lev Vygotsky's idea about how our understanding of the world is mediated by the intellectual tools we use in interacting with it. Vygotsky himself was most interested in how the development of oral language structured our understanding (Vygotsky, 1962, 1978). I want to explore a general level of the effects of literacy's mediation of our experience and of the kind of romantic understanding that ensues.

Psychological, epistemological, and sociological studies of education have not led to a category like romance, and yet I try to show that precisely such categories allow us to address fruitfully educational issues that are important and much neglected. The scientific ambitions of educational psychology and sociology, and the analytic ambitions of educational philosophy, have left them somewhat vulnerable to the reductionist arguments of those who advocate an information processing approach to educational issues. I suggest that romantic understanding, and the other kinds of understanding that I have elaborated elsewhere—the somatic, mythic, philosophic, and ironic (Egan, 1997), are more appropriate categories for dealing with education and are irreducible to information processing models.

I suppose there are more densely laid intellectual minefields than those I try to negotiate here. The "literacy hypothesis" (Olson, 1994; Olson & Torrance, 1991) is fraught with experimental, interpretative, and ideological problems. The study of romance, and its relation romanticism, has been an intellectual battlefield for much longer. The analytic categories appropriate for adequately capturing the complex phenomena of education have been fought over through the 20th century with no clear resolution. Even so, I try to show, first, how Vygotsky leads us in the direction of the category of "kind of understanding"; second, how literacy is responsible for generating a kind of understanding that is sensibly called romantic; third, why romantic understanding is a fruitful category for addressing important educational issues; and finally, with all that precariously in place, why this educational category of romance is irreducible to any form of information processing.

Making Sense of How We Make Sense

Vygotsky (1929) was critical of Piaget's theory about how we develop distinctive and increasingly adequate ways of making sense of the world. Piaget represented the process as an interaction between the individual and the environment such that, given adequate interactions, individuals develop through the regular sequence of stages that his theory described. The fundamental problem with this account, according to Vygotsky, is its focus on an internal developmental process at the expense of a recognition of the shaping power of the sociocultural context within which the individual develops. It is as though Piaget conceived of the psyche as like the body; a wide array of different foods would suffice to fuel the body through its regular developmental stages, and similarly a wide array of different "figurative" learnings can fuel the mind through its regular "operative" developmental stages. Vygotsky argued that this analogy is inappropriate because the mind, unlike the body, takes on, in significant degree, the shape of what it "eats." In Vygotsky's view, the kind of sense we make of the world is in significant part because of the particular intellectual tools we learn to use by growing up in a particular sociocultural milieu.

What changes, then, are brought about in our minds if we replace oral mediational intellectual tools with those of literacy? Or, rather, it would be better to say "add" literacy's tools to those of orality. This question has yielded much discussion and controversy but not a conclusive answer (e.g., see Havelock, 1963, 1982, 1986; Olson & Torrance, 1991; Ong, 1971, 1977, 1982; Street, 1984). I want to approach it at a rather different level and in a rather different way from what has been common. I want to consider some intellectual tools that come along with literacy and try to show that they form a set whose most prominent features are "romantic," as that disputed term is generally used in literary criticism. The set of intellectual tools together form, or mediate, a distinctive kind of understanding, which I am consequently calling romantic. My argument, then, is that whenever these intellectual tools are learned along with literacy, this distinctive romantic kind of understanding will come into play; it will mediate the way the world is understood. If this is true, we should find this romantic understanding wherever and whenever literacy's intellectual tools are used. Other kinds of understanding come into play when further intellectual tools are learned—tools like abstract, theoretic linguistic forms or ironic reflexiveness. So, my focus is on the period after literacy has become fluent, and before abstract theoretical forms become prominent.

But in what sense does literacy *cause* romantic understanding? I have tried to explain this at length elsewhere (Egan, 1997) and should note here, first, that literacy doesn't *necessarily* cause it. Many people learn literacy in a fashion that stimulates romantic understanding hardly at all. Rather, literacy might be better seen as its necessary condition or major stimulant or, to use again the phrase used above, romantic understanding is what commonly comes along with literacy. The conditions that ensure that literacy develops into a rich romantic understanding include stimulation of the set of intellectual characteristics that I describe below. But the causal relationship between them seems tied in with the kind of consciousness that literacy can generate. Written descriptions of events or written claims about the nature of the world encourage a kind of reflection and testing that is less easy in oral societies. The written description can always be returned to; there is no fear of its being lost or forgotten or changed by the attrition of time. It can provide a basis for testing or further descriptions that claim greater representational accuracy. It invents a sense of external, distanced, testable, describable reality about which one can hope to discover more. The text that seeks accuracy in describing the world is far more easily and comprehensively analyzed than the spoken word. The transition from oral to literate mingles one form of consciousness (personal, direct) with another (indirect, analytic) and the peculiar stance with regard to reality that is generated forms what I call romantic understanding.

This is a somewhat unconventional inquiry, I recognize, and setting it up raises a range of preliminary questions, responding to which might fill the rest of the chapter. Very briefly, by **literacy**, I mean Western alphabetic literacy tied in with the kinds of intellectual activities for which it has been most used. The "different level" of "intellectual tools" of literacy not commonly discussed include things like the sense of wonder, the attraction to the extremes of experience and the limits of reality, the forming of associations with heroic or transcendent qualities, and others I touch on below. The empirical data I draw on will not be from typical psychological studies, but from cultural history.

The procedure I follow is to try to show that literacy—in the sense indicated too briefly above—causes romantic understanding regardless of when or where an individual learns it. I take two widely divergent cases in which literacy has become fluent and significant in structuring thinking but before it has become elaborated toward a "philosophic" language of theoretical abstractions. The two cases, then, are of modern students between roughly ages 8 and 15 and of the early writers of prose inquiries in ancient Greece. I try to show quite precise parallels in the kind of understanding deployed by both. This unlikely pairing will help characterize romantic understanding and indicate why it should be considered a useful educational category. Then we can see why it resists information processing ambitions.

ANCIENT GREEK ROMANCE

The early period of Greek writing is marked by the work of the *logographoi* (Fornara, 1983; Pearson, 1939). Their work is distinguished by its use of prose, rather than the poetry of their predecessors, such as Homer and Hesiod, by its rational attempts to discover and disclose the truth about reality, and by its refusal to consider gods as any part of providing a rational account of events. Many of these early prose works involved gathering traditional stories about the past, travelers' tales of foreign places, and various assorted lore about the world—to all of which they applied the new rational criteria that came along with prose inquiries. Inquiries (*historia*) were also occasionally quite specialized, such as the Hippocratic writers' focus on medicine, the Miletan proto-physicists' inquiries into nature (the *physis* of things), and the attempt to describe and account for a particular historical event, such as the recently past Persian Wars. I focus on this last because it is one of the few complete works from this group of writers that has come down to us. It is not a simple history, in the sense of that word today, but is rather a more varied inquiry into the customs, folktales, biographies, natural environments, and climates of all the groups who became embroiled in the great war between the Persian Empire and the Greek states.

I take Herodotus's *The Histories* (trans. 1954) as a case study to show how early literacy, before the development of systematic theoretic thinking, has some specific effects on how the world is understood. These effects are not unique to Herodotus, of course. Indeed, they persist today and are prominent in all Western sociocultural milieu. They are prominent during other historical periods when communities expand into alphabetic literacy, and also when students today similarly absorb into their minds, or expand their minds into, the intellectual tools of literacy.

The Histories recount the origins and events of the Persian Wars (*Persian* in Greek is derived from *destroyer*). But it is unlike a modern academic history in sev-

eral ways. Most obviously, it represents the Greeks, and particularly Athens, as the small, courageous, and civilized underdog and the vast and arrogant Persian Empire as contemptuously assuming victory. The first books are made up of Herodotus's inquiries into the various lands that had been incorporated into the Persian Empire or from whom the Persians could exact tribute in money or troops to support its vast army and navy. The overall plot of the work follows the fortunes of the arrogant Persian troops coming into conflict with the smaller but clever and courageous Greeks until the latter beat off the supposedly invincible imperial troops and they were scattered in disarray. The plot does not simply give us a detailed account of events; it is organized so that our sympathies are with the doomed Greeks, whose virtues, including the democratic spirit of Athens in particular, bring them a victory in whose relief and joy the readers, or hearers, share. (It would not be surprising if, as was later claimed, Herodotus was paid by the state to give public readings from *The Histories* in Athens.) The overall plot, that is, follows the typical pattern of a romantic story, and the narrative is shaped with great artistry to have the appropriate ego-supporting and ego-stroking effects on its audience.

If we look in detail at the early books, which describe the geography, customs, and climate of the Lydians, Persians, Babylonians, Messagetae, Egyptians, Sythians, Libyans, and others, we find that, in addition to those results of his inquiries, the accounts are also crammed with anecdotes, scandals, dramatic events, gossip, and seemingly every bizarre and exotic snippet he picked up. So, for example, we learn that the people of Pedasus received warnings of disasters by the priestess of Athene growing a long beard; or that Mycerinus, on receiving an oracle that he was only to live a further 6 years, had innumerable lamps made, turning night into day, and "never ceased from the pursuit of pleasure" and so extended his 6 years to the equivalent of 12; or that one cannot travel through the region to the north of Scythia because the earth and the air are clogged with falling feathers; and so on and on. He does tell us at the beginning that his purpose is "to preserve the memory of the past by putting on record the astonishing achievements both of our own and of the Asiatic peoples" (Herodotus, trans. 1954, p. 13).

Herodotus certainly keeps his promise to record whatever astonishing achievements he has discovered. In the process, he delivers to us a romantic historical story embedded in a kind of *Guinness Book of Ancient Records*. He spends much of the early books detailing the weirdnesses of the Egyptians and the wonders of their culture. He is like a tourist, taking in most eagerly what is most strange and striking. This "preoccupation with otherness, with what is different, remote, mysterious, inaccessible, exotic, even bizarre" as Ong notes (1971, p. 255), has been a prominent feature of any romantic perspective. (I note, delightedly, that both Herodotus and *The Guinness Book of Records* include the fact that King Psammetichus of Egypt was engaged in a siege around Azotus in Syria for 29 years. Both include the fact for no other reason than because "it was the longest of any in history" [Herodotus, trans. 1954, p. 157; cf. MacWerter, 1992, p. 241]).

Herodotus's narrative of the war between the Greeks and the Persian Empire has many story-like features not much in evidence in modern academic histories. Among its story-like features is the sense of causality that works within the narrative.

Each major event is explained in terms of an individual person's emotion causing his or her will to be exerted, which then causes the events that follow. A modern historian commonly searches for causes in economic and social conditions, but Herodotus searched leaders' minds and emotions. He tried to capture these causes of events in an engaging anecdote, with exotic incidents, where possible. Why did Darius become king of Persia? It was decided by Darius and five others sitting on their horses at dawn; the rider of the first horse to neigh after the sun rose would become king. One of Darius's grooms, Oebares, rubbed the genitals of Darius's horse's favorite mare and then kept his hand covered inside his breeches. When the sun was rising, he drew his hand out and put it to the nostrils of Darius's horse, which at once neighed, and Darius was made king. This is not exactly the kind of account one would expect to find today, except perhaps in the *National Enquirer.* Similarly, the causes of the great war are to be sought in Croesus's greed and his anger at the Greeks; once the emotions are accounted for, the events are seen as a direct result of them. Such a means of explaining events is characteristically romantic; the great person's will is the source of action, and so the great and heroic are made central to a romantic understanding of events. So, romantically, events are seen in terms of human emotions; they become meaningful as products of individuals' fear, hope, greed, compassion, and so on.

Such a sense of causality connects with that most characteristic feature of romance—the hero. **Heroes** are those who possess in transcendent degree some valued human quality. Herodotus's *The Histories* is full of men and women who exhibit transcendent degrees of cleverness, courage, patience, energy, tenacity, compassion, and so on. One main motive for writing romantic histories is to preserve the memory of these heroic people. This characteristic of romantic history shows its derivation from epic poems and myths of the preceding preliterate era, in which gods transcended the constraints that hem in everyday human lives. The hero is, as it were, a god confined within reality. The hero's life asserts that the constraints—of fear, anger, meanness of spirit, stupidity, and so on—that prevent us from living as we would wish can be transcended. The hero's life encourages us to act a little more heroically, to feel less bound by conventions and constraints. So, after the conclusion of each battle that Herodotus describes, we have a roll call of those who fought most courageously or who displayed unusual strategic skill.

The romantic imagination focuses on outstanding events and people; or rather, the nature of romantic imagining is what makes them stand out. Everything else is equivalently suppressed into the background. The romantic view of history is one in which powerful leaders and dramatic events are prominent, with the added sparkle of vivid anecdotes about them, and so they shine against a background of unheroic, undramatic everyday drabness. The ability to see a person or an institution or anything else as heroic shows that the romantic mind can, as it were, enlarge and brighten certain things at the expense of everything else. What Herodotus does for Athens, the romantic mind can do for sports heroes, pop stars, institutions, or the content of the school curriculum.

What was primarily the excited discovery of the *logographoi* was what we now rather warily call "reality." In their rational prose writings, they tried to represent what was really the case about the world. They saw themselves as having broken free from the confusions and delusions of myth and the oral past. As one of Herodotus's contemporaries, Hecateus of Miletus began his *Genealogies*, "The stories of the Greeks are many and in my opinion ridiculous" (cf. Pearson, 1939, p. 20).

Once one could represent the world in writing, one could then reflect on the representation and compare it to the reality it was supposed to represent. If one found the representation inadequate, as we might today assume must inevitably be the case, one could revise it to match the reality better. This process of seeking ever more precise representation, which requires scholarly virtues and disciplines, has been central to the Western intellectual tradition. It has been assumed that ever more refined scholarly inquiry would allow us eventually to represent reality accurately and properly.

This vision of capturing reality in symbols was initially romantic. And it is important here to note that romance, which is often seen as exclusively involved with the mysterious and exotic, is most energetically involved with the excitement of believing that the mind *can* adequately capture reality, can generate forms that correspond with the real world "out there." For creatures whose sense of intellectual security seems closely tied to believing that their mental representations of the world correspond with reality, this is no small matter. For the early users of alphabetic writing, it seemed possible in a way never before imagined to put "the world on paper"—to use the title of David Olson's (1994) book. Herodotus thought that he was recording what had *really* happened; the Hippocratic writers thought that they were describing how the body *really* functioned; and the proto-physicists assumed that their speculations and experiments were disclosing how the physical world *really* worked.

The fact that this initial excitement of discovering reality is closely associated with the mysterious and exotic is not so hard to explain. In trying initially to grasp reality, one useful strategy is to try to discover its limits, its extent and boundaries. You might see the general utility of such a strategy if you were to compare it to being put into a hill town in Italy, say, and having to explore it. You might sensibly begin by heading out of your hotel and looking for the main square, the cathedral, the town walls, the main street, and so on. You attend to the unusual sights, the unfamiliar features of the architecture, the strange customs of the locals. That is, you explore much as Herodotus and his contemporaries inquired into what was for them an unknown world suddenly opened to the intellectual tools that literacy provided. Much the same kind of romantic exploration is commonly stimulated in the student today after literacy becomes fluent.

Romance and the Modern Student

I want to indicate clear parallels between modern students' romantic thinking and that of the *logographoi*. I do not approach it through the somewhat dramatic claims of those theorists of literacy who claim that it transforms thought, or shifts the bias of the mind, or restructures our understanding. In certain conditions, such claims seem reasonable, but here I want to work in a more pragmatic way. I simply point to fairly clear parallels between Herodotus's romantic understanding and that of students today. I have considered among the clearly romantic characteristics of Herodotus's work the importance of a new sense of reality, the causal narrative moved by an individual's emotions, the association with characters who exhibit courage, virtue, compassion, cleverness, and so on in transcendent degree, the fascination with limits, the extreme and exotic, and vivid and scandalous anecdotes.

The fairy stories that a 4-year-old enjoys might involve talking and clothed middle-class rabbits and bears, or witches who build houses of gingerbread and sweets, or poisoned apples that might make a woman sleep for 100 years until awakened by a prince's kiss. The typical 4-year-old does not ask how Peter Rabbit can hold a nice cup of chamomile tea with a paw, or how gingerbread walls could bear the weight of an adequate roof, or what physiological processes might preserve the sleeper in a condition a prince might want to kiss 100 years later. If one tells equally fantastic stories to a 10-year-old, about Superman or hobbits or Dark Age queens with magic powers, one has to create a plausible, even if fictive, reality for the characters. One cannot simply assert magic; it must conform with some sense of reality, of a kind that is not needed by the 4-year-old. The rabbits Bigwig and Hazel of Richard Adams's *Watership Down* (1974) could not give each other cups of tea, as Peter Rabbit's mother gives to him. The "mythic" Peter Rabbit inhabits a different intellectual universe from the "romantic" Hazel and Bigwig. They both involve sets of talking rabbits, but Adams's are confined by a set of realistic constraints that do not bind Peter.

The uncertain boundaries of reality that one finds in romantic fiction generally will be familiar to readers of Herodotus. His avowed rationality and careful inquiries go hand in hand with a clear acceptance of prophecy and oracles—or some prophecies and some oracles—and with beard-growing priestesses and feather-clogged regions, and so on. But we see in newly literate students a similar uncertainty about the limits of reality and a similar drive to explore those limits to get some grasp on the extent of this real world being exposed. However we characterize the complex change that we see between Cinderella and Anne of Green Gables or between the fantasies of Peter Rabbit and Superman, an undeniable feature of it has to do with a new relationship between the audience and reality. It is a relationship that seems to me best characterized as romantic.

The modern 10-year-old is involved in a similar, uncertain accommodation with reality as were the *logographoi.* As Herodotus's exploration of reality is full of discussions of the exotic and strange, of the limits of the world and the extremes of human experience, so we find typical students' early attempts to gain a better hold on the extent of reality following a similar pattern. It is the limits, the extreme, the strange that is most directly engaging to the typical 10-year-old today. So, from this perspective, it is no surprise to find that favorite reading among "romantic" boys and girls is *The Guinness Book of Records* and similar compilations of the limits of reality and the extremes of human experience. A joke example that I sometimes use with teachers to illustrate this point is to ask them: If a colleague is sick and you have to take her Grade 6 class on a Friday afternoon and two lessons are already prepared, would you choose, in order to keep the students engaged, the one on "The structure of your local neighborhood" or the one on "Torture instruments through the ages"? Now, there are lots of good reasons why one would choose not to teach the latter, and the example is a joke only because it is so obvious that typical students would be agog to find out about the latter and generally bored by the promise of the former. But the prevailing educational dogma would predict that the former should be more engaging because that dogma is derived from logical and psychological principles that have been unable to grasp or create a category like romance.

Herodotus's highlighting of heroic characters or of qualities in transcendent degree is also echoed by typical newly literate students today, although the modern object of the romantic association is more likely to be a pop star or sports hero. When one is 10 years old, one is at the mercy of endless constraints over which one has very little power—such constraints as parents' rules, school regulations, and bus timetables. There is an indeterminately large and powerful reality out there to which one has to conform. Yet, one retains the mythic or magic wish to transcend it. Romance is, as it were, myth confined within reality. The romantic urge is to associate with those forces or characters or institutions or whatever that seem best able to transcend the threats of this indeterminate reality. For Herodotus and his Athenian listeners and readers it is courage, democratic love of freedom, vigorous innovation, and enterprise that provide the objects of the romantic association; for today's students, it is the pop stars, the movie stars, the hockey or football players, or whoever seems least constrained by what most constrains the student. So, the 12-year-old girl forms a romantic association with the daring, power, and recklessness of Madonna, and the boy with the near supernatural soccer skill of Maradona. In both Herodotus and in modern students, we can see a similar romantic process at work: They associate with whoever or whatever best exemplifies transcendence over the kinds of constraints that most threaten them. (These characteristics do not simply go away as we grow older. Readers may want to reflect on whom or what they romantically associate with. Identifying the objects of our romantic associations gives us straightforward clues to what we are most insecure about.)

The narratives that romantic students find engaging and meaningful also share with Herodotus their fundamental sense of causality. Not only in fiction, but in any area that hopes to represent the world meaningfully to students between ages 8 and 15, the causal mechanism needs to be tied in to individuals' decisions and emotions. Abstract causal mechanisms are not so much meaningless, but their meaning is relatively difficult to grasp until students develop an elaborated theoretic language. Romantic causality may be seen most commonly in popular media, which aim at an intellectual level of around Grade 8, assume literacy, and avoid theoretic forms of expression. Editors of such media require "a human interest angle" on a story; indeed, they require, not coincidentally, the set of characteristics identified above in Herodotus's work.

I could go on elaborating parallels between *logographoi* like Herodotus and typical students today. The similarities all follow from the way alphabetic literacy mediates our understanding of the world, and each of the similarities is constitutive of what is commonly described as a romantic perspective. It is generally a narrativized understanding, whose causality is an externalization of a naive sense of one's emotions and will causing events. It focuses on exploring the sense of reality that alphabetic literacy opens and is engaged principally by the extremes and limits of that reality and with its more exotic and strange features. Such an understanding defends the ego threatened by this indeterminate reality by associating with heroes who exhibit in transcendent degree the qualities best able to overcome the threats most evident to each student.

Romance and Education

What educational value does the category of romantic understanding have? The characteristics mentioned in the previous section can be used to build a distinctive profile of a general mediator of understanding. It claims to represent—albeit too briefly and somewhat haphazardly—the way students who have become fluently literate in the Western tradition of literacy but who have not yet become fluent users of the kind of theoretic abstractions that come with more sophisticated literacy make sense of the world. These tools mediate their understanding, act as filters for the sense they can make. If this general claim is even moderately accurate, it suggests how we might represent knowledge to students at this age to make it readily comprehensible and engaging.

"Romantic understanding" is an odd category in current educational discourse; it is not the kind of category disclosed by research that draws on psychology, sociology, or philosophy for its models. And as these have been dominant for so long, we have had nothing like this category to "think with" about education. I want to argue, further, that precisely such educationally fruitful categories provide the clearest resistance to the reductionist claims of information processing models. But first, I should try to indicate, however briefly, that Romantic understanding *is* an educationally fruitful category.

I try to show just one of the, I think, several ways in which Romantic understanding can bear educational fruit. Currently, planning teaching, organizing content for presentation to students, tends to be based on logical principles of content organization allied with some psychological principles derived from theories of learning, development, and motivation. These principles can be augmented by, or can be incorporated into, planning frameworks, such as those derived from Ralph Tyler's (1949) work—in which statements of objectives lead to selection of appropriate content, which leads to choice of optimal methods of instruction, all of which guide one to decide on appropriate procedures for evaluation. Below, I show how the characteristics of romantic understanding can also lead to a planning framework, but one that is significantly different from those derived from Tyler's model and one better attuned to the "romantic" thinking of students between ages 8 and 15. I first sketch the framework and then briefly discuss just the first few segments of it—enough, I hope, to clarify its usefulness and distinctness from currently available models for planning teaching.

The Romantic Planning Framework

1. **Identifying transcendent qualities**
   What transcendent qualities can be seen and felt as central to the topic? What affective images do they evoke? What within the topic can best evoke wonder?
2. **Organizing the topic into a narrative structure**
   - 2.1 **Initial access**
     What aspect of the topic best embodies the transcendent qualities identified as central to the topic? Does this expose some extreme of experience or limit of reality? What image can help capture this aspect?
   - 2.2 **Composing the body of the lesson or unit**
     What content best articulates the topic into a clear narrative structure? Sketch the main narrative line and fit the content to it.
   - 2.3 **Humanizing the content**
     How can the content be shown in terms of human hopes, fears, intentions, or other emotions? What aspect of the content can best stimulate a sense of wonder? What ideals and/or revolts against convention are evident in the content?
   - 2.4 **Pursuing details**
     What parts of the topic can students best explore in exhaustive detail?
3. **Concluding**
   How can one best bring the topic to satisfactory closure? How can the student feel this satisfaction?
4. **Evaluating**
   How can one know that the content has been learned and understood and has engaged and stimulated students' imaginations?

Space constraints prevent me from elaborating the framework with an example (but see Egan, 1992, for examples in a variety of curriculum areas). The framework is designed to provide guidance in composing a lesson or unit of study in such a way as to appeal to students at the height of romantic understanding. By answering the questions in the spirit of the discussion of the nature of romantic understanding, one can compose a lesson or unit well tempered to the middle school student.

The first segment of the framework asks us to reflect on our topic with our affective sensors alert, as it were, to identify whatever aspects of it are most accessibly romantic. This is the most important part of the planning but also probably the most difficult for teachers trained to look primarily at the logical structure of the content and consider students' thinking in terms of psychological theories of learning and development. The romantic framework asks teachers to be romantic about the content, to feel about it as well as think about it, to identify their own emotional responses to it, to be alert to strange and exotic extremes within it, and to look for heroic transcendence and for a narrative rather than a logical structure, for human hopes, fears, and intentions. By "turning on" our romantic understanding—which persists in adults even though overlaid with further kinds of understanding—we can locate some of these features in anything, any content. By looking at it romantically, one can see even a broken Styrofoam cup in a gutter, not simply as a piece of environmentally destructive detritus but as a remarkable product of human ingenuity that allows us comfortably to hold scalding liquids millimeters from our fingers. The dedication, ingenuity, and persistence that went into the invention of such an object can stimulate our sense of romantic wonder. Seeing it so is not a matter of creating a romantic "hook," but rather a matter of taking a romantic perspective. By seeing content romantically, the teacher has a key to making it engaging and meaningful for "romantic" students.

At the beginning of the second part of the framework, we are directed to consider the initial introduction of the topic to the students. We are asked to consider what best embodies the transcendent qualities. This, again, doesn't mean looking for some "relevant hook," but rather asks the teacher to identify the most central transcendent quality. The contrast may be exemplified in teaching, say, the Industrial Revolution. In the former case, looking for "relevant hooks" might lead to people of the students' age working in coal mines or of having to climb up soot-filled chimneys to clean them with their bodies. In the latter, it means finding something that embodies the quality we have selected that in transcendent degree captures what the Industrial Revolution is about. We could choose either "reckless and destructive exploitation" or "outburst of human ingenuity and energy" as our transcendent qualities, depending on what we wished to teach about it (or we could use both in turn). Let us take the latter. We are then directed to select some aspect of the content that best exemplifies it. So, we might choose to begin with Isambard Kingdom Brunel's ambition to build an iron road from London, in England, to Boston, in the United States. One can describe Brunel's stunning, bold ingenious and energetic feats of engineering and construction that allowed him to achieve his aim—in a way. Certainly, Brunel's achievements involve extremes and limits—impossible tunnels and beautiful bridges, ships on an unheard of scale, like the Great Eastern (part of his iron road to America) that was a near disaster to float. Everything he did was at or beyond the limit of engineering competence at his time, which accounts for the nervousness he caused shareholders. Our introduction to the Industrial Revolution, then, will be through one of its central figures, and one who embodies precisely those "romantic" characteristics we are using to make the topic engaging and meaningful to "romantic" students.

Let me leave elaborating the framework at this point. I hope that it is clear how it can help in planning engaging lessons for students at this "romantic" period of their educational development. Readers might also be able to see ways the characteristics discussed earlier also lead to principles for selecting a new curriculum for the middle school years.

The usefulness of romance as a category for educational thinking has, of course, been noted before. Geoffrey Elton (1967) has discussed its importance to a rich understanding of history and how its absence can lead to desiccation and dullness and a significant loss of meaning. More elaborately, A. N. Whitehead has suggested that students' educational development should be seen as involving a "romantic stage" lasting from about 8 years until 12 or 13. "Romantic emotion is essentially the excitement consequent on the transition from the bare facts to the first realization of the import of their unexplored relationships" (Whitehead, 1967, p. 18). He talks about romance being the vividness, ferment, the excitement without which learning is barren; learning without romance remains "inert" in the mind. During this "romantic stage," Whitehead thinks, it is necessary for the child to be deluged with "ideas, facts, relationships, stories, histories, possibilities, artistry in words, in sounds, in form and in color" . . . in order to "stir . . . feelings, excite . . . appreciation, and incite . . . impulses to kindred activities" (Whitehead, 1967, p. 21). This "great romance is the flood which bears on the child towards the life of the spirit" (Whitehead, 1967, p. 22).

This has in common with my discussion of romantic understanding a recognition that, during early adolescence, there seems to be a common development of a set of interests, intellectual capacities and inclinations, and sensitivities that invite the description "romantic." Whitehead seems ambivalent about whether this set of intellectual characteristics is caused by subject-matter and its novelty or whether it is a result of a "natural" psychological development (see my discussion in Egan, 1990, p. 206). I take, rather, the Vygotskian approach and see romance as caused by the tools of alphabetic literacy being used to mediate the world to the mind. This is not to deny that psychological developments may be influencing the forms of romance, and epistemological influences too. But I am suggesting, first, that these are rather difficult to characterize apart from the sociocultural environments in which they are expressed, and second, as explanatory sources, they are relatively insignificant in accounting for phenomena like romance compared with the mediational influence of intellectual tools such as literacy.

Now romance is hardly a novel category even though it has been used in education very little, compared with the epistemological categories promoted by, say, R. S. Peters and Paul Hirst and the psychological categories familiar from the work of Piaget and Bruner, for example. Although there is no shortage of controversy about the nature of romance or its meaning within the romantic movement, that it constitutes a recognizable stance that one may take in the world is beyond dispute.

I am suggesting that this stance, this romantic perspective on things, this romantic understanding, is a product of a particular technology being incorporated into our minds, and at a particular time in our lives it is particularly prominent. It can be stimulated or suppressed by the way we present and represent the world to children. My general observation of schools suggests that because romance plays virtually no role in thinking about education at present, it is largely ignored and is consequently commonly suppressed. Good teachers, however, recognize the characteristics of romance intuitively. It would indeed be fair to say that the framework I sketched above is simply a systematization of what good teachers do intuitively.

I hope it may be granted that, as a category, romantic understanding captures something educationally important and that, although the framework is too sketchy to support this claim conclusively, it provides a hint of support, and so it is not simply fanciful to consider romance an educationally fruitful category. What remains, then, is to consider why romance offers a resistance to information processing in education.

ROMANCE AND INFORMATION PROCESSING

Information processing approaches draw more or less on computer operations. The information that flows in computer operations is without meaning; meaning is added by the programs the information informs. The crucial recognition of information processing models is the distinction to be drawn between information and meaning:

> Once this distinction is clearly understood, one is free to think about information (though not meaning) as an objective commodity, something whose generation, transmission, and reception do not require or in any way presuppose interpretive processes. One is therefore given a framework for understanding how meaning can evolve, how genuine cognitive systems—those with resources for interpreting signals, holding beliefs, and acquiring knowledge—can develop out of lower-order, purely physical, information-processing mechanisms. The higher-level accomplishments associated with intelligent life can then be seen as manifestations of progressively more efficient ways of handling and coding information. Meaning, and the constellation of mental attitudes that exhibit it, are manufactured products. The raw material is information. (Dretske, 1981, p. vii)

Information processing entails a solution to the Cartesian question of how immaterial minds can cause material actions by arguing that one can describe the typical stuff of minds—like beliefs and knowledge—in terms of complexes of physical systems that process information or, to use Dretske's nice phrase, that one can bake a mental cake by using only physical yeast and flour. I want to suggest that one cannot bake a romantic cake out of only physical yeast and flour. Or rather, because it is working the other round by deconstructing the mental cake into physical ingredients that is at issue here, one cannot reduce a romantic cake into its informational ingredients without leaving an unaccountable residue.

A preliminary thing to note is that romantic understanding does not on the face of it look like the kinds of objects that information processing models commonly claim are complexes of information. It is not a concept or a set of concepts; it is not a belief or a set of beliefs; and it is not an interpretation. These can be decomposed into sets of propositions, or at least, it can be difficult to show why, in principle, they cannot. And sets of propositions can be accommodated to models of information flow. The claim of the information processing proponents is that there is no quantum leap, no qualitative change, in going from information up to belief; it is simply the complexity of the processors that changes. The principle of agglomeration, it is claimed, accounts for all the changes one may observe, as the information flow in a computer can be seen not to involve quantum changes by being organized by different programs. Other essays in this book challenge that claim, but I have the task of arguing that romance, as I have characterized it, is not simply a complex of processed information; it requires some additional component to account for it.

My first line of argument is an extension of the naive observation above—that romance just doesn't look like the kinds of things that information processing claims have commonly addressed, all of which can plausibly be decomposed to propositions. Consider the Industrial Revolution as discussed in the Romantic Planning Framework. One may accumulate any amount of information about it but not come to feel about it in the manner the framework requires. One may know as much as can be known about Isambard Kingdom Brunel but still not make the romantic association with his ingenuity and energy as recommended in that example and may not carry that association to influence the quality of understanding one constructs of the Industrial Revolution as a whole—as the framework recommends one should. A romantic understanding of the Industrial Revolution does not necessarily involve any propositional knowledge or beliefs or concepts that may not be equally possessed by someone who knows a great deal about the revolution but who lacks whatever constitutes the romantic orientation to it. What distinguishes the romantic understanding is an affective orientation, a quality of understanding, that remains when the knowledge, concepts, and beliefs are decomposed. It is unclear how one could reduce that affective orientation, that quality of understanding, into its informational components.

To continue at the naive level: The computer analogies that inform so much information processing thinking make it difficult to suggest how romantic understanding might be conceived in such terms. It doesn't fit any common analogies; it doesn't look like what are usually represented as analogies of a program the mind is running; and it isn't well represented as a different operating system: Programs and operating systems manipulate the flow of information, whereas romantic understanding is an affective orientation to the products of the manipulations of programs and operating systems. The clumsiness of that analogy indicates how the kinds of analogies that information processing has relied on do not readily adapt to something like romance. The problem is that if one looks at intellectual processes through analogies with computer manipulation of information flow, one cannot recognize processes that cannot be made to fit. One may reasonably draw the skeptical conclusion that romance is not like anything that computers do with information; the analogies that have seemed plausible in the information processing arguments break down.

Something of the difficulty may be seen by considering how the information—the interference pattern—of a holographic plate is composed by a laser into a three-dimensional image. If one breaks the holographic plate and shines a laser through a part of it, one will be able to see the whole image but in a fuzzy form. If one puts back further pieces of the plate, the laser will reveal a clearer image. In the case of a two-dimensional photographic plate, if a part is broken off, one loses the whole of a part of the image and the rest remains intact. In the case of a computer program, if one destroys a chunk of a program's code, one will commonly get chaos, or one might find just that a particular component will not run. The information processing advocate might at this point want to say that the information is just differently organized in the holographic plate than in the other two technologies and would perhaps want to add that a computer could simulate a holograph creating a three-dimensional effect. But the point of this analogy lies elsewhere. My intention is to point out that some intellectual processes—like developing a romantic understanding of an event—are as different from any process a computer can simulate or from any process that can be represented by analogy with a computer as some modes of technically organizing and transforming information are different from each other. I mean that analogies with computer transformation of information do not map in any straightforward way onto holographic transformations of information even though they are both fairly similar basic technologies, so the strain in analogies with romantic understanding is hardly surprising. What is surprising, in these circumstances, is the persistence of the analogies.

Simulation of students' reaction time in a problem situation, or of processes of short-term memory and movement to long-term memory, or of scanning patterns, or of capacity to handle a number of pieces of information in a given time, and so on—the everyday stuff of information processing research in education—seem a far cry from the affective processes that are significant constituents of romantic understanding. Assertions that such affective processes and other sophisticated intellectual processes are simply agglomerations of increasingly complex layered information processes ring hollow—indeed, ring rather like the claims that B. F. Skinner made about language learning behavior and the contingencies of reinforcement that accounted for language learning, which Chomsky (1959) laid waste. Skinner's claims about language learning rode on inadequate analogies. The confident assertion that analogies that look plausible when dealing with very simple behaviors or with very simple information processing tasks can be extended to all human learning or intellectual activity suffers from rhetorical overreach.

It might seem that my manner of accounting for romantic understanding should be hospitable to an information processing approach. After all, I suggest that romance is a product of literacy, in some way, and that literacy is a general technology that, in turn, is responsible for the development of the set of intellectual tools that constitute romantic understanding. All I am describing, it might be claimed, are the particular complexes through which information is composed into romantic meaning. It is always difficult to point out to someone who is a captive of some analogy that the analogy is inadequate; they are inclined not to see what the analogy does not expose. What is not exposed by laying the Procrustean analogy underlying information processing on romantic understanding is the way the affective component that is a part of romance (and a part of all human intellectual activity) is not a product of information. This is quite different from the claim that information can influence one's affective response to something. Romance is a capacity fostered through literacy that one can apply to knowledge to change how one feels about it, but it is not itself made up of knowledge.

The intellectual implications of having evolved into a language-using animal are still very far from clear to us. Language is a tool whose incorporation—genetically into our mental structure—has given us an elaborating power of understanding and a generative power of bootstrapping into increasingly elaborate understandings as we unfold the unguessable potentials of language. Among the bootstrapped implications of language, that we have still not come to comfortable terms with, is literacy. Literacy has, in turn, been unfolded into theoretical abstractions and to the extreme reflexiveness on language that yields irony. These complexities do not seem adequately analogized as more sophisticated programs our minds are running or more powerful operating systems. Our minds in odd ways incorporate the tools they use. The computer's operating system is not transformed by the programs it runs, and its motherboard is not reconfigured by the programs. The human mind's incorporation of intellectual tools involves qualitative changes to the system. Romantic understanding is a qualitative change to modes of sense making. Once the tools that constitute it are learned, they effect a change that cannot simply be undone.

I have looked briefly at some general characteristics of a qualitative change in understanding that I have called romantic. One of its components is a particular affective orientation to knowledge that cannot itself be construed as knowledge, nor as a different layer of informational complexity.

References

Adams, R. (1974). *Watership down.* New York: Simon & Schuster.

Chomsky, N. (1959). Review of Skinner's *Verbal behavior*. *Language, 35,* 26-58.

Dretske, F. L. (1981). *Knowledge and the flow of information*. Cambridge: MIT Press.

Egan, K. (1990). *Romantic understanding*. New York: Routledge.

Egan, K. (1992). *Imagination in teaching and learning*. Chicago: University of Chicago Press.

Egan, K. (1997). *The educated mind: How cognitive tools shape our understanding*. Chicago: University of Chicago Press.

Elton, G. R. (1967). *The practice of history*. Sydney, Australia: Sydney University Press.

Fornara, C. W. (1983). *The nature of history in ancient Greece and Rome*. Berkeley: University of California Press.

Gardner, H. (1991). *The unschooled mind*. New York: Basic Books.

Havelock, E. A. (1963). *Preface to Plato.* Cambridge, MA: Harvard University Press.

Havelock, E. A. (1982). *The literate revolution in Greece and its cultural consequences*. Princeton, NJ: Princeton University Press.

Havelock, E. A. (1986). *The muse learns to write*. New Haven, CT: Yale University Press.

Herodotus. (1954). *The histories* (A. de Sélincourt, Trans.). Harmondsworth, UK: Penguin.

MacWerter, N. (1992). *Guinness book of records.* New York: Bantam.

Olson, D. (1994). *The world on paper*. Cambridge, UK: Cambridge University Press.

Olson, D. R., & Torrance, N. (Eds.). (1991). *Literacy and orality*. Cambridge, UK: Cambridge University Press.

Ong, W. J. (1971). *Rhetoric, romance, and technology*. Ithaca, NY: Cornell University Press.

Ong, W. J. (1977). *Interfaces of the word*. Ithaca, NY: Cornell University Press.

Ong, W. J. (1982). *Orality and literacy*. London: Methuen.

Pearson, L. (1939). *Early Ionian historians*. Oxford, UK: Clarendon Press.

Pinker, S. (1994). *The language instinct.* New York: Morrow.

Polanyi, M. (1967). *The tacit dimension*. New York: Anchor Books.

Street, B. V. (1984). *Literacy in theory and practice*. Cambridge, UK: Cambridge University Press.

Tyler, R. (1949). *Basic principles of curriculum and instruction*. Chicago: University of Chicago Press.

Vygotsky, L. (1929). The problem of the cultural development of the child. *Journal of Genetic Psychology, 36,* 414–434.

Vygotsky, L. (1962). *Thought and language* (E. Hanfmann & G. Vakar, Trans.). Cambridge: MIT Press.

Vygotsky, L. (1978). *Mind in society: The development of higher psychological processes* (M. Cole, V. John-Steiner, S. Scribner, & E. Souberman, Eds.). Cambridge, MA: Harvard University Press.

Whitehead, A. N. (1967). *The aims of education.* New York: Free Press.

BIOGRAPHY

KIERAN EGAN is Professor of Education at Simon Fraser University in British Columbia, Canada. He is the 1991 recipient of the Grawemeyer Award in Education and a Fellow of the Royal Society of Canada. His most recent book is *The Educated Mind: How Cognitive Tools Shape Our Understanding.*

Stories and Conversation in Schools

Nel Noddings

Introduction

In 1983, the Reagan administration placed education center stage in American politics. Concluding that the future of the nation was at risk because of "the rising tide of mediocrity" in American schools, the administration began a campaign for educational reform relative to the economy. President Bush attempted to create a system of national standards and examinations to ensure "world class" educational achievement, and President Clinton has moved some of the agenda through Congress with the passage of "Goals 2000."

Through the last 15 years, the national trend has been to raise and enforce academic standards. Although numerous educational thinkers have cautioned against such narrow emphasis, state education departments and local school authorities have been relentless in their insistence on finding means and measures to make schools more effective and efficient in meeting prescribed standards. The defining goals have been to increase student content acquisition and to develop critical-thinking or problem-solving skills.

In this chapter, educational philosopher and former secondary mathematics teacher Nel Noddings accepts the notion of high academic standards but explains that the focus on facts and skills to process information can and often does leave students disengaged, morally adrift, and culturally illiterate. Her suggestion is to use story and conversation in secondary classrooms to introduce the most central and vital issues of human values, to provide rich contexts for learning through great literature, to enlist students in their own education, and to create dynamic learning communities.

Conversation, for Noddings, is not time away from formal study, but a means of exploring concepts and ideas with depth, clarity, and expansive relevance. Various forms of conversation provide differing levels of informality and personal context for studying everything from mathematics to history. Noddings sees these forms of conversation as a means of overcoming the social, intellectual, and existential detachment that students often experience.

Noddings reminds us that conversation can provide a social foundation in which students can explore virtually all subject areas and the fundamental questions of human meaning, purpose, and identity. Conversation also enhances the sense of community and support for the student grappling with the most profound and commonplace of concerns. Noddings provides some vivid examples of how secondary teachers can approach their subjects with rigor and their students with care.

—*Jeffrey Kane*

Many people today are deeply concerned about the apparent decline in moral standards among young people. Sharing the concern but beleaguered by demands for higher academic standards, educators wonder what role they can and should play in moral education. If we accept the premise that education by its very nature has a moral dimension, there is no question that educators must play a role in moral education. It is reasonable to ask whether academic and moral goals might be approached together in such a way that both are more likely to be attained. As we consider this important educational task, it will be clear that genuine moral education requires the construction of shared meanings and not simply the processing of information.

In an earlier article, I described three forms of conversation that can be useful in moral education (Noddings, 1994). In this chapter, I consider ways in which these three forms can be used in connection with stories. The discussion focuses on secondary education for two reasons: First, stories have always been a large part of the best elementary education, and several fine literature-based programs in moral education are already in use there. Second, secondary schools today are almost universally described as "boring"; many are also described as dangerous and nasty places, so the need to do something in the line of moral education is especially pressing at that level. A program that includes stories can combat the complaint of boredom, increase moral sensitivity, and add to cultural literacy.

THREE FORMS OF CONVERSATIONS

Forms of conversation that have an obvious place in schools include the *formal conversation* typical of scholarly debate and discourse ethics, talk (formal or informal) centered on topics often included in the *immortal conversation,* and the *ordinary conversation* of everyday life. Oddly, although all three are appropriate in education, none of the three appear regularly in secondary schools. Far more frequently, we see the typical pattern of teacher elicitation, student response, teacher evaluation (Mehan, 1979). Even in teachers' lectures, we rarely hear what might be called a "conversational style"—that is, a presentation that includes stories, controversial comments, and statements of puzzlement and wonder, one that is clearly intended to invite eventual conversation.

Formal conversation is perhaps best captured in philosophy, where it is conducted more often in writing than in oral discussion. It is characterized by a "serious" content—something at issue, a problematic matter to be settled—and by a set of widely recognized procedural rules. People engaged in such conversations agree (at least tacitly) to a number of conventions, among them to take turns speaking, to address the issue and not to attack their partners in conversation, to define new terms as they are introduced, to tell the truth, to give credit to others for words or ideas deliberately borrowed, to use universally accepted rules of logic, and to accept the force of the better argument in coming to conclusions. When this form is discussed in the next section, we see that opportunities for such conversations arise in all parts of the curriculum. We see also that when competent thinkers engage in this form of conversation, grasp of "the facts"—even agreement on facts—is insufficient to settle most controversial issues. Interpretation of the facts is crucial.

Talk that can be described as part of "the immortal conversation" might fall into the above pattern, but it might also be more like everyday conversation. Questions about the origin of the universe, the meaning of life, death, suffering, and goodness are asked not only by philosophers but also by Zane Grey's cowboys riding the range under starry skies, old ladies in their rocking chairs shelling peas as the evening cuts off the light of a summer day, lone fishermen standing on rocky jetties in the twilight, and even by that obnoxious little boy in *Calvin and Hobbes*. Again, although the opportunities are numerous, actual participation in the immortal conversation is rare in secondary schools.

Even everyday conversation is rare between teachers and students. Everything is businesslike. Teachers teach, and students either do what they are told or resist. In neither case does conversation usually occur. Yet, children long for conversation with adults. In *Voices From the Inside* (1992), one high school student says:

> Teachers should get to know their students a little better, not to where they bowl together but at least know if they have any brothers or sisters. I have found that if I know my teacher I feel more obliged to do the work so I don't disappoint them. Once my trust is gained I feel I should work for myself and also for the teacher. (p. 21)

When students are recognized in conversation, they often respond with touching gratitude. Another student remarks:

> My teacher shows an honest concern about how we feel. He'll give us time to let our emotions out instead of just work, work, work. Like, for example, today he asked how I felt about the Rodney King trial. That's something I needed to release. I've walked around all day with a frown until my feeling was expressed. Thanx 2 him. (p. 29)

Statements like these should help convince educators that ordinary conversation with students should not always be considered time "off-task" or time wasted. As the first student so poignantly shows, time in conversation often means trust gained, and trust gained means that the teacher acquires a partner in the effort to educate.

In the next three sections, we look more deeply into the three forms of conversation and the kinds of stories that might be used to initiate or enhance them.

Formal Conversation

Some conventions of **formal conversation** are well taught in schools—for example, turn-taking and not attacking one's opponent personally (Hansen, 1993). Other aspects are less well treated. The greatest deficiency, of course, is the lack of conversation itself. But even preparation for formal conversation is widely neglected. It is not unusual to find students in good graduate schools who have not been exposed to the elements of logic that are assumed in formal conversation, and many are reluctant to evaluate the force of the better argument, preferring instead to adopt a politically correct position and defend it emotionally. Others prefer to give back their teachers' words in the simplest form of information processing. Both groups—those who employ emotional rhetoric and those who want only an exchange of facts—are unable to engage adequately in formal conversation.

It is important to understand that I do not argue that training in logic will automatically increase attention to formal conversation (it may even have the opposite effect); nor do I argue that such training will necessarily have beneficial transfer effects in mathematics or any other subject. Typically, educators ask for too much assurance along these lines before they risk experimenting with promising approaches.

I make the following claims for teaching basic logic: Teaching basic logic in mathematics classes gives teachers opportunities to talk about matters that have relevance well beyond mathematics yet are not irrelevant to mathematics. Basic training in logic *may* encourage students to examine all sorts of arguments for logical validity and thus enhance the quest for meaning. Exposure to logic may open a fascinating field of recreation for some students. Finally, such exposure can broaden culture literacy.

In my years as a high school mathematics teacher, I included a unit on logic in many of my classes, and now in graduate courses in philosophy of education, I still find such a unit useful. Consider what can be done with material from *Alice in Wonderland* (Carroll, 1963). The book is so rich in logical, historical, linguistic, and philosophical material that I cannot do it justice here, but let's examine one scene. Alice has stopped to ask directions from the Cheshire Cat and is told that whatever direction she chooses, she'll encounter someone who is mad. The following conversation takes place:

> "But, I don't want to go among mad people," Alice remarked.
> "Oh, you can't help that," said the Cat: "we're all mad here. I'm mad. You're mad."
> "How do you know I'm mad?" said Alice.
> "You must be," said the Cat, "or you wouldn't have come here."
> Alice didn't think that proved it at all: however, she went on: "And how do you know you're mad?"
> "To begin with," said the Cat, "a dog's not mad. You grant that?"
> "I suppose so," said Alice.
> "Well, then," the Cat went on, "you see a dog growls when it's angry, and wags its tail when it's pleased. Now *I* growl when I'm pleased, and wag my tail when I'm angry. Therefore, I'm mad." (p. 89)[1]

I usually ask students to discuss both parts of the Cat's argument. Under what premises is the first part of the argument valid (that Alice must be mad)? Why is the second argument invalid even if we grant the premises (e.g., that a dog's not mad, that it growls when angry)? A careful examination of the two arguments gives us an opportunity to talk about the differences between truth and validity and to employ some skills that should be developed before tackling this exercise. I usually give students experience with basic truth tables for atomic sentences including negation, converse, inverse, and contrapositive. They also know the basic syllogistic form or

1. From *Annotated Alice* by Lewis Carrol. Introduction and notes by Martin Gardner. Copyright © 1960 by Martin Gardner. Reprinted by permission of Bramhall House, a division of Clarkson N. Potter, a division of Crown Publishers, Inc.

law of detachment. Most eventually unravel the second argument and decide that the Cat has only "proved" that a cat is not a dog, not that cats must be mad.

But beyond the basic logic that *may* prove useful in both mathematics and everyday life, the topic may be expanded in many directions. At the beginning of their conversation, the Cat tells Alice that, in one direction lives a "Mad Hatter." Where did such an expression come from? It turns out that, before people knew about the bad effects of mercury, hatters often did go mad. Mercury was used in curing felt for hats, and hatters often exhibited the signs of mercury poisoning: shaking, addled speech, hallucinations, and other psychotic symptoms (Carroll, 1993, p. 90). Do we have reason today, then, to be concerned about mercury in fish and other food products? How much contaminated tuna (and at what level of contamination) would we have to eat to be afflicted with "hatter's shakes"?

Besides looking at the etymology of terms and the direct use of logic, we might induce an interest in biography. In recent years, interest in the life and times of Charles Dodgson (Lewis Carroll) has increased (Cohen, 1995). Was his interest in little girls innocent? What contributions did he make to logic proper? What events in his life contributed to his shyness? Why have Freudians been so interested in *Alice*? (And what *is* a Freudian?) These questions illustrate the possibilities for widening conversation in secondary school classrooms. Students are encouraged to think beyond the mere algorithms of logic and processing of information.

The effort to use *Alice* for educational purposes might also lead to poking a little fun at ourselves, and students will surely enjoy that diversion. G. K. Chesterton understood the teacher's mind. He wrote:

> Poor, poor, little Alice! She has not only been caught and made to do lessons; she has been forced to inflict lessons on others. Alice is now not only a school girl but a school mistress. The holiday is over and Dodgson is again a don. There will be lots and lots of examination papers, with questions like: (1) What do you know about the following: mimsy, gimble, haddocks' eyes, treacle-wells, beautiful soup? (2) Record all the moves in the chess game in *Through the Looking-Glass*, and give diagrams. (3) Outline the practical policy of the White Knight for dealing with the social problem of green whiskers. (4) Distinguish between Tweedledum and Tweedledee.[2]

Chesterton is right, of course. The teaching mind too often bogs down in information processing and retelling on tests. But we need not make our questions into *examination* questions; rather, we can make them into topics of conversation, and the topics of conversation may focus on almost any academic discipline or on a host of everyday interests.

I'll give one more example of what might be done with basic logic. A syllogism that has been used for years in philosophy is this one:

---

2. From *Annotated Alice* by Lewis Carroll. Introduction and notes by Martin Gardner. Copyright © 1960 by Martin Gardner. Reprinted by permission of Bramhall House, a division of Clarkson N. Potter, a division of Crown Publishers, Inc.

All men are mortal.
Socrates is a man.
Socrates is mortal.

In teaching the basic form of the syllogism, we emphasize that only three terms are allowed in a valid syllogism. Here, they are *men* (or *man*), *Socrates*, and *mortal*. Feminist philosophers have recently pointed out that the syllogism as constructed really has four terms. *Men* is used in the major premise as a generic term for "human being," but in the minor premise, *man* seems to mean *male*. Does this construal seem reasonable? Consider what happens when we substitute *Cleopatra* for *Socrates.* We get something called the "bizarreness response" (Moulton, 1977):

All men are mortal.
Cleopatra is a man.
Cleopatra is mortal.

Now, the question is why logicians, the fussiest of all thinkers, did not notice this. At least one answer is that they associated maleness with humanness and failed to acknowledge women as fully human. Such a suggestion could lead to a lively formal conversation and to much reading in current feminist theory.

The syllogism above, in contrast to the discussion of *Alice in Wonderland,* is more typical of routine work in philosophy. Philosophers often use stories called "philosophical fictions" to challenge the theoretical positions of other philosophers. The scenarios are designed to illustrate an unhappy effect of a particular position or a contingency that cannot be handled easily from that perspective. Then a philosopher defending the initial position has to show how the unhappy effect can be blocked or how the contingency can be met. Such work is far more demanding than simply collecting and organizing information.

Fascinating as this work is, it does not have the multifaceted power of literary stories. In addition to providing exercise in logical applications, stories borrowed from real literature reach beyond the purpose at hand and enhance cultural literacy, make connections to other disciplines, and offer intrinsic value. They are in themselves worth talking about.

There is another reason why teachers today might be interested in promoting the skills required by formal conversation. These skills are necessary for civil public life. Indeed, a prominent philosopher, Jûrgen Habermas, has placed conversation at the center of ethics. The idea is that people, following the rules of formal conversation, must communicate with one another and come to agreement on the norms that will govern their lives. "Only those norms can claim to be valid that meet (or could meet) with the approval of all affected in their capacity *as participants in a practical* discourse" (Habermas, 1990, p. 66). Students can be given practice in such discourse through class meetings and like strategies. Opportunities to engage in formal conversation about the rules that govern their own classroom lives should help convince students that there are political and social uses for this form of conversation.

We should not, however, exaggerate the usefulness of formal conversation. History is liberally sprinkled with examples of highly trained people who knew the conventions of formal conversation and quickly cast them aside in the heat of emotional debate. Political debate is rife with *ad hominem* attacks, non sequiturs, and other gross violations of the rules. Scientific debate has not been without its emotional clashes, and even philosophical discourse has suffered from various lapses (Eiseley, 1958; Moorehead, 1969). Further, philosophical debate reveals a difficulty that may be impossible to overcome. Even the best trained people find it hard to judge which are the best arguments. Richard Bernstein (1992) comments on this difficulty:

> Abstractly there is something enormously attractive about Habermas's appeal to the "force of the better argument" until we ask ourselves what this means and presupposes. Even under "ideal" conditions where participants are committed to discursive argumentation, there is rarely agreement about what constitutes "the force of the better argument." We philosophers, for example, cannot even agree what are the arguments advanced in any of our canonical texts, whether Plato, Aristotle, Kant or Hegel, etc.—and there is certainly no consensus about who has advanced the better argument. (p. 220)

Difficulties such as these have to be faced squarely. Consensus is not always possible, and many postmodern thinkers advise that it is often not even desirable. Basic differences between individuals and groups must be recognized and, if they are not morally reprehensible, respected (Derrida, 1978). But the fact that consensus is often either unlikely or undesirable does not imply that we should abandon norms of civility and logical debate. It means, rather, that we need more than procedural conventions to guide our lives, and that observation brings us to the next form of conversation.

The Immortal Conversation

Since humans have been capable of conversation, they have engaged in the **immortal conversation**. In this conversation, we are more deeply concerned with the content than with the process. Matters of birth, death, cruelty, pain, misfortune, love, good fortune—all the topics central to fairy tales, legends, and religions—are of interest to people everywhere, and they get far too little attention in schools obsessed with short answers and the accumulation of information.

Let's consider an example. Among the matters that arise perennially are questions about origins and creation. Universal interest in these questions suggests that science teachers might do well to discuss creation stories with their students. Not only should a wide range of creation stories be told but so should the stories of the debates involving these stories. Instead of hiding the debates behind school board meeting doors, the debates should be an exciting part of the curriculum—an opportunity to learn the skills of formal conversation and an initiation into the immortal conversation.

Students should hear about the highly emotional exchanges between Bishop Wilberforce and T. H. Huxley, Darwin's doubts about a loving Creator in the wake of the natural horrors he observed, the Scopes trial, and present-day arguments over evolution and creation. They should be introduced to literature and poetry that include explorations of these issues, and they should be invited to join that great conversation (Noddings, 1993). They should hear, too, some of the humor on the subject. Here, for example, is a comment from Stephen Leacock (1956) on how things proceeded after the start:

> Once started, the nebulous world condensed into suns, the suns threw off planets, the planets cooled, life resulted and presently became conscious, conscious life got higher up and higher up till you had apes, then Bishop Wilberforce, and then Professor Huxley. (p. 2463)

The great conversation includes many other topics. Another of special importance to high school students centers on the good life. What constitutes a good life? Teachers might note that, at least from the time of Aristotle, thoughtful people have discussed two aspects of the good life: (a) the material conditions or "goods" required and (b) the personal development characteristic of a good life. *Having* goods and *being* good are both part of the good life and interact to enhance one another.

It is widely observed today—and difficult to challenge—that we live in a highly materialistic society. Material goods seem to define the good life almost entirely for many people. It might be good for high school students to hear about people who lacked these goods and nevertheless possessed or at least strove for other goods. The object here is not to minimize the suffering and deprivation of our present students but to arouse in them both pity and admiration for the many, many generations of people who struggled and suffered with far less hope of achieving either material goods or personal recognition. Again, the object is not simply to provide students with more information, although the expanded conversation will certainly do that. Instead, the object is to arouse sensibilities, to get students to think and feel beyond the facts, to reach for what all this means for their own lives and the lives of others.

The teaching of literature provides a wonderful opportunity for the discussion of moral sentiments. Even if insufficient time is available for a high school class to read all of Dickens's *Bleak House* (1853), teachers might combine telling and reading to convey the multitude of life stories dramatized by Dickens. Portraits are painted vividly: of faith, constancy, unselfishness, greediness, shiftiness, cruelty, cleverness, shame, regret, pompousness, and "rising above it all." Parts should be read to convey the life of Jo, a boy growing up without home or family. Dickens, simultaneously mocking the "good" ladies whose efforts are directed to faraway places and hoping to shame his countrymen into doing something to relieve the lives on their doorsteps, describes Jo:

> He is not one of Mrs. Pardiggle's Tockahoopo Indians; he is not one of Mrs. Jellyby's lambs, . . . he is not softened by distance and unfamiliarity; he is not a genuine foreign-grown savage; he is the ordinary home-made article. Dirty, ugly, disagreeable to all the senses, in body a common creature of the common streets, only in soul a heathen.

> Homely filthe begrimes him, homely parasites devour him, homely sores are in him, homely rags are on him; native ignorance, the growth of English soil and climate, sinks his immortal nature lower then the beasts that perish.[3]

Yet, when he is questioned and charged to tell the truth about an event he witnessed, Jo responds:

> "Wisher may die if I don't, sir," says Jo, reverting to his favorite declaration. "I never done anythink yit, but wot you knows on, to get myself into no trouble. I never was in no other trouble at all, sir—'sept not knowin' nothink and starwation." (p. 259)

One cannot argue that Jo, who died shortly after this exchange, lived the "good life" merely because he had a basic desire to be good. He lacked entirely the material resources for a good life and lived one of lonely misery. The story should induce pity, indignation, and humility. Cultural literacy and human feeling need not be mutually exclusive.

So often, even in English classes, opportunities to engage in the immortal conversation are ignored in favor of teaching material or literary facts and techniques. But one can admire the literary mastery of Dickens without neglecting the great human stories in his work. *Bleak House* presents a panorama of characters who are personifications of human attributes. Scarcely any real human being could be as greedy and nasty as old Mr. Smallweed, as cheerfully parasitic as Skimpole, as deluded and lost as Richard, as steady and decent as Mr. Jarndyce, as obtuse and self-righteous as Mrs. Jellyby, as wise and selfless as Esther, as crafty and just as Mr. Bucket, as egotistical and stupid as Mr. Guppy. Yet, all of these characters ring true, and we learn from them. By contrasting Jarndyce and Richard, we see that desire for more wealth—especially contingent and unearned wealth—can actually weaken and even destroy happiness. Jarndyce resolutely refuses to think about a possible legacy that is under litigation and lives a contented life; Richard pins all his hopes on the possibility and thereby loses every chance at happiness.

In every school subject, it is possible to introduce discussion of the good life and what it might comprise. Students might well be deeply touched by the story of Josie told by W. E. B. DuBois (1989). Already 20 years old when she met DuBois who was hired to teach in her poor community, "she herself longed to learn" (p. 44). What happened to Josie? For a while, at least, she came to school with her younger brothers and sisters, and DuBois loved visiting her and her family:

> Best of all I loved to go to Josie's, and sit on the porch, eating peaches, while the mother hustled and talked: how Josie had bought the sewing-machine; how Josie worked at service in winter, but that four dollars a month was "mighty little" wages; how Josie longed to go away to school, but that it "looked like" they never would get far enough ahead to let her. (pp. 47–48)

---

3. From *Dickens: The Bleak House*, by G. Storey, 1987, New York: Cambridge University Press. Reprinted with permission.

DuBois taught for 2 years in Josie's community and then left to further his own education. In that short time, Josie's appetite was "whetted . . . by school and story and half-awakened thought." But what came of this appetite, this awakening? DuBois returned 10 years later: "Josie was dead, and the gray-haired mother said simply, 'we've had a heap of trouble since you've been away'" (p. 50).

Through all this time, Josie had worked for her family—worked and scraped. Then one year when the spring came,

> and the birds twittered, and the stream ran proud and full, little sister Lizzie, bold and thoughtless, flushed with the passion of youth, bestowed herself on the tempter, and brought home a nameless child. Josie shivered and worked on, with the vision of school-days all fled, with a face worn and tired,—worked until, on a summer's day, someone married another; then Josie crept to her mother like a hurt child, and slept—and sleeps. (p. 50)

It is difficult to read this account even now, separated by time and space, without crying. How many lives, potentially so rich, have been lost? Might such stories increase the resolve of students to do something with their own lives? Again, one can see that students may react to this story in a variety of ways. As teachers, we are not trying to get students to memorize paragraphs from DuBois or to answer short questions about life in Appalachia. We want them *to think,* and if some decide—like Scarlet O'Hara—that they will never go hungry or lack material resources, we should be ready with stories that prompt still deeper thought.

Besides material resources, human beings need *projects*, forms of work that they can embrace wholeheartedly. Mathematics teachers might tell the story of the great mathematician James Sylvester, who had to overcome the overt prejudice against Jews in British academic establishments. Still, mathematics was the great project at the center of his life. Of it, he said:

> There is no study in the world which brings into more harmonious action all the faculties of the mind than (mathematics) . . . the mathematician lives long and lives young; the wings of the soul do not early drop off, nor do its pores become clogged with the earthy particles blown from the dusty highways of vulgar life. (in Bell, 1965, p. 405)

Sylvester's language is a bit flowery for our times, but the message and its enthusiasm are clear. Sylvester himself lived a long life, productive to the end, and remained enthusiastic not only about mathematics but also about music and poetry. Teachers can find similar stories about musicians, artists, farmers, nurses, naturalists, priests, and—yes—teachers.

In addition to material resources and projects, the good life according to Aristotle—and few of us would disagree—requires friends. Friends (Aristotle contended) not only provide companionship in shared recreations but also encourage us to be the best persons we can be. Students should be invited to look at friendship in this way. Again, good literature abounds in stories that illustrate this feature of Aristotelian friendship and also the many failures of friends to understand and support one another.

If teachers and curriculum makers thought first in terms of themes such as the good life and its components and second about the literature to be selected, high school education might gain in coherence as well as relevance. For example, in choosing literature on the friendship theme, we might think of John Knowles' *A Separate Peace,* which is usually in the curriculum anyway, but now its inclusion would have special significance. The friendship of Gene and Finny is flawed by Gene's competitiveness and the projection of his own rivalry onto Finny. Teachers can move in many directions with the ideas found here. They can explore rivalry and competitiveness. When is it healthy and when not? What is its relation to enmity and war? What is the school's role in producing and maintaining rivalries? Sticking close to the theme of friendship, however, teachers might want to concentrate on what friends mean to one another, the nature of respect, the need for openness, the obligation to protect, the gift of forgiveness, and the guilt suffered when friends hurt one another.

When a theme has been chosen, it is logical to ask what other works might be read that illustrate the theme. That question is very different from the more general and academic question, What else (e.g., from the canon) should they read? Instead, given the theme of friendship, we ask, Where do interesting friendships appear? Teachers might think of the friendship between Huck and the slave Jim in Mark Twain's *Huckleberry Finn*. This friendship is an anomalous one—even illegal. What makes it a friendship? Discussion of anomalous friendships might lead to consideration of John Steinbeck's *Of Mice and Men,* in which the friendship between Lenny and George illustrates another kind of friendship across difference.[4] Mary Gordon's *The Company of Women* (1980) describes a beautiful lifelong friendship among women, and it also introduces the dilemma of "particular friendships" and the proscription against them for members of the Catholic priesthood and orders. Was Cyprian, the priest in Gordon's story, a failure because he needed and welcomed the warmth of particular human beings? Near death, Cyprian blames himself for his priestly failure but also looks longingly and appreciatively on his human connections. He confesses:

> I think it is unbearable that one day I will not see their faces. I fear the moment of death when one longs only for a human face, that beat, that second between death and life eternal when there is nothing, and for a moment one is utterly alone before entering the terrible, beautiful room of judgment.[5]

In planning for such a thematic unit, one need not ignore current literary crazes. Jane Austen's *Pride and Prejudice* yields two lovely friendships for discussion: that

---

4. For other examples of friendships across differences, see Cronin (1941)—friendship between a priest and an atheist physician; Lessing (1984)—friendship between a lower-class elderly woman and an elegant fashion editor/writer; Brooks (1956)—friendship between the triply disabled Helen Keller and her teacher, Anne Sullivan; O'Brian (various years)—friendship between a rugged naval officer and a pacifist physician/botanist/spy.

5. From *The Company of Women* (p. 287), by M. Gordon, 1980, New York: Ballantine Books. Reprinted with permission.

between the sisters Jane and Elizabeth (can sisters be friends?) and the one between Bingley and Darcy. In the latter, was it right for Darcy to protect Bingley from what he (Darcy) mistakenly judged to be an inappropriate or potentially painful relationship?

Throughout this section, I've concentrated on stories that have direct academic relevance and a high level of intellectual respectability, but of course, teachers might add stories from teenage literature, television dramas, news, sports, or any other source, and some of these possibilities are addressed in the final section on ordinary conversation. My point has been to show that we can enhance intellectual literacy (if we want to do so) without sacrificing what is more universally important—understanding the existential condition.

Finally, in promoting the idea of "the immortal conversation" as central to education, Frederick Turner (1991) reminds us:

> [T]he heart of the immortality of the great conversation lies outside the conventional objects, skills, traditions, and expertise of discourse. It is not, as we said, merely immortality for the Great Minds; for it is precisely when these great minds give up being great minds—being experts, authorities, professionals—and become amateurs, laypersons—bullshitters if you like—that they begin to become immortal. It was the sophists who were the experts. Socrates and company jumped all the fences, like sophomores. They even jumped the sexual fence in some ways; and Socrates finds his best conversational partner, on the most important of all subjects, Love, in Diotima the wise woman of the *Symposium*. (p. 107)

Ordinary Conversation

The three types of conversation are not discrete; they run into each other, and one cannot always tell when the conversational switch has occurred. For example, a group might be involved in discussing friendship as a necessary component of the good life. An example chosen, say, Elizabeth and Jane in *Pride and Prejudice*, might lead to discussion of the movie, and some students might begin talking about other movies they've seen recently, with whom they attend shows, and what they eat before, during, and after shows. It has always been a problem for teachers to decide when to bring the class back to the topic and when to let the conversation run on. Teachers often feel intuitively that these digressions are somehow important, but they do not know exactly why, and they feel guilty—sometimes "used" or "had"—when students effectively steer the conversation away from the initial subject matter.

Let me try to defend the intuitive notion that these conversations can be important. Both teachers and students often feel closer to life's core during these conversations, but the emphasis on information processing and the accumulation of facts gives such conversation an illicit appearance. Here, again, cultural literacy and existential explanation need not be at odds. As students talk, teachers come to know them better. As teachers join the conversation, students get glimpses of the teacher as a human being. Recall the longing expressed by the student in *Voices From the Inside* (1992). Students want to know their teachers better, and when they do, they "feel obliged" to work not only for themselves but also for the teacher whom they now trust. In today's large schools and fragmented communities, trust is not easily established. Students and teachers rarely meet each other in a market, church, or community gathering, and the relationship between them has become more and more professional—professional in the sense of marked status difference, detachment, and goal orientation.

As students and teachers slip into **ordinary conversation**, they learn about one another. But they also learn *from* one another. Without imposing their values, teachers can convey all sorts of messages about respect, taste, choice, time management, humor, human foibles, fears, disappointments. It is difficult to exaggerate how much it might mean to a particular student to hear a teacher say, "That happened to me once too." And sometimes students disclose things about themselves that change the opinion of a teacher drastically.

I recall talking with a general mathematics class years ago about their participation in nighttime demonstrations. This was during the time of racial disturbances back in the 1960s. I told the students frankly that I was afraid someone would get hurt. My remarks opened a conversation that threatened to become explosive. White boys in the class bragged that they "were ready"—armed to the teeth, if one could believe them. Black boys laughed and scoffed. They were already engaged in "busting heads" and committing all sorts of mayhem—if one could believe *them*. Then the white boys described their guns, and one tough guy challenged the most outspoken black boy to describe his gun. "I don't have one," he replied. "Oh, come on," urged the white boy, "how about your hunting gun?" "I don't hunt," James blurted out, "I've always been afraid of hurting someone." Dead silence followed this admission. The threat was over. And the relationship between James and me was ever after one of mutual appreciation. His name was not "James," but I remember his real name, and details of his difficult life stay with me. I no longer remember the white boy's name.

My story of one ordinary conversation is unique in its details, as all stories are, but its form and effects are repeated elsewhere. Lee Colsant (1995) recounts a series of such stories in the tale of his transformation as a teacher. Attempting to teach French culture to inner-city Chicago students in the same way he had successfully taught students in Quebec, Colsant found himself sliding into despair. In an account that is touchingly honest, Colsant admits that he came to hate his first-period class. The students despise him, and he despises them. But then he decides to make peace and start over. He listens; he reasons openly with them about their mutual problem; he tries group work. The initial result is a melange of voices, messages, resolutions, and debacles. Colsant admits:

> I try to acknowledge my failure and their resistance while giving them a choice, even an invitation to join and work. Instead, I make them feel they are outsiders, wrong if they don't join the rest. I am still pushing French on them. My old self speaks while I try to find my new voice. The dilemma is not resolved. I am not making it. (p. 69)

But Colsant does make it. He does not ever teach French in the way he once taught it, but he connects with teenagers who need the trust, respect, and example of an adult who cares for them, and he does teach some French, albeit a far different one from the old standard curriculum. From him, the students learn something about cooperation, polite modes of exchange, persistence, and concern for the feelings of others. They begin to use French expressions to convey short messages. From them, Colsant learns what it means to live life on the border—no security of place, no recognition, no security even for one's life. And, of course, in the end, Colsant suffers a loss when students move away suddenly, leaving unanswered the tacit questions, Why? to Where? with Whom? The loss is even greater when a student or former student is shot dead. Suffering is one of the costs of relating. Thinking back on the student who moved (Where?) and the one who died, Colsant knows the debt he owes them—what he learned from them. He sees them in his new students: "New lads are there all right, not remote antagonists, but alive in the toil of listening. New conversations will surely emerge" (p. 89).

Conversations reveal care, promote trust, and invite remembrance. Colsant's students began to repeat his often-used response, "I don't know; think it through!" They may use it with their own children some day. Slogan-like expressions that emerge either in conversations or in routines can reverberate years later in the memory of students. Philip Jackson (1992) recalls a favorite teacher and how her slogan recurs in his reflective thinking: "Keep your wits about you!" And he reminds us of something especially relevant to the current discussion. He says, "I think it would be hard to say which came first, my liking for Mrs. Henzi or my successful mastery of the material she taught" (p. 89). Whether that liking comes through masterfully run routines, personal kindness, or spontaneous conversation, it is something too often overlooked in the study and practice of teaching. It *matters* whether or not students like their teachers and teachers like their students. It matters to the teachers, and it matters to the students. "I feel more obliged . . ." "I don't want to disappoint them." This could be a teacher's voice as easily as a student's.

Ordinary conversations, if they are more than mere banter, provide opportunities for telling personal stories. Students get to reveal something of themselves (e.g., whether they have brothers and sisters), and teachers become real persons. The latter may be especially important for students who have no other models of educated persons in their lives. Uneducated parents, no matter how much they love their children, cannot provide such models. To be effective as models, however, teachers have to be real people, people whose life experiences, desires, and disappointments seem realistic and lead students to believe that they can also become educated persons—without becoming alien creatures.

Legitimate questions arise about the length and scope of ordinary conversations in the classroom. Teachers who have achieved a high level of artistry seem able to bring even the most esoteric conversations back to the initial topic at just the right time. How do they do this? How do great violinists and cellists produce the effects that set them apart from run-of-the-mill musicians? Practice, sensitivity, and a great love for what they are doing seem paramount. In teaching, a wide repertoire of stories, careful planning, and passionate interest seem vital. As David Hawkins (1973) pointed out years ago, one has *to plan* for spontaneity.

Planning might be thought of in two ways: (a) planning for the upcoming lesson and (b) preparing more generally for one's future teaching. Both senses of planning have been badly treated in teacher education and supervision. Teachers are encouraged (coerced?) by supervision in schools to plan skimpily—learning objectives, page numbers, and assignment crammed into small spaces. This is another example of the horrible overemphasis on mere facts. In contrast, a teacher-artist plans far more extensively. A mathematics teacher, for example, may work all of the problems she plans to assign, noting carefully places where alternative methods are possible, places where mistakes are likely, prerequisite skills for certain moves, interesting shortcuts, interesting numbers, and interesting mathematicians who spring to mind as the interesting numbers are considered. Her planning may involve charts and diagrams, but it is, in its entirety, more like a growing web or even a stellar explosion than a flowchart. Such planning is deeply satisfying in itself and is directed at both the immediate lesson and future lessons. Much that appears in this kind of planning is not actually used in the lesson that instigates it; rather, it becomes material for possible conversations and contributes to the growth of the teacher. Indeed, we might say that it enriches the teacher's internal conversation. Further, teachers who plan in this way are perpetually alive to all the possibilities around them that might contribute to their classroom virtuosity.

Teachers with this sort of mastery have little need for the mechanistic forms of control so popular today. Like other artists, they have control of the artistic medium. They know where most conversations might go, and they are prepared to change course when a change seems appropriate. They can take risks because they know that they will be able to handle most problems likely to arise.

I have been arguing that ordinary conversations in classrooms are important in themselves. Their occurrence *in a rich learning environment* is a sign that relationships of care and trust are being established. I have emphasized the phrase "in a rich learning environment" because I do not mean to suggest that ordinary conversation should fill the entire school day. Clearly, time must be available for the practice of technical skills, teacher-telling, formal conversation, and the semifocused conversation that we call "the immortal conversation" among other familiar school activities. Students themselves are often the best judges of balance among activities. When teachers use conversation—banter—to cover for lack of preparation and when that conversation goes nowhere or creates no need to think or evaluate, students lose interest in it and lose respect for such teachers.

It may be especially important today for teachers to participate in conversations with their students because conversation in homes seems to have diminished. Working parents, tight schedules, and television have all contributed to the reduction in conversation. In a rich learning environment, however, students regard ordinary conversations as a mark of respect. In such conversations, students learn all sorts of things—facts, the rules of polite conversation, manner and style, trust and confidence, how to listen, how to respond without hurting one another, and a host of other things. These conversations are essential to moral life. They are part of moral education because, properly conducted, we learn through them how to meet and treat one another. They are part of moral life because such exchanges with other people are essential to the good life.

Conclusion

I have argued that conversation should play a much larger role in classrooms than it does today, and I have tried to show how stories can be used in these conversations. Sometimes the stories provide starting points for conversation, and sometimes conversations provide the setting in which stories emerge. Guided by a sensitive and well-prepared teacher, these stories and conversations have the potential to contribute significantly to moral life and education.

Three kinds of conversation were discussed: (a) formal conversation—the sort of serious, rule-bound conversation characteristic of philosophy; (b) the immortal conversation, which may be formal or informal but is distinguished by its subject matter—the great existential questions; and (c) ordinary conversation—the sort in which friends and acquaintances regularly engage. All of these forms are likely to increase engagement, enhance cultural literacy, and contribute to the construction of relations of care and trust. An education rich in conversation clearly goes well beyond information processing and the accumulation of facts. It addresses matters central to life itself.

References

Bell, E. T. (1965). *Men of mathematics*. New York: Simon & Schuster.

Bernstein, R. (1992). *The new constellation*. Cambridge: MIT Press.

Brooks, V-W. (1956). *Helen Keller*. New York: E. P. Dutton.

Carroll, L. (1993). *The annotated Alice* (M. Gardner, Ed.). New York: Random House.

Cohen, M. (1995). *Lewis Carroll*. New York: Knopf.

Colsant, L. (1995). "Hey, Man, why do we gotta take this . . . ?" In J. G. Nicholls & T. A. Thorkildsen (Eds.), *Reasons for learning.* New York: Teachers College Press.

Cronin, A. J. (1941). *The keys of the kingdom*. Boston: Little, Brown.

Derrida, J. (1978). *Writing and difference* (A. Bass, Trans.). Chicago: University of Chicago Press.

DuBois, W. E. B. (1989). *The souls of Black folk*. New York: Bantam Books.

Eiseley, L. (1958). *Darwin's century: Evolution and the men who discovered it*. Garden City, NY: Doubleday.

Gordon, M. (1980). *The company of women*. New York: Ballantine Books.

Habermas, J. (1990). *Moral consciousness and communicative action* (C. Lenhardt & S. W. Nicholsen, Trans.). Cambridge: MIT Press.

Hansen, D. (1993). From role to person: The moral layeredness of classroom teaching. *American Educational Research Journal, 30*, 651–674.

Hawkins, D. (1973). How to plan for spontaneity. In C. E. Silberman (Ed.), *The open classroom reader* (pp. 486–503). New York: Vintage Books.

Jackson, P. W. (1992). *Untaught lesson*. New York: Teachers College Press.

Leacock, S. (1956). Common sense and the universe. In J. R. Newman (Ed.), *The world of mathematics* (Vol. 4). New York: Simon & Schuster.

Lessing, D. (1984). *The diaries of Jane Somers*. New York: Vintage Books.

Mehan, H. (1979). *Learning lessons*. Cambridge, MA: Harvard University Press.

Moorehead, A. (1969). *Darwin and the Beagle*. New York: Harper & Row.

Moulton, J. (1977). The myth of the neutral "man." In M. Vetterling-Braggin, F. Elliston, & J. English (Eds.), *Feminism and philosophy.* Totowa, NJ: Littlefield, Adams.

Noddings, N. (1993). *Educating for intelligent belief or unbelief.* New York: Teachers College Press.

Noddings, N. (1994). Conversation as moral education. *Journal of Moral Education, 23*(2), 107–118.

O'Brian, P. (various years). Aubrey/Maturin series (17 books). New York: Norton.

Storey, G. (1987). *Dickens: The bleak house.* New York: Cambridge University Press.

Turner, F. (1991). *Rebirth of value*. Albany: State University of New York Press.

Voices From the Inside. (1992). Claremont: Claremont Graduate School, Institute for Education in Transformation.

Biography

Nel Noddings is Lee L. Jacks Professor of Child Education at Stanford University. Her area of special interest is philosophy of education and, within that, ethics, moral education, and mathematics education. She is Past-President of both the national Philosophy of Education Society and the John Dewey Society. She was a Phi Beta Kappa Visiting Scholar for the year 1989–1990. In addition to nine books—among them, *Caring: A Feminine Approach to Ethics and Moral Education*, *Women and Evil*, *The Challenge to Care in Schools*, *Education for Intelligent Belief or Unbelief*, and *Philosophy of Education*, she is the author of more than 125 articles and chapters on various topics as diverse as the ethics of caring and mathematical problem solving.

INDEX